THE MAKING OF THE
RESTORATION SETTLEMENT

THE MAKING OF THE RESTORATION SETTLEMENT

The Influence of the Laudians
1649-1662

BY

ROBERT S. BOSHER

THE GENERAL THEOLOGICAL SEMINARY
NEW YORK

dacre press
westminster

FIRST PUBLISHED 1951
REPRINTED, WITH SLIGHT REVISION, 1957
DACRE PRESS: A. AND C. BLACK LTD
4, 5 AND 6 SOHO SQUARE LONDON W.1

MADE IN GREAT BRITAIN
PRINTED BY LATIMER TREND AND CO LTD PLYMOUTH

To

The Reverend POWEL MILLS DAWLEY, *Ph.D.*

Professor of Ecclesiastical History
of
The General Theological Seminary
New York City

MAGISTRO DISCIPVLVS AMICO AMICVS
MAXIMIS PRO BENEFICIIS TRIBVIT

CONTENTS

FOREWORD

by NORMAN SYKES, M.A., D.D.
Dixie Professor of Ecclesiastical History in the
University of Cambridge

IT is both a privilege and a pleasure to accept the invitation of my friend
and pupil Dr. Robert S. Bosher to write a brief foreword to his book.
To the careful reader it will be evident indeed that his work needs no
commendation save its own merits. But I am glad to have the opportunity of recording the profit and pleasure which I enjoyed from our
association in Cambridge, and of emphasizing my conviction that his
researches have resulted in an original contribution to our knowledge
and interpretation of the Restoration settlement of the Church of
England.

Dr. Bosher attaches greater importance than most previous historians of the ecclesiastical history of the Interregnum to the personali-
ties and principles of the Anglicans in exile rather than to their brethren
who remained at home, in regard to their several contributions to the
church settlement of Charles II. Of the latter indeed his general account
is less that of a heroic company of confessors, not to say martyrs, than
of a painful example, especially so far as concerned the bishops, of the
traditional tag *episcopi Anglicani semper pavidi*; and he censures particularly their failure to take steps to ensure the perpetuation of the
apostolic succession at a time when its proximate extinction seemed
by no means impossible. At the same time he emphasizes the extent
to which under the Commonwealth the Puritan system of Lectureships was diverted to become a means of preserving the Anglican
tradition. But the heat and burden of the day fell upon the exiles;
and a detailed account is given of the apologetic of the clergy in behalf
of the *via media* against both papist and presbyterian in circumstances
when its temporary eclipse seemed likely to be but the prelude to permanent extinction. The chief success of the exiled clergy, however, lay
in their conversion of Edward Hyde to their principle that the *Ecclesia
Anglicana* must be restored with the monarchy and without compro-
mising concessions to the Presbyterians at home. Dr. Bosher argues, to
my mind convincingly, that this was the corner-stone of their policy,

and that Hyde accepted it *ex animo* and not merely as a matter of expediency.

It is no part of a preface to steal the author's thunder; and it must, therefore, be left to the reader to learn how Dr. Bosher traces and interprets the complex strand of events between the actual restoration of Charles II and the passing and enforcement of the Act of Uniformity in accordance with this major premiss of his argument. It must suffice to say that in my judgment his skilful and careful record covers more of the facts than any other explanation of which I have knowledge; and, whilst he would not claim that he has the answers to all the questions, nor that all the several pieces of an unusually complicated puzzle fit perfectly, I think that his interpretation holds the field, and will not be easily dislodged. It is true that a good many individual reputations suffer in the exposition. The picture of Hyde and his ecclesiastical counsellors playing off their opponents one against another, on the ancient maxim of *divide et impera*, using the royal Declaration concerning ecclesiastical affairs, the offer of bishoprics, and the summons of the Savoy Conference as means of procrastination with the Presbyterians until the Convention parliament could be dissolved and the ecclesiastical settlement left to the Cavalier parliament: this is not altogether edifying nor always creditable to the individual actors. But attention should be drawn on the other side to Dr. Bosher's insistence that the revision of the Book of Common Prayer was moderate and designed to make possible the continued ministry within the Church of England of Puritan-minded clergy who were willing to accept episcopal ordination and to promise conformity to the Prayer Book. Likewise Dr. Bosher maintains an attitude of scrupulous fairness and understanding in estimating the policies of Hyde, Sheldon, and Baxter, typical leaders of the several contending interests.

The unfolding of a story whose foci are consistency of end and variability of means cannot be an heroic or even edificatory exercise in all details. Some readers may think that the combination of rigid principles with expediency, not to say duplicity, in their realization is a curious bulwark for the cause of truth and righteousness. To such may be commended for careful consideration Dr. Bosher's conclusion that "the Lord who rules the destinies of the Church can turn even the wrath of man to His praise". There is a saying of Thomas Fuller in relation to the Articles of Religion: "children's clothes ought to be made of the biggest, because afterwards their bodies will grow up to their garments". In my judgment Dr. Bosher is right in appealing to the subsequent history and growth of the *Ecclesia Anglicana* into the Anglican Communion as evidence of the wisdom of the policy of our forefathers who laboured in the restoration of church and crown in 1660 to preserve and enrich the Anglican tradition of comprehensiveness by keeping "the mean between the two extremes", in the spirit of George Herbert's suffrage:

The mean thy praise and glory is,
And long may be.

N.S.

Emmanuel College,
Cambridge.

PREFACE

"THE overturning of all the Reformation of England, without a contrary petition, to me was strange, and very grievous, and I suspect we know not yet the bottom of that mystery"[1]—so wrote in 1661 the Scottish divine, Robert Baillie, as he reflected on events in the southern kingdom. Even today, after three centuries of historical study, some mystery still attaches to the ecclesiastical settlement of the Restoration. Its uncompromising character stands in marked contrast to the spirit of moderation which prevailed in other matters at issue. The political policy adopted by Edward Hyde was generous and conciliatory, and early signs indicated that a similar line would be followed in dealing with the Puritans. Various plans were sponsored for remodelling the Church in the interests of comprehensiveness, and men remembered that the Royalist party in the past had shown little sympathy to High Church pretensions. Despite this beginning, the second year of the Restoration saw the triumph of a militant High Anglicanism in the Establishment, and the final exclusion of all the nonconforming clergy. The church settlement of 1662 was thus a vindication of the religious programme of Archbishop Laud, and a partial abandonment of the position held by Hyde and other Royalists in 1641.

The events which led to this dénouement form a pattern which is inconsistent and puzzling, and the original intentions of the Royalist statesmen and clergy have never been satisfactorily determined. First-hand evidence is scanty and open to different interpretations; as a result, the judgments of historians have varied according to their prepossessions. Anglican writers have tended to telescope the progressive stages of the settlement, and to suggest that the restoration of the old Church followed automatically on the King's return, supported by a wave of Anglican sentiment throughout the nation. Nonconformist historians have simplified the story no less drastically, appealing for justification to two standard sources—Baxter's memoirs and Clarendon's autobiography. In their version, the Royalist government and Anglican clergy were united from first to last in a determination to drive Puritans from the Establishment, and the attempts at conciliation

[1] *Baillie*, iii, 444.

were a means of temporizing until the end could be achieved. More recently, a third view has been advanced—that the Chancellor was essentially an Anglican latitudinarian, desiring to unite the conservative religious parties in a comprehensive State Church. On this theory, the negotiations with the Presbyterians were entirely *bona fide*, and were only frustrated by the obstinacy of the bishops and the anti-Puritan violence of the old Cavaliers. But serious difficulties remain. Many of the government's actions during 1660 are hard to understand on this basis, nor does the theory explain why Hyde's first step was to fill the episcopal bench with the men most likely to oppose his liberal views.

A book which deals with a subject so often explored requires some apology. During the course of a year's research on Anglican activity in exile during the Protectorate, I was led to the conclusion that developments within Anglicanism both at home and abroad threw light on the problems of the Restoration settlement. In particular, it seemed possible that the relations between Royalist statesmen and church leaders might be clarified when seen in proper perspective against the background of the years of exile. Because of the scarcity of material little effort has been made heretofore to write the story of the church settlement in terms of its Anglican protagonists. This aspect of the total picture is further obscured by the lack of an adequate history of the Church of England during the Commonwealth period. The fact that the greater part of the old Church was quietly absorbed into the Cromwellian Establishment has received little attention; but it was of immense consequence at the Restoration. By that time the role of a self-conscious and vocal Anglicanism had entirely devolved on the minority which had maintained a separate and independent existence. In the crucial years before and during the settlement, the Anglican cause was effectively represented only by this well-organized group of High Churchmen. It was one of the rare occasions when the Church of England was able to act as a unity, free from inner tension; its babel of voices was stilled, and only one voice spoke in the silence.

This work, therefore, endeavours to trace the fortunes of an ecclesiastical group during the years when it existed partly in exile, and partly as an underground movement in Cromwellian England. At the Restoration the Laudian party emerged as the dominant force on the religious scene, and we shall then consider the part it played in the events of 1660-2, with the hope of reaching some further understanding of the church settlement.

A word of explanation should be added about the term "Laudian party", which may be thought open to exception. The members of the group in question were not in most cases personal disciples of Archbishop Laud, nor did they constitute in the modern sense an ecclesiastical party within the Church of England. They were High Churchmen who shared the religious viewpoint of Laud, and who were in wholehearted agreement in their method of defending the Church's interests both before and after the Restoration. In their attitude on controversial issues and their policy of dealing with the Puritans they may be easily distinguished from other groups of Anglicans. But it should be emphasized that they were not conscious of being one party among several; they thought of themselves rather as the faithful remnant of a persecuted Church, from which all others had fallen away. I have described them as the "Laudian party" for lack of a more convenient title, and trust that with this explanation the term will not prove misleading.

I would gratefully acknowledge the help I have received from many persons in the preparation of this book. I am deeply conscious of all that I owe to Professor Norman Sykes; his interest and encouragement have been unfailing at every stage of the work, and his criticism and advice have proved invaluable in bringing it to completion. The profit I derived from his careful scholarship and wide learning in the field of English Church History was only equalled by the pleasure of a very happy association during two years in Cambridge. I am also grateful to Professor Claude Jenkins of Oxford for reading the book in manuscript, and saving me from a number of errors and omissions. The Rev. B. H. G. Wormald, Fellow of Peterhouse, was generous in giving me opportunities to discuss with him the problems of Clarendon's ecclesiastical policy, and helped clarify many obscure points. An eminent Nonconformist scholar, the Rev. A. G. Matthews, has placed all Anglican students of the period in his debt by his exhaustive research into the personal histories of the sequestered clergy, and was more than kind in answering the questions I put to him. I owe several important suggestions to the Rev. Douglas Popplewell, who read and criticized the manuscript. Professor Bruce Dickins and Professor E. R. P. Vincent of Corpus Christi College also gave me kind assistance on various points. Not the least heartfelt of my acknowledgments is to the Rev. C. L. Gage-Brown, vicar of St. Cuthbert's Church, London, who welcomed me as a guest on so many occasions, and made it possible for me to work at leisure in the British Museum and Public Record Office.

Finally, I pay my grateful thanks to the Master, Fellows, and Junior Members of Corpus Christi College for the hospitality and friendship which have made my years of study in Cambridge so delightful to remember.

ROBERT S. BOSHER.

CHAPTER I

THE LAUDIAN REVIVAL UNDER THE COMMONWEALTH

1649-1660

ON a winter morning in January, 1645, a weary old man went bravely from prison to his execution on Tower Hill. Though his way led through hostile, jeering crowds, he appeared lost in prayer and oblivious to the insults. Silence fell when he mounted the scaffold, and delivered the customary last speech; then, while the executioner waited, he prayed earnestly for "the preservation of this poor Church of England in her truth, peace, and patrimony". A few moments more, and his stormy life had ended. "Thus Laud fell", wrote his first biographer, "and the Church fell with him." We may suppose that death was not unwelcome; as Dr. Heylyn remarks: "He that had so long been a confessor, could not but think it a release of miseries to be made a martyr."[1] For it was Archbishop Laud's tragedy to survive the ruin of his life's work—to see his Church overthrown and despoiled, his King hard pressed by rebel armies, his social and political programme utterly discredited. His trial and execution were something of an anticlimax to his dramatic fall from power five years before, and caused little stir in a nation plunged in civil war and revolution.

Yet, a quarter of a century later, when Peter Heylyn set himself to recount that pathetic scene, a curious text came to his mind. "As it is said of Samson in the Book of Judges, that the men which he slew at his death, were more than they which he slew in his life", he wrote, "so may it be affirmed of this famous prelate, that he gave a greater blow unto the enemies of the Church and the King at the hour of his death than he had given them in his whole life before."[2] Heylyn's judgments are more those of the hagiographer than the historian, but there is a sense in which his simile is remarkably apt. In 1668, when he wrote, the Church

[1] P. Heylyn, *Cyprianus Anglicanus: the History of the Life and Death of William, Lord Archbishop of Canterbury* (Lond. 1668), 529, 535, 539.

[2] *Ibid.*, 530.

for which Laud died was re-established on firmer foundations than it had ever known in his lifetime. His spiritual sons filled its bishoprics and dictated its policies. Conformity to the Prayer Book and Church canons was more rigidly enforced than ever before. His Puritan enemies were a persecuted and outcast minority. In the House of Commons, where angry protests against the bishops and their tyranny had been heard on all sides in 1641, a fanatical loyalty to the Church now reigned supreme, opposing any leniency towards dissenters. In short, the struggle waged between Anglicans and Puritans for possession of the Established Church had ended in total victory for Laud's followers within a generation of his overthrow. His spirit had indeed wrought more mightily in death than in his whole life before.

That there were important limitations to this victory must be at once added. The resurgent Laudianism of the Restoration was a creed shorn of the political and economic aims by which Laud had alienated the propertied classes of England, and the new alliance of parson and squire was cemented by the Church's surrender of any pretension to political independence.[1] Nevertheless, the triumph of the Laudian party in the ecclesiastical sphere should not be minimized, for it found a permanent expression in the religious settlement of 1662, and this settlement, in the long view, may be said to have given to the English Reformation its definitive character.[2]

That the religious aims of Archbishop Laud would one day be secured with the enthusiastic support of Parliament could hardly have been dreamed in the year 1640. Historians of the Civil War period agree that loyalty to the Church of England was a real and widespread sentiment at that time, and a powerful factor in the emergence of a Royalist party. But the Laudian bishops and clergy, on the other hand, were

---

[1] In his *Archbishop Laud* (Lond. 1940), 429 ff., Mr. H. R. Trevor Roper argues that a victory so qualified was no victory at all. Although he disclaims the intention of dealing with the purely ecclesiastical aspect of the archbishop's career, in effect he denies any real significance to Laud as the leader of a religious movement. Any such judgment, we may suggest, would have baffled the seventeenth-century Englishman. Whatever the other issues at stake, the conflict which Laud raised was in the minds of both sides essentially religious. In any case, Laudian ascendency in the Church after 1660 had important repercussions in the religious and social life of the nation, and was not without consequence in the political struggles of the next half-century.

[2] Cf. N. Pocock, "Restoration Settlement of the English Church", *E.H.R.*, i, 677 ff.

universally detested. The Catholic revival of the early seventeenth century numbered in its ranks learned scholars, able theologians, and saintly priests, but it had remained almost exclusively an academic and clerical movement, and only the circumstance of royal favour had enabled Laud and his supporters to impose their will on Church and nation. A laity by no means predominantly Puritan had come to share the Puritan indignation against the bishops, fiercely resenting the arbitrary powers of the Court of High Commission, and opposing with stubborn conservatism the ceremonial innovations of the new school. In the great debate on ecclesiastical matters in the Long Parliament, scarcely a voice was raised in defence of the Laudian régime. One of the leaders of the Church party, Lord Digby, declared: "There is no man within these walls more sensible of the heavy grievance of Church government than myself, nor whose affections are keener to the clipping of these wings of the prelates, whereby they have mounted to such insolencies; nor whose zeal is more ardent to the searing them so as they may never spring again."[1] Men like Lord Falkland, Lord Hopton, and Edward Hyde were in full accord with the speaker, and are said to have approved the introduction of a Bill for Church Reform which would drastically have reduced episcopal powers.[2]

Under this pressure of hostility, and with the King now powerless to interfere, the Laudian rule collapsed almost overnight. So rapidly did the attack on the bishops develop into a Puritan onslaught on the entire Anglican system that the overthrow of the High Church party cannot be seen separately from the destruction of the Church itself. In the general disintegration of the old system in Church and State, divisions among Anglicans faded into insignificance, and for the next ten years the Laudian party ceased to exist as a recognizable group with a distinctive policy. A few individuals like Bishop Brian Duppa, Henry Hammond, and Gilbert Sheldon continued to have influence in the counsels of the King; but Dr. W. K. Jordan is largely justified when he writes at length in his *History of Toleration* of "the collapse of the Anglo-Catholic leadership".[3]

[1] J. Rushworth, *Historical Collections* (1682), iv, 170.
[2] The bill is printed in S. R. Gardiner, *Constitutional Documents of thePuritan Revolution* (1900), 167. Cf. J. R. Tanner, *English Constitutional Conflicts of the Seventeenth Century* (Camb. 1928), 102.
[3] W. K. Jordan, *Development of Religious Toleration in England* (Lond. 1938), iii, 194; iv, 361.

The persistence of a Laudian viewpoint among the harassed and scattered clergy might be expected, but more remarkable was the re-emergence of a strong and determined High Church party as the principal legatee of the Anglican tradition in Cromwellian England. It will be our aim in this chapter to examine the circumstances which encouraged this development, and to show how the younger generation of Laudians, by a consistent and unyielding opposition to the new order both religious and political, were able to rally the Cavalier party to their cause, and earn the gratitude and favour of the future Royalist government. Laudian policy during the Interregnum may be epitomized as an ecclesiastical preparation for the Restoration; when Charles II returned in 1660 the party was once more in position to exploit fully the old alliance of Church and Crown.

Paradoxically, the renewal of Laudian activity dates roughly from 1649, the year of King Charles I's execution. That event marked the nadir of Anglican fortunes; for the King's strong convictions on the subject of episcopacy had offered some semblance of hope that the Church might yet be saved, and his death seemed the final blow. Eight years of Presbyterian ascendency in Parliament had already revolutionized the century-old religious system of England. The abolition of episcopal government and the seizure of Church lands had been followed by the work of the Westminster Assembly in imposing the Solemn League and Covenant, revising the Thirty-Nine Articles, and substituting for the Book of Common Prayer a Puritan Directory of Worship. From the remodelled Establishment clergy faithful to Anglican standards of doctrine and worship had been ruthlessly expelled, often under circumstances of cruelty and extreme hardship. Identification of religious and political loyalties in the heat of war, and the bitter resentment of Puritans against the Laudian policy of past years, made any moderation or fairness impossible in the treatment of such men. Early in 1643, a series of committees had been created by Parliamentary ordinance "for the sequestration of notorious delinquents' estates", and though the measure was directed only against those assisting the Royalist forces in any way, great numbers of the clergy were naturally affected. In August of the same year a further ordinance empowered the Earl of Manchester to set up county committees to examine all university and parochial clergy charged with scandalous life or political disaffection. If found guilty, they were to be ejected from their livings. The work was greatly facilitated six months later, when subscription to the Covenant was imposed on all citizens over eighteen. "Instead of the trouble of depositions and evidence, summoning witnesses, and judicially examining", writes Perry, "the committees simply tendered the Covenant to any clerk suspected of malignancy, and upon his refusal to take it, deprived him of his living."[1] First to suffer were the London clergy, more than a hundred being expelled from livings in 1643; but many others were made to share their confinement in the various bishops' houses in the capital. Numbers suffered a cruel imprisonment beneath the hatches of ships anchored in the Thames, and in the countryside there were many cases of "rabbling" at the hands of fanatical mobs. The "regulation" of Cambridge University, which began in 1643, resulted in the expulsion of some 230 masters, fellows, and chaplains, and more than 400 scholars and exhibitioners. The purging of Oxford took place at a later date, and caused a similar exodus.

The total number of sequestered clergy has long been a matter of controversy, but the publication of A. G. Matthews's scholarly revision of Walker's *Sufferings of the Clergy* has made available figures unlikely to be challenged.[2] Of the some 8,600 livings then existing, Matthews estimates that approximately 2,425 were sequestered. The number ejected from cathedral and collegiate churches totals 650, and from Oxford and Cambridge 829. However, since some three-quarters of the cathedral clergy and a quarter of the university clergy held parochial benefices in plurality, only 780 names can be added to the first figure without duplication. A further group of four hundred "harassed but not expelled from their livings, together with curates, perpetual and assistant, and schoolmasters", swells the grand total to the round figure of 3,600. This number undoubtedly represented the bulk of the Laudian clergy, who were thus reduced to a condition of extreme destitution and suffering. It is important to note, however, that some 70 per cent of the parishes were unaffected by the upheaval. Few would suggest that this was the proportion of Puritan sentiment in the old Church —rather, the figure indicates that many of the poorer and more remote benefices escaped the attentions of sequestration committees, and that numbers of moderate men whose Anglicanism was rather a matter of preference than conviction accepted the new order. As will be seen, Anglicanism as a point of view continued to exist both within and without the Establishment. It is only when it is equated with the Laudian

---

[1] G. G. Perry, *History of the Church of England* (Lond. 1862), ii, 109-10.
[2] *Matt. W.R.*, Introduction, pp. xiii ff.

position that the conventional church history is justified in telling its story in terms of a persecuted underground movement.

The year 1649 was the beginning of a new era in religious as well as political affairs. January 30 was to the Presbyterian no less than the Anglican a day of calamity and mourning, for the King's execution set the seal on the triumph of the Independent party, equally hostile to both. By his drastic purging of the Presbyterian House of Commons and his summary treatment of the monarch, Cromwell had shown that the real power lay in the army. Sectarian dominance was firmly established, and the nation moved forward into an uncharted experiment of religious toleration which few could have foreseen in the early days of the Civil War.

Inevitably a study of developments within Anglicanism during this period must begin with some discussion of Cromwell's religious policy. The ecclesiastical history of the Commonwealth has been summed up by a leading authority as "simply a record of confusion",[1] and in terms of the previous conception of a national Church with a definite polity, theology, and form of worship, this description can hardly be challenged. Religion seemed to keep a semblance of corporate life merely in the survival of parochial machinery and in the momentum of clerical professionalism. Nor was there any attempt by the new government to find a solution along traditional lines for the religious disunity of the nation. The Protector's policy, says Dr. Clark, "was not so much a settling of the problem [of] what shall the national Church be, as a pretending that the problem did not exist".[2]

Nonetheless, beneath the anarchy of a national Church based on the merely negative principle of tolerance, a coherent policy can be discerned, radically different from the old. The clue to the Cromwellian Church is to be found in the vehement "religiousness" of the new régime, in its profound conviction of the religious character of the State, its endless legislation upon matters of private and public morality. Unlike previous governments, it was utterly non-ecclesiastical and non-clerical in its attitude toward the State Church. The questions of ordination, sacramental administration, liturgy, and ceremonial, which, as the symbols of church order and unity, had been bones of contention in the past, were now ignored. Every attempt to elaborate a doctrinal

[1] W. A. Shaw, "The Commonwealth and the Protectorate", in *Cambridge Modern History* (Ed. 1934), iv, 453.
[2] H. W. Clark, *History of English Nonconformity* (Lond. 1911), i, 378.

basis for the Church beyond the simple requirement of "faith in God by Jesus Christ" was resolutely opposed by the Protector. To a recalcitrant Parliament he declared that "whoever hath this faith, let his form be what it will: he walking peaceably, without the prejudicing of others under another form" would be guaranteed full liberty of worship.[1]

The new conception was unashamedly Erastian, but Erastian with a novel twist. The authority of the State was to be exercised not for regulating religious doctrine and practice, but for preventing any such regulation. To make the Establishment the instrument for enforcing an almost unlimited tolerance of opinion, and for uniting the warring groups in a common zeal for godliness was Cromwell's ideal. Hence he could regard with equanimity the crazy patchwork of the Commonwealth Church at the parish level—a spectacle that to Anglican and Presbyterian alike seemed an intolerable nightmare.

A brief sketch of religious legislation will serve to illustrate the practical evolution of Cromwell's policy. The Presbyterian classis system, originally designed to replace the Anglican structure throughout England, had been only partially erected when the rise of the New Model Army in 1647–8 checked its further growth. The events of the following winter finally destroyed its chance of becoming the national church order. But despite prolonged debates, the Rump Parliament took no positive step toward a religious settlement, its only real achievement being the *Act for relief of religious and peaceable people* of September, 1650, whereby all previous legislation enforcing uniformity was repealed. Curiously, the religious revolution of 1648–9 was never reflected in legislation—no formal action was ever taken to disestablish the Presbyterian system, and invest Independency with official privileges.

In the brief experiment of the Barebones Parliament, sectarianism proved equally incompetent to deal with the problem of a National Church, and it was not until 1654 that Cromwell created that minimum of organization needed for the settlement he envisaged. The ordinance of March 20 regulated the selection of ministers for the Establishment; thirty-eight commissioners or "Triers" were named to examine the qualifications of candidates. Including Presbyterians, Independents, and Anabaptists, the commission determined whether the applicant was of "known godliness and integrity" and of "holy and good conversation"; it was not empowered to deal with questions of ordination or doctrine. A further ordinance of August 28 established machinery for

[1] O. Cromwell, *Letters and Speeches* (Lond. 1904), ii, 535–7.

continued supervision of ministers. A second commission could call "before it any preachers, lecturers, and schoolmasters who are ignorant, scandalous, insufficient, or negligent in their several and respective places".[1] Here political distrust of Anglicans was allowed to limit tolerance, for "scandal" was defined not only in terms of blasphemy, immorality, and offences against the Puritan moral code, but as including any public use of the Prayer Book since the beginning of 1653. These two ordinances provided an administrative framework adequate for the government's purpose, and remained in effect until the end of the period. That they did nothing to check ecclesiastical chaos was irrelevant to their author; they served his purpose in imposing a wide comprehensiveness on the structure of the Establishment.

To maintain this settlement against the opposition of all the conservative elements of the nation involved Cromwell in continual dissension with Parliament. In April, 1657, by accepting the *Humble Petition and Advice* as the constitution of the State, he finally assented to a definition limiting toleration to believers in the Holy Trinity who acknowledged the Bible as the revealed Word of God. Anglicans and papists, however, were expressly excluded. This proved to be the final enactment on religion during the Protector's lifetime, and in the growing confusion of the next two years no further legislation was practicable.

Thus, church life in England and during the Commonwealth became largely congregationalist in pattern, each parish tending to reflect the religious views of its own minister, and to a lesser extent, of the local community. Some degree of association was provided by what survived of the old ecclesiastical structure, and by the operation of the government commissions; but in fierce tension the multifarious sects jostled side by side with remnants of the older systems. Inevitably, attempts were made on a regional scale to fill the ecclesiastical vacuum, but the resolute pressure of the civil power prevented the predominance of any one group, and kept the uneasy peace. It is in this setting that the development of Anglican activity and policy must be studied.

In the beginning, Cromwell's assumption of power served only to deepen the gloom and despair of the ejected clergy. Dispersed as refugees in their own land, they lived precariously on the bounty of patrons and neighbours, viewing the Army's triumph as an earnest of continued

[1] H. Scobell, *Acts and Ordinances*, ii, 340.

persecution and severity. Young William Sancroft wrote his father:

"When we meet it is but to consult to what foreign plantation we shall fly, where we may enjoy any liberty of our conscience, or lay down a weary head with the least repose; for the Church here will never rise again, though the Kingdom should. . . . The doors of that Church we frequented will be shut up, and conscientious men will refuse to preach, where they cannot (without danger of a pistol) do what is more necessary, pray according to their duty. For my part I have given over all thoughts of that exercise in public. . . . In the meantime, there are caves and dens of the earth, and upper rooms and secret chambers for a Church in persecution to flee to; and there is all our refuge."[1]

The learned Dr. Henry Hammond felt a similar foreboding, and declared to his friend, Gilbert Sheldon: "Whether the judgments that hang over us should at all incline us to leave this nation which yet is our lot, I am as unresolved as you."[2]

But though churchmen were as yet unaware of it, the worst period of persecution was past. The establishment of a stable government, the breakdown of the Presbyterian attempt to impose its system on the nation, and the initiation of Cromwell's policy of toleration opened the way to a rallying of Anglican forces. By 1650 it was apparent that leniency was the order of the day; no attempt was made to harass the clergy with close surveillance, nor to disturb the Prayer Book services that were conducted privately. Dr. Hammond now commented to Sheldon that the flight of many of their friends to the Continent had been premature: "Truly we are so oft deceived in what we choose unnecessarily upon foresights that I am yet more inclined to wish those friends here again which have gone on those terms, than to follow them, if I had a sufficient stock to support me, and no care of any but myself. . . . Methinks yet a man may do some good here, and I see no way of doing any anywhere else."[3]

There is good evidence that the government's policy during these years sought to move beyond a limited indulgence of Anglicans. Cromwell certainly explored the possibility of including them in the official toleration, for early in January, 1652, he invited Ralph Brownrigg, Bishop of Exeter, to London for a conference. Brownrigg was well known for his moderate views, but the negotiation proved premature. "The overtures that were made to me are laid aside (as I am told)",

[1] H. Cary, *Memorials of the Great Civil War in England* (Lond. 1842), ii, 118 ff.
[2] *Harl.* 6942, f. 14.
[3] *Ibid.*, f. 68.

he wrote Sancroft, "till some greater affairs may be transacted, and some differences composed. . . . I am requested still to stay by those that conceive some hope that good may be done, which in truth I do not see makes any approach towards us; but I will not desert any opportunity so long as it offers itself." A few weeks later, he added: "[The business] hath been retarded, if not disappointed, *contra molitiones Presbyterorum*. I assure you, the Independents are of a more moderate disposition."[1]

Despite the disclosure of widespread Royalist plotting in the year following, Cromwell remained conciliatory. A staunch Anglican squire was informed by a London correspondent in January, 1654: "The news is very current about the town that the Protector expresses thus much that the ministry would discreetly use the Common Prayer; I hear this from persons of great credit."[2] The Dutch Ambassador reported that the Protector was busy with church affairs, "to bring the same by some toleration and connivance into a considerable and peaceable condition to the content of all differing parties". A conference was preparing, to which "it is firmly agreed that the bishops and anabaptists shall be admitted, as well as the Independents and Presbyterians—but yet with this proviso, that they shall not dispute one another's *principia*, but labour to agree in union; and it is believed that the effects thereof will be to be seen in a short time".[3] Those who sympathized with Cromwell's aim were too few to achieve any such co-operation. Anglican opinion, however, came gradually to see that the real danger of oppression lay in a Parliament still Presbyterian in sentiment. Its sympathies in the struggle between Cromwell and the Rump are indicated by a ballad written on the latter's dissolution in April, 1653:

> 'Twas that which turned our bishops out
> Of house and home, both branch and root,
>   And gave no reason why;
> And all our clergy did expel
> That would not do like that rebel—
>   This no man can deny.
>
> It was that Parliament that took
> Out of our churches our Service-Book,
>   A Book without compare;

[1] *Tann.*, 55, f. 128; H. Cary, *op. cit.*, ii, 402, 415.
[2] Northamptonshire Record Society, *Lamport MSS.* 332.
[3] *Thurl.*, ii, 67.

And made God's House (to all our griefs),
That House of Prayer a den of thiefs,
Both here and everywhere.

The tale's now done, the Speaker's dumb,
Thanks to the trumpet and the drum;
And now I hope to see
A Parliament that will restore
All things that were undone before
That we may Christians be.[1]

Though legal measures against Anglican worship were not repealed, the comparative mildness of the new régime encouraged a widespread resumption of clerical ministrations. It was probably at this time that, according to Matthew Griffith, "some of us [i.e. 'the ancient Orthodox clergy who had been sequestered and silenced'] . . . took the confidence (being partly emboldened by the connivance of the higher Powers that then were) to fall to the exercise of our ministerial function again, in such poor parishes as would admit us".[2] Many Royalist households enjoyed the regular services of a chaplain, and Prayer Book worship was held privately wherever an ejected minister could find a handful of loyal churchmen. In parish churches throughout the land, the use of the Liturgy, discreetly modified, was revived. "In a few years [after the King's death]", Dr. Heylyn's biographer tells us, "the rage of the higher Powers abating, the Liturgy of the Church began in some places to be publicly read; and Mr. [Anthony] Huish in Abingdon had a numerous auditory of loyal persons."[3] Examples could be multiplied, but one need only glance at the situation in the nation's capital.

"The clergy of the old model begin to be very dear to the people in many parts of the nation: conventicles for Common Prayer are frequent and much desired in London," declared a newsletter of 1653.[4] At the Church of St. Peter's, Paul's Wharf, where John Williams and Robert Mossom officiated, "the Common Prayer was much read therein, and the Holy Sacrament of the Lord's Supper duly administered according to the Liturgy of the Church of England, which brought a great concourse and resort to it".[5] At St. Bennet's the rector

[1] W. W. Wilkins, *Political Ballads* (Lon. 1860), i, 118 ff.
[2] M. Griffith, *The Fear of God and the King* (Lond. 1660), Epistle Dedicatory, n.p.
[3] G. Vernon, *The Life of Dr. Peter Heylyn* (Lond. 1682), 147.
[4] *C.S.P.C.*, ii, 234.
[5] *The Churchman*, xlviii, No. 1 (Jan. 1934), pp. 33 ff; *Matt. W.R.*, 54, 261.

and churchwardens continued the use of the Prayer Book, and maintained regular Eucharists.[1] Anthony Farindon was doing the same thing at St. Mary Magdalen's, Milk Street, while under Matthew Styles, George Wilde, and John Hewett, the Anglican use was so openly followed at St. Gregory's that that church gained the reputation of being licensed by the government.[2] At the chapel of Exeter House, Peter Gunning and Jeremy Taylor had gathered so large a congregation that it was popularly known as "the Grand Assembly" of the Church of England.[3] By a curious historical reversal, Anglicans were able to use an old Puritan device to regain the legal right to preach. A Parliamentary ordinance of 1641 had allowed parishioners "to maintain an orthodox minister at their own expense to preach every Lord's Day where there is no preaching, and to preach one day in every week where there is no weekly lecture".[4] Groups of Anglican laity in the capital now took full advantage of this loophole, and lectureships multiplied. John Pearson was preaching at St. Clement Eastcheap, Bruno Ryves at Lincoln's Inn, and Evelyn tells us that on several occasions he went to hear Anglican sermons at St. Leonard's.[5] Nathaniel Hardy, recently converted by Dr. Hammond from Presbyterianism, was preacher at St. Dionis Backchurch. He maintained a "loyal lecture" at which monthly collections were made for the deprived clergy, with an annual funeral sermon on the anniversary of the Royal Martyrdom.[6] Thomas Warmestry assumed the lectureship at St. Margaret's, Westminster, and George Hall preached at St. Bartholomew's, Exchange.[7] In addition, sequestered clergy like Matthew Griffith, Timothy Thurscross, and Thomas Warmestry were known to officiate in private congregations.[8]

If in the seat of government Anglican activity was so unhampered in the years 1650–5, we may accept Jordan's conclusion that in the country at large "Puritan rigour . . . against the Anglican clergy was slowly

[1] J. E. Bailey, *Life of Thomas Fuller* (Lond. 1874), 507.
[2] *Matt. W.R.*, 59, 68; *Evel.*, ii, 71, 101.
[3] W. Kennett, *History of England* (Lon. 1706), iii, 223; *Merc. Pol.*, No. 396, pp. 199–200.
[4] J. Pearson, *Works* (Oxf. 1844), i, pp. xxxi ff; G. B. Tatham, *The Puritans in Power* (Camb. 1913), 229 ff.
[5] *Matt. W.R.*, 57, 340; *Evel.*, ii, 53, 64.
[6] *Athen. Oxon.*, 11, 465.
[7] Articles on Warmestry and Hall in *D.N.B.*
[8] *Matt. W.R.*, *op. cit.*, 49, 178; *Yorkshire Diaries* (Surtees Soc. 1877), 420 ff.

but progressively relaxed", and that "in numerous rural counties ministers conducted the traditional services throughout the period without molestation".[1] Matthews's recent work reveals that in some counties sequestrations continued into the early fifties; but on the other hand there are numerous instances of the ejected clergy being admitted to vacant benefices. In Cheshire, for example, out of some fifty sequestered ministers, by 1655 nine were once more in livings.[2] One example will indicate what freedom obtained in the small rural parishes. In 1650 Henry Tilson, deprived Bishop of Elphin in Ireland, was appointed by Sir William Wentworth to the incumbency of Cumberworth in Yorkshire. One might suppose that the enemies of prelacy would keep an eye on the new vicar, who had resolved "to do God service in the exercise of my ministry among that Moorish and late rebellious plundering people". But early in October, 1650, the bishop was occupied in publicly ordaining the Rev. Christian Binns to the priesthood in Emley Parish Church, and by the following year had erected a new chapel with Anglican appointments in the neighbouring village of Meltham. This he consecrated in August, 1651, with traditional rites. Binns was appointed curate to the new church. It is not surprising that for the next few years most of the candidates for Holy Orders in the north of England found their way to Cumberworth. In 1654, only a few weeks after the Triers had completed a visitation of Yorkshire, the bishop performed his last ordination, when he made Henry Pigot a priest in his oratory at Soothill Hall. He died the next year, unmolested to the end.[3] The remoteness of the parish, the strong Anglicanism of the district, and the fact that Tilson habitually used the Directory rather than the Prayer Book in Sunday worship help to explain his immunity, but his story illustrates how ineffective the laws might be.

In such circumstances, the need for a common Anglican policy on the question of government restrictions became pressing. Underlying all the controversy of the next few years was a fundamental issue— should Anglicans coalesce into an organized movement of opposition to the new order in religion, after the model of the papist recusants? Or,

[1] W. K. Jordan, *op. cit.,* iii, 195, 200.
[2] *Matt. W.R.,* 88 ff.
[3] *Church Quarterly Review*, vol. 132, no. 263, April–June, 1941, pp. 54 ff. C. L. Berry, "Henry Tilson, Bishop of Elphin, and his ministry during the suppression of the Church".

like Puritanism in former times, should Anglicanism be merely a
general viewpoint, content to influence the Cromwellian Establishment from within? The question was not one which could be decided
on grounds of expediency. As was soon evident, the decision depended
on one's conception of what Anglicanism really was. To the Laudian
party, the Church of England, as the national embodiment of historic
Catholic faith and order, continued to exist by divine right though
ousted from the Establishment. Its legal status but not its constitution
could be affected by the action of a usurping government. Its mission
was to go out into the wilderness, and maintain its witness unimpaired
in opposition to the schismatic body that had dispossessed it. To those
termed "moderate Episcopalians", Anglicanism was a matter of conservative sentiment rather than ecclesiastical allegiance. So long as
liberty of conscience was secured, accommodation within the Establishment was perfectly possible, even though rival views were for the
time being predominant.

The problem of the "Engagement" first brought disagreement into
the open. In January, 1650, Parliament imposed on all the following
oath of allegiance: "I do promise to be true and faithful to the Commonwealth of England, as it is now established without King and Lords."
The form was studiously moderate, and a stronger phrase—"to maintain the same as it is now established against King and Lords"—had
been voted down. The question of conscience which confronted the
clergy was one of civil allegiance, but the result foreshadowed divisions
on religious policy. Churchmen differed as to whether the oath might
be taken according to a private interpretation, or must be accepted in
the sense of those imposing it. In the universities some clergy preferred
to resign office rather than "engage", among them such men as William
Sancroft, Edmond Pocock, and Edward Rainbow. But a friend wrote
to Sancroft from Cambridge: "Some have subscribed that were never
dreamed on; others quite contrary, whence I have learned not to think
of men by this touchstone. The great party [is] laying in during this
cessation provision of arguments to satisfy themselves in what least
binding sense to engage; for my part, would I subscribe, I would do it
to the full intention of the urgers, otherwise I should think myself . . .
in the briars, turn things how they will."[1] Thomas Washbourne, a
Gloucestershire rector, sought guidance from Dr. Robert Sanderson
whether for the sake of wife and children he might, "without making

[1] H. Cary, *op. cit.*, ii, 244 ff.

shipwreck of a good conscience, take the Engagement, which many do who are more learned, and would be thought as conscientious as the best". The doctor's reply was distinctly encouraging to those who would take the oath, and his reputation as the foremost casuist of the day caused his opinion to be widely circulated in manuscript.[1] Robert Payne, a former Canon of Christ Church, mentioned to Sheldon that Dr. Sanderson's tract seemed to allow great liberty—"A friend of yours and mine [Dr. Pocock] hath suffered very deeply for want of making use of that liberty, and if the laws of conscience permit, I am sorry his error should have cost him so dear."[2]

The eminent Dr. Hammond, then in retirement in Bedfordshire at the home of Sir Philip Warwick, took a more rigid line. Consulted by Richard Lovell, who feared to lose his post as tutor to the young Duke of Gloucester if he refused the Engagement, Hammond wrote to Sheldon, "I could not advise him to take it, though I think his excuse is more justifiable than any man's."[3] Both men exerted all possible influence against any concession to the ruling power. But on the whole, the Anglican clergy were far more compliant than the Presbyterian. A Nonconformist historian of Chester points out that many Episco-palians who in 1643 had refused the Covenant with its repudiation of prelacy now accepted the Engagement without scruple, and in some cases were approved by the Triers and appointed to livings.[4] Richard Baxter was critical of Anglican policy: "Some Episcopal divines that were not so scrupulous it seems as we, did write for [the Engagement] . . . and plead the irresistibility of the Imposers, and they found starting holes in the terms . . . but I endeavoured to evince that this is mere juggling and jesting with matters too great to be jested with." But he admits that "the prelatical divines of the King's party" refused it for the most part; he was probably mistaken in believing that "the moder-ate Episcopal men" did so likewise.[5]

The events of the next year were not calculated to heighten the Royalist fervour of Anglicans. The young King's acceptance of the Covenant in return for the Scottish crown was a cruel blow to old Cavaliers, though his advisers were chiefly blamed. His invasion of

[1] *Sand.*, v. 17 ff.
[2] *Harl.* 6942, f. 131.
[3] *Ibid.*, f. 4.
[4] W. Urwick, *Nonconformity in Chester* (Lond. 1864), xxxii, xxxiv.
[5] *Rel. Baxt.*, 64–5.

England in the summer of 1651 met with complete apathy on the part of churchmen; no effort whatever was made to unite with the Presbyterian party in the King's cause. Baxter remarks bitterly in this connection: "The Prelatical divines, instead of drawing nearer those they differed from for peace, had gone farther from them by Dr. Hammond's new way than their predecessors were before them . . . the very cause they contended for being not concord and neighbourhood, but domination."[1] Following the disastrous defeat at Worcester, Dr. Payne could write to Sheldon with some complacence: "I am the less troubled at it, since most of the ill success is fallen on some of those who were the first agents to contrive the misery, and for aught I know, had they prospered, would have been no easy masters for those of our profession and principles."[2]

By 1653 another issue was agitating the Church, this time in the realm of ecclesiastical authority. The crisis which resulted was the most important in Anglican history during the Commonwealth; for in effect it was to determine whether churchmen would unite in an organized body under duly constituted authority, or whether a *laissez-faire* attitude on the part of the bishops would give free rein to a determined group like the Laudian party. We have noticed the widespread use of the Prayer Book; but it is also true that to comply with the letter of the law, and to disarm Puritan prejudice, many clergy used the Book only in disguised form. Edward Rainbow, former President of Magdalen College, Oxford, in an Essex parish "composed such prayers as he used in the church out of those in the Liturgy; and so gradually brought the ignorant people to affect the Common Prayers a little transformed and altered, who disliked the Common Prayer Book itself, they knew not why".[3] George Bull in Bristol "formed all the devotions he offered up in public out of the Book of Common Prayer, which did not fail to supply him with fit material and proper words".[4] Sanderson has left a full description of the way in which he altered the order of service, and expanded the wording of prayers.[5] Against this practice, however, strong objection was raised by many Laudian church-

[1] *Ibid.*, 68.
[2] *Harl.* 6942, f. 31.
[3] J. Banks, *Life of Bishop Rainbow* (Lond. 1688), 48.
[4] G. Bull, *Works* (Oxf., 1827), i, 33–5.
[5] *Sand.*, v. 40–2. For the similar practice of John Hacket at Cheam, cf. T. Plume, *Life and Death of Bishop Hacket* (Lond. 1865), 65–7.

men. Until some recognized authority had modified the Act of Uniformity, they held that no priest in good conscience could disregard
the plain requirements of the Church of England.

In November, 1652, Sanderson was consulted by a clergyman disturbed in conscience "as to the use or forbearing of the established
Liturgy", and once more employed his skill in casuistry to resolve the
problem. Briefly, he held that the real purpose of the Church's rule
would be defeated if a too literal observance of it should result in depriving the faithful of the Liturgy altogether. All danger of scandal to
the laity could be obviated if care were taken to observe the spirit of
the Prayer Book. Finally, the reproach of schism was groundless, since
"we do not lay aside Common Prayer of our own accord . . . neither
in contempt of our lawful Governors; but . . . by such a necessity as
we cannot otherwise avoid".[1] This decision was widely circulated in
manuscript in 1653, and the controversy began to rage in earnest. Hammond, who had long been critical of Sanderson's views in this matter,[2] was the oracle of the High Church party, and his strong dissent
gave weight to the opposition. Gilbert Sheldon, in retirement in Nottinghamshire, was given the views of both sides. Herbert Thorndike,
after a hasty perusal of Sanderson's tract, informed him: "For his practice I confess I cannot approve it, upon this score that . . . he hath
several parts of service of his own making . . . and so directly against
the negative command which prescribes [the Prayer Book] and no
other." He held that whatever might be said for omitting parts of the
Liturgy, Sanderson's reasoning for the substitution of other forms was
mere casuistry which would nullify any inconvenient law. He warned
of impending schism among Anglicans—"the setting up *Altare contra
Altare* (not Presbytery against Episcopacy but) Directory against
Liturgy".[3] Another Laudian stalwart, Bishop Duppa of Salisbury,
wrote in different strain: "I have . . . met with a little tract of your
neighbour Dr. Sanderson . . . how, without any shipwreck of a good
conscience, [the clergy] may keep their cures and prudentially manage

---

[1] *Sand.*, v. 35 ff.

[2] Cf. *Harl.* 6942, f. 62: Hammond to Sheldon, 14 October 1649(?): "I think
when I saw Dr. S[anderson] last . . . certainly he told me he used the
Common Prayer; otherwise I wonder not that he that disuses it should think
fit to go to their churches that do omit it. When you meet him, endeavour to
infuse some courage into him, the want of which may betray his reason. His
opinion expressed will betray many."

[3] H. Thorndike, *Works* (Oxf. 1844–56), vi, 116 ff.

c

the duty they owe to the public worship enjoined. There are some very severe men among us that will dispense with nothing; but I profess I am not of their mind, and I have in some measure suffered in their esteem for it. But I am sufficiently satisfied that I find that judicious friend of ours of the same opinion."[1]

At this point a schism was threatening not unlike that between the *assermentés* and *réfractaires* of the French Revolution. The clergy who had lost their livings and could officiate only in private were not minded to be indulgent toward their more compliant brethren, and the issue of ecclesiastical obedience was a convenient stick to beat them with. The beneficed ministers, on the other hand, were faced with a hard dilemma, in which loyalty to church order had somehow to be reconciled with the only conditions on which they could serve their congregations. Dr. Sheldon described the resulting chaos as follows:

"He that hath either his eyes or ears open must needs know the confusion to be great, and the state of [this poor Church] most lamentable; and that not only in regard of the wild schismatics, but even of those who would be owned, and may pass for the better and sounder part. . . . Amongst those that either are, or would be thought loyal subjects to the King and obedient sons of this Church, there is great diversity of opinion and practice about [Common] Prayer and the public worship of God; some believing themselves excused by the times, if they wholly omit it, some contriving the substance of it into a prayer of their own making; supposing they have done their duty, if they pray nothing against the old form; others retain part, some more, some less, according to their several judgments; and some again holding themselves obliged to use all, according to their former engagements; and not so much as to communicate with any that use it not (supposing them schismatical) . . . to the greater scandal of the well affected laity.

"Thus it is already; and 'tis like time will produce more divisions, both in this particular, and many others; and in that confusion the Church is wholly lost, if timely remedies be not applied. The persons thus divided in judgment are men of worth; there being on all sides some most to be valued both for their piety and learning . . . so like enough to give reputation to their several opinions and practices; and so continue the breach, God knows how long."[2]

[1] *Tann.* 53, f. 110.
[2] Letter of Gilbert Sheldon to John Barwick, 10 January 1653; printed in *Barwick*, 537 ff. The original of this letter, deposited in the library of St. John's College, Cambridge, is unsigned and dated only "Jan. 10". The handwriting has been identified by the Rev. B. H. G. Wormald of Peterhouse, Cambridge, as that of Sheldon, and a letter of Barwick of 17 January 1653 (*Tan.* 52, f. 5) obviously written in reply, establishes the year.

To the wiser men on both sides it was plain that only one solution could satisfy all parties—dispensation from the bishops to relax strict conformity to the Prayer Book. Sheldon had begun to apply himself to this end in the autumn of 1652, but on January 10 of the following year he wrote to John Barwick in some discouragement: "At present I take myself the unfittest person that can be thought on to pass between the bishops, both for divers other reasons, and likewise because I have found that averseness in some of them already, as they would not admit any discourse about it, but have desired me to mention it no more to them." Barwick, one of the most active and capable of the Royalist clergy, had been lately released from the Tower, and had been in consultation there with his fellow-prisoner, the Bishop of Ely. On Matthew Wren, the ablest of Laud's coadjutors, Sheldon fixed his hopes. "The truth is", he confided to Barwick, "I shall sooner expect so great a blessing from his Lordship's wisdom, courage, and goodness, than from any; and if I should say, from all the rest of his Order, I should but speak my thoughts."[1]

With Barwick acting as intermediary, Sheldon now laid before Bishop Wren proposals that were both far-sighted and moderate in tone. Originating as they did from one of the most influential Laudian leaders, they suggest that the High Church clergy were ready and anxious to accept episcopal leadership, and to effect the union of all convinced Episcopalians. "There is no way . . . to me imaginable left", he began, "to settle a Church of any one Communion among us (without which we cannot long subsist) but by giving such a temper and moderation to the old laws in all matters, as these times will bear, and by casting the form of God's public worship in the same mold; keeping still to the duty we owe to God and the King, and receding as little as may be from the old way in all. And this was it [i.e. what] I meant by regulating the Church; and if it were first done in Prayers, other matters might be proceeded unto, as occasion is offered, and the times give advantage." Two alternatives were suggested for dealing with the immediate situation. The episcopate, Sheldon pointed out, was now "in the state and condition of primitive bishops, and under a civil authority, though not pagan, yet clearly antichristian, and such as endeavour to destroy the Church of God." In the present exigency, they were "necessarily freed from the obligation of such former laws, as violence and rebellion have made utterly impractical". Therefore,

[1] *Barwick*, 546–7, 538–9.

the bishops should agree "how far this remission [of conformity to the Prayer Book] ought to extend", and "either command, or but recommend it to the practice of the clergy". An episcopal ruling would be accepted, "if not by all, yet by the most and best of them".

However, if Barwick felt that " 'tis not very likely the bishops themselves would easily agree, some being more remiss in judgment, others more rigid", the writer suggested another possibility—"more effectual though not altogether so safe as the former". A commission should be obtained from the King in exile, "leaving . . . the whole business of giving temper to the old laws to the bishops' discretions". But this authority should not "be given to above three bishops at the most, both for more secrecy, and for avoiding diversity of opinion among them". No matter which plan were adopted, the power of dispensation should be used for "making the . . . conditions of the Communion as large as may be, excluding none which possibly may be kept within it".[1]

In effect, Sheldon was merely proposing that an episcopal Church should act as such. The bishops alone were in a position to adjust ecclesiastical discipline to the new conditions, and enable the Church to meet the menace of persecution as a united body. The policy advocated was both realistic and generous, and might well have achieved the end in view. If the question of the Prayer Book had been thus settled, and "other matters . . . proceeded unto, as occasion . . . offered", the history of Anglicanism during the Commonwealth would have been a different story. But all depended on the resolution and energy of the surviving bishops.

Fortunately, Barwick's account of his interview with Bishop Wren has survived. If that prelate did indeed excel his brethren in wisdom and courage, then such qualities were certainly not conspicuous on the episcopal bench.

"As to the business itself", Sheldon was informed by his friend on 17 January, "he [Wren] seemeth to rest satisfied with the reasons in your letter so far forth as he hath taken notice of it. Only, he sticks upon this point, that such a regulation would be the way of hardening men's hearts in the Schism, and that it were better to forbear all the public worship of God till such time as by preaching and the want of it men were brought into an hungering desire to accept of it all. I know not what you will think of such a way, but am certain enough how little it satisfied me. . . ."

[1] *Ibid.*, 541 ff.

"It was his own wish that such a commission were obtained, being satisfied with your reason, that perhaps it could not be got so conveniently hereafter. But [he] thinks it were better to have all the bishops named in it, though the power be granted to a small number to despatch it. And indeed, the way of a commission is that only which he thinks feasible in this business.

"I am of opinion (though he doth not express it) that, if he could foresee an alteration to the better before the condition of the Church were brought to be worse than now it is, he would not consent that anything should be done by way of regulation, for fear of opening a gap to future inconveniences; which made him in discussing that point before mentioned prescind from past and future, and state the question as to the present advantage of the Church— whether it might receive more advantage or danger by such a regulation; and again to consider it *quoad bonum publicum* (which I cannot but yield to him is to be preferred before the private), for he readily grants that such regulation would much advantage many dutiful sons of the Church in several respects."[1]

What the bishop gave with one hand, he promptly took back with the other. *Episcopi Anglicani semper pavidi.* Certainly Wren showed himself a prelate of familiar type, preferring to have the Church bear those ills it had than fly to others that it knew not of. Since any positive course of action threatened a myriad dangers, the only possible policy was one of cautious delay. It was a state of mind fatal to any exercise of episcopal leadership in a disintegrating Church.

Barwick retired baffled, but two months later nerved himself for another conference in the Tower. He found that a period of reflection had merely confirmed the bishop's misgivings.

"The thing that he allegeth", he informed Sheldon, "is that it would foment the Schism. I made bold to propose one query whether the contrary did not more, by suggesting to every man in Holy Orders a faculty of dispensing with themselves in some things while they officiate, which necessity will not permit them to use, and thereby opening a gap to those to whom they officiate to think they may dispense with more, and to be ready to desert them, if they do not dispense in every thing which they fancy not."

But the bishop remained "still tenacious of his former opinion". Barwick could only groan, "I see God is angry with us, and punisheth us several ways, even by such means as we might have hoped for relief".[2]

The agitation for a settlement, however, continued. Jeremy Taylor, who had issued a revision of the Prayer Book offices to comply with the letter of the civil law, voiced the uneasiness of the orthodox clergy in a *caveat*: "The offices themselves. . . . I submit to the judgment of

[1] *Tann.*, 52, f. 5.   [2] *Ibid.*, f. 5.

my afflicted mother the Church of England, and particularly to the censure of my spiritual superiors: and I desire that these prayers may no longer be used in any public place, than my lords the bishops . . . shall perceive them useful to the present or future necessities . . . of the Church."[1] In May he was laying before Warner, Bishop of Rochester, "the clergy's desire to have the Common Prayer taken off, and some other forms made".[2] The episcopate was at length moved to take cautious action. Before the end of the month Duppa was arranging a conference of the leading clergy in London, and Hammond wrote in some concern to Sheldon: "I apprehend your presence very useful . . . at Richmond or London at this time, where some of our ecclesiastical affairs are now afoot, and by what I hear . . . I cannot but wish you were there to interpose your judgment and authority. . . . The Bishop of Sarum much depends upon your coming. And Dr. Henchman who was by him solicited to come up, is, I think, likely to meet you."[3] On June 17 he added: "I am told from Richmond that a journey that way will be expected from both of us ere long, to which I suppose neither of us will willingly deny obedience."[4]

From the fragmentary correspondence which survives, it is not easy to determine what happened. A letter from Bishop Duppa of August 28 informed Sheldon: "When your friends had the last meeting together, the result was that they should meet again toward the latter end of September to consult farther *ne ecclesia aliquid detrimenti caperet.* . . . And to this end your presence and advice is very necessary where that excellent good man Dr. Sanderson is, or whether you may prevail with him to accompany you I know not. But if you can obtain it of him, there may be great use of him. When you come, you must resolve to stay some time, for a business of this nature will require it."[5] This further meeting seems never to have taken place, and certainly no pronouncement was ever issued by the bishops regulating the use of the Prayer Book. Sheldon regarded the project as virtually abandoned after the inconclusive meeting in August. On September 1 Dr. Henry Ferne replied to him: "What you write of the business of the Church as laid aside, I am sorry for, yet do not marvel so much at their failing in duty,

[1] J. Taylor, *Works* (Lond. 1847–54), viii, 575.
[2] *Harl.* 6942, f.24.
[3] *Ibid.*, f. 24.
[4] *Ibid.*, f. 26.
[5] *Tann.* 52, f. 41.

as at the reason of it (which you mention)—their waiting to see what those in power will do, as if there could possibly be any expectation of advantage either from them or by that delay of time."[1]

A little further light is thrown on the matter by a somewhat garbled account given to Bishop Barlow years later:

"Some of the most eminent divines of the Church of England met in London . . . and determined to excommunicate all those who forbore reading the Common Prayer: because . . . they did actually disobey the Established Law, and disown their allegiance to their lawful though depressed Sovereign, and their obedience to the Bishops and Church of England. But hearing of Dr. Sanderson's practice, they suspended the business till his judgment could be had. The return he made them was that which here follows ['The Case of the Use of the Liturgy']; which being received by them and read, it put an end . . . to their design."[2]

It is probably true, as the letters of Hammond and Duppa suggest, that Sanderson's opinion prevented a decision against the conformists. But the failure to issue episcopal dispensation may be attributed to two other considerations. In the event of a Restoration, the Puritans would obviously make capital of any such precedent. Also, Cromwell, as we have noted, was in 1653 conciliatory towards the Anglicans, and Ferne's letter reveals the hope that the lifting of the ban on the Prayer Book might clear up the whole difficulty. In any case, the outcome was prophetic of a future Anglican pattern—no official action was taken, the *status quo* was tacitly accepted, and a decision in the matter was left to the individual conscience.

The Prayer Book controversy is important as the only attempt of the Church in these years to adopt a common policy, and act corporately under its bishops. The failure of the attempt had lasting consequences; the adherents of the old Church remained a disorganized multitude, mostly living in some degree of uneasy relationship with the Cromwellian Establishment. More and more, the authentic voice of Anglicanism came to be identified with that of the smaller group which remained severely aloof and unassimilable. The Laudians had all the strength of a clear dogmatic position, committing them to the straight-

[1] *Ibid.*, f. 42.
[2] *Sand.*, v, 37. Bishop Barlow heard this tale in 1670 from Henry Bankes, Fellow of Winchester College. The date given for the meeting (1652) is mistaken by one year. Further, we know that Sanderson's tract was occasioned by a different circumstance, and that church leaders were already well acquainted with it.

forward course of unyielding opposition to the new régime in Church and State. If the study of Anglican policy can be confined hereafter to the views of this party, it is because leadership in every movement of resistance quickly gravitates into the hands of extremists, whose aims are uncomplicated and action unhampered by any compromise with the enemy.[1]

Why was Anglicanism as a whole unable to achieve the organized and united front of Romanism in England and Presbyterianism in Scotland in time of oppression? The resistance of the Covenanters moved Dr. Ferne to an unfavourable comparison with his own Church: "Well fares the Presbyterian in Scotland", he wrote to Sheldon at this time, "who goes his own way and prays and preaches accordingly, even to the face of them that are there in power, as I find acknowledged in your diurnals."[2] As we have seen, the type of persecution which arouses heroic resistance did not continue long in England; the nature of the Cromwellian Church soon made conformity possible to moderate Anglicans. Even more weighty was the comprehensiveness of the Anglican settlement, which had united in a state church men who came to interpret that settlement in widely different ways. Once the century-old bond of unity was destroyed, it was difficult for those who still preferred the old way to find a basis for common action. The problems of relationship with the remodelled Establishment raised just those issues on which Anglicans had always been divided doctrinally,

[1] It would be misleading, however, to suggest that the history of the Church of England during the Interregnum can be written exclusively in terms of this minority party. The now well-established tradition of depicting Anglicanism as a persecuted underground movement began soon after the Restoration, when Laudian writers preferred to ignore the inconvenient truth that Anglican conformity to the Cromwellian Church was widespread. For example, cf. T. Washbourn, *Sermon preached on May 29*, 1661 (Lond. 1661); J. Beaumont, *Some Observations upon the Apologie of Dr. Henry More* (Camb. 1665), 175, 179 ff.; *Morley*, "Answer to Fr. Cressey", 16 ff. Another Laudian priest, Jasper Mayne, was much more candid: "In those days of public calamity, I saw some take for their pattern the prophet Jonas, and sleep securely in the storm; others to preserve their wretched fortune compounded with the tempest, and made a league and friendship with the winds; others of a nobler and more Christian temper (whose just reward was now to shine like stars of honour in the Church) immoveably resolved to maintain their loyalty and conscience with the loss of their lives, as they had already with their fortunes." *A Remembrancer of Excellent Men* (Lond. 1670), 110.

[2] *Tann.*, 52, f. 42.

and conscientious men reacted to them in opposite ways. Angry recrimination followed, and the taunts of "rigorist" and "timeserver" were freely exchanged.

Above all, the one factor which might have preserved some sense of solidarity among the parties was wholly absent—episcopal leadership. A chief source of unity in Anglican tradition was the value set on episcopal government, and the persistent failure of the bishops to assume responsibility was disastrous for the Church's solidarity. This failure was widely deplored; Dr. Hammond mentioned to Sheldon in 1654:

"I might far oblige you to all diligence in the business whereof I wrote to Richmond [Bishop Duppa's home] by telling you that last week I received two letters from clergymen of several parts, the one of an intention to petition [the Bishops] to take the care of us and press it as a duty to children, and to get many hands to this purpose; the other a beneficed man in Sarum diocese to petition the Fathers surviving to live in their dioceses, and to act as primitive Bishops, adding that the greatest part of incumbents would submit to them. But I desired both to have patience, and leave things to the most prudent managery."[1]

In a work published in 1655 Henry Ferne rebuked the bishops in scarcely veiled terms:

"If our Pilots, tired out with the storm, did think it best . . . to 'let the Ship drive' awhile . . . this indeed might be prudence for the then pressing exigency . . . yet now it calls for the more courage and zeal, in providing for that which seems to have been too long neglected (a more regular Church-way of Communion and worship) . . . not 'forsaking the assembling of ourselves together', as the manner of too many among us is . . . or indifferent where or with whom they meet; nothing scrupling that promiscuous Communion, which is yet seen in too many places, and should (I confess) be provided against. If any ask how? How but by the power of the Keys, which the sword of violence cannot cut in sunder, nor the Church loose, unless they that hold them, cast them away? The use of that power is to separate . . . the peaceable Christian from the factious Schismatic. . . . And were this done . . . there would be no occasion for the adversaries to mock, or for others to complain. . . . 'There is none to guide her of all the sons whom she hath brought forth, neither is there any that taketh her by the hand, of all the sons that she hath brought up.' "[2]

A year later, a zealous layman, Sir Robert Shirley, reported to the King that "the inferior clergy and laity much complain" of the lack of episcopal supervision, and urged the necessity of "a right correspon-

---

[1] *Harl.* 6942, f. 97.
[2] H. Ferne, *Of the Division between the English and Romish Church* (Lond. 1655), "Foreword to the Reader", n.p.

dence and organization" among Anglicans. "The Anabaptists, Presbyterians, and Papists all have it; only amongst ourselves each man shifts
for himself, and unless some speedy course be taken, the wisest part
will become Papists or Socinians, and the more foolish Anabaptists or
Atheists. The bishops (whose duty it is) should be commanded to take
the government."[1]

But neither criticism nor appeal could stir the bishops. Scattered in
various refuges throughout England, the aged prelates lived in fearful
remembrance of the stormy scenes of 1641–2, of their imprisonment in
the Tower, of the execution of Laud. The conviction held them that
only obscurity and inaction could preserve them from the attentions
of a suspicious government. "I secure myself the same way as the tortoise doth, by not going out of my shell," wrote Duppa, probably the
boldest of the lot.[2] There is no reason to think that any of them, except
perhaps Skinner of Oxford, felt a sense of responsibility for his diocese;
Brownrigg is known never to have set foot in Exeter from his consecration in 1642 to his death in 1659.[3] There is little evidence of consultation among them, and indeed they were rarely in contact with one
another; Duppa could write of Juxon: "My Lord of London is so remote from me that I shall despair of having any intelligence from him.
What he is about I know not. ..."[4] Wren of Ely remained in easy confinement in the Tower, nursing a sense of injury and unconcerned with
the Church's need of leadership. His reply to Cromwell's offer of release was singularly unhelpful: "This was not the first time he had received the like intimation from that miscreant, but he disdained the
terms projected for his enlargement, which were to be a mean acknowledgement of his favour, and an abject submission to his detestable
tyranny—he was determined patiently to tarry the Lord's leisure, and
owe his deliverance . . . to Him only."[5]

Even the most pious Anglican chronicler of these confessors can hardly
conceal the fact that Juxon is chiefly remembered during these years for
possessing the finest pack of hounds in the Midlands, King of

[1] C.S.P.C., iii, 49, 142.
[2] Duppa, 20 Jan. 1651 or 1652.
[3] R. J. E. Boggis, History of the Diocese of Exeter (Exeter 1922), 405. Skinner's
apologia is to be found in Tann. 48, f. 25; cf. also T. Wharton, Life of Ralph
Bathurst (Lond. 1761), 36 ff.
[4] Duppa, 10 Nov. 1657.
[5] C. Wren, Parentalia (Lond. 1750), 34.

Chichester for his slender output of romantic verse, and Morton of Durham for his incredible longevity. Goodman was discredited by his leanings to Rome; Hall, Winniffe, and Frewen disappear into impenetrable obscurity. Bishop Warner was later to claim proudly that "he had not forgot in any kind to discharge the part of a . . . dutiful son to my holy Mother the Church", and justified himself by this account: "While I lived in my own house . . . I read the Liturgy morning and evening; weekly I preached privately or publicly; monthly I administered the Sacrament; and I confirmed such as came to me, or I went and confirmed them in orthodox congregations."[1] There is no hint of any sense of larger responsibility. Only Brian Duppa of Salisbury, living in the environs of the capital, remained closely in touch with ecclesiastical affairs, and was frequently consulted by the leading clergy.

Thus the leadership of the Church passed by default to other hands. With the failure of the one attempt at a united policy, we may pause to consider the three parties into which Anglican clergy were now roughly divided. There was, first, the large group who despite a preference for the old order, felt able to join in the life of the Establishment and who may be accounted loyal "conformists". Baxter refers to them often as "those of episcopal persuasion" or "moderate conformists that were for the old Episcopacy", as contrasted with "the new Prelatical divines".[2] Of this type, such men as Thomas Fuller, John Gauden, Edward Reynolds, Edward Stillingfleet, and Benjamin Whichcote are familiar examples; but the fact that two-thirds of the old beneficed clergy remained in their cures suggests that their name was legion. Since theirs was a course involving no material hardship, their ranks were inevitably swelled by the timeservers and "Vicars of Bray". But there is nothing insincere about Fuller's apologia:

"Not to dissemble in the sight of God and man, I do ingenuously protest that I affect the Episcopal government . . . best of any other, as conceiving it most consonant to the word of God and practice of the Primitive Church. . . . But I know that religion and learning hath flourished under the Presbyterian government in France, Germany, the Low Countries. . . . I know the most learned and moderate English divines . . . have allowed the Reformed Churches under the

[1] *Tann.* 49, f. 23; Bod. Lib., *Smith MSS.* 22, f. 21. Cf. Warner's address to the clergy of his diocese in 1662, quoted on p. 236 *infra*. Sheldon remarked of him in 1653: "The Bishop of Rochester I have no interest at all in, nor I believe any else, so much as to get an hand into his purse." *Barwick*, 547.

[2] *Rel. Baxt.*, 64, 97, 149.

[Presbyterian] discipline for sound and perfect in all essentials necessary to salvation. If, therefore, denied my first desire, to live under that Church government I best affected, I will contentedly conform to the Presbyterian government, and endeavour to deport myself quietly and comfortably under the same."[1]

A second group, whose numbers are more difficult to estimate, might be termed "disaffected conformists". They continued to hold parochial benefices—or formerly ejected, were admitted to new livings by the Triers—but had no mind "contentedly to conform" or to "deport themselves quietly and comfortably". Unalterably opposed to the existing régime, they observed the restrictions on Anglican worship only so far as compelled, and increased the chaos of the Establishment by passive resistance to all efforts for greater order and unity within it. It is difficult to determine how far Anglicans of this type made a show of conformity to the new customs. Anthony Huish, for example, held the incumbency of St. Nicholas's, Abingdon, until 1655, "having escaped the danger of the sword of the Commission"; yet a militant Laudian like Peter Heylyn could reckon him among "that poor remnant of the regular and orthodox clergy, which have not yet bowed their knees to the golden calves of late erected".[2] Such men as John Lake, Isaac Allen, and John Lightfoot were a perpetual grief to the Presbyterian classes in Lancashire.[3] Others like John Hacket, Nathaniel

[1] T. Fuller, Collected Sermons (Lond. 1891), ii, 317–18. An interesting statement of the principles of the conformists is given in C. Barksdale, Disputation at Winchcombe (Lond. 1654), preface, n.p. The following may be noted: 1. "We content ourselves with the present state, not seditiously seeking after changes.' 2. "We do honour the Church of England . . . as in Queen Elizabeth's time." 5. "The Liturgy of the Church of England . . . we heartily embrace; but . . . shall not retain anything offensive and opposite to the present government." 7. "We will communicate with any Christians in the world in all that is good and lawful." 11. We will be "in preparation of mind to conform unto any church government which the Superior Power shall settle over us according to the Word of God."

[2] P. Heylyn, Historical and Miscellaneous Tracts (London. 1681), pp. xxii ff. A. E. Preston, The Church and Parish of St. Nicholas, Abingdon (Oxf. 1935), 94 ff.

[3] These Episcopalians defied classis discipline on the ground that "it hath pleased his Highness . . . to secure all godly and peaceable men . . . from those ordinances which the rigour of Presbytery had mounted against them; but where he gives the least encouragement for this power usurped by them we find not." Excommunicatio Excommunicata, or a Censure of the Presbyterian Censures (Lond. 1658), preface, n.p. The response of the classis was: "If they had the judging of us by such a circumstance they would not stick to say that we strove

Hardy, Simon Patrick, and Jasper Mayne made their parishes centres of propaganda for the Anglican cause, and constituted, from the Protector's viewpoint, a dangerous fifth column within the Establishment. They themselves justified their attitude by a simple denial of the legitimacy of the new order. To the party that remained wholly aloof from the Establishment, their respectful veneration was like that of the High Church clergy of Queen Anne's day toward the Non-Jurors.

In this final category is to be found the product of the Laudian régime in the Church and universities, and the outstanding ability of so many of them is an impressive testimony to Laud's success in attracting the most gifted of the younger clergy. The recognized leaders of the High Church party were the two intimates, Henry Hammond and Gilbert Sheldon, former Oxford dons, and trusted advisers of Charles I in his last years. Energetic and profoundly learned, Hammond might well have been the dominant figure in the Restoration Church but for his untimely death in 1660. Though he was a strict High Churchman, his true spirituality and Christian temper made him esteemed in all quarters. Even Baxter, who regarded him as the *fons et origo* of the prelatical bigotry of his day, could write: "Yet I must say, I took the death of Dr. Hammond . . . for a very great loss; for his piety and wisdom would sure have hindered much of the violence which after followed."[1] Sheldon is a more enigmatic figure, grave and reserved in religious matters, yet withal an accomplished courtier. His administrative ability and single-minded devotion to the Church have never been questioned; but historians in general have fixed on him the character of a worldly ecclesiastic and callous persecutor. Against such charges must be set the fact that he enjoyed the intimate friendship of some of the noblest men of his time, and that in the days of his obscurity he was much loved and trusted by his fellow clergy. Feiling's verdict seems the fairest— "strength, not charity, must cover his faults, and strength we find in all his actions".[2] Associated with these leaders was a truly notable band.

for anarchy in the Church, whilst we refused a government settled, with which we might accommodate, under pretence for one we more fancied that was quite abolished. . . . We know some that are of the Episcopal way, that notwithstanding their difference in judgment with us, yet would heartily close with the Presbyterian government . . . rather than have the Church of God lie in such anarchy, as in most part of the nation it doth at this day." *The Censures of the Church Revived* (Lond. 1659) Narrative, n.p.

[1] *Rel. Baxt.*, 208.
[2] *Feil.*, 127.

There were scholars and theologians like Brian Walton, Herbert Thorndike, John Pearson, and Jeremy Taylor, and controversialists like Peter Heylyn, Thomas Pierce, and Henry Ferne. Such men as Richard Sterne, John Fell, John Dolben, and William Sancroft provided contact with university circles. Peter Gunning, Humphrey Henchman, Bruno Ryves, Anthony Sparrow, and George Wilde were parish priests. Richard Allestree and John Barwick were royalist agents who provided means of communication with the exiled court. Among the bishops, Wren and Duppa were active sympathizers. Friendship linked Robert Sanderson to the circle, but his deviations from party orthodoxy were a constant source of anxiety. A study of Hammond's correspondence in the Harleian collection reveals how close-knit was the association of these men; their steady collaboration and clear-cut policy prepared the way for the Laudian triumph in the future settlement.

It is necessary, therefore, to examine this policy in some detail. Its basis was simple and traditional—the complete identification of the Anglican and Royalist causes. Every one of this party was either potentially or actually a Royalist agent, and it speaks much for the Protector's leniency that John Hewett and Peter Vowel were its only martyrs among the clergy. For a characteristic party document, we may look at the detailed scheme submitted to the King by Sir Robert Shirley, one of Hammond's closest friends. Drawn up in 1655, its purpose was to promote "a right understanding among the King's friends . . . by settling the Church", on the principle that "whoso in these times of persecution professes himself a son of the Church will also by the same principles be a loyal subject". The writer goes on, "when once a settlement is made under bishops, it will not be hard for them to know their clergy, nor for the latter to know every distinct member in their congregations, and so be able to direct the King's agents to those best able to do him service." Then he sets forth the measures desired for welding Anglicans into a church militant, organized to defend its integrity and advance the interests of the Crown. First, adequate leadership must be provided—the penalty of Praemunire should be lifted to permit free episcopal elections "according to the ancient Canons", and timorous bishops should make way for others "of more active and passive courage". Thereafter each bishop must assume oversight of the priests in his diocese willing to render him canonical obedience, and churchmen be required to refuse the ministrations of all others. Weekly or frequent

Communions should be held, and alms provided thereby for the support of clergy. Schismatics and heretics must be rigorously excluded from Communion. Canon law should be revised "with regard to apostolical tradition", and new canons drawn up as necessary. Public penance is to be enforced, and the power of excommunication limited to ecclesiastics, with no easy commutation of penance. Forms are desired for the consecration of churches "and the utensils thereof". In view of the difficulties connected with the use of the Prayer Book, the King should order the bishops "to draw up a perfect form of Liturgy, not open to the just exception of Papist or Puritan, and with regard had to the ancient Church and to the present Eastern and Western Churches, that the desire for unity with the whole Christian world be testified". The Articles might be cleared of obscurity, with such caution "as may preserve Catholic truth and peace". A formal apologia for the persecuted Church should be drawn up by the bishops, to "be sent to all neighbouring Churches and Princes, and to . . . the Greeks and other Eastern Churches". Finally, the King should solemnly engage himself to restore Church lands.[1]

Later, Shirley further developed that part of his plan which would be most attractive to Charles—"Some prudent and learned clergymen will be licensed by the bishops to minister in the associations allotted to them (the kingdom being divided into fifteen parts) who shall also carry intelligence to some chief person appointed for that purpose . . . in this way the Church will be in some degree provided for, and the whole party brought to understand and assist each other."[2] Not long after, Shirley succumbed to smallpox, and no more is heard of the scheme. But the practice of using the loyal clergy as agents continued unabated.

If the High Church party was secure in its loyalty to the Crown, there was more doubt as to Charles's devotion to the Church of England. The Scottish venture of 1650–1 had shaken the confidence of Anglican leaders in the traditional alliance of Church and King. Though they were ready to accept Charles's assurance of renewed allegiance, they were keenly aware of the dangers inherent in his situation abroad. Old friendship between the Laudians in England and the leading clergy in exile enabled Hammond and Sheldon to keep a watchful eye on affairs at court. In 1652 Hammond informed the latter: "I am told there be some clergymen beyond seas fit to have wages of

[1] C.S.P.C., iii, 47 ff.   [2] Ibid., iii, 192.

subsistence gotten them, and that if there be not some able to attend the King without bringing charge to him, the consequences of it will be very dangerous."[1] The following year, Dr. Sheldon was worrying about the problem, and wrote to John Barwick: "I cannot say Dr. Cosin is provided for, but I have reason to believe that both he and Dr. Earle will be; and if I find they be not, I will try some other way to do it."[2] Funds were in fact provided for two court chaplains, Cosin and John Lloyd, but the need was recurrent. "I had a letter this week from [Dr. Earle]", Hammond notified Sheldon in 1654, "who acknowledges his condition low . . . but the want yet of Dr. Cosin lower, having but oblations to live on. Whilst there, they two divide the preaching part, but when they remove hence, Dr. Cosin being to stay behind, he shall want an assistant. He hopes for one of his late companions' return, but in case it fail . . . he desires us to choose and send one, and provide him a subsistence."[3] Later he wrote: "I now hear that Mr. Lloyd is returned to [Dr. Earle's] relief, and methinks he should go provided against a siege. And therefore I hope all will do well there for a while, for truly unless [Dr. Morley] would be persuaded to make a third, I know not whom to pitch upon. And these two I am confident will not suddenly want greater supplies than . . . I conclude to be provided for them."[4] This collaboration between the two groups of clergy lasted until the Restoration, when it was to have important consequences.

Meanwhile, the High Anglican policy was being further implemented by a campaign to detach the Royalist laity from the Cromwellian Establishment, and to advertise the continued existence and separateness of the true Church of England. Henry Ferne warned:

"Lest there be any mistake in names (because all the sects in this nation call themselves. . . . Churches of England) . . . by the Church of England is understood the Church of Christ in this land established upon the Reformation, holding out her doctrine and government in the 39 Articles, her liturgy and public divine service in the Book of Common Prayer: and all those are called 'Sectaries' and are proved so to be who (of what persuasion soever) have departed from, or refused to hold communion with this Church upon dislike of doctrine, government, liturgy, rites, and ceremonies, or any of these."[5]

[1] *Harl.* 6942, f. 110.
[2] *Barwick*, 547.
[3] *Harl.* 6942, f. 91.
[4] *Ibid.*, f. 103; cf. f. 52.
[5] H. Ferne, *A Compendious Discourse upon the Case* (Lond. 1655), 1 ff.

There could be no question about the schismatic character of the Cromwellian Church; as Lawrence Womock asserted:

"These men have razed the very foundations of the Church of England . . . and made it their design to erect a new fabric upon the platform of a new confession, a new catechism, a new directory, and a new government."[1]

Hammond and others were concerned to demonstrate the visibility of the old Church, though driven from its ancient parish churches to private shelters.

"As yet, blessed be God, the Church of England is not invisible; it is still preserved in the bishops and presbyters rightly ordained, and multitudes rightly baptized. . . . Schism hath so far been extended by force that many, if not most churches parochial are filled by those who have set up a new, or a non-form of worship, and so that many men cannot any other wise than in private families serve God after the Church way. . . . The night meetings of the Primitive Christians in dens and caves are as pertinent to the justifying of our condition as they can be of any."[2]

"I should speak to that seeming advantage they would make of our disturbed condition to the abusing of unwary Protestants . . . that we have no Government, no Communion, no Church," wrote Henry Ferne. After many pages describing persecutions in the Roman Empire, he continues:

"During these perilous times there was nothing done in the way of the Church for worship or discipline, but 'tis or may be done in this Church. . . . For notwithstanding the attempts of violence, there is the same doctrine and power of discipline remaining, the same liturgy and form of worship, the same government by bishops and other inferior pastors; and were there the same zeal as was in the Christians of the ancient Church under the heathen or Arian violence, there would be no cause of complaint."[3]

Dr. Thomas Swadlin besought his readers:

"I hope you will not deny us the form and being of a Church, since I believe there is so much ingenuity and wisdom in you, as to distinguish between a Church extinguished and eclipsed or persecuted. The Church of England I acknowledge is under a cloud and eclipsed; but the candle is not quite out and extinguished. Wheresoever two or three (of the Catholic Church) are gathered together, there is Christ in the midst of them, so was his promise; and whereso-

---

[1] L.Womock, *Arcana Dogmaticum* (Lon. 1659), Prefatory Epistle, n.p.
[2] H. Hammond, *Of Schism* (Lond. 1654), 179 ff.
[3] H. Ferne, *Of the Division between the English and Romish Church* (Lond. 1655), Foreword, n.p. Cf. W. Brough, *A Preservative against the Plague of Schism* (Lond. 1652), 53 ff.

D

ever a lawful priest or pastor of the English Church is with two or three of his congregation, I will not, I dare not doubt of the performance."[1]

Dr. William Stamp sent a trumpet blast to his former parishioners at Stepney:

"We are not to think the worse but the better of our Religion for the crue persecution which the Devil, by these infernal instruments, hath raised against it. As the King's power (however trampled upon by rebels and regicides) lives still; . . . so our Holy Religion, like the late martyred Defender of it, will improve by sufferings, and appear more glorious and celestial, when these black clouds and fogs shall be dissolved and scattered into nothing."[2]

The same sentiments were expressed in popular verse by Edward Sparke:

> Meantime, a faithful Spouse o' th' King of Kings,
> Thou show'st thyself, by's echo'd sufferings!
>
> Thy little flock yet (through their Lion's aid)
> Shall have their fights, with crowns of conquest paid:
> Then cheer up (Honour'd Mother) cease your grief,
> And let me bring your tears this handkerchief,
> Millions of sons their duty still retain,
> And at least, pray for your fair days again:
> But though your emblem were a waning moon,
> And that too here eclips'd a while, yet soon
> Thou shalt be clothed with the glorious Sun,
> And be as bright as now thou seemest dun;
> Crowned with the sparkling jewels of the sky,
> The moon thy footstool, for all change too high:
> While thy fierce, numerous, oppressive foes,
> Shall be sequestered to continual woes![3]

A constant appeal was made to those who by habit or ignorance continued to frequent parish churches where "schismatic" ministers had been intruded. "All my complaisance", wrote Humphrey Henchman to Bishop Duppa of his work among the laity, "was . . . to continue them in the communion of a persecuted Church."[4] A renegade

---

[1] T. Swadlin, *Whether it is better to turn Presbyterian, Roman, or to continue what I am, Catholic in matter of Religion* (Lond. 1658), 9.

[2] W. Stamp, *A Treatise of Spiritual Infatuation*, 1650 (Reprint, Lond. 1716), 61.

[3] E. Sparke, *Scintullula Altaris, or a Pious Reflection on Primitive Devotion* (Lond. 1652), n.p.

[4] *Duppa*, 1 Nov. 1653. For a similar description of John Hacket's activity, cf. T. Plume, *op. cit.*, 70–1.

Cavalier speaks angrily of "those censures which passed on me and others for hearing or receiving where Common Prayer or other ceremonies were not used, or for hearing of such as (I might suspect at least) were not ordained as heretofore".[1]

"I speak to and of those men especially", Dr. Edward Hyde prefaced his work, "who are so ready not only to forsake, but also to condemn their poor Mother, this distressed Church of England. . . . The intent of this treatise . . . is to bring these men back again to their Saviour Christ, and to the ordinary way of their salvation, His Church. . . . For I may not forsake the true Christian Religion without being a rebel against my God, nor the true Christian Communion without being a Separatist from Him."[2]

Herbert Thorndike was even more sweeping in denunciation of schismatic worship. In his *Letter concerning the Present State of Religion*, circulated anonymously in the mid-fifties, he declared roundly that

"[those are] no more ministers of the Church, that are made by Assemblies of Divines and Presbyteries, than those that are made by Commission of Triers. . . . They can no more be acknowledged by those that pretend to adhere to the Church of England, than Belial by Christ, or darkness by light." They constitute not a Church, but a conventicle of schismatics. "And therefore their Priesthood is no Priesthood, their Eucharist is no Eucharist, but sacrilege against God's ordinance." He concludes: "If you demand what means I can show you to exercise your religion, withdrawing from the means which these Acts provide, I answer that there are hitherto everywhere of the clergy that adhere to the Church, who will find it their duty to see your infants christened, your children catechized, the Eucharist communicated to all that shall withdraw from Churches forcibly possessed by them whom you own not for pastors.

"And if they cannot minister to you, so dispersed . . . you have the service of God according to the order of the Church, you have the Scriptures to read for part of it, you have store of sermons manifestly allowed by the Church to read, you have prayers prescribed for all your own necessities. . . . To serve God with these in private. . . . I do believe an acceptable sacrifice to God, which you cannot offer at the Church in such case. . . . The refusing to hear 'the voice of strangers' will unite us to make a flock under those whom we acknowledge our lawful Pastors."[3]

We have quoted at some length in order to make clear that the views set forth were not confined to a few extremists, but expressed the considered policy of the whole party. The course of the ecclesiastical settle-

[1] J. Hall, *The True Cavalier examined by his Principles* (Lond. 1656), Preface, n.p.
[2] E. Hyde, *Christ and His Church, or Christianity Exposed* (Lond. 1658), Preface, and pp. 523 ff.
[3] H. Thorndike, *op. cit.*, v, 19 ff. Cf. F. Peck, *Nineteen Letters of the Rev'd. Henry Hammond* (Lond. 1739), 49 ff.

ment of 1660–2 becomes more intelligible when we realize that these men were consistently applying the same unyielding principles to an altered situation.

Such men as Hammond, however, were well aware that the Church could not survive its days of adversity by a policy of mere aloofness and obstruction, but must justify its intransigence on theological and historical grounds. It is due in large measure to his efforts and his encouragement of others that the Interregnum became in fact a golden age of High Anglican theology and apologetic. The need was urgent; at the beginning of the period Bishop Duppa had lamented: "What amongst these late philosophies and the Erastian and Socinian opinions too much in request, I doubt the Church is likely to be stripped by learned hands, which seems sadder to me than all her sufferings from the rabble."[1] Hammond set himself to the task of building an intellectual defence for the faith whose outward structure lay in ruins. The number and range of his own works during this period is astonishing; he published more than twenty-five in the period 1649–60. They included volumes of sermons, biblical works, cases of conscience, manuals of prayer; apologies for the Church of England, for episcopacy, ceremonies, and infant baptism; and numerous controversial writings against Puritans and Papists. But he desired mainly to set a standard of scholarly activity that others would emulate. "Dr. Owen tells me that the whole weight of the Episcopal cause seems especially to be devolved upon me," he wrote to his friend Sheldon, "which particular I should be glad Dr. Sanderson or you or some others would confute, for the truth is my appearing thus alone will go for little."[2] Sheldon was directed to "cull out the chief testimonies produced by Mr. Cressey, Dr. Vane, Dr. Bayly, and Mr. Knott [Roman controversialists], and render punctual answer to them." Again: "I have assigned you two little pieces, one in answer to Mr. T., the other to my old friend Mr. Owen."[3] He was concerned to provide funds for theological students, and in 1654 conceived an ambitious scheme.

"Let me mention to you an hasty undigested fancy of mine suggested by reading the conclusion of Bishop Bramhall's excellent book on Schism. What if you and Dr. Henchman and I should endeavour to raise £600 per annum

[1] *Duppa*, 8 April 1650.
[2] *Harl.* 6942, f. 39.
[3] *Ibid.* f. 31, f. 34. Cf. *Lambeth Palace MSS.* 595, f. 14, where Hammond suggests projects for Jeremy Taylor and John Pearson.

. . . for seven years to maintain a society of twenty exiled scholars, and when we discern the thing feasible, communicate it to Bishop Bramhall, and require of him a catalogue of twenty such, whose wants and desires of such a recess in some convenient place . . . might make it a fit charity to recommend to pious persons. . . . Tell me . . . what else you can think of to perfect and form this sudden rude conceit; which when I have also communicated to Dr. Henchman, I shall be content to be laughed at by either of you."[1]

Others sympathized with Hammond's aims. Bishop Duppa wrote to Anthony Farindon: "Certainly there was never more need of the press, than when the pulpits . . . are shut up. . . . Let all good sons of the Church go on in their duty, and when they can no longer preach to the ears of men, let them preach to their eyes."[2] Hammond's friend Sir Robert Shirley had been infected by his zeal, and determined to provide an annuity of £100 for Peter Gunning, with Wren, Hammond, and Sheldon as trustees of the fund. Gunning was to employ himself in "writing such things as might be most advantageous for the present state of the Church of England". But the donor soon decided that "the course adopted by Mr. Gunning of disputing with the Papists, Socinians, Anabaptists, and other sectaries" was not quite what he expected, and died leaving on record his fervent wish that "Mr. Gunning would betake himself to the business intended".[3] Hammond wrote to Sheldon: "I believe Mr. Gunning acknowledges all which the paper you sent me testifies, and that he is upon a large design agreeable to what is there mentioned . . . and that what may be objected from his spending of time in preaching, he is very well able to answer, because all his sermons are upon subjects which are but branches of that design . . . *viva voce* to confirm and continue in our Communion those that are any way doubtful."[4]

Despite such contretemps, Hammond's dream was more than realized. The theological output of the decade was an impressive witness to the strength of the Anglican position. One need only mention such classics as Pearson's *Exposition of the Creed*, Thorndike's *Epilogue to the Tragedy of the Church of England*, Taylor's *The Real Presence* and *Ductor Dubitantium*, Sparrow's *Rationale upon the Book of Common Prayer*, and Walton's *Biblia Sacra Polyglotta*. Alongside this solid array of learning, there appeared a host of popular controversial works, now forgotten,

---

[1] *Harl.* 6942, f. 18. The passage from Bishop Bramhall's work mentioned by the writer is quoted on p. 66, *infra.*

[2] *Tann.* 52, f. 207.   [3] *C.S.P.C.*, iii, 385.   [4] *Harl.* 6942, f. 80.

but effective propaganda in their day. Peter Heylyn, Thomas Pierce, William Nicholson, Henry Ferne, Jeffry Watts, William Ley, Thomas Swadling, Edward Boughen, Lawrence Womock, Edward Hyde, Lionel Gatford, William Brough, even an unbalanced Welsh visionary named Arise Evans—all championed the Laudian viewpoint in popular treatises. The effect of these publications on public opinion is hard to estimate, but one result may be seen in the steady demand for episcopal ordination.[1] We know that George Bull and Simon Patrick were influenced by the writings of Hammond and Thorndike to take this step, and Nathaniel Hardy was in the same way converted from Presbyterianism.[2] Sancroft mentions the conversion of a prominent Norwich divine in 1655: "Mr. Gibson Lucas is become a zealous man for the Church of England, and upon profession of his hearty repentance for what he hath done against it, and his resolution to preach up what he had before persecuted, was ordained priest by my Lord Bishop of Norwich. . . . The Presbyterians of Norwich being . . . full of rage to have lost a brother."[3] Richard Kidder describes how acute the issue of episcopal ordination had once more become in academic circles by 1657, when "there were great disputes" about it in Emmanuel College; he too sought Holy Orders from a bishop.[4] Furthermore, Baxter testifies that Laudian views on Church and Ministry came now to be regarded in most quarters as orthodox Anglicanism.[5]

In a day when the pulpit was a public platform and theological debate a public entertainment, the Laudians did not hesitate to make use of "disputations" to broadcast their views. This practice, as we have seen,

[1] Results of recent research on Commonwealth Ordinations will be found in *Theology*, xliv (1942), 341 ff., and xlv (1943), 37, 210, 254; H. Smith, *Ecclesiastical History of Essex under the Commonwealth* (1932), 327 ff. Cf. also J. B. Mullinger, *Cambridge in the 17th Century* (1884), iii, 542–4, 680–1. The *Libri Exhibitorum Cleri* of the Restoration period show that Bishops Brownrigg, Duppa, King, and Hall held ordinations in the decade 1650–60. Bishop Skinner of Oxford (*Tann.* 48, f. 25) claims to have ordained "betwixt 4 & 500"; but as his name occurs so rarely among ordaining bishops, this is probably an exaggeration. It is significant that the vast majority of candidates seem to have received Orders from three Irish bishops resident in England, Tilson of Elphin, Maxwell of Kilmore, and Fulwer of Ardfert.

[2] R. Nelson, *Life of Bishop Bull* (Ed. Oxf. 1840), 37 ff; S. Patrick, *Autobiography* (Lond. 1839), 23; J. Pearson, *op. cit.*, i, xxxii.

[3] *Tann.* 52, f. 97; cf. *ibid.*, f. 11.

[4] R. Kidder, *Autobiography* (Ed. A. R. Robinson, Lond. 1924), 5 ff.

[5] *Rel. Baxt.*, Pt. iii, Appendix viii, 124 ff.

was Gunning's delight; "on the week days", says Wood, "he would look out all sorts of sectaries, and dispute with them openly in their own congregations. Nor was there any considerable sect, whether Presbyterian, Independent, Anabaptist, Quaker, Brownist, Socinian, etc., but that he held with them some time or other a set public disputation in defence of the Church of England."[1] Two accounts survive; one a disputation between Gunning and Pearson and the papists Thomas Lenthall and John Spencer, another "before thousands of people at Clement Dane Church" between Gunning and the Anabaptist Henry Denne.[2] In 1652 a great congregation assembled in Winchcombe Church, Gloucestershire, to hear Clement Barksdale defend episcopacy and the Eucharist against the Fifth Monarchy preacher Helme.[3] In Wales Dr. George Griffith engaged a more famous radical, Vavasour Powell, and in Berkshire and Oxfordshire Dr. Jasper Mayne debated with the Baptist John Pendarves, denouncing schism amidst riotous interruptions from the audience.[4]

The Laudian party was concerned also with a quieter and more effective way of propagating its views. Constant efforts were made to introduce "orthodox" divines into the homes of the nobility and gentry as tutors and chaplains; one is struck with the frequency in Hammond's letters of such references as this—"I had a letter this week from Mr. Rawson of Brasenose, whose health permits not his stay with Lady Ormond. Tell me whether he be fit for Sir G[eorge] Sa[vile]."[5] In this way, a generation of young English squires absorbed the principles of "a proscribed and persecuted Church", and came to cherish with romantic devotion the Faith of the Royal Martyr.[6] The importance

[1] *Athen. Oxon.*, ii, 765.

[2] *Athen. Oxon.*, ii, 766; *Schism Unmasked* (Paris 1658); *A Contention for Truth* (Lond. 1658).

[3] C. Barksdale, *Disputation at Winchcombe* (Lond. 1654).

[4] *A Relation of a Disputation* (Lond. 1653); *A Welsh Narrative* (Lond. 1653); J. Mayne, *Certain Sermons and Letters* (Lond. 1653); Matt. *W.R.*, 298.

[5] *Harl.* 6942, f. 92; cf. *ibid.*, ff. 54, 57, 58, 61, 74, 75, 83, 93, 98. For similar interest on the part of Bishop Duppa, cf. *Duppa*, 30 July 1651.

[6] A typical example is given by Walker. The Puritan Parliamentarian, Sir Christopher Yelverton, took Bishop Morton of Durham into his home, "where he became tutor to that son of his, which was afterwards the incomparably learned Sir Henry Yelverton ... whom the good old bishop made a true son of the Church of England and endeared to himself with the affection of a most tender child." *Walker*, ii, 18. Henry Yelverton was a zealous member of the Church Party in the Cavalier Parliament.

of this training can hardly be exaggerated, for it cemented an alliance between the High Church clergy and the Squires or "Country Party" which was to figure in politics for the next hundred years. We have already noted the grounds for Trevelyan's verdict that in 1640-1 "the Bishops were hated not only by the City mob but by the whole body of gentry".[1] Now there was a drastic realignment of forces. The Cavalier landowner, compounding for his estates by huge fines, hating the new order and all its works, was not likely to find kinship with the moderate Anglicans who had made their peace with the Puritan Church. But the uncompromising Royalism of the ejected clergy and their sufferings for conscience's sake warmed his heart. In country manors throughout the land the destitute parson found shelter and a warm welcome in the family circle. The proscribed services of the Church were performed with new devotion, and friendship and mutual sympathy accomplished the work which Laud's discipline had signally failed to do. The new alliance did not pass unnoticed. Cromwell complained bitterly that the Royalists had "bred and educated their children by the sequestered and ejected clergy . . . as if they meant to entail their quarrel and prevent the means to reconcile posterity".[2] Baxter declared "I gave notice to the gentry and others of the Royalists in England of the great dangers they were in of changing their ecclesiastical cause, by following new leaders . . . yet Dr. Hammond and the few that at first followed him, by their parts and interest in the nobility and gentry, did carry it at last against the other [Episcopal] party."[3] It is this development which explains a phenomenon noted with surprise in the Parliament of 1660—a solid block of "young men", zealous for episcopacy.[4]

By the middle fifties the Laudian party had thus assumed an importance which could scarcely have been predicted a decade earlier. Its activities were not likely to conciliate the Protector, who now deemed it a source of disaffection to be reckoned with. The abortive rebellions

---

[1] G. M. Trevelyan, *England under the Stuarts* (Ed. Lond. 1947), 168.

[2] *A Declaration of His Highness* (Lond. 1656), 38.

[3] *Rel. Baxt.*, 112, 149.

[4] Cf. pp. 146-7, 170, *infra*. In 1662 Sir John Robartes, Lord Privy Seal, declared in the House of Lords (quoting Mr. Serjeant Charlton): "The Commons observed the force of education was great . . .; for so many of the gentry and nobility found in the Long Parliament differing from the Church of England did . . . arise from this root. It was an oversight in the Usurping Powers that they took no care in this particular, whereby many young persons were well seasoned in their judgments as to the King." *J.L.*, xi, 217.

of 1655 touched off the spark, and in November of that year Cromwell announced stern measures of repression against the sequestered clergy. Royalists would be heavily fined for employing them as chaplains or tutors, and they were debarred from teaching, preaching, administering Sacraments, celebrating marriages, and using the Prayer Book for any purpose. Imprisonment was to be the penalty for the first conviction, and banishment for the third. The ordinance was slightly mitigated a few weeks later by an assurance that "towards such ... as shall give a real testimony of their godliness and good affection to the present government, so much tenderness shall be used as may consist with the safety and good of the nation."[1] The blow was not unexpected,[2] but it was a heavy one. Unwilling to compromise on the political issue, church leaders gloomily prepared for an era of persecution. "We here know nothing of the particular severity which is to find us out," wrote Hammond to Sheldon on November 27, "only general threats we have from all hands. Methinks your condition and mine should be safe from this danger, and yet they say it is not ... God avert his farther judgments from this poor vanquished Church."[3] Sancroft was considering removal into exile, but wrote to his brother that he "would stand to gaze awhile to see what will be the issue of these expectations, and where the storm will fall. ..."[4] Duppa predicted in December that "when the persecution goes higher, we must continue to go lower, and to serve our God as the ancient Christians did, in dens, and caves, and deserts".[5] He found some consolation in seeing his worst suspicions of Cromwell now confirmed, confiding to Sheldon: "As for this desolation which is brought upon the Church, it hath been for these many years so far foreseen by me that I am no way astonished at it, for though the utmost of the activity of this poison hath been suspended for a time, and hath wrought by some degrees upon us, yet the very first workings of it were enough to show us what would be the issue of them."[6]

---

[1] S. R. Gardiner, *History of the Commonwealth and Protectorate* (Lond. 1901), iii, 190–1.

[2] Cf. John Evelyn's letter to Jeremy Taylor, 18 May 1655 (J. Taylor, *op. cit.*, i, p. cclxxvii). One sentence indicates how openly Anglican worship was performed during 1650–5; "For to this pass it is come, Sir ... we are now preparing to take our last farewell (as they threaten) of God's service in this city, or anywhere else in public. ..."

[3] *Harl.* 6942, f. 76.

[4] *Tann.* 52, f. 97.

[5] *Duppa*, 16 December 1655.

[6] *Tann.* 52, f. 105.

Efforts were made to secure modification of the harsh terms. Arch-bishop Ussher, who enjoyed some favour with Cromwell, and rather less with the High Church clergy, sought an audience to plead for sus-pension of the edict. His brother of Salisbury put small stock in such dallying with tyranny, and resolutely expected the worst: "I hear that some hopes have been conceived by our clergy about London that by the mediation of the Primate [of Ireland] the extremity of the late Act might be abated. But when I consider what the main design is, to root us out so that our name may be no more in emembrance, I look upon it as a flattering dream. When the petitioners are awake, they will find their hands empty."[1] Cromwell was non-committal with Ussher—"yet some Court holy water was bestowed on the old man, besides a dinner and confirmation of church leases to him in Ireland", observed a cynical Royalist.[2] Later in the month, however, the Protector sum-moned a group of Anglican clergy to Whitehall, and offered to with-draw the ordinance on their undertaking to abandon Royalist intrigue.[3]

Gardiner has maintained that Cromwell intended his declaration of 1655 as a threat to intimidate the Anglicans, and finds no evidence that it was actually enforced. There are some grounds for modifying this judgment, especially as regards London. Anthony Farindon and Robert Mossom were certainly ejected from their churches at this time. Bishop Duppa wrote from Richmond in January: "As yet I am undisturbed, but not secure, for I see as low shrubs as myself rooted up."[4] In June, 1656, it was reported to Sancroft that "Dr. Hewett continues yet silenced; but hopes (in vain 'tis supposed) for his restoration. Common Prayer is down at St. Peter's. . . . No Communion at St. Gregory's on Whitsunday: but yesterday (being the monthly Sunday) they had one without the exhortation."[5] Martin Blake was expelled from his Devonshire parish by reason of the ordinance, and John Hales lost his chaplaincy.[6] Thomas Holbech, rector of Chastleton, Oxfordshire, acquainted Sancroft with his plight: "If my [previous] sequestration had not been taken notice of, I might have adventured to have gone on,

---

[1] *Ibid.*, f. 105.

[2] *C.S.P.D., Commonwealth*, 1655–6, 109.

[3] *Add.* 17, 677 W, f. 232.

[4] *Matt. W.R.*, 68; Article on R. Mossom in *D.N.B.*; *Duppa*, 16 January 1656.

[5] *Tann.* 52, f. 144.

[6] J. F. Chanter, *Life and Times of Martin Blake* (Lond. 1910), 134 ff.; *Matt. W.R.*, 21.

but the malice of some made that known soon enough to cut the throat of any such purpose." He was now required by the Triers to pledge his "approbation and affection to the present government, and whether I have such or no, I would not willingly be asked". He was, in fact, soon ejected.[1]

It seems plain that open performance of Anglican worship now ceased, and that on occasions local prejudice incited action against individual clergymen. In any case, relations with the government had definitely worsened, and the relative freedom of previous years was never enjoyed again by the Anglican party. We hear of a remonstrance in 1657 against persecution by a "century" of ministers,[2] and later in the year the Council of State begged Cromwell to act against Gunning and Jeremy Taylor for violation of the ordinance.[3] The Protector's death did not ease the situation. In December, 1658, Richard Cromwell instructed the Mayor and Aldermen of London to enforce the laws against the Prayer Book and the observance of Christmas and Easter. Two months later, a Committee in Parliament was engaged on a bill "to supply defects in the act for abolishing Common Prayer . . . and to provide against the use of other superstitious ceremonies and practices in divine worship".[4] This general disquiet resulted in a sporadic harassing of Anglican congregations in the capital. "I had usually frequented St. Gregory's, Dr. Mossom's, Dr. Wilde's, Dr. Gunning's, or some other congregations where the orthodox clergy preached and administered the Sacraments", a layman recalled long after; "but the soldiers often disturbing those congregations, it was not convenient for my father to appear there."[5] Evelyn wrote in 1656 that "the Church of

[1] *Tann.*, 52, ff. 109, 113.
[2] *Ibid.*, f. 190.
[3] *C.S.P.D.*, 1657-8, 226. Taylor wrote to Sheldon on 19 December 1657: "I do not know whether we shall have cause to fear this Parliament or no; for I suppose we shall be suppressed before the Parliament shall sit; we are every day threatened, we are fiercely petitioned against by the Presbyterians, we are agitated at the Council Table; only we yet go on, and shall till we can go on no longer." *Works*, i, p. lxxii. The House of Commons was also striking at the Anglican lecturers, and in June of that year (1657) desired Cromwell to remove Dr. Thomas Warmestry, "a notorious delinquent", from his post at St. Margaret's, Westminster. H. F. Westlake, *St. Margaret's, Westminster* (Lond. 1914), 110.
[4] *Merc. Pol.*, No. 547, p. 118 (23 December 1658); *ibid.*, No. 556, p. 261 (21 February 1659).
[5] *Autobiography of Sir John Bramston* (Camden Soc. 1845), 91-2.

England was reduced to a chamber and conventicle, so sharp was the persecution", and his account of the raid on Christmas Day, 1657, is well known.[1] Again, in 1658, Sancroft heard that "Mr. Gunning, Dr. Wilde, and Mr. Thurscross were silenced a fortnight since".[2] Government action never went beyond this petty persecution, the effect of which was merely to publicize the staunch loyalty of Anglican separatists to Church and Crown.

One final subject demands notice because of its bearing on the future religious settlement. During the later years of the Protectorate, a change may be noticed in the relations of Anglicans and Presbyterians, largely due to the growing difficulties of the latter. The days were long past when a triumphant Presbyterian party had set itself to destroy the episcopal régime "root and branch", and erect its godly order and discipline throughout England. Dr. W. A. Shaw has described in detail the steady decay of the classis system even in those regions where it had been most firmly established.[3] Once the support of the civil power was withdrawn, the Presbyterians were increasingly frustrated by popular apathy and the recalcitrance of many of the clergy. The old Puritan zealot William Prynne expressed the dismay of his fellows when, with "bleeding soul and mournful spirit", he addressed "the over-sadly divided, misguided ministers of the miserable, distracted, undermined, almost ruined Church of England", and used his redoubtable pen to denounce the religious chaos.[4]

Anglican apologists did not fail to exploit this weakness. "I would very fain know", was Heylyn's taunt, "why the Ordinance of 1644 should be in force as to the taking away of the Book of Common Prayer, and yet be absolutely void or of no effect as to the establishing and imposing of the Directory thereby authorized . . . or why the Ordinance of 1646 for abolishing Archbishops and Bishops should be still in credit, and yet so many Ordinances for settling the Presbyterian

---

[1] *Evel.*, ii, 116, 125 ff. For an interesting official version of the Christmas raid, cf. *Merc. Pol.* No. 396, pp. 199–200 (25 December 1657). Cf. also *Suth.*, 165–166, and C. H. Firth (Ed.), *Clarke Papers* (Lond. 1899), iii, 130.

[2] *Harl.* 3783, f. 194.

[3] W. A. Shaw, *History of the English Church under the Commonwealth* (Lond. 1900), ii, 98 ff. Cf. also the same writer's article in *Vict. Co. Hist.*, Lancaster, ii, 65 ff. For account of the Anglican disruption of the Manchester classis, cf. R. L. Halley, *Lancashire Its Puritanism and Nonconformity* (Manch., 1869), ii, 49 ff.

[4] W. Prynne, *A Seasonable Vindication* (Lond. 1656), Dedicatory letter, n.p.

government (in order whereunto the hierarchy of bishops was to be abolished) should be as short-lived as Jonah's gourd?"[1] Sanderson, in a work published in 1657, held up before the Presbyterians the dire results of their destruction of the old Church. The purpose of his attack, he declared, was "by putting the patient to a little smart at the first piercing of the sore, to give future ease to the part affected". He begged for a change of heart among the moderate divines of the party —"of which sort I know many, whom I verily believe to be godly and conscientious men, though in error. . . . These are the only adversaries in this controversy whose spirits are in a disposition and capacity to be wrought upon in a rational way."[2]

The discomfiture of the Presbyterians, and their increasing sentiment for a restoration of the monarchy, did in fact result in a desire for reconciliation with the Anglicans. The need for co-operation among all Royalists was obvious, and in view of the position of Hyde and other Anglicans at court, there was now little likelihood of agreement with the King on strictly Presbyterian lines. Therefore, when in the autumn of 1656 Archbishop Ussher's plan for combining Presbyterian and Episcopal government was published for the first time, moderate Puritans welcomed it as a means of uniting orthodox religious parties. Shirley wrote to the King that a paper was being "dispersed by the Presbyterians amongst their friends under the name of the Bishop of Armagh, wherein they profess to be inclinable to a moderate episcopacy".[3] The Manchester classis viewed Ussher's scheme sympathetically, but declared: "We have many reasons why we dare not admit of moderate Episcopacy." They added, however, that "as for such as are moderate and godly Episcopal men . . . though we may differ from them in judgment in some points . . . yet they are such as we do heartily desire to accommodate with, and we believe that such terms might be propounded, that betwixt them and us there might be an happy union".[4] Nor were signs absent of a desire for agreement on the other side. Dr. Nicholas Bernard had published Ussher's tract, "wishing that such as do consent in substantials for matter of doctrine, would consider of some

---

[1] P. Heylyn, *Ecclesia Vindicata* (Lond. 1657), general pref., n.p.

[2] *Sand.*, ii, pp. liv ff. Notice of Sanderson's words was taken by the Manchester classis; cf. W. A. Shaw, *Minutes of the Manchester Classis* (Chetham Soc. 1891), ii, 312.

[3] *C.S.P.C.*, iii, 192.

[4] *The Censures of the Church Revived* (Lond. 1659), 85.

conjunction in point of discipline".[1] John Gauden wrote to him, observing that "not only Presbyterians and Independents . . . but even Episcopal men are upon a very calm temper". Two prominent Presbyterian divines had expressed to him their willingness to accept a limited episcopacy, and he himself heartily welcomed Ussher's proposal.[2]

It was in this spirit of accommodation that the "Association" movement began to spread through the country, aiming to unite the parish clergy "in the practice of so much of discipline as the Episcopal, Presbyterians, and Independents are agreed in, and as crosseth none of their principles".[3] Baxter notes that "three or four moderate conformists that were for the old Episcopacy" were willing to join his Worcester Association, and this was common elsewhere. In Devon "the far greater and better part of the Episcopal persuasion joined". The Cornish "voluntary classis" established in 1655 also contained a number of Anglicans.[4]

But among the Laudian party the overtures for peace met with no response whatever. According to Baxter, "those of the new Prelatical way, Dr. Hammond's followers", stayed rigidly aloof from the county Association, and his own approach to Hammond met with a polite rebuff.[5] Promising negotiations with Episcopalians in Shropshire, represented by Thomas Warmestry and Thomas Good, were quickly ended when Warmestry sought the advice of Peter Gunning and other London clergy.[6] To Dr. Sanderson's enquiry whether he might properly join with certain Presbyterian ministers in Lincolnshire, Hammond replied indignantly. If the bishop [Winniffe] could exercise his authority, he would certainly forbid Presbyterian services; how could his friend consider "joining with Schismatics in Schism"? He added a significant comment: "To sweeten them by complying with them in schismatical acts, and making them believe themselves pardonable whilst they continue and remain unreformed in their Schism, is to confirm them in their course. . . . Certainly the greater charity to those

[1] N. Bernard, *The Reduction of Episcopacy unto the Form of Synodical Government by Dr. James Ussher* (Lond. 1656), pref. to the reader, n.p.

[2] *Thur.*, v, 598.

[3] *Rel. Baxt.*, 167. For Association movement, cf. W. A. Shaw, *History of the English Church under the Commonwealth*, ii, 152 ff.

[4] *Rel. Baxt.*, 97; *Matt. C. R.*, 281; M. Coate, *Cornwall in the Great Civil War* (1933), 339.

[5] *Rel. Baxt.*, 97, 112, 149, 208.

[6] *Ibid.*, 149 ff.

moderate reformable Presbyterians were to assist and hasten the per-fecting of their repentance, and recovering of their erroneous prac-tices. . . . For those that mean not this, 'tis certain that they are not to be persuaded that, if the laws regain their power, they shall be tolerated, their way being so unreconcileable with Prelacy." Poor Sanderson meekly complied, sadly hoping that "I may not seem to be the chiefest instrument in hindering that meeting, which to some men's apprehen-sion seemeth to tend so much to Christian peace and edification".[1]

The attitude of the High Church clergy had an emotional as well as a doctrinal basis. No one reading their correspondence can fail to notice the inveterate hostility which singles out the Presbyterians as the real authors of all the Church's sufferings. We need not look to such em-bittered controversialists as Peter Heylyn and Thomas Pierce for evi-dence of this feeling; it is a common theme. The mild Sancroft could write: "I look upon that cursed Puritan faction as the ruin of the most glorious Church upon earth."[2] When a correspondent inquired of Bishop Duppa whether the Jesuits or the Presbyterians were more dangerous to the Church, the good prelate replied: "Both of them (though never so distant one from another) are united in their infinite malice towards this poor Church. But if there be any difference, I shall absolutely cast it on the Presbyterians, whose business it hath been from the beginning of the troubles [to destroy us], and [who] will never cease till they have perfected it."[3] Much the same sentiment is ex-pressed in an Anglican ballad:

> "Papists took one away, but you combine
> To rob the people both of bread and wine;
> They blame us 'cause we have not rites so many,
> But you condemn us more 'cause we have any;
> They will not call us Catholics, you can
> Scarce yield us the first name of Christian.
> Poor English Church, thy enemies from Rome
> Were cruel, more unkind are those at home."[4]

It was idle to expect such prejudice to be dispelled by what, in Laudian eyes, was nothing more than the shameless opportunism of Presby-terian policy.

[1] *Sand.*, vi, 379–80.
[2] *Theologian and Ecclesiastic*, viii, 167.
[3] *Tann.* 52, f. 106.
[4] C. Barksdale, *Disputation at Winchcombe* (Lond. 1653), 2.

The closing years of the Interregnum undoubtedly found Anglican-ism in a much stronger position than at the beginning of the decade. Public opinion, moved by dislike of the change and uncertainty of army rule and by repugnance to Puritan moral legislation, was reacting steadily in favour of the old order in Church as well as State. To the man in the street the Church of England seemed to have suffered many things of many physicians, and to have grown nothing better but rather worse. To some who had once fretted under the Laudian discipline, the days of prelacy now suggested a newly valued uniformity and order in religion. Many complaints recorded in the State Papers of 1658–60 witness to the growing popularity of "prelatical" worship.[1] This re-vival profited by the reactionary trend in political sentiment; soon the watchwords of the hour would be "legitimacy" and "the old Constitu-tion".

It was for this turn of events that the Laudians had planned from the beginning. Other religious groups hoped to profit by a Restoration, and each had its characteristic view of "a right settlement of the Church". But the High Church party could now reap the timely fruits of a consistent policy; even among Anglicans in general its tacti-cal advantage was clear. Its unblemished record of loyalty and its intimate ties with the exiled Court laid a strong claim on Royal favour. The ability and learning of its leaders marked them out for high office in a restored Church. The Cavalier gentry had been largely won over, and gave the party a prospect of political strength. These were powerful assets, but it should be noted that they were largely unsuspected at the time of the Restoration. Even a wise observer would scarcely have predicted in May, 1660, the religious settlement actually arrived at two years later. In order to understand fully the forces working for a Laud-ian triumph, we must examine the religious policy of the Royalist exiles now recalled to power.

---

[1] Cf. the examples gathered by G. B. Tatham, op. cit., 226 ff.; also, W. K. Jordan, op. cit., iii, 201 ff. Samuel Pepys provides a good example of the change of sentiment; cf. A. Bryant, Samuel Pepys, the Man in the Making (Lond. 1933), 59 ff.

CHAPTER II

ANGLICANS IN EXILE
1645–1660

IN these troubled years of the Interregnum other Anglicans were contending for their faith in a setting far different from that of Cromwellian England. The clergy who shared in the Royalist emigration
abroad faced no easier task than their fellows at home, but so much
greater was their freedom of action that some historians have affirmed
that during this period the real centre of Anglican church life was on
the Continent.[1] Certain it is that the course pursued by the exiled
churchmen was to have a profound influence on the religious situation
in 1660, when the King and his followers returned to England.

Following the disastrous battle of Marston Moor and the flight of the
Queen to France in 1644, a growing stream of refugees crossed the
Channel to seek asylum in France and the Low Countries. As the
Royalist cause steadily declined, the emigration assumed proportions
which suggest that of the French Revolution 150 years later. Many
Cavaliers were drawn to Paris to be near the Court of the exiled Queen,
but others found life easier in the provincial towns of Rouen, Caen,
Blois, Saumur, and Angers. Still others settled in the commercial
centres of Holland and the Spanish Netherlands, and in this region
Charles II maintained his little court in later years. Colonies of English
merchants had long existed in the Dutch cities, and the sympathy of the
ruling house was assured by the fact that the Princess of Orange was a
daughter of Charles I. In this host of émigrés were over a hundred
clergy of the Church of England, rendered notorious at home by their
Laudian views and Royalist activity.[2]

There were notable men among them. John Cosin, Dean of Peterborough, had been a target of Puritan attack in the ceremonial con-

---

[1] Cf. W. J. Sparrow Simpson, *Archbishop Bramhall* (Lond. 1927), 75; H. W.
Clark, *History of English Nonconformity* (Lond. 1911), i, 390; H. H. Henson,
Studies in English Religion in the 17th Century (Lond. 1903), 257 ff.

[2] Cf. Appendix, "A List of Anglican Clergy in Exile, 1645–60".

troversies; by a wise choice of Charles I he was appointed chaplain to the Anglicans of Queen Henrietta's Court. A plain blunt man of indomitable spirit, he was well fitted to bear the brunt of the Romanist onslaught on the exiled Church, and proved an untiring pastor and vigorous controversialist. To Richard Steward, Dean of St. Paul's, whom he greatly loved and trusted, the King had given the spiritual charge of the young Prince of Wales. Until his death in 1651 Steward was a tower of strength to the Anglican cause; Evelyn eulogized him as a man "of incomparable parts and great learning, of exemplary life, and a very great loss to the whole Church".[1] John Earle, Chancellor of Salisbury, succeeded him as chaplain; he combined a gift for satire with a characteristically Anglican piety which caused Walton to compare him to Hooker. According to Bishop Burnet, "Earle was a man of all the clergy for whom the King had the greatest esteem. He had been his sub-tutor, and followed him in all his exile with so clear a character that the King . . . who had a secret pleasure in finding out anything that lessened a man esteemed for piety, yet had a value for him beyond all the men of his order."[2]

Another well-known divine was George Morley, Canon of Christ Church, and for some years chaplain to the Hyde family. Like his close friend Gilbert Sheldon, Morley was a complex figure. Shrewd and resourceful, he was a staunch churchman, and much esteemed in religious circles. Yet one is left with the impression of a reserved and subtle nature, having none of the winsomeness of Earle or the frank combativeness of Cosin. Intellectually pre-eminent in the group was John Bramhall, Bishop of Derry, already well known as Strafford's ally in the struggle with Puritanism in Ireland. During his frequent wanderings through western Europe he found time to defend the Anglican position with some of the ablest controversial works of the century, thereby earning from his foes the sobriquet of "Bishop Bramble". Associated with these leaders were other divines of reputation—Edward Martin, Richard Watson, Robert Creighton, Peter Mewes, Guy Carleton, Joseph Crowther, John Lloyd, Eleazor Duncon, Michael Honywood, Benjamin Laney—some destined to high office in the Restoration Church. Again one is impressed by the close friendship which linked these clergy, and made possible solidarity of policy and

---

[1] *Evel.*, 11, 46: cf. letters of Charles I to the Prince of Wales, *S.P.C.*, 11, 253.

[2] I. Walton, *Lives* (Ed. Lond. 1927), 213–14; G. Burnet, *History of His Own Time* (Ed. Lond. 1840), i, 152.

action. We have noted already how closely in touch were Morley, Cosin, and Earle with church leaders in England.

In addition to the threat of imprisonment which decided these men to seek refuge on the Continent, the desire for spiritual freedom was a strong motive. Convinced that their Church faced suppression at home, they were further alarmed by the Presbyterian argument that the Church of England was being not abolished, but merely subjected to a final reformation on the Continental pattern. Though the Westminster Assembly had done away with episcopacy and the Prayer Book, and introduced a new Confession of Faith, it claimed that the Establishment thus altered remained the legitimate Church of the English people. If the identity of Anglican faith and order were not to be obscured and lost, there was urgent need for the true Church of England to maintain a visible existence in the freedom of exile. Such witness was held to be impossible in England:

"What will you say if they be exiles too, worse exiles than ourselves?" demanded Dr. Henry Byam in a sermon preached in 1649 before Charles II. "They cannot breathe one gust of free air. . . . Can he [the Englishman] tell of what religion he is to-day, or must profess to-morrow? Can he find him any rules or statutes, by which he may frame himself to walk in some security? Is there any face of a Church or Commonwealth left? Nay, can he find one corner in that Hell of Confusion where he may sit down, and without fear of a Committee bloodhound lament the times? No sure. . . . So that we may say, If we had stayed with them, we must have strayed with them; and whilst we sought to keep our homes, we might have lost that Home the saints did seek for and enjoy.'[1]

A similar belief in the mission of the exiled Church was expressed by Dean Steward in a sermon in Paris:

"I must hence hold it a duty I owe to that venerable Church that baptized us all, though our now afflicted Mother, to keep the fruit of her own womb from thus trampling on her, to keep them, as much as in me lies, from being gulled and cheated from her unity, and withal from communicating too deeply in sin with those who have now cast her on the ground."[2]

---

[1] H. Byam, *Thirteen Sermons* (Lond. 1675), 113–14. Cf. Hyde's reference to Sheldon in a letter to his wife from Madrid, 13 May 1650: "Can it be possible that in the midst of these new threats and others, the Warden [of All Souls' College, Oxford] can find it safe to stay in that cursed country? There can be no doubt, but they will enjoin all the obligations upon all people who live within their dominions which may secure them of their fidelity and allegiance to them, and therefore it is madness to stay upon the confidence that they can get away, when they will." *Hist. MSS. Com., Bath MSS.* (1907), ii. p. 90.

[2] R. Steward, *The English Case Exactly Set Down* (Lond. 1659), 23–4.

But the situation abroad hardly favoured such a plan. Beset by the poverty and insecurity which are the common lot of refugees, the clergy could expect no aid or sympathy from the Churches dominant in Europe; on the contrary, they were often subject to petty persecution and hostile propaganda. "I do not remember in ecclesiastical history", wrote Richard Watson bitterly, "to have read of any number of orthodox Christians chased out of their own country, at loss for a safe communion in some one or other elsewhere; that [was] our special difficulty or misfortune."[1] In the eyes of the world the English exiles were partisans of a wholly discredited faith. As between a victorious Puritanism in Britain, and Rome at the height of her Counter-Reformation triumphs in Europe, Anglicanism seemed the sorry shade of a Church, ἐγγὺς ἀφανισμοῦ. To the Continental mind it was the natural fate of an illogical compromise in religion, maintained hitherto only by the vagaries of the English State. But even more disheartening to churchmen was the knowledge that the English communities themselves were deeply divided on religious policy.

Inevitably the refugees saw all things in terms of one problem—what steps would bring about the King's restoration, and their own return to forfeited homes and possessions. Royalist resistance in England was now crushed; the former King's obstinate clinging to his Anglican principles had brought him to his death, and reduced his party to impotence. A reorientation of policy seemed urgent to many if the Royalist cause were to find new strength. Since the end of the first Civil War there had been many to protest against the idea that "monarchy ought to fall, because Episcopacy cannot stand".[2] By 1650 the conviction was even more widespread that the first step in recovery must be to disembarrass the King of a moribund Anglicanism. On one side, the French pamphleteer, de la Milletière, was stating that the English Church "had perished by the proper axioms of its own Reformation, and hath no more subsistence in the world, nor pretence to the privilege of a Church". On these grounds he invited Charles in a public letter to embrace the Roman Catholic faith.[3] On the other, Francis Wentworth was writing from Amsterdam to one of the King's Council:

"As for what concerns his Majesty's interest with foreign states (in relation to the religious professions in Christendom), 'tis surely unquestionably . . . in

[1] R. Watson, *Bishop Cosin's Opinion for Communicating rather with Genevv than Rome* (Lond. 1684), 16.

[2] *S.P.C.*, ii, 263.   [3] *Bramhall*, i, 63.

ANGLICANS IN EXILE

[either] the Popish or Reformed. The Prelatical or Episcopal I mention not in regard that there is no such thing in the least owned by any Protestant Church this day in the world. . . . Were not these Councillors mad upon their lusts and ecclesiastical preferments . . . their understandings could not possibly be as besotted as to affirm his Majesty's interest to lie in a non-entity or a thing that hath not so much as any being."

After discounting the advantages of a Romanist policy, he concluded:

"Whence, my Lord, I hope 'tis clear that if there be any interest his Majesty hath to own in order to his restoration, it must rationally be that of the Reformed Churches . . . [and] the policy of engaging the Protestant party both at home and abroad firmly to adhere unto him. And therefore they that advise his Majesty to desert or decline it for that which is not only without a being but is universally reprobated and exploded, it were easy to determine what ill friends such are."[1]

So in an age when political action in Europe was inseparable from religious policy, three courses were hotly debated among Royalist leaders. To conservatives like Hyde, Hopton, and Nicholas, breaking the old alliance of Church and Crown was unthinkable. In their view the very basis of the Royalist party was its claim to "stand fast upon the old rock of established law", and the Church was "as much fenced and secured by the laws as Monarchy itself, and an entire part of the frame and constitution of the kingdom".[2] But in terms of quick results this policy was bankrupt—its supporters could only advise an attitude of watchful waiting, until the factions within the Commonwealth "at last determine the confusion and be each other's executioners".[3] Alliance with the Presbyterians, on the other hand, offered the immediate prospect of winning back the kingdom with a powerful Scottish army; overtures from Scotland had reached the young King within a month of his father's execution. If the price of aid was acceptance of the Covenant, so often refused by his father, there were many to remind the prince that he was also a grandson of Henry of Navarre, who had found a kingdom well worth a change of faith. Finally, if the King were to favour or even adopt Roman Catholicism, the hope of engaging the Pope and Catholic monarchs in a crusade against Cromwell seemed promising. Even the Presbyterian Wentworth confessed: "Could his Majesty be supposed willing to espouse the cause of that anti-Christian religion, it cannot be denied . . . but he were likely enough to have store of assistants who might be sufficiently considerable."[4] To Anglican

1 *Orm. II*, i, 284–5.   2 *S.P.C.*, ii, 308, 326.
3 *Ibid.*, iii, 198.   4 *Orm.* II, i, 284.

statesmen these latter alternatives were counsels of despair, as injurious to the true welfare of the Crown as they were fatal to the Church. A rhyme from *Mercurius Pragmaticus* went the rounds:

> *A Scot and a Jesuit, joined in hand*
> *First told the world to say,*
> *That subjects ought to have command*
> *And princes to obey.*[1]

The story of the exile becomes one of jealous and embittered factions, with religious policy the chief bone of contention.

The Romanizing party naturally centred in the court of the Queen Mother, Henrietta Maria. From the time of her marriage the Queen had regarded the promotion of the Roman Catholic cause as her mission, and worked openly to win converts. Now, a refugee in her nephew's court, she saw in the disintegration of the Church of England a golden opportunity for a mass conversion. To win over the bulk of Royalist exiles, many of them of great prominence, might be the starting-point of an English Counter-Reformation, and was a stake well worth the effort. Certainly Rome could exercise a more powerful appeal than ever before. Papists were no longer under suspicion of disloyalty to the Crown, since they had fought manfully for the King in the Civil War. The pressure of a dominant and flourishing religion would be strong on a tiny and discouraged minority group far from home. Finally, the provision of financial relief for converts would have its effect on the destitute English.

Needless to say, the Queen believed that alliance with the power of Rome was the surest path to a Restoration, and never ceased to urge this on her son. Her essential stupidity and bigotry eventually destroyed the influence she might have had in Cavalier circles; only the intermittent support of Cardinal Mazarin and the French Court, together with the activity of such confederates as her secretary Lord Jermyn, her almoner Walter Montague, Sir Marmaduke Langdale, and the Jesuit Peter Talbot, gave her policy any consequence. Considered today, the grand schemes and fantastic intrigues of the Court circle have an air of opera-bouffe; but there can be no doubt that Charles toyed with a papal alliance in his more desperate moments, and never lost hope of aid from a Catholic coalition.

However alarming Romanist intrigue might seem, the Presbyterian

---

[1] *Mercurius Pragmaticus*, 12 to 20 October 1647.

party was in reality a far more dangerous threat to Anglican hopes. "In the whole period up to the Restoration", says Keith Feiling, ". . . alliance with Presbyterianism was more than once within an ace of success, and between 1646 and 1651 was the ever-present nightmare of the Anglican Cavaliers."[1] Made up partly of Scottish Royalists and partly of English Puritans disgruntled with the army's rule, a faction of Royalists in exile proclaimed in season and out that Charles could only be restored on Presbyterian terms. These usually included the religious and political concessions made by the late King at the Isle of Wight, and the re-establishment of the Long Parliament, now purged by Cromwell. Leaders of the party were the Earl of Balcarres, with whom Hyde waged an endless feud, Lord Culpeper, Major-General Edward Massey, and James Bunce, while such opportunists as the Duke of Buckingham, Prince Rupert, and Lord Wilmot usually lent their support. An unnatural alliance developed between them and the Queen, who as a means of achieving her own aims eagerly joined in schemes to destroy the influence of Anglican statesmen.

It was fortunate that the Church of England could count on the devotion of a group of laymen of proven ability and integrity. The long years of poverty and disappointment played havoc with Royalist morale. The shabby court was the prey of faction and jealousy, disgraced by open vice and shameless opportunism. In this atmosphere the uprightness and disinterested patriotism of the Anglican leaders stand out clearly. It was for such qualities as these that Charles, cynical but discerning, came to rely on Edward Hyde as on no other man. Hyde's devotion to the Church had been already apparent when he was a conservative reformer in the Long Parliament, but like many others he seems to have been influenced by association with the Laudian clergy in the years of adversity. In the beginning he probably shared the latitudinarian views of Lord Falkland's circle; certainly he was an unsparing critic of the bishops and their policy in the Parliament of 1641. A growing intimacy with such men as Sheldon, Morley, and Cosin soon had its effect. In 1649 he could write to Sheldon: "You are one of those few by whose advice and example I shall most absolutely guide myself, and upon whose friendship I have an entire and absolute dependence."[2] Two illustrations will indicate the new temper of his churchmanship. To Lord Hopton he stated his belief that the acts of a non-episcopal

---

[1] Feil., 75. [2] Add. 4162, f. 20.

ministry were completely invalid, and dissented from "that charitable opinion, that some of the offices [of an Episcopal ministry] may in case of extremity be performed by others, when . . . with the same charity and with more reason, they might conclude that God would rather in those cases dispense with the offices, than with the officers . . . as it were better that I being cast into the Indies should live there all the days of my life without receiving the Sacrament, than that I should receive it from the hands of one who had no other authority to give it than that he was chosen by the company to that office".[1] In 1656 he begged Cosin to compose a treatise on sacramental Confession, "in the handling whereof you will vindicate an excellent pious institution".[2] Since Hyde's sympathy with the Laudian party has occasionally been challenged, the point is worth labouring that his clerical friendships were exclusively with that group at home and abroad, and that in his correspondence with them no hint of theological difference ever arises.

Associated with Hyde in the Anglican party were Sir Edward Nicholas, the shrewd and devoted Secretary of State, and his son-in-law Joseph Jane; garrulous old Lord Hatton, whose home in Paris was a gathering-place for churchmen; Sir George Radcliffe, a friend of Strafford and Laud, with a consuming interest in church affairs; and Sir Richard Browne and Sir Henry de Vic, the King's Residents in Paris and Brussels respectively. Early in 1651 the party was immensely strengthened by the arrival in France of James Butler, Marquis of Ormond, who had struggled vainly to retrieve the Royalist cause in Ireland. Ormond represented the best of the Cavalier ideal, and commanded the respect and admiration of all. Steadfast and serene in his loyalty to King and Church, almost alone he remained untouched by the intrigues and jealousies of the exiled court. He fully shared Hyde's love of the Church; it was said of him later that "whoever notes the smiles and frowns which his Grace of Ormond received at different seasons from the court, may form a good judgment of the situation of the Church of England at those times".[3]

With the encouragement of these men, the clergy set themselves to the difficult work of shepherding their scattered flocks, and reviving some measure of church life. Handicapped as they were, they possessed one great asset. Whatever the defects of the Laudian movement, it had

[1] *S.P.C.*, ii, 403.
[2] *Clar.* 51, f. 115.
[3] T. Carte, *Life of James Duke of Ormond* (Oxf. 1851), iv, 705.

undeniably bred a generation of clergy who believed passionately in
the truth and rightness of their Anglican faith. The Church of England
was for them no haphazard product of political compromise, but the
one pure and authentic embodiment of primitive tradition. We need
only compare them with the Marian exiles of a previous generation to
note the profound change which a century had made in Anglican self-
confidence. Remembering those bishops-to-be who sat humbly at the
feet of Calvin, deprecated their Prayer Book and its minimum of ceremonial, and studied eagerly in Zürich, Basle, and Geneva "the best
models of the foreign Reformed Churches", we may find it hard to
recognize their spiritual descendants. We hear of Dr. Cosin "supporting the honour of the Church of England to admiration in an open
chapel at Paris with the solemnity of a cathedral service", and "per-
stringing those of Geneva for their irreverence of the Blessed Virgin".[1]
Preaching in the Calvinist Hague, Dr. William Stamp "was eloquently
zealous in condemning all reformed Churches of simple ignorance for
rejecting the English liturgy . . . an antidote of all sects and heresies,
and the pith and marrow of all piety".[2] Dr. Byam's sermons were even
less conciliatory:

"This was the Religion, the reformed, refined, and new Religion! A Religion but of yesterday, however they pretend to the Apostles' days. But 'twere
very strange, it hath much outslept Endymion and the seven sleepers, and fifteen
hundred years could scarce awake it. Well, 'tis up at last; and no sooner up, but
up in blood, bred and fed with treason and rebellion. I might call Germany and
Geneva to be witnesses, but we have many nearer home. . . .When men grow
weary of the old ways, and seek them out by-paths to wander in; when the
primitive Church is counted but an embryo, which must be licked into a better
form by future ages (vide Calvin); when the best of the Fathers are but dish-
clouts; when men gape for new doctrines as oysters do for new tides . . . beware
of such prophets! . . . Let us lay before our eyes the harmony of the two tests,
the general practice of antiquity; the consent of the Fathers, Councils, all the
world, till those worst of times. And for those who are otherwise minded, God
reveal it to them."[3]

The thought of the earlier days filled Richard Watson with horror:

"Though I reverence the Church of England so far as she doth [reverence]
the authority of the primitive Christian or right reason, yet [I] am not so fond
of her as to follow her in all her little policies of complying with all Protestants
of whom no parties ever were or will be consistent, and varnishing her articles

[1] D. Granville, *Remains* (Surtees Soc. 1865), ii, p. viii; *Evel.*, ii, 36.
[2] *Merc. Pol.*, No. 37, 16 February 1651.
[3] H. Byam, *op. cit.*, pp. 37, 92, 98.

with words capable of two senses to cement different opinions. Nor ever will I have such canonical obedience for a Morton or a Brownrigg as for a Montague, to whose sense of our articles rather than I'll ever swear, I'll burn at a stake if my courage fail not. . . . The more I look into antiquity, the more I discover the partiality and fraud of many forsooth our reverend divines, unworthy hypocrites as they were, and foul imposters."[1]

Unshaken by the disaster which had overtaken their Church, these divines faced the future with a confidence impervious to the gibes of Romanist and Presbyterian. "Our Church is as much misunderstood and misconstrued here abroad, as it is misused and maligned at home," wrote Dean Cosin to Watson, "and I have had experience enough of both. . . . In the meantime I will be glad to hear of your resolution still to be constant in the maintenance of the ancient Catholic Faith and Government of the Church of Christ, which the Church of England hath professed and taught us. . . . God ever preserve you and me in our old way of truth, from which no persecution shall ever drive us."[2] Bramhall proclaimed to the world: "If it please God, we may yet see the Church of England, which is now frying in the fire, come out like gold out of the furnace, more pure, and more full of lustre."[3]

In all the large towns of western Europe where the English had gathered, endeavour was made to provide Anglican ministrations. A good idea of clerical zeal is given by George Morley:

"We were then in Antwerp, where no religion but that of Rome is either professed or tolerated; yet there I read the divine service of our Church twice a day at the canonical hours; and celebrated the Sacrament of the Eucharist once a month, admitting thereunto, as likewise to our daily prayers, as many of our countrymen as were willing to communicate with us; as Sir John Shaw and his family, the Duke of Newcastle and his family . . . besides divers others. I did there likewise bury the dead, and baptize children according to the form prescribed in our liturgy. . . . Besides this, I did once a week at least catechize the whole family wherein I lived . . . in the principles of Christian doctrine and practice as they are taught in our Church Catechism, to the end that . . . they might not easily be seduced to Popery while they were abroad; or to Presbytery or to any other schismatical sect when they came home."[4]

Vesey tells how Bishop Bramhall while in Brussels "preached constantly every Lord's Day, frequently administering the Sacrament, and confirming such as desired it"—among them the Princess Royal, and the Dukes of York and Gloucester.[5]

[1] *Clar.* 46, f. 95.   [2] *Cosin*, iv, 385–9.   [3] *Bramhall*, i, 64.
[4] *Morley*, pp. v, vi.   [5] *Bramhall*, i, pp. x, lxx.

Places of worship were of several types. The most fortunately situated were those claiming the privileges of an ambassador's oratory; nowhere else could Anglican services be publicly performed in France and the Spanish Netherlands. Most important of these was the chapel of Sir Richard Browne in the Faubourg St. Germain at Paris, which could contain "an infinite crowd of people", and where every Sunday Royalists flocked to see the King and Dukes at worship and hear a distinguished divine.[1] Puritan and Huguenot visitors were scandalized by the splendour of the ceremonial, the copes, incense, and profound reverences to the Altar;[2] but Cosin was resolved to "omit nothing that we were wont to practise in England", and Sir George Radcliffe delighted to have "Roman Catholics see that the Church of England desires to serve God decently".[3] Sir Henry de Vic kept a similar chapel in Brussels, to which the English came from great distances.[4] Hyde relates that after his mission to Spain in 1650, the Archduke Leopold accorded him an ambassador's oratory in Antwerp—"all the English who were numerous then in that city repaired thither with all freedom for their devotion and the exercise of their religion; which liberty had never been before granted to any man there, and which the English and Irish priests and all the Roman Catholics of those nations exceedingly murmured at, and used all the endeavours they could to have taken away, though in vain."[5]

In Holland there were available the churches provided by the Dutch government for the companies of Merchant Adventurers. Anglican

[1] *Orns.*, i, 283; *Evel.*, *passim*.

[2] Letter of Samuel Brett, quoted in J. Stoughton, *History of Religion in England* (Lond. 1901), ii, 304; *Hyde I*, iii, 1187.

[3] *Cosin.*, iv, 387; W. N. Darnell, *Correspondence of Isaac Basire* (Lond. 1831), 66. An anecdote of Richard Watson throws further light on the Laudian pleasure in dignified ceremonial, and also informs us of the Roman Catholic reaction. "I remember, when I was in Flanders, an old Benedictine asking me how I liked the decency of their churches, and solemnity of their service, or public worship. I answered to this purpose, that I observed little more in substance than what he might have formerly seen, if he had pleased, in our King's Chapel, St. Paul's, London, and St. Peter's, Westminster, with the other Cathedrals that we had in England. Whereto he somewhat sarcastically replied, that in Archbishop Laud's time indeed, your Church washed and beautified her face a little; but, for all that, more intrinsically she was a very slut." R. Watson, *Answer to Elymas the Sorcerer* (Lond. 1682), 7.

[4] *Bramhall*, i, p. x.

[5] *Hyde I*, v, 2577.

conformity had been enforced in these congregations by Archbishop Laud in the previous reign, and the services of the refugee clergy were welcomed. Two former Oxford dons, Richard Chalfont and Henry Tozer, ministered to the congregation at Rotterdam. Dr. Thomas Marshall took over the church at Dort. In Amsterdam were Richard Maden, ejected from St. Mildred Poultry, London, and William Price, fellow of Jesus College, Cambridge. In the words of Cromwell's outraged ambassador, they made the pulpit ring with "invectives against the State of England and the Council of State . . . they poison the Dutch more than any".[1] Morley's friend George Beaumont officiated at the Hague, and Robert Creighton and Michael Honywood at Utrecht. There were also established congregations at Breda, Delft, Flushing, and Middleburg.

In other cities congregations gathered in private homes. At Caen, for example, Sunday services were held by Morley and Watson in the house of the Marchioness of Ormond, and a similar arrangement existed at Rouen.[2] In some places, however, Anglicans were dependent on the occasional visits of clergy; in Blois Sir Ralph Verney wrote to a neighbour in 1649: "I forgot to tell you that on Saturday next (my wife being ill), a friend will give us a sermon and the Sacrament (after the honest old way at home), and if either yourself or your son please to communicate with us you shall be very welcome."[3] Similarly, Sir Henry de Vic in Brussels informed Nicholas in 1657: "Tomorrow morning I receive the Sacrament, and it is high time, not having had it this fifteen or sixteen months. I hope whatever else we suffer here we shall not be so long without it."[4] The following year Joseph Jane was also seeking the Secretary's aid for the Anglicans at Bruges: "We have a small congregation here, but expect its increase by the return of some from Brussels. . . . The Bishop of Derry is now with us, but will not stay long. I wish one of the chaplains would help us."[5]

The most urgent problem faced by the clergy was Romanist proselytizing. Scarcely had the Royalists settled in their new homes before the Queen's party became active. In Cosin's words:

[1] *Thurl.*, i, 118; cf. *ibid*, i, 514; ii, 374.
[2] *Morley*, p. viii; *Theologian and Ecclesiastic*, x, 330; *ibid.*, xi, 87.
[3] F. P. Verney, *Memoirs of the Verney Family* (Lond. 1892–9), ii, 413.
[4] P.R.O., *Flanders Papers*, S.P. 77/32, April 11–21, 1657.
[5] *S.P.D. Commonwealth*, 1658–9, pp. 4, 22.

"At my first coming into France, I found many of the Roman profession (both priests and others) very busy and industrious in persuading them of our religion ... to turn papists; for which purpose the chief arguments that they used were such as these: 'You have lived a long while in heresy, which hath brought God's anger and indignation upon you; your kingdom of England is ruined; your Church is lost; your Bishops and priests are put out of their places, and are never likely to be restored; ... your Service-Book and your Sacraments are come into the contempt and scorn of the world; the head of your Church aches, and is ready to perish; the members are scattered and torn in pieces.... There is no safety, no salvation for you to be had but in the bosom of [Rome]!' "[1]

This type of persuasion was effective, for there began a series of conversions that dismayed the English clergy. A churchman wrote indignantly to Dean Steward:

"As ridiculous and impious as you think the change of those persons will be, yet those persons are changed and gone. They say the Church of England is lost, and this fond reason (for others they allege none) hath carried them away to ruin themselves. All hath been said and done that you could wish to hinder it, and more than they will ever be able to answer either to us or their own consciences. They came at last to this, that they neither desired nor were willing to receive any satisfaction from us, for they were resolved what to do and do it they would, let others think what they pleased."[2]

The Queen's agents did not hesitate to trade on the desperate poverty of the exiles. One lady reported that Walter Montague "says he will take care of her and of the old woman too, and as many as have a mind to lapse after them".[3] Another convert priest, Stephen Goffe, offered to make ample provision for all proselytes, and with the Queen's help was as good as his word.[4] The poets Richard Crashaw and William Davenant were relieved from penury after their conversions by Henrietta's bounty, and the prospect of relief was a sore temptation to many. Pressure of various kinds was brought to bear in court circles. "I wish you would get the King to put in a word or two that Dean Cosin might have some pay," wrote Lord Hatton to Nicholas in 1649, "for they give him not a penny, and when every groom and lackey was paid this Christmas in some proportion, Sir Henry Wood told him there was order for four pistoles for him, which was intended as a scorn ... they have found a neater way of starving out their parson, and then they think

[1] *Cosin*, iv, 242.   [2] *Theologian and Ecclesiastic*, vii, 380.   [3] *Ibid.*, vii, 381.
[4] J. Gillow, *Bibliographical Dictionary of the English Catholics* (Lond. 1885), ii, 506 ff.

the congregation will dissolve quietly."[1] The young courtier Stephen Fox found himself in a not uncommon plight:

"Amongst others, I was laid siege to [by the priests] with uncommon ardour; but what through the grace of God, with the remembrance of those instructions I had received from the most orthodox and truly primitive divines, and what through an innate aversion I had always entertained for popish superstition, I was no way prevailed upon; but so irritated the Father who had made sure of my perversion that he gave a very untoward report of my obstinacy to the Queen; which would have had very ill consequences, had not the Chancellor [Hyde] stepped in between me and the danger that threatened me, and spoke . . . much in favour of me to the King."[2]

The danger that the Church might disintegrate under this pressure was very real; from letters of the period we glimpse something of the strenuous efforts of the clergy to halt the flow of secessions. Dean Steward's words to the volatile Lady Kynalmeaky, niece of the Duke of Buckingham, certainly minced no matters:

"Madam, ask your own heart if there be no discontent, or secular by-end, that has brought you into this staggering. . . . 'Tis a poor thing, Madam, and unworthy the candour not only of a Christian, but of any person that pretends to honour, to resolve first to leave us without so much as consulting with our priests, and then to pretend to admit of discourse only to take occasion to deride it, as if so goodly a victory were the most meritorious entrance into a religion that commands simplicity. . . . Cut no feathers with God, Madam, lest you cut more than your fingers. . . . The Christian Religion was not made to serve turns, and therefore stay where I left you, Madam, and remember what I told you when you stumbled at first, that it would trouble you on your deathbed to have left a Church that gave you Christ's whole institution, to embrace another that will rob you."[3]

Cosin advised his fellow-clergy in the same year to "propound cases of conscience . . . whether it be lawful to go against one's conscience? to do that willfully which they know will offend God and all good people? to bear us in hand . . . to be satisfied, having beforehand made a desperate resolution not to receive any satisfaction at all?"[4] He himself was a tireless pastor, and according to John Evelyn who was then in Paris, "in this time of temptation and apostasy held and confirmed many to our Church".[5] "The Duchess of Richmond hath been sick in her chamber a whole month together," the Dean informed Hyde,

---

[1] *Nich.*, i, 159.   [2] *Memoirs of the Life of Sir Stephen Fox* (Lond. 1717), 14.
[3] *Orns.*, i, 279.   [4] *Ibid.*, i, 278.   [5] *Evel.*, ii, 44.

"and I have gone daily hence fifteen days to attend her there; she promiseth to be firm in Religion, for which purpose I wish the King would now and then put a line in his letters to her."[1] A young Englishman at court reported: "I had the advantage of Dr. Cosin's company often, [who] took great pains to confirm me in the Protestant Religion."[2]

Nor was Cosin backward in accepting challenges to the formal debates in which the seventeenth century delighted. In 1645 he defended the validity of Anglican ordinations against Fr. Paul Robinson, prior of the English Benedictines in France, to the satisfaction of a group of English laymen.[3] Evelyn describes a similar conference six years later which Cosin and Earle held with the friar Fr. Coniers in order to regain one Thomas Keightley for the Church of England. The diarist was more impressed with the Anglican armoury than was Mr. Keightley, who was not reclaimed—"finding himself worsted upon every point, the friar was forced to use a thousand subterfuges: the Church of England not visible, no due ordination or succession, etc., and at last to have recourse to miracles . . . of some famous relic, with abundance of such stuff."[4] Similarly, in Brussels Dr. Morley and Dr. Creighton engaged the Jesuit Fr. Darcy before a group of noble auditors on the differences between their Churches.[5]

The need for an Anglican apologetic adapted to the Church's present situation was obvious, and the major works of both Cosin and Bramhall were occasioned by the pastoral problems which confronted them. Out of his debate with Robinson, Cosin developed his *Validity of the Ordination of Priests in the Church of England*, in which he showed that the formula declared requisite for validity by the Roman Church was contrary to the judgment of the early Fathers, was unknown for many centuries in the Western Church, and had never been used in Eastern Christendom. In 1652 he produced the Latin treatise *Regni Angliae Religio Catholica* at the request of Hyde, who wanted a work that would give foreign Christians a true picture of the doctrine and discipline of the English Church. The book was typical of the Laudian viewpoint, maintaining emphatically that the Church of England was Catholic

---

[1] *S.P.C.*, iii, 418; cf. *Clar.* 58, f. 271.
[2] *Memoirs of Sir John Reresby* (Ed. A. Browning, Glasgow 1936), 29.
[3] *Cosin*, iv, 241 ff.
[4] *Orns.*, i, 283.
[5] *Morley*, 3 ff.

in retaining the apostolic faith, ministry, and sacraments, and Protestant in rejecting the novelties added by Rome. Three years later, when Cosin heard that the Court, then in Cologne, was discussing a Jesuit tract charging Anglicanism with eucharistic heresy, he wrote in a few months' time his *History of Popish Transubstantiation*. With considerable learning, he argued that Roman Catholics wrongly apply to the medieval scholastic doctrine expressions which the Fathers had used to affirm belief in the Real Presence of Christ in the Sacrament, and that that belief was firmly maintained by the Church of England.

Meantime, the Bishop of Derry was engaged in a similar task in Flanders. In Bramhall, wrote Jeremy Taylor, "were visible the great lines of Hooker's judiciousness, of Jewel's learning, of the acuteness of Bishop Andrewes".[1] The Bishop first entered the lists with his *Answer to M. de la Milletière*. The Frenchman's public letter to Charles II, inviting him to embrace the Roman Faith, had been remarkable for its naïveté and ignorance of the English Church; but Bramhall's reply was a powerful defence of the principles of the English Reformation. In Anglicanism, he maintained, "all genuine universal Apostolical traditions" had been preserved in their purity, and concluded: "The truths received by our Church are sufficient in point of faith to make his Majesty a good Catholic. More than this your Roman bishops, your Roman Church, your Tridentine Council may not, cannot, obtrude upon him."[2]

The following year (1654), Bramhall produced what is probably his most celebrated writing, *A Just Vindication of the Church of England from the Unjust Aspersion of Criminal Schism*. In it he declared: "I make not the least doubt in the world, but that the Church of England before the Reformation and the Church of England after the Reformation are as much the same Church, as a garden before it is weeded and after it is weeded is the same garden." He supported his thesis on four grounds: (1) The rejection of the Roman jurisdiction was endorsed by Roman Catholics themselves, "with the concurrence and approbation of four and twenty bishops and nine and twenty abbots then and there present". (2) The separation was justified by the ancient laws and statutes of the realm. (3) "The English Church was under no foreign jurisdiction for the first six hundred years, and ought to continue in the same condition." (4) Rulers have power to alter whatsoever is of human

---

[1] *Bramhall*, i, p. lxxv.
[2] *Ibid.*, i, 25.

institution in the external discipline of the Church. He concluded that the Church of Rome had throughout history been the real cause of division within the Church, and that "we are ready . . . to believe and practise, whatever the Catholic Church (even of this present age) doth universally and unanimously believe and hold".

Bramhall's *Vindication* was widely read, and two replies were made on the Roman side, both of which the Bishop answered in detail. Against Dr. Richard Smith, who was titular Bishop of Chalcedon, and head of the Roman clergy in England, he wrote his *Replication*—in the main a defence and explanation of the Anglican position towards other reformed bodies—pointing out that the present plight of his Church arose from its refusal to be implicated in Protestant error. The other opponent was an ex-Anglican, John Sergeant, whose two works *Schism Disarmed* and *Schism Despatched*—with an appendix happily entitled *Down Derry*—drew from Bramhall the rebuttal *Schism Guarded*. This treatise somewhat belied its opening plea for controversial meekness, and vehemently attacked the claim that Romanism and Catholicism are identical.

Like Cosin, Bramhall was drawn into controversy over the validity of Anglican Orders. In 1645 he had written a short answer to two Roman attacks about which a Captain Steward had consulted him; and somewhat later he published his *Protestants' Ordination Defended*. This was in answer to *The Guide of Faith*, written by the English Jesuit Sylvester Norris, a quarter of a century before. Bramhall's work was much wider in scope than Cosin's, and dealt cogently with all the now familiar Roman objections, historical, theological, and liturgical. But in 1657, a situation arose which drew from him an historical essay, *The Consecration of Protestant Bishops Vindicated*. In Charles's Court at Bruges the Jesuits had revived the old story of the Nag's Head Tavern, spreading rumours that the Bishop of Durham had now publicly acknowledged the truth of the tale, and also that Bramhall had been pitifully worsted in a debate with Fr. Peter Talbot in the King's presence. Bramhall was able to procure a solemn declaration from the aged prelate, then ninety-four, rejecting the assertion about him as a notorious slander. Then he himself proceeded to subject the legend to searching analysis, adding a compilation of the documents which established the facts of Archbishop Parker's consecration.

Other clergy, too, were aroused to the defence of their Church. Isaac Basire wrote *The Ancient Liberty of the Britannic Church*, maintaining

F

"the legitimate exemption thereof from the Roman Patriarchate".
George Morley composed a learned treatise on the invocation of saints
in his *Letter to Janus Ulitius*, and in Bruges wrote the *Vindication of the
Argument from Sense against Transubstantiation*, for Ormond's nephew
James Hamilton, who soon after became an Anglican.[1] Robert Creighton wrote a Latin history of the Council of Florence, in which he
emphasized the historical precedents for the Anglican position. Richard
Watson argued against the Presbyterians in *Akolouthos*, published at the
time of Charles II's treaty with the Scots.

All this was a considerable achievement for a small community of
refugees, and Bramhall gives some idea of the difficulties encountered:
"Those who have composed minds free from distracting cares, and
means to maintain them, and friends to assist them, and their books and
notes by them, do little imagine with what difficulties poor exiles
struggle, whose minds are more intent on what they should eat to-
morrow than what they should write, being chased as vagabonds into
the merciless world to beg relief of strangers."[2] His controversial
labours were typical of many other divines: "Since I came into exile
these sixteen years, where have my weak endeavours ever been wanting
to the Church of England? Who hath had more disputes with their
seculars and regulars of all sorts, French, Italian, Dutch, English, in
word, in writing, to maintain the honour of the Church of England?"[3]

These efforts were not without effect in reviving church loyalty
among the refugees. The numerous congregations were a refutation of
the charge that the Church of England was no longer visible. "He must
be as blind as Bartimaeus that cannot see the English Church," declared
Bramhall. "Wheresoever there is a lawful English pastor and an English flock, and a subordination of this flock to that pastor, there is a
branch of the true English Protestant Church. Do you make no difference between a Church persecuted and a Church extinguished?"[4] Both
Evelyn and Watson mention that in controversies with papists and sectaries the divines in Paris argued for the visibility of their Church on
the evidence of the flourishing chapel there.[5] Cosin could say with satis-

---

[1] Cf. Hamilton's letter to Ormond in *Carte* 213, ff. 391–2.
[2] *Bramhall*, i, 276.
[3] *Ibid.*, iii, 540.
[4] *Ibid.*, i, 64.
[5] *Evel.*, ii, 146; "Dedicatory Epistle" by R. Watson (n.p.) in I. Basire,
Ancient Liberty of the Britannic Church (Lond. 1660).

faction: "I have by God's blessing reduced some and preserved many others from communicating with the papists," and wrote in sprightly vein to the old Bishop of Durham in England:

"Many controversies I have had . . . but especially with those limitors that come creeping into our pale and hunt for proselytes, whereof they have not (God be thanked) been able for these four years' space to get one, unless it were a poor footman (whom they trapped with a female French bait too) and have lost some others of more considerable quality, whom they had lured into their nets before."[1]

And there were other clergy who, like Edward Martin, "by regular life and good doctrine reduced some recusants to, and confirmed more doubters in the Protestant Religion".[2]

But at the beginning of 1650, the other danger to the Church materialized. The long drawn-out negotiations between Charles and the Scottish commissioners in Holland came to a conclusion, and it was soon apparent that the young King by successive capitulations had agreed to terms that were nothing short of disastrous to the Church of England. At Breda in March, 1650, the treaty was signed restoring him to his northern kingdom. When he reached Scotland a few months later, he was forced to take the Covenant, "desiring to be humbled for his father's opposition to it, for the idolatry of his mother, acknowledging his own sins and the sins of his father's house, and abhorring popery, superstition, idolatry, and prelacy". He promised further "to confirm the church government agreed upon by the Synod of Westminster, and in matters of religion to prefer the council of [Presbyterian] ministers before any other".[3] The Anglican party was in total eclipse; Nicholas and Hopton had fought manfully against the inevitable until the King excluded them from the Council. From Spain, Hyde wrote with passion: "It is such folly and atheism that we should be ashamed to avow or think of it. If there be a judgment from Heaven upon [the King], I can only pray it may fall as light on him as may be," but hoped that "all your dexterous compliers will be exposed to the infamy they deserve".[4]

It is a curious paradox that Charles's feeling for his Anglican faith was probably never more real than in this moment of forswearing it.

---

[1] *Cosin*, iv, 398–9, 472.
[2] *Walker*, Pt. ii, 156.
[3] *S.P.D. Commonwealth*, 1650, 291 ff.
[4] *S.P.C.*, iii, 14, 22.

When the commissioners refused his request that three of his chaplains might go with him to Scotland, "as altogether against their Covenant and against Presbytery", they were shocked to see him "break out into a great passion and bitter execration".[1] A curious scene occurred on the eve of his departure, May 25. News reached the Scottish ministers that the King was preparing to communicate on the morrow according to the Anglican rite. "We showed the sin of so doing", reports Commissioner Livingstone, "and that it would provoke God to blast all his designs . . . and how it was against that which he had granted in his concessions . . . but we found him tenaciously resolute to continue his purpose. He said his father used always to communicate at Christmas, Easter and Whitsunday, and that he behoved to do so likewise . . . to procure a blessing from God on his intended voyage." So in the morning he knelt before the altar in his chapel as the Bishop of Derry administered the Sacrament and blessed him.[2] Months later in Scotland, sorely harassed by the bigotry of the Kirk, he received in secret audience Dr. John King, Dean of Tuam, and declared with pathetic earnestness: "I do give you assurance that however I am forced by the necessity of my affairs to appear otherwise, yet that I am a true child of the Church of England, and shall remain firm unto my first principles; Mr. King, I am a true Cavalier."[3] And to Nicholas he wrote with undoubted feeling: "You cannot imagine the villainy of their party: indeed it has done me a great deal of good, for nothing could have confirmed me more to the Church of England than being here seeing their hypocrisy."[4]

But for the moment such feelings were little help to the exiles, to whom news of the Scottish treaty was a staggering blow. The policy of separating the Stuart cause from that of the Church of England had triumphed, and probably at no other time in history have the Church's fortunes sunk so low, or its future seemed so dark. A cry of despair went up on all sides.

"We are here in an amaze to understand that the King is gone for Scotland," wrote Dean Steward to Nicholas. . . . "The King's hasty counsellors . . . without any consideration of honour or conscience, are still crying out, what else have we to do? when indeed there are times when honest men must pray and do

[1] S. R. Gardiner, *Charles II and Scotland in 1650* (Edin. 1894), 74.
[2] *Life of John Livingstone* (Edin. 1848), 124–5.
[3] *Orm. I*, i, 391.
[4] W. Bray, *Diary and Correspondence of John Evelyn* (Lond. 1881), iv. 195.

nothing else until God's providence open a way fit for them to take. . . . I should give the poor Church for utterly lost, but that I believe there is a good God in heaven."[1]

Richard Watson wrote mournfully from Breda:

"It is now ended, and so much of the mystery revealed as makes every honest subject's heart ache. Our religion is gone, and within a few days is expected the funeral of our Liturgy, which is dead already. The Scottish ministers were yesterday with Rivet to consult what way best to take to remove the King's chaplains and place themselves about him. When that is once done, the fine new pageant will be seen, or heard rather in their preachments. . . . What becomes of us I know not, but we wash our hands of all iniquity as in reference to treachery and treaty."[2]

Sir George Radcliffe proposed to Nicholas that they should quietly withdraw from public life: "We may retreat to Gallion or some other quiet private cheap place, and there wear out a year or two. . . . The Dean of the Chapel would willingly live with us, and either he or some other will be had to help us to serve God after our old English manner."[3] Lord Hatton's report from Paris was no less gloomy:

"We are daily now jeered at the Louvre with the inconstancy of our master and told we are content to be fooled with good words, whilst his enemies enjoy good deeds. . . . And, good sir, let us know from the fountain head whether he intend to command an extirpation of our Liturgy and forbid the use of it here at the Louvre and his Resident's house, that we may in time know how to dispose of ourselves and settle where we may buy the exercise of that religion which we are forbid by our own Prince."[4]

Even the Queen was appalled. Lord Hatton told of seeing her in tears at Chaillot when the news came that Charles had taken the Covenant. By this act, she complained, "the King of England . . . had so justly exasperated and incensed all Popish Princes by engaging himself to persecute their religion within all his kingdom, that he could not expect any assistance from them, nay she herself was hereby disabled to serve him".[5] But the Queen's tears soon dried as she became agreeably occupied in putting into effect the one aspect of the new policy she approved—the suppression of Anglican worship. Unluckily for the

[1] *S.P.D. Commonwealth*, June 2, 1650. Stewart signs the letter with his usual pseudonym "Nicholson".
[2] *Clar.* 39, f. 196.
[3] *Nich*, i, 274.
[4] *Ibid.*, i, 174-7.
[5] *Ibid.*, i, 174.

English, the Queen Regent of France happened to decide just at this moment "(upon most deep and solemn grounds) that her son's late troubles [of the Fronde] had been in part caused by the public permission of heretical worship in his own Palace".[1]

The first intimation of what was planned came in May, 1650, from Lady Kynalmeaky, now become, according to Hatton, "Lord Jermyn's echo". This lady with some zest "did tell Dr. Cosin that the King would shortly send to the Louvre and to Sir R. Browne's to command at both places to desist from the use of the Common Prayer Book, and then she said there would be an end of our Religion".[2] It was not Charles, however, who acted; an order came from the French Regent forbidding in the name of King Louis "the exercise of any other religion in any of his houses than the Roman Catholic". Henrietta gave notice to Cosin of his discharge, merely remarking that "she was no longer able to continue the payment of the exhibition she had formerly assigned to him".[3] Early in 1651 she had excuse to take more drastic action. The clergy of France offered to raise a pension for her on condition that none of it went to the support of Protestants. In April Nicholas wrote to Ormond, "there is warning given at the Louvre to all the Queen's servants that will not change their religion or serve for nothing to be gone and provide for themselves". He was pessimistic over the outcome: "I believe there are many at the Louvre . . . that will make no more scruple to comply for their advantage with Popery than Presbytery."[4] He added to Lord Hopton that "some of the female sex begin already to have scruples".[5] Evelyn noted some months later: "The Dean of Peterborough preached on Job 13: 15 ('Though he slay me, yet will I trust in him') encouraging our trust in God on all events and extremities, and for establishing and comforting some ladies of great quality, who were then to be discharged from our Queen Mother's service, unless they would go over to the Romish Mass."[6]

An anonymous observer now prophesied an exodus from the English Church comparable to the flight of rats from a doomed ship.[7] Such was the hope at Court. "Since the warning given at the Louvre to the Queen's servants," Nicholas informed the Marquis, "the Queen is very

[1] T. Brown (ed.), *Miscellanea Aulica* (Lond. 1702), 142.
[2] *Nich.*, i, 174.   [3] *Hyde I*, v, 2586 ff.
[4] *Orm. I*, i, 451.   [5] *Ibid.*, ii, 24.
[6] *Evel.*, ii, 43.
[7] P. H. Osmond, *Life of John Cosin* (Lond. 1913), 122.

active . . . in persuading many there to turn Papists; the main arguments are the King's forsaking the Church of England by taking the Covenant, and that he rather favours the Papists than us by permitting his sister to be brought up in that religion; and above all, the Queen's exorbitant and ruling power with the King, by which she intends to give the law, and beyond all others to countenance her own converts."[1] When the Duke of York arrived in Paris a month later, a further insult was offered to the Church; the prince was refused the customary privilege of his own worship in the Louvre. Ormond, much concerned, could only advise him "to go more frequently and solemnly to Sir Richard Browne's".[2]

What might have been the result if the pressure had continued, it is impossible to say. With the King's return in October, 1651, after a miraculous escape from Cromwell's armies, all was changed. Charles came back with a rooted dislike of the Presbyterians that was to last a lifetime, and at once and openly renewed his allegiance to his old Church. He gave gratifying evidence of his new disposition. "A pretty discourse" made by him to Dr. Steward quite set his chaplain's mind at rest, and the King's regular attendance in state at the Embassy Chapel was thankfully observed. "The English Prayer Book is become again the only rosary of his devotions, his chapel being crowded with copes, surplices, and bishops that would be," sourly noted *Mercurius Politicus*.[3] "Whatsoever your politic friends at the Hague have designed," Hyde joyfully wrote to Nicholas, "there is no more danger of Presbytery!"[4]

A Royal Declaration issued in December gave formal expression to the King's return to traditional policy. "Whereas some jealousies have lately arisen that I am in a declining way from the government of the Church by bishops," his Majesty asserted, with engaging candour, "I . . . must in charity be thought desirous to preserve that government in its right constitution . . . wherein my judgment is fully satisfied that it hath of all other the fullest scripture grounds and also the constant practice of all other Christian Churches till of late years. . . ." His attitude was conciliatory, however, towards his late allies; they were assured that "Presbytery is never so considerable or effectual, as when it is joined to, and crowned with Episcopacy". Though the King was "firm

---

[1] *Orm.*, I, i, 453.
[2] *Ibid.*, ii, 37, 41.
[3] *Merc. Pol.*, No. 78, p. 1248, 25 November 1651.
[4] *S.P.C.*, iii, 37.

to primitive Episcopacy", he held out the prospect that "discretion without passion might easily reform whatever the rust of time, or indulgence of laws, or corruption of manners have brought upon it". The Presbyterians were reminded that their method of reform by violence was a dangerous weapon only too likely to be turned against them when the Sects got "but number, strength, and opportunity". The Declaration concluded with the pious wish to "leave the success of all to God, who hath many ways to teach us those rules of true reason and peaceable wisdom ... tending most to God's glory and the Church's good".[1]

We may observe in passing that Charles's brief excursion into Presbyterianism had served to underline a significant development in Anglican theology. In the century of its independent existence, Anglicanism had become something much more than the religion of the King of England. Under the Tudor monarchs the doctrine of the royal supremacy had been not merely a convenient administrative device; it had been a corner-stone of the theological structure of the Church, and an evident spiritual reality to Christians of the Reformation period. A change in the religious viewpoint of the Crown had involved Archbishop Cranmer in an acute problem of conscience, and other such changes had been genuinely held to justify the Vicar of Bray attitude adopted by most English clergy in those years. But the rise of the High Church school at the beginning of the seventeenth century caused a radical alteration in the doctrine. The royal prerogative in matters ecclesiastical was asserted to be merely the duty of defending the Faith and enforcing its acceptance; only a divinely instituted Episcopate was empowered to define the truths of religion.[2] The implications of this new

---

[1] *A Declaration of the King of Scots concerning the Presbyterians* (Rep. Lond. 1651), pp. 4–7. It is possible that this tract is a contemporary English forgery, since the French original from which it purports to be copied is not listed in *Catalogue Générale de la Bibliothèque Nationale*, nor is the proclamation to be found in R. Steele, *Tudor and Stuart Proclamations* (Oxf. 1910). However, its moderation of tone, and the fact that it fits the situation at court in December, 1651, are arguments for its genuineness.

[2] Cf. George Carleton, *Jurisdiction, Regal, Episcopal, Papal* (Lond. 1610), 44: "For the preservation of true doctrine, the Bishops are the great watchmen. Herein they are authorized by God. If Princes withstand them in these things, they have warrant not to obey Princes." Similarly, Richard Field, *Of the Church*, Bk. V, p. 426. For an excellent discussion of this change, cf. J.W. Allen, *English Political Thought*, 1603–1660 (Lond. 1938), i, 129 ff.

teaching were for a time obscured by the agreeably Anglican policy of the first two Stuarts; but the Puritans were alert to the new note, and charged the "Arminians" with intent to usurp the power of the Crown and nullify the royal supremacy.

It is no matter for surprise, therefore, that when Charles took the Covenant in 1650, his act caused little searching of conscience among his Anglican followers. There is no suggestion in the correspondence of that year that the apostasy of the King could affect the theological position of the Church of England. Long before, the Laudians had developed a positive doctrine of the Church's nature and function in virtual independence of the royal prerogative; now, the circumstances of the Interregnum made the fact fully apparent for the first time.

Of Charles's true religious convictions in the years ahead, it is impossible to speak with any certainty. Roman Catholic writers have sometimes claimed that he was received into their Church in 1655, though the secret was known to only three or four people.[1] But a recent historian on that side, David Mathew, has declared: "The date and extent of any such change of attitude remains conjectural . . . all that concerns the King's beliefs is an enigma, probably incapable of solution."[2] One of the most acute observers of his own time comments thus:

"The ill bred familiarity of the Scotch divines had given him a distaste of that part of the Protestant Religion. He was left then to the little remnant of the Church of England in the Faubourg St. Germain, which made such a kind of figure as might easily be turned in such a manner as to make him lose his veneration for it. In a refined country where religion appeared in pomp and splendour, the outward appearance of such unfashionable men was made an argument against their religion; and a young Prince not averse to raillery was the more susceptible of a contempt for it."[3]

One fact, however, is indisputable; to all outward appearances Charles now threw in his lot with the Church of England party. Hyde, Nicholas, and Ormond became his chosen mentors in state policy, and the King adopted their belief that his fortunes were inseparably bound to those of the Anglican Church. One of Cromwell's agents in Paris

---

[1] Cf. M. Faillon, *Vie de M. Olier* (Paris 1873) ii, 320–34; M. V. Hay, *The Blairs Papers* (Lond. 1929), 45 ff.

[2] D. Mathew, *Catholicism in England* (Lond. 1948), 96.

[3] G. Savile, Marquis of Halifax, *A Character of Charles II* (Lond. 1750), 2.

could write in November, 1651: "The dissensions of the Royalists are
. . . not so much national, because the Scotch agree with the Louvrians,
i.e. the Queen and Jermyn, but the rigid Royalists are so implacable
against them that they rather rejoice at the late miscarriage. . . . They
are overjoyed that the King, through what has befallen him in England
and Scotland, is wholly come over to their party."[1] Three years later
another spy reported to Secretary Thurloe: "Ormond, Hyde, and their
party have, contrary to the sense of the rest [of the Council], advised
and prevailed with the King totally to abandon both the party and the
principles of the Presbyterians, and to rely entirely upon his old Episcopal party, which they persuade him comprehends the nobility, gentry,
and bulk of the kingdom of England."[2] The Queen intrigued frantically with the Presbyterians to destroy the hated alliance, but to no avail
—Lord Jermyn had finally to admit that "Hyde could lead the King to
any resolution he pleased".[3] Moreover, if Charles at this period was in-
wardly disloyal to the Church, he never gave his closest advisers reason
to suspect it. Mathew admits that "his public attitude towards religion
was remarkably consistent, a strong dignified attachment to the Anglican Church".[4] He wrote affectionately of "our small visible Church",
and Hyde could confide to Nicholas, "the King is as firm in his religion
as ever his blessed father was, and you know a higher expression I
cannot make".[5]

Inevitably, Anglican spirits revived upon the abandonment of the
Presbyterian policy, and it was felt that the Church had weathered
its gravest peril. The King's favour also weakened greatly the effect of
Romanist propaganda. When Charles left for Germany in the summer
of 1654, he made every effort to protect the interests of the Anglicans
in Paris. "I assure you", Hyde notified Browne, "the King takes all
possible care that the house receives no affront, and to that purpose
hath had a consideration of it in Council these three days . . . for the
keeping up the service carefully when he leaves this place."[6] Charles
directed to the Dean a solemn mandate:

[1] *S.P.D. Commonwealth*, 1651–2, p. 2.
[2] *Thurl.*, ii, 510.
[3] *C.S.P.C.*, iv, 622.
[4] D. Mathew, *op. cit.*, 98.
[5] T. Brown, *op. cit.*, 113; *S.P.C.*, iii, 42. Cf. a similar assertion of Nicholas
to Sir R. Browne in *S.P.D. Commonwealth*, 1659–60, p. 271.
[6] W. Bray, *op. cit.*, iv, 281.

"to continue the same your care and diligence in the performing all divine offices to all those our servants of the Protestant Religion in the family of our Royal Mother the Queen, and in keeping up that form of service in our Chapel at our Resident's house here, to the end that no discountenance or discouragement, in these ill times, may dissolve that congregation . . . holding ourself to be the more obliged to use all possible means within our power for the maintenance and profession of that our Religion in these times of slander, reproach, and persecution."[1]

Hardly had the King left Paris, however, than the fanatic Queen precipitated a crisis which was to have unexpected consequences in Royalist affairs. Henry Stuart, Duke of Gloucester, the youngest son of Charles I, was at this time a boy of fourteen. Early in 1653 Parliament had released him from Carisbrooke Castle, and allowed him to join his sister the Princess of Orange in Holland. Shortly after, Charles summoned his brother to Paris at the urgent wish of the Queen, and the Princess, who had some acquaintance with her Royal Mother's methods, confided to Nicholas with many tears that "she doth with too much reason apprehend that this may be an artifice of some Papists powerful with the Queen (besides her Majesty's intention and perhaps inclination) . . . to gain this young Duke . . . to turn Roman Catholic, upon some large promises to make him Cardinal and to settle on him other great preferments".[2]

This indeed was Henrietta's intention, despite solemn promises made to the King before his departure. In October, 1654, Henry was moved to Montague's establishment at Pontoise. His chaplain and tutor, Richard Lovell, was dismissed, and members of his Church forbidden access to him. Montague pressed him constantly with the spiritual and material advantages of conversion, and he was told by the Queen of

"the desperateness of his condition in respect of the King his brother's fortune, and the little hope that appeared that his Majesty could ever be restored, at least if he did not himself become Roman Catholic; whereby the Pope and other princes of that religion might be united in his quarrel . . . by which he [the Duke] might be able to do the King much service, and contribute to his recovery; whereas, without this, he must be exposed to great necessity and misery, for that she was not able any longer to give him maintenance."[3]

Despite his youth, and the influence brought to bear on him now and later, the Duke never showed the slightest sign of wavering. Back in Paris for a day, he sent for Cosin and asked for help "in the great task

---

[1] Quoted in P. H. Osmond, *op. cit.*, 132.
[2] *Nich.*, ii, 7.   [3] *Hyde I*, vi, 2773 ff.

he had to undergo without authorized assistance". Before Montague could interrupt them, Cosin learned that not only a Cardinal's hat but the Crown of England had been mentioned to the prince as a possible reward if he submitted to Rome.[1]

News of what was now believed to be a Romanist design on the throne spread like wildfire, and the English colony was in a fever of excitement and anxiety. Lord Hatton, who undoubtedly enjoyed a crisis, wrote that "next the murder of my beloved master I never was in such confusion of thoughts"—the Papists were busy with their old prophecy that Henry IX must repair what Henry VIII ruined.[2] Sir George Radcliffe roundly declared to Nicholas that "this is one of the greatest actions now on foot in Christendom, wherein all the Protestants of all countries will think themselves concerned".[3] The Princess of Orange, "in great trouble", wrote frantically to the King, "as well for his soul's good as his body's, to take some resolution to hinder this great mischief".[4] Though the Queen had arranged for the detention of all letters to England or Cologne, it was impossible to keep the news from the Court. For once the King reacted as energetically as his ministers could wish—"I never in my life saw the King our master in so great trouble and perplexity, nor of that quickness and sharpness in providing against a mischief," wrote Hyde.[5]

Letters of passionate urgency were despatched to Henry and the Duke of York, while to the Queen and Lord Jermyn Charles wrote with a bitterness he seldom used. The dependable Ormond was sent hurriedly off to Paris to demand the Duke of Gloucester's person, though the operations of Condé's troops made the journey hazardous. He arrived late in November to find matters at a new crisis. Angered by the King's letters and her failure to move the stubborn Henry, Henrietta was arranging to hold him in strict isolation at the Jesuit College in Clermont. The French Court was supporting her, and the protests of the Duke of York and even of Jermyn had been futile. The Marquis faced the Queen with imperturbable assurance, and by prompt action secured the boy's return to Paris. Two days later the Queen Regent

[1] *Nich.*, ii, 119 ff. Cf. P. H. Osmond, *op. cit.*, 135; T. Carte, *Life of James Duke of Ormond* (Oxf. 1851), iii, 636.
[2] *Nich.*, ii, 119, 112.
[3] *Ibid.*, ii, 132.
[4] *C.S.P.C.*, 11, 419.
[5] *Clar.* 49, f. 159.

and Cardinal Mazarin came to urge him to obey his mother, claiming him as "a child of France".[1] Henrietta made one last effort; overwhelming her son with loving words and caresses, she sought desperately to move him. His blunt refusal enraged her. "She told him", Ormond wrote to the King, "that she would no more own him as her son, commanded him out of her presence, forbad him any more to set foot in her lodging, and told him she would allow him nothing but his chamber to lie in till I should provide for him."[2] Ormond was reduced to raise money for the return journey by pawning his last jewels, and soon after left Paris with his charge.

The attempt to convert a prince in direct line of succession to the English Throne became overnight a *cause célèbre* throughout Europe, and had astonishing reverberations. Not least important was the effect on Anglican prospects. Just as the threat from Presbyterianism was checked by the defeat at Worcester, so the danger of an alliance with Rome was now banished by Charles's forceful action to protect his brother. The resentment of the disappointed Papists was out of all proportion. The Jesuit Talbot reported the anger of the papal nuncio in Germany, and his fear that "many more may be misled, to the prejudice of the business in Germany, by this particular of the Duke of Gloucester".[3] Another Jesuit visiting Rome the following May found Pope Alexander VII entirely hostile to Charles—"He seemed to dislike that the King of England had diverted the Duke his brother from the Catholic Religion".[4] From Cologne Thurloe received word in January, 1655: "All the Catholics here in Rome, France, Spain, etc., do speak against R.C. [Rex Carolus] and disaffect him for hindering his brother to be a Catholic", and later, "the Catholic princes of Germany are resolved not to give any more relief to the King because he hinders his brother from being a Catholic."[5]

The King's own Papist subjects were equally affronted. Cromwell's agent in Paris declared: "That action hath extremely vexed all the English, Scotch, and Irish Roman Catholics who are in this city."[6] To one of these it seemed that the King had deprived his party of "the

[1] E. Scott, *The Travels of the King*, 1654–1660 (Lond. 1907), 44.
[2] *C.S.P.C.*, ii, 433.
[3] *Ibid.*, ii, 437–8.
[4] *Ibid.*, iii, 35, 37; *S.C.P.*, iii, 260.
[5] *Thurl.*, iii, 44, 69.
[6] *Ibid.*, ii, 739.

most solid security he can give us for the performance of those graces and favours he shall please to promise us in case of his restoring".[1] In 1657 Lord Aubigny was still pleading with Charles to give way in the matter, declaring that no other assurance would satisfy Roman Catholics. The King's refusal had been represented at Rome "in the worst sense by those who had judged the missing of the Duke an affront to their order", and "the court of Rome looked upon your Majesty as a prince more inclined to persecute than to favour Catholics".[2]

Some indication of the King's motives is given by his dry comment on Aubigny's petition: "As I very well know, the person is very much mistaken in the temper of England as to its indifference in religion, and inclination to Catholics, of which I may be reasonably thought to understand somewhat, by having opportunity for many weeks during my last being there, to discover the humours of the people without dissimulation, myself being unknown amongst them."[3] Whether or not the politic Charles would ever have risked a less drastic concession, his potential allies in that quarter were now largely alienated. If his action was, as Gardiner declares, "a magnificent advertisement" for him in the eyes of Protestants,[4] it indicated no less to Roman Catholics that they might expect from him words but not deeds. His later tentative approaches to the Vatican were met with chill indifference,[5] and he found himself now doubly limited to an Anglican policy.

Nor was peace restored between Charles and his mother until the eve of the Restoration, and she never again exercised the slightest influence on his policies. The Queen's party had not only over-reached itself in a base attempt to proselytize a mere boy, but with its whisperings of "Henry IX" had become tainted with treason. Old Lord Hatton wrote incoherently: "My hand trembles, and I vow to God my heart, to think how they would dispose of the King and the Duke of York, if once they had got into their claws the Duke of Gloucester."[6] The play had been for great stakes, and had aroused the attention of all Europe. The reaction was proportionately strong, and sentiment for the English Church deepened as once more men came to feel that disloyalty to the old Church meant disloyalty to the King. The conflict

---

[1] *Orm. I*, ii, 100.   [2] *Thurl.*, i, 743.   [3] *Ibid.*, i, 744.
[4] S. R. Gardiner, *History of the Commonwealth and Protectorate* (Lond. 1894-1901), iii, 124.
[5] Cf. E. Scott, *op. cit.*, 159 ff, 169, 363 ff.
[6] *Nich.*, ii, 112.

with Romanism went on intermittently, but the danger that the small islands of Anglicanism would be engulfed grew perceptibly less.

What were the ultimate effects of Rome's prolonged assault on the exiled Church? It may be safely asserted that both in the impression made on the body of Anglicans, and in the number and quality of converts, the results were negligible. Mathew's comment supports this conclusion: "It appears to be a fact that the Laudian ideal was singularly impervious to the assaults of Rome."[1] Clerical converts were few indeed. Apart from men like Hugh Cressey, Thomas Bayly, and Stephen Goffe, the half-dozen others who seceded are little more than names to us. The chief conversions among the laity were in the Court circle where French influence was strongest; but even here the proselytizing hardly realized the Queen's hopes. "All this new Catholicism", admits Mathew, "was in fact poured out upon the sand."[2] The *Legenda Lignea*, a contemporary account of conversions during the exile, is one of the most scurrilous little books ever written, but its main contention seems justified—that most of those who left the Church of England "strained their consciences to supply their conveniencies".[3] That the conversions did not in fact reach serious proportions nor gravely compromise the English Church was due largely to the constancy and pastoral work of her clergy. The loyalty of these men was sternly tested by the loss of so much that seemed an inalienable part of the Anglican settlement, as well as by the formidable combination of influences against them; but their confidence in the theological and historical soundness of their position grew the stronger. "Truly," says one historian, "whereas the exile under Queen Mary was one of the greatest evils that ever befell the English Church, the exile under the Commonwealth and Protectorate was one of the greatest blessings; for it purified and spiritualized men's conceptions of the Church, and made them realize their Churchmanship as they had never done before."[4]

Such a judgment is perhaps influenced by the prepossessions of the writer, and it is possible to take a less favourable view of the undoubted effect on Anglican thought of this intensified struggle with Rome. Frequently an apologist is unconsciously influenced by the very terms of

[1] D. Mathew, *op. cit.*, 91.

[2] *Ibid.*, 87.

[3] E. Lee, *Legenda Lignea* (Lond. 1653), 206.

[4] W. E. Collins (ed.), *Typical English Churchmen* (Lond. 1902), essay by the editor on "John Bramhall", 104.

debate imposed by his opponents. Since Anglican theologians were forced to defend their tradition on the side of sacramental doctrine, of ecclesiastical polity and continuity, they emphasized ever more insistently its Catholic elements. In Bishop Henson's view, this trend was the worst legacy of the Interregnum: "Anglican apologists, almost in spite of themselves, contracted from contact with the Roman adversary a habit and a temper which were incompatible with the larger and more reasonable Protestantism of the previous period."[1] We may agree that the experience of exile widened the theological breach with Puritanism, and rendered the task of accommodation more difficult at the Restoration.

In anticipation of this problem, some account must be given of the Anglican attitude during these years to Presbyterianism at home and abroad. It is a story parallel to that of the Laudian party in England— the old hostility deepened into hatred that was almost an obsession. It became a matter of faith with churchmen that the Presbyterians were responsible for all their ills. Puritanism was incompatible with decency in religion and order in the state. "I believe if you speak with any zealous Presbyterian", wrote Richard Watson, "and he freely [speaks] his mind to you, he will tell you he not only wisheth but is bound in conscience to endeavour the setting up his religion and republic over all the world, one being the right of God . . . and the other of God's people; from which two heresies I am sure he is immoveable."[2] The growth of a Royalist party among the Presbyterians, with its demand for drastic concessions, merely increased the tension.

"Where be those people we would have him brought unto?" declaimed Dr. Byam. "Shall the Presbyterians be the men? 'Twere strange they should. They that brought the first fuel to that prodigious fire; they that swore against him, betrayed, sold their innocent Master. They that disavowed that cement by which the Church of Christ hath been firmly knit together ever since there was a Church Apostolic upon the earth; I mean Episcopacy. . . . To give these men the right hand of fellowship . . . were to partake of their sins, and render ourselves guilty of that sacred blood their hands have spilt, to join with them were to justify all their infernal and unparalleled actions."[3]

[1] H. H. Henson, *The Relation of the Church of England to the Other Reformed Churches* (Lond. 1911), 56.
[2] *Clar.* 46, f. 95.
[3] H. Byam, *op. cit.*, 13.

William Stamp, preaching in the Hague, exhibited the same spirit:

"The name of Gospel Purity and Reformation hath been used to distinguish and palliate the blackest designs the sun ever looked upon. . . . Our religion could never have received so deep a wound from any infernal stratagem, as from the plausible pretences of *refining* and *securing* it unto us. How well it is refined and secured, yourselves may judge by the present melancholy complexion of our dear Mother, stripped, mangled, and wounded unto death, by the sons of her own bowels."[1]

In a Latin epistle to the famous Huguenot Samuel Bouchard, George Morley gave an impassioned recital of Presbyterian crimes "contra omnia Divina humanaque apud nos Jura, Potestatem tam civilem quam ecclesiasticam", and concluded, "Hac et his similia facinora facinorosissima, schismatici nostri, qui se Presbyterianos appellant, ediderunt."[2] Cosin denied hotly that he could ever say anything to excuse "their voluntary and transcendent impiety that have endeavoured to destroy [Episcopacy] in the Church of England".[3] "That accursed Genevan tyranny" is the constant refrain of Edward Martin's letters.[4] Such quotations could be multiplied indefinitely, and exhibit a state of mind fully shared by the Anglican laity.

It was thus inevitable that when co-operation with the Presbyterian party became a political necessity, Anglicans entered on that course resentfully and with dissimulation of their real feelings. Jane's comment to Nicholas is typical: "Though I think no trust at all to be given to those Presbyters, yet I find a necessity of receiving their overtures, and not rejecting their propositions upon the ground of their inclinations, which are still as corrupt as ever. . . . Every man sees that Presbytery is destructive to Monarchy."[5] The real tenor of Royalist policy is summed up in two remarks of the King's most active agent, Mordaunt. The first lays down its fundamental basis: "Nothing can secure the Crown that destroys the Mitre." The second explains the course to be followed: "The chief wheels of this motion being Presbyterian, we ought so to comply with them as to persuade them if possible that we approve of what we do but connive at, and in truth cannot resist."[6]

[1] W. Stamp, *A Treatise of Spiritual Infatuation* (Ed. Lond. 1716), 6 ff.
[2] Bod. Lib., *Corpus Christi College MSS.* E. 314, f. 212.
[3] *Cosin*, iv, 450.
[4] E. Martin, *His opinion . . . communicated by five pious and learned letters* (Ed. R. Watson, Lond. 1662), 72-7.
[5] *Nich.*, iii, 22.
[6] *C.S.P.C.*, iv, 429; *Letter-Book of John Viscount Mordaunt* (Lond. 1945), 169.

G

The attitude of the exiles to the Continental Reformed Churche throws further light on the increasing intransigence of the Laudian party. The friendly relations between these bodies and the Church of England had already somewhat cooled. A French historian notes a change on the part of the English in Paris after the accession of James I. Previous ambassadors had worshipped freely at the Huguenot temple at Ablon, but under the Stuarts this practice was discouraged.[1] Lord Scudamore "was careful to publish upon all occasions . . . that the Church of England looked not on the Huguenots as a part of their Communion".[2] Laud, informed of the ambassador's refusal to join in Huguenot worship, answered: "He is the wiser."[3]

The decision of the Royal Family in the matter weighed heavily with the exiles, and was not reached without discussion. In December, 1651, after Charles's return from England, Lord Jermyn and the Queen entered upon a campaign to have him attend service at Charenton. Jermyn, remarks Hyde bitterly, "in his own judgment, was very indifferent in all matters relating to religion, [but] always of some faction that regarded it", and he pressed the move as a "thing that ought in policy and discretion to be done . . . which would draw to [the King] all the foreign Churches and thereby he might receive considerable assistance". The Queen was in favour of any policy that would detach her son from the Anglican Church. The Huguenot pastors added their pleas. But the Chancellor passionately opposed the scheme, partly on political grounds, and partly because the King's going to Charenton "could not be without this effect, that it would be concluded everywhere that his Majesty had renounced the Church of England, and betaken himself to that of Charenton, at least that he thought the one and the other to be indifferent; which would be one of the most deadly wounds to the Church of England that it had yet ever suffered". In view of Charles's now well-developed aversion to anything that smacked of Presbyterianism, Hyde had no difficulty in prevailing, and the King vowed that "he would never go to Charenton".[4] Though strong political inducements were later offered him, he never wavered in his decision.[5] The Duke of York took a similar stand. Of the Princess of Orange, Hyde wrote to Cosin:

[1] J. Pannier, *L'Eglise Reformée de Paris sous Henri IV*, (Paris 1911), 471.
[2] *Hyde I*, iii, 1187.
[3] R. A. Blencowe (Ed.) *Sydney Papers* (Lond. 1825), 261 ff.
[4] *Hyde I*, v, 2648–51.
[5] Cf. *C.S.P.C.*, ii, 172, 193; *Orm. II*, i, 284 ff.

"The Charenton elders may be as easily answered upon any invitation they shall make [her] as the Dutch elders have been, nor can they expect that she shall come to their Kirk in France, when she declines it at home in Holland."[1]

The attitude of the exiled clergy to Huguenot overtures has been frequently discussed in recent years, too often without adequate knowledge of the facts. Puritan writers of the time affirmed unanimously and positively that the Laudian clergy "do disown all [the foreign Protestant Churches] as no true Churches ... separate from their communion, and teach the people to do so, supposing sacramental ministrations to be there performed by men that are no ministers, and have no authority".[2] But in fact the stated views of High Church theologians were non-committal. Morley, upon demand that he either admit the Reformed bodies to be true Churches or condemn them as no Churches, replied: "As we need not do the one, so we list not to do the other.... We are sure our Church is truly Apostolical, and that for government and discipline, as well as doctrine. Whether the Christian congregations in other Protestant countries be so or no, *aetatem habent, respondeant pro semetipsis, et Domino suo stent vel cadant.*"[3] Bramhall's verdict is much the same: "I cannot assent ... that either all or any considerable part of the Episcopal divines ... do unchurch either all or the most part of the Protestant Churches. No man is hurt but by himself. They unchurch none at all, but leave them to stand or fall to their own Master."[4] Similarly Hyde: "The Church of England judged none but her own children, nor did determine that other Protestant Churches were without ordination. It is a thing without her cognizance."[5]

On the practical point of intercommunion, however, there was more justification for the Puritan charge. Morley is emphatic that he "never had anything to do with the Classis, nor they with me ... all the while I was in the Presbyterian [country]." Later in France, he "never went to the Presbyterian Church at Charenton, no more than afterwards to that of Caen in Normandy".[6] Bramhall equally refrained from any

---

[1] *Nich.*, ii, 246; *Clar* 51, f. 115.

[2] R. Baxter, *Five Disputations of Church Government* (Lond. 1659), 8. Cf. J. Corbett, *Interest of England in the Matter of Religion* (Lond. 1660), 77; J. Gailhard, *The Right of the Church Asserted* (Lond. 1660), 21–2; H. Hickman, *Laudensium Apostasia* (Lond. 1660), 58 ff.

[3] *Morley*, 'Answer to Fr. Cressey', p. 31.

[4] *Bramhall*, iii, 517.   [5] *Hyde II*, ii, 131.   [6] *Morley*, p. vii ff.

measure of fellowship with the Reformed congregations.[1] Dean Steward was inflexible in his opposition to intercommunion.[2] The pastors of Charenton sent a particular invitation to Bishop Sydserf to join with them, which he refused.[3] The only known exception is Dean Cosin, whose letter to Thomas Cordell of Blois advocating intercommunion is frequently cited. For this stand, however, he was fiercely denounced by Edward Martin and Richard Watson, and faced the disapproval of his congregation in Paris.[4]

The general attitude of the Anglicans was marked with astonishment and resentment by the French. "Rogaveram cur vestrates hic in Gallia pro causa regis exules, a communione cum nostris ecclesiis fere abstinerent," wrote Samuel Bouchard to Morley.[5] Drélincourt of Charenton, defending Charles as a true Protestant, observes: "Il y a des Anglois . . . qui luy font grand tort. Car sur des faux préjugés, ils se sont abstenus de notre communion." He mentions Cosin as an exception.[6] "Nous sçavons qu'il y a des personnes considérables de ce party qui étans à Paris, ont . . . refusé d'aller à Charenton, adjoutans . . . que les Eglises Reformées de France n'étoyent que des conventicules des Calvinistes", observed another author.[7] Years later, an English visitor to Paris found unhappy memories still lingering: "the famous M. Claude, the chief minister at Charenton, inveighed bitterly against [the Lord Chancellor Clarendon] and Dr. Morley and others for refusing communion with them."[8]

[1] A. J. Mason, *The Church of England and Episcopacy* (Camb. 1914), 171; W. J. Sparrow Simpson, *op. cit.*, 82.

[2] N. Pocock, *Life of Richard Steward* (Lond. 1908), 131; *Theologian and Ecclesiastic*, vi, 73.

[3] D. Dalrymple, *Memorials and Letters of the Reign of Charles I* (Glasgow 1766), 72–4.

[4] E. Martin, *op. cit.*, 72–7, 90, 101 ff.; R. Watson, *Bishop Cosin's Opinion* (Lond. 1684), 6 ff.; *Nich.*, iv, 93. Watson sums up the matter as follows: ". . . In our state of exile, wheresoever we found no oratories of our own, we asked admission neither into the churches of the Roman Catholics, nor the temples or meeting-places of the Lay-Reformed Calvinists (for ecclesiastics I dare not acknowledge those whom they pretend to make such.)" *Op. cit.*, 7.

[5] S. Bouchard, *Epistola qua respondetur ad tres questiones* (Paris 1650), 1–2.

[6] *Certain Letters Evidencing the King's Steadfastness in the Protestant Religion* (Lond. 1660), 43–4.

[7] *Apologie des Puritains d'Angleterre* (n.a.) (Geneva 1663), 34.

[8] G. Hickes, *Two Treatises* (Lond. 1707), pp. ccv–vi. Cf. also the conversation of Hickes with M. Diodati at Geneva, quoted in P. Bayle, *General Dictionary, Historical and Critical* (London. 1737–41), vi, p. 159, note.

To one small group, refugees from the Isle of Jersey, this breach in friendship between Anglicans and Huguenots was a serious embarrassment. The Church in the French-speaking Channel Islands had been reformed along purely Calvinist lines, and the Stuart kings had been only partially successful in imposing Anglican ways. To France came Jean Durel, Daniel Brévint, and Philippe Le Couteur when Jersey surrendered to Parliament in 1651; associated with them was another cleric of Huguenot extraction, Isaac Basire de Preaumont. Not surprisingly, these clergy saw no real distinction between the English and French Churches, and readily accepted posts in Huguenot congregations. Their importance for our story is that they entertained an ambitious design—to make a complete breach between the Calvinists in France and those in Britain, and to induce the Huguenot Church to recognize the Anglican as the one orthodox Protestant body in England. However they differed from the Laudians in other respects, they shared an implacable hostility towards the Presbyterians who had rebelled against the King and overthrown their Church.

Basire made the first move by the publication of a book entitled "Défence de la Religion Reformée et de la Monarchie et Eglise Anglicane contre l'Impiété et Tyrannie de la Ligue Rebelle d'Angleterre, à messieurs de l'Eglise Reformée de Paris". To a second edition of 1660 he gave an even more descriptive title—"Histoire des Nouveaux Presbitériens Anglois et Ecossois, où est monstré la Différence de leur Doctrine et Discipline en Religion, d'avec celle de France et autres Protestants". The real affinity of the Reformed Churches on the Continent, the author argues, is not with the factious and antinomian dissenters, but with the Church of England, since the Huguenot want of episcopacy is not deliberate but accidental.[1] Shortly afterwards, Durel and his fellows were eloquent on the same theme in the Huguenot synod at Caen, and the assembly was led to voice "much grief for the sad condition of our King and Church". Furthermore, the synod

---

[1] This book is anonymous in both editions, and the authorship has been disputed. The *Dictionary of Anonymous and Pseudonymous English Literature* (Lond. 1928), iii, 80, suggests that the author is Pierre du Moulin II (though it also names Basire). However, *Athen. Oxon.*, i (fasti), p. 286; the *Catalogue Générale de la Bibliothèque Nationale* (Paris 1901), viii, 487; the *Catalogue of the McAlpin Collection* (New York 1928), iii, 340, all ascribe the work to Basire. In any case the book was written by someone who closely shared the aims of the Jersey group.

unanimously censured one Coignart of Rouen for his "scandalous expressions against the Church of England" in a recent book. "We rejoiced to see so much right done to our Church, and that so handsomely, so unanimously, in such a juncture of affairs," wrote Durel.[1]

On the subject of their recalcitrant fellow-Anglicans, the group took a somewhat disingenuous line. In a letter to the ministers at Charenton, they acknowledged with regret the "evil understanding between you and some of ours . . . [who] have declared themselves contrary to the doctrine of the Reformed Churches . . . despised your assemblies . . . and maintained that there could be no Church where there was no bishop". Asserting that it was well known that the circumstances of the French Church made it impossible for the present to adopt episcopacy, the letter passed off the matter playfully: "You then, gentlemen, joining to your Christian charity the French courtesy, pardon our English scholars, who peradventure have brought with them from the University an humour a little affirmative, and from the fresh remembrance of their glorious Church retain yet an admiration of home things; which is an humour neighbour nations observe in the English, and which those that heretofore have known England will easily pardon."[2]

A typical illustration of the propaganda carried on is the exchange of letters between Durel and the pastor Gayon of Bordeaux. Durel artfully set forth the character of English Presbyterianism in the following terms:

"(1) That they had no set forms, nor indeed would admit of any, whether for Common Prayer, or for administration of Sacraments, etc. (2) That for a long time many of them had left off using that very form our Lord hath taught us. (3) That most of them likewise wholly neglected the use of the Lord's Supper for many years. (4) That there was a great irreverence at prayer in their congregations, very few kneeling, and many not so much as pulling off their hats; but either not uncovering their heads at all, or only a little their pole, as if they were playing at Bo Peep, or laying their hat on one ear like fools and fanfaroons."

It is not surprising that Gayon's regard for his co-religionists in Britain was decidedly dampened by this account. His reaction was gratifying:

[1] J. Durel, A View of the Government and Public Worship in the Reformed Churches (Lond. 1662), pp. 69, 95.
[2] "Letter to the Ministers of the Reformed Church at Paris" (n.p.), in History of the English and Scotch Presbytery (Villa Franca, 1660).

"Il faut avouer que l'on nous a bien trompés en ce pays lorsqu'on nous a parlé des Presbitériens Anglois. Je m'estois toujours imaginé que c'estoit un ordre de gens qui se conduisoit comme nos Eglises en France. Cependant ce n'est rien moins que cela. La description que vous m'en faites, fait voir que ce ne sont que des sectes estranges et qui ne peuvent point estre tolérées. Et j'estime que le meilleur rémède que l'on puisse apporter à cette confusion, . . . , c'est de réduire le tout sous le régime de l'Episcopat, ne jugeant pas que l'Eglise d'Angleterre puisse jamais fleurir autrement ni estre en repos."[1]

After ten years of converse with the Huguenots on these lines, the French Anglicans, one can believe, had achieved a considerable re-orientation of church relations. So at least Durel boasted: "It hath been observed . . . that the Presbyterians have always pretended a conformity with the Reformed Churches beyond the Seas; giving out that the said Churches are of the same judgment with them . . . and they have therein gained belief not only from the simpler sort of their disciples . . . but also from most of the Protestants abroad at first, till they were better informed. . . . But our brethren of the Reformed Churches have long since been undeceived by those whom God was pleased to disperse amongst them, during the late captivity of this Church and usurpation of his Majesty's authority."[2] This claim was to be amply justified by the attitude of the French pastors at the Restoration.

The full significance of Anglican activity on the Continent will become apparent in succeeding chapters, but one point may properly be stressed here. It has been sometimes rashly assumed that the re-establishment of Anglicanism was the inevitable result of a Stuart king's return to power. But this sequence of events was not a matter of course, as is indicated by the Scottish alliance of 1650. Not until the achievement of ascendency by Hyde and the Anglican party in 1651–2 was it possible to foretell with any probability the ecclesiastical colour of a Restoration. For some years after, that ascendency was precarious, for, as we have seen, popular opinion regarded the Church of England as virtually dead. The success of the exiled clergy in witnessing to its continued life, and in retaining the allegiance of the "legitimate" government, made Anglicanism once more a factor to be considered. Thus, at the Restoration, the problem was not whether the remnants of the old Church at home survived in enough strength to justify the support of the new ruler. The government itself was part of a returning stream of Anglicanism which had preserved its traditions intact, and which had long since committed Royalist leaders to a pro-Anglican policy.

[1] J. Durel, *op. cit.*, 144, 146.   [2] *Ibid.*, pp. 1–2.

CHAPTER III

LAUDIAN PREPARATION FOR THE RESTORATION
MAY, 1659 TO MAY, 1660

IN the preceding chapters we have traced the growing influence of the High Church party in Royalist circles both at home and abroad. At the beginning of 1660 responsible leaders of the Cavaliers fully shared the Laudian view that no plan of Restoration was acceptable which did not mean a return to the old order in Church as well as State— "Nothing can secure the Crown which destroys the Mitre." The exiled government never openly avowed this programme; to have done so would have rendered impossible that co-operation of parties on which success depended. But if one turns from the generalities of the Declaration of Breda to examine the policy of Hyde's clerical agents in 1659–60, it becomes clear that the Chancellor's real purpose was to reach power unhampered by any definite concessions to the Presbyterians, and, in the interim, cautiously to prepare the way for Anglican reestablishment. The immediate objective was in fact achieved; the Restoration of May, 1660, was virtually unconditional. So vague was the King's promise of religious toleration, with its reference to a future decision of Parliament, that the actual settlement remained ostensibly an open question, and the Presbyterians were left without those safeguards on which they had always counted.

The negotiations conducted by Barwick, Allestree, and Morley during the final year of the Interregnum have a particular interest, for the correspondence between these clergy and Hyde is the chief evidence we have of the latter's ecclesiastical policy at a crucial stage. Since the meaning of that policy during the next two years is the most controversial aspect of the Restoration settlement, the earlier evidence must be carefully weighed in any attempt to resolve the ambiguity. There is always a temptation to simplify the complex motives at work in any period of crisis and transition, and to credit the actors with our own foreknowledge of events. It is therefore well to keep in mind the caveat of a modern diplomatist: "Nobody who has not watched 'policy' expressing itself in day to day action can realize how seldom is the course of events determined by deliberately planned purpose or how often what in retrospect appears to have been a fully conscious intention was at the time governed and directed by that most potent of all factors—'the chain of circumstance'."[1] At a time when confusion and uncertainty reigned in England, and no man dared predict what the next turn of events might bring, it would indeed be misleading to imply that the negotiations directed by Hyde were one step in a far-sighted and carefully planned strategy—a great "conspiracy", as the Puritans were later to charge.[2] The Anglicans were no more prescient than others; but through all the changes of the Spring, they continued to give proof of that consistency of principle and resistance to compromise which they had shown throughout the Interregnum. However opportunist its tactics, the Laudian party never lost sight of the final goal—complete restoration of the old Church. Two factors in particular combined to make this policy effective; the intransigence of the Laudian divines, determined to secure all or nothing in the religious settlement, and the statesmanship of Hyde, who was able to cloak this aim with a wise and cautious diplomacy.

The mission on which John Barwick and Richard Allestree embarked in May, 1659, concerned a grave problem which had long exercised the minds of churchmen. As early as 1651 anxious comment began to appear in Royalist correspondence about the growing danger of a lapse in the episcopal succession. The last consecrations of bishops had taken place at Magdalen College, Oxford, in 1644. Most of the prelates were now elderly men, and death had already made serious inroads among them, with half the sees now vacant. In October of 1651, John Maplet wrote to Sheldon from Paris, expressing urgent hope that "there will be a course taken to perpetuate that Church, which methinks can never fail",[3] and ten days later Hammond notified Bishop Wren: "I have been put in mind by G[ilbert] S[heldon] to be a remembrancer to some of those who are concerned, to think of doing somewhat to preserve a Church among us, lest it should perish with their order."[4] In the follow-

---

[1] H. Nicholson, *The Congress of Vienna* (Lond. 1946), 17.

[2] For example, in R. Baxter, *Against the Revolt to a Foreign Jurisdiction* (Lond. 1691), chapter xxi.

[3] *Harl.* 6942, f. 163. John Maplet uses the pseudonym "Belleau".

[4] *Theologian and Ecclesiastic*, ix, 294.

ing May Nicholas and Hyde were in consultation on the matter. "I am upon a good and secure way for the making of bishops without noise", wrote the Secretary, "if, when I come, the King shall approve of it, and have already made some preparations for it."[1] But Hyde at this stage was not over-concerned. He replied: "It is well you have found so private and secure a way for the making bishops; I confess I have thought as well as I can upon that argument, and can find none against which there are not weighty objections, and the best comfort is, there is no necessity."[2]

Others were less complacent. Richard Watson wrote to his friend Edgeman, secretary to the Duke of York: "I am satisfied in part with that and the other pretences you send for the non-election of new bishops, though in all circumstances I think they hold not, and if they should, I cannot take all for sufficient to justify so great an hazard." He added with his customary bluntness: "Should the succession or per-petuity of that Holy Order fail in our Church, I know not that man of it more likely to suffer in the disreputation of it . . . than the noble Lord [Hyde]."[3] Sir George Radcliffe in Paris pursued the matter so hotly that Hyde was exasperated: "I do not conceive . . . that Sir G. Radcliffe hath any other title to be solicitous in that matter, but what his own activity suggests to him."[4]

There was some ground for the Chancellor's hesitation. As we have seen, ordinations to the diaconate and priesthood were performed in England with little difficulty; but the consecration of bishops was a different affair, complicated as it was by legal and constitutional proce-dure. This could hardly be brushed aside by men whose constant appeal was to "the old constitution in Church and State", and who were intent to maintain that their Church was still lawfully established. Even when the need for action became urgent, and the very existence of the Church seemed at stake, the plea that necessity knows no law carried small weight with some church leaders. The bishops themselves felt that not to act at all was almost preferable to enduring Puritan gibes that their acts were irregular. Several indeed intimated that "rather than they would, through their default, suffer that necessary function to fail, they would either consecrate bishops without titles; or else assign them to small bishoprics themselves". But the writer hastened to explain to Hyde that such sentiment was expressed "by way of consultation

[1] *Nich.*, i, 302.   [2] *S.P.C.*, iii, 75.
[3] *Clar.* 45, f. 463.   [4] *S.P.C.*, iii, 75; cf. *Nich.*, i, 302.

only, and not by resolution peremptory",[1] and his belief was to be amply justified by the events of the next few years.

The normal method of appointing and consecrating bishops was no longer possible. Upon the vacancy of a see, the dean and chapter always awaited the King's *congé d'élire*, together with a letter missive of nomination, and then formally elected the candidate at a meeting in the chapter house. The King's writ of assent followed, with his mandate ordering three bishops—or four, if the archbishop were unable to preside—to proceed with the consecration. Now, as Barwick made clear to Hyde, "for the dean and chapter to petition for such a licence would be difficult, as to elect if they had it, many of the deans being dead, some chapters extinguished, and all of them so disturbed, as they cannot meet in the chapter house, where such acts regularly are to be performed".[2]

There were, however, several alternative methods which were legally permissible. Since the Crown possessed absolute power of nomination in the Irish Church, the chapters having no electoral function, Bramhall suggested that the King might nominate clergy to the Irish sees, and afterwards translate them to England. It was also pointed out that suffragan bishops could be appointed and consecrated by royal warrant. But on the advice of legal counsel, the bishops in England preferred a plan by which the King, instead of issuing a *congé d'élire*, made a simple collation of the persons to be consecrated, and issued a mandate to all the bishops in England to perform the act. "After this manner", as Cosin remarked, "they proceeded in the consecrating of new bishops at the beginning of Queen Elizabeth's reign, and we cannot have a better pattern."[3]

A decision was not reached without prolonged discussion, but by the spring of 1655 Hyde had despatched to England Eleazor Duncon, a prebendary of York, to make the necessary arrangements with the surviving prelates. He was instructed to consult with five, Wren, Duppa, Warner, Frewen, and King, and reported in June that "they were all very glad to hear that care was taken for the preservation of their Order, and ready to . . . do anything in their power that might further it".[4] King and Frewen volunteered to cross to France if it were desirable to hold the consecrations abroad, while Duppa gave assurance that both Ussher and Brownrigg would join with him in a service in

[1] *S.P.C.*, iii, Appendix, p. ciii. [2] *Ibid.*, iii, 503.
[3] *Ibid.*, iii, Appendix, p. cii. [4] *Ibid.*, iii, Appendix, p. c.

England. But strict secrecy was enjoined, for obedience to the King's mandate might involve "loss of their liberty or life". On receipt of Duncon's report, the Chancellor notified Dean Cosin that "the King is resolved to despatch [the business] one way or other this winter".[1]

After so promising a beginning, the complete failure of the mission is at first sight surprising. Now, as later, the prelates in England were prodigal in grateful assurances to their "nursing father", but exceedingly reluctant to act. Undoubtedly, the severity threatened by Cromwell in October towards Anglicans acting in the King's interests gave them pause. In March, 1656, Hyde assured Cosin: "We are not asleep in that business; there is as much done in it as the present fears and apprehensions of our friends in England will permit, and enough to prevent the mischief we most fear, if men do their duty."[2] Such fears and apprehensions continued to paralyze the bishops, and there for a time the matter rested. Some years later, in a sermon at Bishop Duppa's funeral, Bishop King of Chichester offered an explanation: " 'Tis true divers ways were propounded, yet all found dangerous under the inquisition we then lived, both to the undertakers and the actors. His Majesty therefore at last thought . . . to call over to him two of the remaining bishops, who joined to a worthy prelate residing with him in his exile, might canonically consecrate some . . . divines who then attended him. . . . But great age and greater infirmity denying the concurrence of anyone of the rest (though otherwise most ready) that design fell."[3] In short, the bishops simply concluded that action in England was too dangerous, and a journey abroad too difficult, to warrant the attempt.

For four years no further mission was undertaken from abroad, and the bishops in England showed little eagerness to reopen a negotiation so embarrassing to them. But uneasiness among ch rchmen steadily increased. By 1659, all but eleven of the twenty-seven sees in England and Wales were vacant, and before the end of that year, two more bishops had died. Joseph Jane in Bruges voiced the impatience that many felt at this needless risk. In May, 1658, he was pressing his father-in-law Sir Edward Nicholas on the subject: "I spoke with the Bishop [of Derry] about the making of new bishops, but he knew of none; is the thought of it laid aside? I think it should not be, as the difficulties are not considerable." A few weeks later he renewed the attack: "I

[1] *Ibid.*, iii, Appendix, p. ci.   [2] *Clar.* 51, f. 115.
[3] H. King, *Sermon preached at the Funeral of Brian Lord Bishop of Winchester* (Lond. 1662).

am told that some of the bishops offer to come over, and serious trial should be made whether any will do it; if not, it lies at their doors. But I cannot understand that there has ever been an endeavour but in general words. I am sorry it is so slackly pursued."[1]

When in January, 1658, the King delivered to Hyde the Great Seal, and named him Lord High Chancellor of England, the step was interpreted as final proof of the ascendency of the old Anglican leadership, and the clergy felt renewed confidence that, whatever happened in political affairs, the interests of the Church would not be sacrificed. Richard Watson wrote in congratulation: ". . . the fainting Church will resume spirits to claim support and what re-advancement your hand can give it by this high confirmation of your interest in his Majesty's grace and favour".[2] Cromwell's death in September was a great stimulus to Royalist hopes, and though for the moment those hopes were dashed, the growing confusion and disunity in England made the prospect of a Restoration more encouraging than for many years past. But Hyde was loath to gamble the Church's very existence on expectations, and wrote to John Barwick in May, 1659, that though he believed "the time is drawing on that we may enjoy each other—sure if some . . . do not think so, it would be impossible that they should so much neglect an affair of importance, which you . . . will well understand by this insinuation, and upon which the hearts of your best friends are so much fixed". He hoped the bishops realized "what hath been done here towards it, and what importunity hath been used from hence, how ineffectually soever". He concluded with an annoyed comment on Herbert Thorndike's recently published *Epilogue to the Tragedy of the Church of England*. Its author had maintained that the one hope of raising the Church from ruins was in a drastic reconstruction of its constitution along more primitive and Catholic lines; he clearly despaired of any return to the old ecclesiastical order. Hyde's reaction showed how definitely he himself envisaged such a return:

"I pray tell me, what melancholy hath possessed poor Mr. Thorndike? . . . His name and reputation in learning is too much made use of, to the discountenance of the poor Church; and though it might not be in his power to be without some doubts and scruples; I do not know what impulsion of conscience there could be to publish those doubts to the world in a time when he might reasonably believe the worst use would be made, and the greatest scandal proceed from them."[3]

[1] *S.P.D. Commonwealth*, 1658–9, pp. 21, 32.　　[2] *Clar.* 57, f. 166.
[3] *Barwick*, 400 ff.

This letter marked the beginning of the Chancellor's second effort to ensure the episcopal succession, and the story of its frustration is among the least creditable episodes in Anglican history. Before the end of May Richard Allestree, one of the most trusted agents among the clergy, arrived at Court, and was commissioned to renew negotiations with the bishops. His own account has been preserved.

"In May 1659 I being at Brussels received from King Charles II a paper, wherein were these names, Dr. Sheldon, Dr. Hammond, Dr. Lucy, Dr. Ferne, Dr. Walton, with one other which I have forgot, in cypher, which I was commanded when I came into England, whither I was then going, to decipher and carry from him to the Bishop then of Salisbury, Dr. Duppa, with a message to this purpose, that he did desire him as his tutor, and require him as his subject, all pretences whatsoever laid aside, without delay to cause the bishops then alive to meet together and consecrate the above-named persons bishops, to secure the continuation of the Order in the Church of England. The dioceses they were to be consecrated to were also named in the same paper. The paper and message I did deliver to the Bishop of Salisbury, Dr. Barwick, afterward Dean of St. Paul's, going with me to him to Richmond."[1]

The stringency of the command laid upon the bishops was deliberate. Hyde had every reason to anticipate their reluctance, and in a letter to Barwick in June alluded to "the great Affair, which considering the delays [which] have been hitherto used, is not like to move as it ought to do without another kind of prosecution; and the King is very impatient to have that work done[2]". The character of the appointments is also noteworthy. The Chancellor explained that "the care that was taken in the nomination of those who were sent to you was that fit men might be appointed; nothing being so evident . . . that nothing but the great merit of churchmen can buoy up the Church[3]". Four of the five named by Allestree were leaders of the Laudian party, and William Lucy, designated to St. David's, was of the same stamp, though less prominent. Two others on Allestree's list were Francis Mansell, Principal of Jesus College, Oxford, and Matthew Nicholas, Dean of Bristol, both Laudian stalwarts of an older generation.[4] Barwick himself was designated either for Sodor and Man or Carlisle, and only Benjamin Laney's unwillingness and Robert Sanderson's age and infirmity prevented their inclusion among the names chosen.[5] A number of other

[1] Quoted in Coxe's *Catalogue of Oxford College MSS.*, vol. ii, Collegii Vigorniensis, MS. liv, p. 15.
[2] *Barwick*, 405–6.   [3] *Ibid.*, 463.   [4] *Ibid.*, 438, 464.   [5] *Ibid.*, 463.

church appointments were made at this time; among them, Dr. Edward Hyde to the Deanery of Windsor, Morley to that of Christ Church, Oxford; and Earle to Westminster.[1] Nothing could indicate more clearly the position of the Laudian party in Court favour, and the direction of Hyde's own preference, than the exclusive character of the selection.

John Barwick now assumed responsibility for the negotiations in England, while Allestree continued to act as intermediary between the bishops and the Court. The former entered on his work with enthusiasm, assuring Hyde that "the grand affair of the Church is still in motion towards that happy conclusion, which his sacred Majesty is so piously zealous for, with what speed may reasonably be used in a matter of so great importance and difficulty". The bishops, as usual, were profuse in assurances of good will, "tendering the most humble submission . . . to his sacred Majesty . . . and their dutiful acknowledgement of his pious and princely care". But they also exhibited considerable skill in the tactics of delay. The old method of procedure approved in 1655 was now reconsidered and rejected; they desired the King instead to grant a commission to the bishops of each province to elect and consecrate fit persons to the several sees, "either assembled in provincial council, or otherwise, as they should find most convenient . . . and then afterward . . . to have his Majesty's ratification and confirmation of the whole process". Though they were well pleased with the persons designated to office, the Bishop of Ely with a certain inconsequence wished to remind the King "that it hath been always the prudence of our former princes to keep some equality of the balance between the two universities (*caeteris paribus*) for the general encouragement of learning . . . which he observeth will be overpoised, when he considers both who are already in the stock, and who are designed for the supply".[2]

Hyde was determined to give no excuse for delay, and replied speedily from Brussels: "His Majesty is very willing to change, and acquiesce in the opinion and resolution now proposed; and leaves the whole despatch of it entirely to their care, both for the time and the manner." Again he urged "all possible haste in the finishing it", and explained that his impatience was due not merely to the age of the consecrators, but to a "fancy" of his own, "never yet communicated

---

[1] *Matt., W.R.*, 69; *C.S.P.C.*, iv., 273.
[2] *Barwick*, 410 ff.

to any person". This reflection is interesting enough to quote at length:

"The late revolutions in England, and the . . . jealousies in several factions amongst themselves make it a very natural supposition that there may fall out some avowed treaty with the King; and then the Presbyterians will not be over-modest in valuing and computing their own power. . . . If I were a Presbyterian (and they have many wiser men, and who know better how to compass what themselves desire) I would not propose to the King to do any formed act to the prejudice of the Church, because I should despair of prevailing with him; but I would beseech him to suspend the doing anything that should contribute to the former Establishment, till there might be such a mature deliberation, that the best provision might be made to compose all differences: and if I could pre-vail thus far, I should hope by some continued suggestions . . . to spin out the time till all the bishops were dead. . . . Such an overture . . . would be grateful to too many, and not resolutely enough opposed by others, who in truth mean well, but are not yet convinced of the mischief of compliance in things which they call small."[1]

Clearly, the Chancellor already saw in the Presbyterian party the chief obstacle to setting up the former Establishment, and sensed a danger in complying with that party "in small things". But the kind of strategy he feared as so effective bears a curious resemblance, *mutatis mutandis*, to the policy of skilfully disguised obstruction which the Presbyterians were to attribute to him at a later time.

John Barwick spent the month of July travelling through the coun-try to interview the widely scattered bishops. He found them "very ready and willing", but obviously hoping that the rumoured Royalist uprising would make the work unnecessary. By September he could only trust that "they are still of the same mind and affections, seeing the same reason that damps those hopes, makes the work more necessary". He begged Hyde to "lay as many and strict commands upon me from his Majesty as you please to quicken them in it".[2] The summer of 1659 had indeed proved discouraging to the King's friends; the premature Royalist plot had utterly failed by reason of the treason of one of the conspirators. Hundreds of suspects were arrested. The King's affairs appeared "hopelesser" than ever, and he was warned to "expect no more risings".[3] This increase of surveillance put the seal on the hesitations and fears of the aged prelates. Duppa's house was ran-sacked by government agents in September, and his correspondence thoroughly examined. A letter referring to the passage of the Israelites

---

[1] *Ibid.*, 425 ff.   [2] *Ibid.*, 436 ff.
[3] E. Scott, *The Travels of the King* (Lond. 1907), 395.

through the Red Sea received particular attention, "but the riddle (had there been any) being not unriddled, the innocent paper was laid down again".[1] In these circumstances the bishops were far too frightened to heed the Chancellor's reproaches or the King's commands. Before the end of September, Hyde wrote in desperation:

"The King hath done all that is in his power to do; and if my Lords the Bishops will not do the rest, what can become of the Church? The conspiracies to destroy it are very evident, and if there can be no combination to preserve it, it must expire. I do assure you, the names of all the bishops who are alive, and their several ages, are as well known at Rome, as in England; and both the Papist and the Presbyterian value themselves very much upon computing in how few years the Church of England must expire. It may be the hopes which this last summer administered of seeing some short end of these confusions have retarded the work. But sure the disappointment of those hopes ought now to hasten it. And I have the King's commands to write very earnestly to you to speak with the Bishop of Salisbury, and by his advice to press any of the other bishops ... to consecrate those persons which are designed by his Majesty."[2]

Dr. Hammond was no less apprehensive as he continued to wait in Worcestershire for a summons from the bishops; and he replied to a letter from Sheldon: "I hear nothing lately from Mr. Barwick, but I believe you must enlarge your prayer, and extend it not only to danger, but fears, though never so causeless ... or else the granting it will be of no effect to our Church business. God's will be done. I pray do not you give over attempting to awaken those that are concerned, whilst there is any hope of success."[3]

The autumn passed, and still the bishops would not stir. The Chancellor poured out his exasperated complaints to Barwick: "I know not what to add to what I have so often said concerning the business of the Church; the accidents of every day making the work more difficult; which if they are not sensible enough of, who can only prevent the mischief, I hope God Almighty will work one miracle more for the preserving his Church." Again, at the end of November: "I can say no more with reference to the Church, but that if there be nothing hinders it but the winter, it will be quickly over whilst preparations are making; and yet, God knows, it will be almost a miracle if the winter doth not take away half the bishops that are left alive."[4] No apologia

---

[1] *Duppa*, 20 September 1659.   [2] *Barwick*, 449 ff.
[3] *Harl.* 6942, f. 56.   [4] *Barwick*, 457, 462.

H

was forthcoming from the prelates save an injured and enigmatic letter which Duppa addressed to Sheldon on November 16:

> "When I met with the expression of [the Chancellor's] being amazed that there is so little care taken of our great business, I must impute it to the distance of place which is between us, and the misrepresentation of what is past, for otherwise if all circumstances and difficulties were made known to him he might pity some of us, but there would be no place of wonder left. And to this particular I shall give an answer (such as I can for the present), but the best satisfaction will be to send such a person as may do it by an *ore tenus*."[1]

Hyde's analysis of Anglican prospects at the close of 1659 is of considerable interest:

> "Truly I am of opinion that the Church will be either totally ruined (towards which there is too great a conspiracy between persons who agree in nothing else), or else that it will be restored to a great lustre. For all discourses of the Treaty of the Isle of Wight trouble me little; though it comes mentioned sometimes to us by those who pretend no disaffection to the Church, and who pretend all shall be repaired again afterwards. But as I am confident the King will never endure it, so if he should consent to it, it can never be reduced into practice, or a peace be established in the kingdom by it."[2]

If these words may be taken at face value, they seem to imply that in the writer's view Anglican policy must aim at "all or nothing"; certainly there is no anticipation of a compromise settlement with the Presbyterians, or of any concessions which would diminish the full "lustre" of the Church's restoration. He is equally clear that negotiations with the King on the basis of the old Presbyterian platform would lead to mere self-deception, and that a Royalist government in power would never implement such terms.

The new year saw one more effort on the part of the exiled government to force the bishops' hands. Allestree was in Brussels preparing for one of his periodic trips to England, when the King entrusted him with the most explicit command possible to the bishops to perform the consecrations without further delay. Hyde wrote to Barwick at this time: "Concerning the business of the Church, I am always ashamed of mentioning it to his Majesty, who is as much troubled and ashamed that there should be no more care taken of it by those whose part it is, when he hath done all that he can." He begged the agent to accept nomination to the obscure bishopric of Sodor and Man, "so that you

---

[1] *Tann.* 51, f. 159.   [2] *Barwick*, 465–6.

... will give a good example to others, by showing them that for the Church's sake you expose yourself to as much danger as they can do, and when you receive nothing to recompense it". He trusted that "what Mr. Allestree will say from the King . . . will prevail with the bishops to proceed to the despatch of the whole", but had little hope of any action unless the Bishop of Ely were released from the Tower. His comment on Bishop Brownrigg's death in the previous December was almost savage: "I will not enlarge upon the death of the Bishop of Exeter, because I will charge Mr. Allestree with that discourse in which I can use no patience. If that bishop were long sick, I would be glad to hear how he expressed himself to those friends who were about him in those particulars in which he suffered in his reputation, of not being zealous enough for the Church."[1]

Before Barwick could receive this letter, however, two misfortunes occurred, which, when they became known in England, effectually put an end to any chance that the bishops might overcome their fears and act. One of Barwick's letters to Hyde was intercepted by the English garrison at Dunkirk, and deciphered by an agent of Thurloe. Even more serious, Allestree was denounced to the authorities by an English merchant in Brussels, Bedford Whiting, and on his arrival in Dover at the end of January was seized and lodged in the Castle there. The consequences were not really fatal; Allestree was able to save his despatches from capture, and not long after, Barwick was expecting to interview him and receive the King's commands.[2] Nor is there any indication that the Council of State took notice of the project once they had knowledge of it. But belief that the affair was no longer secret "greatly affected the minds of many, everywhere spreading suspicions of deceit and treachery".[3] Though references to the "business of the Church" continue in the correspondence between Hyde and Barwick, they are wholly pessimistic in tone, and it is obvious that the bishops no longer bothered to keep up any pretence of zeal. Barwick wrote: "As for the old business of the Church, I know not what to say of it. I have com-

---

[1] *Ibid.*, 247, 488, 496. Cf. Hammond's similar comment to Sheldon: "You will have heard of the death of the Bishop of Exeter, for which truly I am very sorry, though I believe the business of the Church no whit more backward for it." (*Harl.* 6942, f. 108.)

[2] *Barwick*, 250; *C.S.P.C.*, iv, 531–8, 549; *S.P.D. Commonwealth* (1659–60), p. 324.

[3] *Barwick*, 252.

municated as much of your letters as concerned that business to my Lord of Salisbury from time to time, and proffered all the service I can do to him and the rest, but I hear nothing from him or them."[1] Duppa was once more securing himself "as the tortoise". His Lordship of Oxford, however, was less discreet than his fellows, and incurred the wrath of the Chancellor by protesting against Hammond's appointment to the see of Worcester, as a post too important to be given to a new bishop. "I meet with another objection made by one that I fear will do nothing else," wrote Barwick when reporting this development. "However, Dr. Hammond is very willing to be left out, or put to Exon. or Carlisle, or anything, so the work may be done." Hyde replied angrily: "You have indeed too much reason to doubt that he who makes those scruples will never do anything he should do. I would be very glad, you would tell me who it is."[2] Barwick's considered opinion of the elusive prelates is not surprising: "We now (too late) see the mistake of making bishops upon bye-respects, under which name I understand all things that do not really tend towards the government of the Church, which is a mystery sufficient for a man's study, and yet . . . there are not many of them that have undertaken it who really mind it."[3]

The rapid march of events in England, however, was bringing to the fore more urgent issues, and with the growing certainty of a Restoration the need of providing for the episcopal succession became less immediate. On February 3, 1660, General Monk arrived in London at the head of his army, and became to all intents and purposes the arbiter of events. Cautious and inscrutable, Monk was essentially an opportunist, but fortunately possessed of just those qualities needed to guide the nation peacefully through a period of crisis and transition. He had been drawn south from Scotland by the deadlock between the army leaders and the little group of uncompromising Republicans in the Rump. On his march he gauged accurately the drift of public opinion toward the old constitution, as the only practical safeguard from anarchy on the one side and a military tyranny on the other. Toward that solution he moved in successive stages, never anticipating or forcing the pace of events, but exercising a discreet pressure at each crucial moment. Wisely, he utilized what constitutional machinery was available to give effect to each decision. One after another, the earlier stages

---

[1] S.P.C., iii, 653.   [2] Clar. 69, f. 85; Barwick, 506.
[3] S.P.C., iii, 662.

of the Revolution were retraced in reverse sense until the point was reached where Monk's gradually improvised policy could make a natural juncture with Hyde's—i.e. agreement on the constitutional settlement of 1641.

If today historians are uncertain at what date Monk definitely resolved to restore the King, it is understandable that in the early months of 1660 public opinion was utterly baffled by his equivocal actions. "If you would know in what condition we are here," wrote Bishop Duppa to a correspondent in the country, "I know not how to tell you, for Fame was never more busy than now, *dum vanis rumoribus oppida pulsat.* Never was more said, and less known."[1] Royalists were elated at one moment, and downcast the next. At first the General seemed to side with the Rump in its quarrel with the City of London, but on February 11, he confronted the little clique at Westminster with a peremptory demand. Writs must be issued immediately to fill the vacant seats in Parliament, and order taken in the near future for a new election of the whole body. When it became apparent that the Rump would oppose the free and representative Parliament desired by the nation, Monk reached an agreement with those members who had been excluded since Pride's Purge in 1648, and on February 21 compelled their readmission. "Another strange mutation", was the comment of the irrepressible Lady Willoughby, "the Rump being now enlarged to a Gigot!"[2] The Republican group was now hopelessly outnumbered, and for a brief moment the Presbyterians once more tasted power.

It seems probable that Monk had no strong convictions on the religious issue as such; certainly his policy in this matter was framed on a principle of expediency. To the restored members he gave the following advice on February 21:

"As to a government in the Church, the want whereof hath been no small cause of these nations' distractions, it is most manifest that if it be monarchical in the State, the Church must follow, and prelacy must be brought in, which these nations I know cannot bear, and against which I have so solemnly sworn. Indeed, moderate Presbyterian government, with a sufficient liberty for tender consciences, appears to be the most acceptable way to the settlement of the Church."[3]

To his chaplain that evening the General explained that it was impossible to restore bishops, "for not only their lands are sold, but the temper of the nation is against them". But he took no offence at the cleric's

[1] *Duppa*, 24 January 1660.   [2] *S.P.C.*, iii, 689.   [3] *P.H.E.*, iii, 1580.

Anglican sympathies, and indeed showed no anti-prelatical feeling—"So much I will promise you, that I will not be engaged against bishops."[1] He was still in this frame of mind as late as March 14, when he wrote to the Scottish minister, Robert Douglas: "As for Presbytery, what I declare to the world, which was both my conscience and reason, so I assure you I adjudge it the best expedient to heal the bleeding divisions of these poor nations, so it be moderate and tender, otherwise it will but enrage our disease and increase our wound."[2] But as Monk's words to Parliament really implied, and the Presbyterians were soon to find, his support was contingent on political circumstance.

With such Puritan zealots as William Prynne once more seated, Parliament needed little encouragement to revive Presbyterianism. Since the dissolution was fixed for March 15, and a new Parliament of unpredictable character summoned for April 25, the majority seized the opportunity to give all legal security possible to the favoured system. On paper, the triumph of Presbyterianism was complete, and the Puritan muse declaimed in joyful couplets:

> Thus lay Religion panting for her life,
> Like Isaac, bound under the bloody knife;
> George held the falling weapon, saved the Lamb.
> Let Lambert (in the briars) be the Ram.
> So lay the Royal Virgin (as 'tis told)
> When brave St. George redeemed her life, of old.[3]

The Westminster Confession was officially adopted, and ordered to be published. The Solemn League and Covenant was to be displayed in all churches and publicly read to the congregation once a year. The Committee of Triers was abolished, and a commission largely made up of Presbyterian divines established in Sion College to approve all candidates for livings. Another Act confirmed the rights of ministers in sequestered livings to all revenues enjoyed by the ejected incumbent. The Engagement was repealed, and a beginning even made in restoring to their posts the ministers who had refused it; Edward Reynolds replaced the Independent, Dr. Owen, as Dean of Christ Church, and several canons were restored.[4]

[1] J. Price, The Mystery and Method of his Majesty's Happy Restoration (Lond. 1680), 116–18.
[2] Baillie, iii, 585.
[3] R. Wild, Iter Boreale (Lond. 1660), 17.
[4] Add. 19,526, f. 39; S.P.D. Commonwealth, 1659–60, 392, 394.

In a moment of such political uncertainty, this re-establishment of the old Presbyterian system had inevitably an air of unreality. The hasty legislation was in fact a symptom of the uneasiness of the Puritan party, as the letters of James Sharp, agent of the Scottish Church in London, make clear. "The great fear is", he reported in March, "that the King will come in, and that with him moderate Episcopacy, at the least, will take place here." There was little confidence that the new Parliament would favour the Presbyterian interest; "the Cavalier spirit breaks out very high, and is like to overturn all". Some members were reluctant to support the church legislation, "lest it bar them from being elected next Parliament". Sharp himself was one of a group of divines who waited on General Monk, and "urged much upon him that the Presbyterian interest he had espoused was much concerned in keeping up this [present] House, and settling the government on terms"; but Monk declared that his decision for a new Parliament could not be reversed.[1] Anglicans were not noticeably downcast at the ascendency of their old rivals. Barwick wrote to Hyde: "The business of Presbytery, which makes so much noise in the House, signifies not much with them [the army]: my friend is none, nor I think Monk, more than to serve his own ends."[2] A country squire, Sir Justinian Isham, commented to Duppa: "We have lately had as many several doctrines as there are points in the compass, that they having now gone around, begin Presbyterian again. Who knows not whether this dance may not like others end in the same measure they began, and then men come to be restored to their wits again, when the biting of this cursed Tarantula is wrought out by those various and violent motions?"[3] Even a practised time-server like John Gauden felt it safe publicly to rail against the Presbyterians in their day of triumph. Preaching before the Lord Mayor and Aldermen on February 28, he reminded them that "the Church of England [lived much more freely] under excellent Bishops beyond what they ever will under the rigour of others, who have their horns, though they endure no Head; the little finger of rigid Presbytery hath been heavier than the loins of moderate Episcopacy".[4]

On March 16 the Long Parliament at last dissolved, and for over a month government was in the hands of Monk and a largely Presby-

[1] *Wodrow*, i, 8–11; *C.S.P.C.*, iv, 606.
[2] *S.P.C.*, iii, 698.
[3] *Duppa*, 27 February 1660.
[4] J. Gauden, *Slight Healings of Public Hurts* (Lond. 1660), 59–60.

terian Council of State. There was general expectation of the King's return; "the controversy begins now to be rather upon what terms, than whether the King shall be restored", Barwick informed Hyde.[1] Within two days Monk had accepted a letter from the King, and entered into negotiations with the exiled government. He suggested that Charles agree to a general amnesty; confirm the sale of confiscated lands, including those of the Church; and agree to religious toleration for all his subjects. At the same time the Council of State and a group of Presbyterian peers were engaged in preparing a treaty which would drastically limit the King's power, and ensure the permanent establishment of Presbyterianism—"propositions . . . more insolent than ever they had demanded of the late King", declared a Royalist agent.[2] They hoped to bind Charles to these terms before Parliament could meet. The Presbyterian clergy in London were active in promoting a settlement on these lines,[3] yet it was from the City, once their stronghold, that unexpected opposition came. Commercial leaders had reached the conclusion that only a truly constitutional settlement could restore law and order; there was no desire to see the King return as the puppet of a Presbyterian oligarchy. On March 25 a memorial from the City was laid before the Council urging the recall of Charles without conditions. Three petitions should be presented to him, requesting a general amnesty, payment of the army, and lastly, a lawful assembly of divines to determine religious questions.[4] These proposals made a great impression on the Council, where they were inconclusively debated the same day; more important, they gave Monk needed assurance that public opinion would support the liberal terms on which he was now planning the Restoration. One point is noteworthy. The General, seeing the sectarian army as a potential danger, envisaged the religious settlement in terms of a general toleration. The City, with its awareness of the Anglican-Presbyterian tension, turned rather to the old solution of a synod of orthodox divines to work out an agreement. This latter plan had been the one ostensibly favoured by Hyde;[5] but in the Declaration of Breda, Monk's suggestion was followed.

[1] S.P.C., iii, 698.

[2] Ibid., iii, 705.

[3] Ibid., iii, 723; Wodrow, i, 18.

[4] Tann. 49, ff. 1, 2. Cf. L. von Ranke, History of England in the 17th Century (Oxf. 1875), iii, 295–6.

[5] A preliminary draught of the Declaration of Breda, summarized in C.S.P.C. iv, 633, speaks of referring the religious settlement to a synod.

It was apparent to Royalists that the nature of the Restoration would depend on the balance of power in the new Parliament. "The whole moment will rest in the happiness of the new election", Lady Willoughby declared to Hyde; "in which, my Lord, you may rest assured that his Majesty's friends will use their best industry."[1] During the next month the Cavalier party engaged in frantic activity to win the support of influential persons. In the struggle of conflicting aims, the church settlement was perhaps the chief issue in suspense. In a letter written on March 16, shortly before his death, Dr. Hammond revealed his fears: "It appears not improbable that the tabernacle of David, which hath been in the dust so long, may ere long be re-edified; but whether not with those diminutions which may extort tears from them that compare the second with the former edifice, I am not able to divine."[2] He is evidently thinking of the sentiment for "moderate Episcopacy", a compromise widely favoured as the only means of uniting Anglicans and Presbyterians. Uncertainty continued until the new Parliament convened; on April 23 Bishop Duppa wrote: "It is yet standing water with us; how far the near approaching Parliament may either advance or drive us back I know not. But we hope the best. Many machinations there are, plots under ground and above, to prevent any settling at all; but God keeps His councils apart, and unless our ruin be irreversibly decreed, will at last happily finish what he hath so wonderfully begun. . . . We are all here in great expectations, and if the end answers these blessed beginnings, we may be once more a happy people."[3]

It was during this interval that George Morley arrived in England, commissioned by the Chancellor to act as his agent in promoting the interests of the Church. The latter had written to Barwick on March 2: "That little appearance of more liberty than ordinary makes a very worthy man encouraged to venture over, Dr. Morley, with whom your good friends will bring you acquainted. You will find him a right worthy person, as well of habit as of integrity. . . . He will do all he can to advance this grand affair of the Church, and will be hearkened to by some who may be shy to others. . . . I shall be glad to hear that Mr. Allestree is at liberty . . . in this general gaol delivery." He added

---

[1] *S.P.C.*, iii, 689.
[2] F. Peck, *Nineteen Letters of Dr. Henry Hammond* (Lond. 1739), 50 ff.
[3] *Duppa*, 23 April 1660.

drily: "I hope my Lord of Ely will be even compelled to leave his prison."[1] Morley reached London at the end of March, and almost immediately his mission attracted attention. "Tuesday last," he informed Hyde on April 5, "I was summoned to attend the Council of State, and did so; where, after some questions asked by them and answered by me (of which the most important was, whether I had brought over any commissions with me) I was dismissed, and have leave to stay here, or to dispose of myself where or how I please."[2] The agent Alan Brodrick commented to Hyde: "The Council of State takes notice of Lord Mordaunt's departure and Dr. Morley's arrival, in whom they say is ten Lord Mordaunts. . . . I beseech God he may proceed with more than ordinary coolness, lest it exasperate our Presbyterians to their accustomed insolence, who are now apt for good impressions, if gently applied. A worthier person is nowhere of his profession, nor shall he want any possible assistance from me, and all in whom I have interest, to effect whatever he intends."[3]

What did Morley intend? The answer is important in determining Hyde's religious policy during these crucial weeks, for there can be no doubt that the Doctor acted as his representative. Since no paper has survived setting forth the Chancellor's instructions, we can only surmise them from Morley's periodic reports. The evidence will be considered in due course, but one preliminary observation can be made. Throughout the spring a fundamental ambiguity persisted in the Royalist approach to the church problem. Did the liberal terms held out by Royalist spokesmen envisage wide comprehension within the Establishment, or merely a general toleration of all religious groups? The Sectarians would have been fully content with the latter solution; but the Presbyterians were committed by doctrine and tradition to membership in a national Church. If they failed in the plan of establishing their own system, the obvious alternative was to press for the most drastic modification of Anglicanism which they could obtain. The

[1] *Clar.* 70, f. 61. In this letter, "the grand affair of the Church" seems to refer not to the consecration of bishops, but to the attempt to win over the Presbyterians.

[2] *S.P.C.*, iii, 722. Cf. the letter of Dr. William Denton to Sir Ralph Verney, 4 April 1660: "Dr. Morley has been before the Council, and, as I hear, on his engagement to act nothing prejudicial, is at liberty." (*Hist. MSS. Com., Report VII*, 1879, *Verney Papers*, p. 484.)

[3] *S.P.C.*, iii, 714.

Declaration of Breda, issued on April 4, did not really clear up this confusion; the relevant section reads as follows:

"And because the passion and uncharitableness of the times have produced several opinions in religion, by which men are engaged in parties and animosities against each other; which, when they shall hereafter unite in a freedom of conversation, will be composed, or better understood; we do declare a liberty to tender consciences; and that no man shall be disquieted, or called in question, for differences of opinion in matters of religion which do not disturb the peace of the kingdom; and that we shall be ready to consent to such an act of Parliament, as, upon mature deliberation, shall be offered to us, for the full granting that indulgence."[1]

On this, as on all controversial issues, Hyde made a general assent to Monk's terms, but referred the details of settlement to Parliament. From the Chancellor's viewpoint, it was an expedient which had the double advantage of affirming the constitutional relation of Crown and legislature, and freeing the King from definite commitments which might, in the future, prove embarrassing. Moreover, Anglicans could point out that the Presbyterian party had frequently in the past expressed willingness to accept a Parliamentary decision. As early as 1655, the Puritan leader Lord Balcarres was quoted as follows: "He knows it particularly from the Presbyterian ministers of London . . . that no more is asked of the King in his present condition to their entire satisfaction than the declaring he will refer matters of religion to a free Parliament."[2] In the summer of 1659 another veteran of the party, James Bunce, was assuring the London clergy that the King would grant a free Parliament and a free Synod "to settle the affairs of Church and Kingdom", with the evident belief that such terms were acceptable.[3]

Ostensibly, Morley's visit may have been designed to spur the flagging negotiations with the bishops. "I hope Dr. Morley is by this time with you," Hyde wrote to Barwick on March 23, "and will join with you in the business of the Church, of which I can say no more, but that God Almighty will not put it into their power, who care so little for it, to suffer it to expire." But in the same letter he broaches another matter: "The Presbyterians and their humours and appetites must be now so well known, that I hope no arts or artifices are omitted to dispose them, for their own sakes, as much as is possible to repair the ruins they have made; and then the worst of them will be so contradicted and

[1] D.A.U., 2–3.   [2] Orm. II, i, 317.   [3] C.S.P.C., iv, 340, 348.

controlled by the best, that the schism will appear. There are some of
them who have been eminent enough when they were against us, who
now either really are, or are willing to appear converted as well to a
piety towards the Church, as a loyalty towards the King."[1]

Whatever the original intention, Morley was soon immersed in a
two-fold task—on the one hand, to moderate the indiscreet propaganda of the Laudian party, and on the other, to employ those "arts
and artifices" which might lead to the disruption of Presbyterian solidarity, and reconcile the more moderate ministers to the prospect of
Anglican re-establishment. A serious threat to that prospect had indeed
arisen early in April from the ranks of Morley's own party. At a time
when the Anglican cause could best be served by a show of conciliation,
the old hatred of Presbyterianism was given alarming expression. In
such tracts as *The Grand Rebels Detected or the Presbyterians Unmasked*,
published April 2, the real sentiments of the Laudians were trumpeted
to the world:

> "As for all that show of loyalty now seeming to be in them [the Presby-
> terians] unto his Majesty, it is most manifest that it is out of selfish designs to
> advance their own interest, and upon no other account. . . . 'Tis true, they are
> willing he should come, because they are afraid of the fanatic sectaries, lest they
> should overcome them; and therefore they have revived their Covenant . . .
> against Episcopacy and Bishops, the ancient government of our Church; a
> Monarchy they are for, but it must be a limited Monarchy; a King they are for,
> but they must rule him, and the people too, else 'Curse ye Meroz, curse him
> bitterly, etc.'. . . . For all that is (as they judge) below their Reformation is
> Popery; and all above it, heresy. . . . It was they made the breach in, and brought
> all those sorrows and pains upon our Mother the Holy Church, and I wonder
> with what face these men think their sin should be either forgotten or forgiven
> without repentance and a return from whence they are fallen."[2]

Several Anglican divines in the capital who had conformed to the
Cromwellian Church now took occasion to make up for past arrears
by their militant attacks on the Presbyterians. George Masterson, who
had held the sequestered living of St. Clement Danes since 1650, cried

[1] *Barwick*, 513 ff.
[2] The full title of this tract is "The Grand Rebels Detected or the Presbyterians unmasked, shewing to all loyal hearts who were the first founders of the
King's Majesty's ruin and England's misery, under the pretence of Reform,
who in truth have proved the Instruments of Destruction both to Church and
Kingdom. By a lover of his Country, whose design is to undeceive the deceived,
make known the deceivers, and himself also in convenient season." (Lond.
1660.) Cf. p. 12.

revenge for the blood of Laud and Strafford.[1] A sermon preached by Dr. Matthew Griffith in the Mercer's Chapel on March 25 was speedily published under the title of *Fear God and the King: A brief historical account of the causes of our unhappy distractions*; it so enraged the Presbyterian Council of State that the Doctor shortly found himself in Newgate. The pleasing style of his apologia might surely have disarmed his accusers: "I saw that it was high time . . . to prescribe strong purgative medicines in the pulpit (contempered of the Myrrh of Mortification; the Aloes of Confession and Contrition; the Rhubarb of Restitution and Satisfaction, with divers other safe roots, seeds, and flowers, fit and necessary to help carry away by degrees the incredible confluence of ill-humours and all such malignant matters as offended)."[2] It was small wonder that an observer reported to Hyde at this time: "I find that some of the Presbyterians who have been formerly forward enough, begin a little to flag now, and fear the settlement of Episcopacy."[3]

The Chancellor was greatly perturbed by the reports which reached him at Breda "of the very unskillful passion and distemper of some of our divines in their late sermons", with "such menaces and threats against those who have hitherto had the power of doing hurt, and are not yet so much deprived of it that they ought to be undervalued". The King, he informed Barwick, is "extremely apprehensive of inconvenience and mischief to the Church and himself from offences of that kind; and hath commanded . . . you and Dr. Morley to use your credit and authority with such men, and to let them know . . . the sense he hath of it." Yet he was optimistic: "Truly, I hope, if faults of this kind are not committed, that both the Church and the Kingdom will be better dealt with than is imagined. And I am confident, those good men will be more troubled that the Church should undergo a new suffering by their indiscretion, than for all that they have suffered hitherto themselves."[4] He expressed the same view to Dean Cosin in Paris: "I hope at least, if the unseasonable warmth and indiscretion of our own friends do not do mischief, that the Church will be preserved in a tolerable condition, and by degrees recover what cannot be had at once. I mention the indiscretion of our friends upon some late sermons which have been preached, with such unseasonable menaces, and contempt of the

---

[1] *S.P.C.*, iii, 727.
[2] M. Griffith, *Fear God and the King* (Lond. 1660), Epistle Dedicatory, n.p.
[3] *S.P.C.*, iii, 716.
[4] *Barwick*, 517 ff.

Presbyterians, as if the High Commission were again up, and the Church possessed of her entire jurisdiction."[1] Morley, however, was soon able to reassure the Chancellor: "I have both before and since done what I can in order to the business I came for, particularly by endeavouring to allay the indiscrete and unseasonable zeal of some divines of our party, by representing unto them the ill effects of it in general. . , . And. truly, I am persuaded that almost all our clergy in this place have put on such a temper as the King would have them, and are resolved to expect with patience what it shall please God, and the King, and a free Parliament to do for them."[2]

In order to repair the damage done, and offset the alarm caused by loose talk of retribution among the more embittered Cavaliers, Morley took a leading part in promoting conciliatory declarations from the Royalist party throughout England. These insisted that the Cavaliers were content to bury the past, and professed a degree of submission to the future Parliament that indicated full confidence in its decision. Morley wrote to the Presbyterian John Davys on April 16, with reference to the Declaration of the Somerset gentry:

"I thought of it so well that I hoped and believed there would come forth another shortly, subscribed by all the King's party both clergy and laity . . . [and] give as much satisfaction to the Council of State for us all as that declaration did for some of us only. . . . I add further: that I never knew, heard, or thought of any writing to be published or subscribed to the prejudice or offense of any of the dissenting parties, and much less to the provocation of any that shall be in authority, having already subscribed that I will neither by myself nor by my advice to others do anything to hinder or obstruct the proceedings of the present Council of State, or the ensuing Parliament. . . . Moreover, I will endeavour (as I have already done to the utmost of my power) to make all men both of clergy and laity in whom I have any interest, to be of the same mind that I am in this particular."

His conclusion, however, can only be termed disingenuous:

"I profess that if anything shall be determined either in regard of civil or ecclesiastical government with which I cannot actively comply, I will notwith-

---

[1] S.P.C., iii, 732.

[2] Ibid., iii, 727. It is perhaps significant that Dr. Griffith's indiscretion did not lose him the favour of Royalist leaders. On 8 August of the same year, he mentions that Secretary Nicholas has expressed a desire to serve him, and adds: "I writ to my old schoolfellow and good friend Dr. Morley to let me understand what dignities are yet undisposed of; who sent me word that there be some prebends of Winchester to be had, if I make use of the present opportunity." P.R.O., S.P., 29/10, f.76.

standing passively submit to it, so far as not to oppose it directly or indirectly, the extent of my resolution (even in that case) being no more than this '*Ego cedam, atque abibo, et si Republica frui non possum carebo, mala*. . . ."[1]

Both he and Jeremy Taylor were among those signing the Declaration of the Royalists in London. Similar pronouncements appeared from a number of counties, all alike disavowing a desire for revenge, and promising that "we will thankfully submit and attend the resolutions of the next ensuing Parliament, for a just and happy settlement of Church and State".[2] These measures undoubtedly helped to calm Presbyterian fears, and ease the way for the King's return.[3]

Morley's diplomacy was also called upon to deal with another difficulty. In the middle of April a concerted effort was made by the Presbyterian party to forestall the return of Sir Edward Hyde and the Marquis of Ormond, or at least to insist on their removal from the King's Council. Unquestionably, the Presbyterians looked upon the Chancellor as their most dangerous enemy. "There was to visit me last night of his own accord one Mr. Bates of St. Dunstan's", wrote Morley to Hyde on April 18, "a very moderate man . . . and one of the most learned of the Presbyterian party. He told me there was great fear amongst them of some about the King, and especially of Sir Edward Hyde, who was everywhere spoken against as a proud and implacable person, especially against the Presbyterians, whom he never mentioned nor heard spoken of without some expression of scorn and bitterness."[4] Other enemies of Hyde like the Duke of Buckingham and Lady Newport had been busy; "by stories related both to the General and his Lady, [they] have possessed them both with a very ill opinion of you, which has showed itself by several bitter expressions", Lord Mordaunt reported.[5] It required a firm letter from the King[6] and considerable effort on the part of the Royalist agents to overcome Monk's prejudice. The Presbyterians were never really reconciled to Hyde's leadership of

---

[1] *Carte* 30, f. 566.

[2] "Declaration of the Nobility and Gentry of Essex", in British Museum, vol. 669. f. 25, f. 1. More than a dozen similar declarations are contained in this volume and in 669. f. 24.

[3] Cf. *Rel. Baxt.*, 217. On the other hand, Lady Willoughby remarked acidly: "The poor Cavaliers have declared in many shires their absolute oblivion of all injuries, to sweeten (if it be possible) the crabbed Presbyterians . . . yet will they believe nothing sure, but their own salvation, not their safety." *S.P.C.*, iii, 731.

[4] *Clar.* 71, f. 295.   [5] *S.P.C.*, iii, 738.   [6] *Clar.* 71, f. 299.

the government.[1] "It hath not been a small business [to allay opposition]", Lady Mordaunt informed the Chancellor, "for malice was very high against you, as that good man Dr. Morley can tell you; but in earnest you are very much obliged to the Doctor, and his coming over hath been of great advantage to his Majesty's business."[2]

Morley's rôle in the general work of reconciliation was undoubtedly important. As the Chancellor's personal representative, he was regarded on all sides as a person of weight and influence, and he reassured many doubters by representing Royalist intentions in the most reasonable and moderate light. "Dr. Morley doth his master great service and himself much honour by his prudent and sober temper," wrote one agent. "I heard that excellent character given of him by a person of quality who doth not know him, but took it from public fame."[3] Lord Mordaunt was even more enthusiastic:

"I am now to tell you how happy I am in worthy Dr. Morley's kindnesses, who has been the most useful person in the world here, and makes daily converts; the opinion these people have of him is so great that they let fall the cudgels to his mildness, which they would still have defended their plans with against the rigour of some of our inflexible divines. His great moderation speaks him fit and equal to my undertaking. . . . He is constantly with me, and lodges next door, that with less inconvenience I may have the advantage of his advice."[4]

Even the French Ambassador took note of the Doctor's mission, and reported to his master, "Il y a présentement à Londres un chapelain du Roy d'Angleterre envoyé par ledit Chancelier qui n'oublie rien pour aplanir toutes les difficultés de l'accommodement. Il promet tout à tout le monde, mesme la liberté de conscience aux Trembleurs; beaucoup se confient en ses promesses. . . ."[5]

It is in the examination of Morley's relations with the Puritan ministers that we can determine the true nature of his "mildness" and "great moderation". On his arrival, he had found "the Presbyterian party very

---

[1] Cf. the excerpts from the reports of the French Ambassador quoted on page 140 *infra*.

[2] *Clar.* 72, f. 63b. According to the French Ambassador, Morley was *persona grata* with the General's family—"Au moins, est-il certain que sa famille [i.e. Monk's] a relations particulières avec le ministre Morley, qui a esté envoyé par le chancelier Hyde pour ménager tous les partis. . . ." P.R.O., Transcripts 3/107, f. 222.

[3] *Ibid.*, 71, f. 240.

[4] *Ibid.*, 72, f. 62.

[5] P.R.O., Transcripts 3/107, Bordeaux to Brienne, May 3, 1660 (N.S.).

high in their demands, and exalted in their hopes".[1] But the fact that Parliamentary elections were seen to be strongly in favour of the Royalists was disquieting to them; the outcome in London was an especial blow. "It was almost a miracle that none of the most popular Presbyterian clergy could get any voices (in a manner) at the election of Parliament men for the City," wrote Barwick, who was in high spirits over the trend of public opinion. "I believe at this instant [March 30] there may be as many hands got not only for the King . . . but also for bishops and the Service Book as at first there was against them."[2] But when the Presbyterian ministers reached the point of desiring "a conference with some of the moderate men of the Episcopal persuasion", both Morley and Barwick were perplexed, and reluctant to enter into any discussion of the church settlement. "Whether there may be such a conference admitted on our part without leave from his Majesty, and in what manner, and how far we are to proceed in it," Morley wrote to the Chancellor, "I cannot tell, and therefore desire some particular directions to be sent to that purpose. For the present I am of opinion that all that is in difference betwixt us, is to be referred to the decision of a national Synod and a free Parliament."[3] Barwick was even more dubious.

"Since Monk did make his thoughts known," he reported on April 10, "I have applied myself the more to the business of the Church with Dr. Morley. . . [The Presbyterians] know not well what to say in particulars, but only to make a clamour in the general. They find very little hope to have their interest advanced by the next Parliament; they find the general vote of the people is for the King. . . . But, however, if they desire a conference, I cannot see how it can be refused, though I conceive the best way will be to evade it by delays or any other prudent expedient, for they now play at their last stake."[4]

On April 12 the Chancellor sent the instructions requested, addressing the letter to Barwick, "since Dr. Morley hath not yet his cypher by him". He declared: "The King very well approves and desires that he and you, and other discreet men of the clergy should enter into conversation, and have frequent conferences with those of the Presbyterian party; that if it be possible, you may reduce them to such a temper, as is consistent with the good of the Church." He made a further important suggestion: "It may be it would be no ill expedient to promote that temper, to assure them of present good preferments in the Church. But

---

[1] *S.P.C.*, iii, 722.   [2] *Clar.* 71, ff. 108–10.
[3] *S.P.C.*, iii, 722.   [4] *Clar.* 71, f. 198.

in my own opinion, you should rather endeavour to win over those, who being recovered, will have both reputation and desire to merit from the Church, than be over-solicitous to comply with the pride and passion of those who propose extravagant things.''[1] This latter advice accorded with opinions Barwick had frequently expressed: "How to break the design [of the clergy of that party], whether by mollifying or dividing, is still the great question, though neither way will be left unattempted." Again, "for my part I take the best method to be to begin with the most moderate of them, which will dig up the others by the roots by finding themselves deserted, and in that way I hope I have made some progress. . . ."[2]

While waiting for instructions from abroad, Morley took stock of current opinion among the Presbyterian clergy. He noted, "by what is told me by those that converse with them", that he was considered acceptable as a negotiator, "being thought by them to be somewhat more moderate than others of our clergy are, and than those [Griffith and Masterson] perhaps indeed I am". He commented in his interim report to Hyde:

"Those that are the chief, and have most power amongst them, are content to admit of the name 'bishop', but not with the power which we think to be inseparable from his office. . . . And whereas they thereupon infer that then the Episcopal Government will be arbitrary and tyrannical, I tell them they may be secured from that fear by those canons and ecclesiastical laws whereby he is to govern, and which, if he do transgress, he is answerable for it to a free Synod. With this, I am confident, Dr. Reynolds is fully satisfied, but Calamy and others are not, but perhaps they may be hereafter."

Morley saw no prospect of the "friendly conference" desired by the Presbyterians, before the opening of Parliament.

"Besides, as they do not press it, so have we no reason to desire it; partly, because we have no command nor leave from the King for it; and partly, because there is little or no fruit to be expected from it; neither can anything to oblige either of the parties be concluded in it. And therefore (as we tell them) we think it best for both parties to refer all the differences betwixt us to be disputed there, where they may be decided, viz. in a Synod and a free Parliament."[3]

On April 25 the new Parliament met, and at once the issue of Presbyterian dominance was raised in a new form. "The Presbyterians have

[1] *Barwick*, 525.
[2] *S.P.C.*, iii, 723; *Clar.* 71, f. 110.
[3] *S.P.C.*, iii, 727–8.

brought their business to a considerable height, they have formed their
design, and made their Cabal already what to do as soon as the House
meets," Hyde was informed.[1] The Long Parliament before its dissolution had restored the House of Lords, and thirteen Puritan peers were
on hand at its first sitting. They intended to exclude all their fellows
who had not supported the parliamentary cause during the Civil War;
in addition, the "young lords", who had come into their titles since
1641, and the "king's lords"—those whose titles had been created since
that date—would also be ineligible. In this way control of the House
would remain firmly in the hands of a côterie led by the Earls of Manchester and Northumberland. A similar design was on foot in the House
of Commons. Though elections had strongly favoured the Royalists,
the late Parliament had disqualified Cavaliers and their sons as candidates. If this restriction were upheld, more than a hundred of the new
members would not be seated. By such measures the Presbyterians still
hoped to be in a position to drive a bargain with the King.

Once again Monk's attitude was decisive. Pressure from him enabled
the excluded peers to take their places in the upper House, and prevented any attempt to debar the Cavalier members from the Commons. On the first of May, letters from the King were laid before the
expectant Houses, and they lost no time in concurring that "according
to the ancient and fundamental laws of this kingdom, the government
is, and ought to be, by king, lords, and commons".[2] Likewise the
officers of the army, summoned by Monk to a meeting at St. James's
Palace, "declared all for [the King] according to their General's good
example, with all imaginable cheerfulness and satisfaction".[3] However,
the question of terms was as yet far from settled, and a joint committee
was set up to formulate a reply to the King. On May 4 Mordaunt sent
a worried letter to Hyde: "Last week I sent you word it then clearly
lay in the General's power to restore the King without terms; but last
week is not this week, neither did he strike while the iron was hot. My
opinion is, his interest lessens again . . . either he must own the King yet
farther, or he may own him too late."[4] Brodrick, now a member of
Parliament, wrote in the same sense three days later: "Truly, my Lord,
we must use great despatch in our votes of bringing the King to us, or
we shall, notwithstanding the greatness of our number, be utterly

---

[1] *Ibid.*, iii, 730.   [2] *J.C.*, viii, 8.
[3] *S.P.C.*, iii, 737.   [4] *Ibid.*, iii, 739.

lost."[1] In short, there remained strong sentiment in both Houses for the imposition of terms and specific guarantees; it was even proposed that Parliament should retain control of the militia, and appoint a commission to administer the Great Seal. "The Commons have . . . laboured daily to complete the Acts which are to be presented to the King," reported Bordeaux, the French envoy. " . . . There is a fourth Act which relates to religion, and refers its differences to a national Synod. . . . Those who are called Old Presbyterians desire to have this security before receiving him."[2] But Monk's masterful diplomacy did not fail him; he cut short these deliberations by notifying the legislators that he could not answer for the action of the army and the peace of the nation if the King were not immediately recalled. All resistance to an unconditional Restoration now collapsed, and on May 8 Charles II was solemnly proclaimed in London amid scenes of wild rejoicing. "This day is a day of joy", Bishop Duppa rhapsodized, "for the King so long laid aside is now proclaimed the headstone of the corner. Never was there so miraculous a change as this, nor so great things done in so short a time. . . . I have not leisure to say any more, being overlaid with visitants, for now every man visits every man, and I am not at quiet, for the *Percontatores* will not be satisfied."[3]

These events—above all, Monk's gradual frustration of the Presbyterian strategy—had immediate repercussions on the religious situation. It will be convenient at this point to take stock of the leading parties then represented in the capital.

We have hitherto given little attention to the Independents, who after the downfall of the Rump in February, 1660, had lost the favoured position so long enjoyed under the Army's patronage. Sturdily Republican in sentiment, they could offer no effective opposition to the King's return so long as Monk controlled the army. Since they could not hope for—and probably did not desire—comprehension in a State Church dominated by Presbyterians and Anglicans, they remained wholly in the background in the discussions during the spring, and fastened their hopes on the King's pledge of toleration. At one point they seemed about to cast in their lot with the pro-Royalist parties, but Lambert's abortive uprising in April deflected them from this counsel of despair.

[1] *Ibid.*, iii, 739.
[2] M. Guizot, *History of Richard Cromwell and the Restoration of Charles II* (Lond. 1856), 424–5.
[3] *Duppa*, May 8, 1660.

"The Independents had drawn up propositions to send the King", Hyde
was told, ". . . but the sudden hopes of Lambert's business diverted all,
and they said six days ago that the train was so laid that it was impossible
to miss. Thus you see they are . . . still following that they call providence."[1] Their bitterness towards the Presbyterians, whom they looked
on as traitors to the old cause, was both now and later a factor which
facilitated the Anglican drive for supremacy. Brodrick mentioned on
May 7 that the Independent party had "refused all overtures made by
the rigid Presbyterians, not out of kindness to his Majesty . . . but out
of an established opinion that the Presbyterians are greater rogues than
themselves in their designs and contracts".[2] Barwick had the same
impression: "They [the Presbyterians] have been tampering with the
fanatics, and find them stiffly bent against tithes and ordinations, and
they have no hopes that way."[3] This hostility was maintained during
the crucial months of the Restoration settlement, and was normally
repaid in kind by the Presbyterians. The situation of the Independents
as a religious party is well summed up by a chronicler of the time:
"Lately quelled in some measure as to any outward acts of hostility,
[they] expected so little favour or countenance from his Majesty as to
the toleration of their practices, that they stirred little or nothing at all
for the obtaining thereof; only, they assembled still in their conventicles."[4]

With the collapse of all plans to ensure their own predominance in a
restored monarchy, the Presbyterians tended to divide into two groups.
Some divines there were whose Puritanism had never assumed the

[1] *S.P.C.*, iii, 730.
[2] *Ibid.*, iii, 740.
[3] *Clar.* 71, f. 198.
[4] *Add.* 19, 526, f. 39. According to George Vernon, the Independents maintained a party organization during this period. "Witness his [Dr. Owen's]
fishing out the King's counsels, and enquiring whether things went well as to
his great Diana, Liberty of Conscience? How his Majesty stood affected to it?
Whether he would connive at it, and the execution of laws against it? Who were,
or could be made its friends at Court? What bills were like to be put up in
Parliament? How that assembly was united or divided, etc., and according to
the current and disposition of affairs, he did acquaint his under-officers [eleven
names of Independent divines listed], and they by their letters each post were
to inform their fraternity in each corner of the kingdom how things were likely
to go with them, how they should order their business, and either for a time
omit or continue their conventicles." G. Vernon, *A Letter to A Friend* (Lond.
1670), 34.

rigid cast of their Scottish brethren, among them the more prominent city incumbents. As we have seen, the possibility of an agreement with the Anglicans had aroused their interest several years before, and now again the compromise of "moderate Episcopacy" as outlined by Ussher was discussed. "I smell that moderate Episcopacy is the fairest accommodation which moderate men who wish well to religion expect," James Sharp wrote to his Scottish friends in April.[1] As a *primus inter pares*, bound to act in all matters with the consent of the presbytery, the bishop would not dislocate the essential workings of Calvinist polity. Toward such a compromise a large section of the Puritan party was now drawn, and it is interesting to read the apologia they directed to their disapproving fellow-Presbyterians in Scotland:

"It cannot be hoped for, that the presbyterial government should be owned as the public establishment of this nation, while the tide runneth so strongly [toward the old prelacy].... Therefore, no course seemeth likely to us to secure religion ... but by making presbytery a part of the public establishment; which will not be effected but by moderating and reducing episcopacy to the form of synodical government, and a mutual condescendency of both parties in some lesser things, which fully come within the latitude of allowable differences in the Church. This is all we can for the present hope for; and if we could obtain it, we should account it a mercy. . . ." Their general policy they described as follows: "That, on the one side, we may neither by any forwardness and rigid counsels of our own, hazard the peace and safety of a late sadly distempered, and not yet healed nation, and on the other side, by undue compliances, destroy the hopes of a begun reformation."[2]

This group included some who, in the 1640's, had been among the bitterest opponents of prelacy, but who had come to regard "the formidable power of the sectaries" as an even greater menace. Such were Edmund Calamy, Matthew Newcomen, William Spurstowe, and Simeon Ashe. Associated with them were other prominent ministers of the metropolis—Thomas Manton, Thomas Jacombe, Anthony Tuckney, and Thomas Case. Edward Reynolds, who had been active in the Commonwealth Church, is usually reckoned among them; but there are some grounds for classifying him as essentially an Anglican conformist. He was content to act with his Presbyterian associates during the period of settlement; but Morley had already noted in April that he

[1] *Wodrow*, i, 20.

[2] Printed *ibid.*, p. 54. This letter, dated August 10, 1660, was signed by Calamy, Ashe, and Manton, and sent in answer to a reproachful address from the leading ministers of Edinburgh, dated May 12. Cf. *ibid.*, p. 26.

was "fully satisfied" with the existing canonical safeguards to episcopal government. Even before a tentative agreement was arrived at in October, he accepted a bishopric.[1]

On April 13 there arrived in London the man who was speedily to assume the leadership of these moderate Presbyterians: "Baxter, the Coryphaeus of Worcestershire, is come hither for no good," pronounced that redoubtable Anglican, Lady Willoughby of Parham, for the Chancellor's information.[2] No one appeared better qualified to head the group of "Reconcilers", as he termed them, than the famous pastor of Kidderminster. A Presbyterian in his general sympathies, but holding that no church system was of divine authority, he had laboured for many years with transparent sincerity to draw all parties into a union based on what he conceived to be the "fundamentals" of the gospel. His belief in moderation and tolerance was the governing principle of his ministry, and his purity of intention was beyond question; but in point of fact, on any concrete issue, Baxter could seldom reach an agreement with anyone. The frustration of his life-long efforts at conciliation cannot be altogether blamed on the bigotry and party spirit of his opponents. Baxter's temperament was always at war with his ideals; insatiable love of argument and a passion for self-justification led this peace-maker to become the most prolific and tiresome controversialist of his day. However slight the prospects for comprehension, Baxter's leadership was a grave handicap to the Puritan party, and it is not hard to see why Anglicans came to regard him as the obstructionist *par excellence*.

There were other Presbyterians, however, who could not conscientiously assent to any form of episcopacy, since they held themselves strictly bound by their old Covenant. The Lord Chancellor's hope of fomenting a schism in the party was not wholly disappointed, and under the influence of Lazarus Seaman, Master of Peterhouse, and rector of

---

[1] It is usually asserted on Baxter's authority (cf. *Rel. Baxt.*, 282) that Reynolds accepted the bishopric of Norwich in October, 1660, on the basis of the settlement outlined in the King's Declaration of October 25. But Baxter virtually admits that his friend was committed to the offer before this date, and quotes him as saying, somewhat unconvincingly, "that some friend had taken out the *congé d'élire* for him without his knowledge". (*Ibid.*, 283.) Actually Reynolds's acceptance was known as early as September 9; cf. *S.P.D. Charles II*, 1660, 262. The Letter Missive officially nominating him for election is dated September 30; cf. *ibid.*, Addenda 1660–85 (Lond. 1939), 13.

[2] *S.P.C.*, iii, 731.

All Hallows', Bread Street, and of William Jenkyn, vicar of Christ Church, Newgate, one section of Puritans held aloof from all schemes of reconciliation. Baxter merely says that "Dr. Seaman and Mr. Jenkyn and some few more, were a little estranged from them [Dr. Calamy's party], and hardlier spoken of at Court. . . . Dr. Seaman's party meddled not with them, not as being unwilling, but because the Court did give them no encouragement."[1] But a study of the tracts issued during the next two years makes it clear that even the most modified form of Anglicanism was unacceptable to many Presbyterian divines. Such men as Zachary Crofton, Henry Hickman, John Gailhard, Cornelius Burgess, Arthur Jackson, and Giles Firmin were irreconcilable, and were supported by the exhortations and encouragements of church leaders in Scotland.[2] Though the strict Presbyterians, as well as the Independents, remained in the background, they must not be forgotten if the negotiations of the next two years are to be seen in true perspective. Had Baxter, Calamy, and their fellows secured their aims, a Church would have resulted more broadly comprehensive than before, but dissent would still have persisted on a wide scale. The question at issue in the Savoy Conference and its preliminaries was much more limited in scope than Nonconformist historians have sometimes acknowledged; indeed, the idea of toleration found no support among moderate Presbyterians until they themselves had failed in the struggle for comprehension.

In so far as a vocal and organized party could speak for the Anglicans in London, this was not the moderate wing of Episcopalians. We have seen that there were many clergy whose sympathies were with the old order, but whose views were sufficiently broad to permit their ministering in the Cromwellian Church. These men naturally welcomed the prospect of an Anglican Restoration, and supported a settlement which might happily unite all orthodox parties. Preaching before Monk and the Lord Mayor of London on February 28, John Gauden suggested that one side

---

[1] Rel. Baxt., 229.

[2] Cf. the letters of Robert Douglas in Wodrow, i, pp. 6 ff., and of Robert Baillie in Baillie, iii, pp. 400 ff. The position of the strict English Presbyterians is well stated in H[enry] D[awbeny] A Sober and Temperate Discourse concerning the Interests of Words in Prayer, (Lond. 1661) and in two tracts by J. Gailhard, The Right of the Church Asserted (Lond. 1660) and The Controversy between Episcopacy and Presbytery Stated and Discussed (Lond. 1660).

"did but aim to maintain the order and eminency of presidential Episcopacy, which was so universal, so ancient, so primitive, so apostolic, so prosperous in the Church of Christ; the second designed only to bring Episcopacy to such a paternal temper with Presbytery that the whole clergy of a diocese and the concerns of religion might not be deposed to one man's sole jurisdiction without such joint counsel, consent, and assistance of ministers, as is safest for bishops, presbyters, and people. . . . Indeed," he continued, "the differences of honest Protestants are but small compared to the bonds of union in which they do agree as to doctrinals, morals, and essentials; nor, are we hard, I hope, to be reconciled as to prudentials, if we could meet freely, debate soberly, and submit humbly to the public votes and results of the majority part of Parliaments and Synods."[1]

A contemporary ballad gives popular expression to the same viewpoint:

> "The only way to make Presbytery
> Run diapason with Episcopacy,
> Is to acquaint one th'other with their grieves,
> And stitch up their divisions in Lawn Sleeves.
> This may procure Church union speedily,
> And make our organs whistle cheerfully,
> Which presupposed, no charity can want
> 'Twixt moderate Presbyter and Protestant."[2]

Anglicans of this type, however, were at a decided disadvantage. As conformists, they were now in a somewhat anomalous and embarrassing position. They had no close contact with the Court, were in the dark as to its intentions, and had in any case no mandate to work out a settlement with their Presbyterian associates. Furthermore, there seem to have been few men of influence among them; apart from John Gauden, Nicholas Bernard, Edward Stillingfleet and Thomas Fuller, they are an unknown company. James Sharp refers in general terms to the "moderate Episcopalian party" in the months before the Restoration, and to its endeavours for an accommodation with the Presbyterians, but without specifying its members.[3] Baxter mentions talks he had with "many moderate Episcopal divines . . . for our general concord", and adds: "We agreed as easily among ourselves in private, as if almost all

---

[1] J. Gauden, *Slight Healings of Public Hurts* (Lond. 1660), pp. 104–6.

[2] R. Brathwaite, *To His Majesty upon His Happy Arrival* (Lond. 1660), 12.

[3] *Wodrow*, i, pp. 17 ff. Baxter gives the names of Dr. Gouldson and Dr. Helen as two moderate Episcopalians with whom he negotiated. *Baxter MSS.* quoted in *Stoughton*, 90. The former may have been Joseph Goulson (or Gulson), rector of Bishops Waltham, Hampshire; it is possible, but hardly probable, that the latter was Dr. Peter Heylyn.

our differences were at an end." But it is noteworthy that when Gauden attempted to arrange a full-dress conference, promising "to bring Dr. Morley and many more of that party to meet with some of the other party", the result was a fiasco. Only Gauden and Bernard were on hand to represent the Anglicans—"so, little was done, but only desires of concord expressed".[1]

Though the Laudian party, thanks to Morley's efforts, was for the moment quiescent, its strength was not underestimated by many who feared its rise to power. Robert Baillie in Scotland showed himself a keen observer:

"If it please God . . . to bring home our sweet Prince in peace", he advised James Sharp in April, "I think, in this case, the greatest pull will be about Episcopacy. Concerning this great difficulty I suggest unto you . . . to print the tenets and point out the writes of the present leaders of the Episcopal party, Dr. Taylor, Mr. Pierce, Dr. Hammond, Mr. Thorndike, Dr. Heylyn, Bishop Wren, Bishop Bramhall, and others. Their humour is exceedingly bitter, and high even, in their late writes, not only against the Covenant and all Presbyterians but the Reformers abroad. . . . If shortly and plainly their present tenets . . . were put in the text, and the proofs in the margin in their own words, I think it might prove a notable mean, by God's blessing, either totally to withdraw the heart of the King from them—and the heart of a potent party they have, I doubt not, in England still—or at least to allay and cool all honest Protestants towards their designs. I think . . . Dr. Reynolds, or Mr. Prynne, or sundry others might get it ready for the press . . . for the crushing of that high, proud, malicious, and now very active and dangerous party. . . ."[2]

The Laudians were indeed unobtrusively organizing their forces for action at this time. Many of their leading divines were already resident in the capital—Evelyn speaks of a gathering the previous December at Dr. Gunning's, at which were present, besides the host, "Dr. Ferne, Mr. Thurscross, Mr. Chamberlayne, Dr. Henchman, Dr. Wilde, and other devout and learned divines, firm confessors and excellent persons".[3] Bishop Wren was released from the Tower on March 14. Hammond, after a brief illness, unfortunately died on April 25, but shortly before had been summoned to a meeting in London "there to assist in the great work of the composure of breaches in the Church".[4] Sheldon arrived in the city on April 27, and was soon closeted with Morley;[5] a few days before, Cosin had reported to Hyde: "Dr. Sheldon calls upon me by his letter which I received this day to come over

---

[1] *Rel. Baxt.*, 218.   [2] *Baillie*, iii, 400.   [3] *Evel.*, ii, 141.
[4] J. Fell, *Life of Dr. Henry Hammond*, (Lond. 1661), 208.   [5] *S.P.C.*, iii, 736.

presently, and says there is a great need of it now in these conjunctures of affairs."[1]

The projected meeting of party leaders took place in London on May 4. Wren, Duppa, and Warner were the only members of the episcopate who appeared. Morley and Barwick were present, as were doubtless Sheldon and the other Laudian divines in the city, though their names are not recorded. There was urgent need to reach a clear understanding with the returning government as to the official status of the Church of England. What attitude was to be adopted publicly by Anglicans upon the restoration of the Monarchy was a matter of some delicacy, and it was important that the King should not be embarrassed at this juncture. John Barwick was designated emissary to the Court at Breda to discuss the question and learn the King's pleasure. The official address to Charles reads as follows:

"Most gracious and dread Sovereign:

"Although we your poor outcaste bishops are denied the happiness to join with your Temporal Lords in the expression of our most unfeigned joy for your long wished for return ... and in our most hearty acknowledgement and most bounden thankfulness for those many great invaluable benefits and favours which by your late comforting letter and decision you have been pleased freely to grant to all your people in general, and for one more special mercy to your lately despised clergy, which we hold ourselves bound in all humility to take notice of and to bless God and your Majesty for, in that you have been graciously pleased to keep in your own holy breast and royal power the care and ordering of the Church, not referring it among other most important cases to your Houses of Parliament: yet we trust ... that there neither are nor can be any of your people more earnest in their prayers, more sincere in their endeavours, and ... more ready to perform all possible loyal service to your Majesty than your Bishops, and among them those few now present:

"(Signed) Matt: Elien, Jo: Roffens, Br: Sarum."[2]

This document is interesting for one point. By the phrase "your late comforting letter and decision", the writers are evidently referring not to the Declaration of Breda, but to the Royal letter addressed to the House of Commons, and read before that body on May 1. Whereas the Declaration had spoken of the King's willingness to consent to "such an act of Parliament, as, upon mature deliberation, shall be offered to us", the letter dealt with the question of religion in the following words:

"... Nothing can be proposed to manifest our zeal and affection for it [i.e religion], to which we will not readily consent: and we hope in due time our-

---

[1] *Clar.* 71, f. 328.   [2] *Carte.* 30, f. 613.

124   THE MAKING OF THE RESTORATION SETTLEMENT

self to propose somewhat to you for the propagation of it that will satisfy the world that we have always made it both our care and our study. . . ."[1]

This may seem a somewhat slender basis for the bishops' assurance that the King had determined to keep in his "own holy breast and royal power the care and ordering of the Church, not referring it among other most important cases" to Parliament; but it is difficult to believe that, with Morley and Barwick to advise them, they were under a complete misapprehension. We can only assume that they had received a private assurance from Charles on this point. It was unquestionably Anglican policy during the summer of 1660 to prevent any action on the church question by Parliament, and the King's own course during this crucial period was quite in accord with the intention the bishops ascribed to him in May. Thus, the bishops' address would seem to corroborate the view that the Declaration of Breda concealed rather than declared the real purpose of Hyde and the exiled government.

Barwick bore, in addition, letters to the three leading Anglicans abroad—Hyde, Ormond, and Nicholas. The one to the Marquis survives in the *Carte Manuscripts*, and indicates the assurance of the Church party that the King's chief councillors were their firm allies:

"It is no small comfort to us and to the rest of our afflicted brethren to understand by common report and particularly by Dr. Morley, the great zeal that your Excellency hath been pleased to express toward our poor Church in these times of her so grievous persecution and when she hath so few friends left. Wherefore we think it our duty to take notice of this your pious affection, and to give you humble thanks in the name of ourselves, our brethren, and of the whole Church of England. . . ."[2]

According to his biographer's account, Barwick's mission was chiefly to establish liaison with the Court. He was "to give his Majesty a distinct account of the present state of the Church in all the particulars wherein his Majesty desired to be informed, and to bring the bishops back his Majesty's commands with regard to all that should be thought proper for them . . . to do". In particular, the prelates desired to know whether the Church should be officially represented at the King's landing in England. Should they "attend him . . . in their Episcopal habit, and at what time and place, and how many?" Should the Royal chaplains be on hand? Were they to arrange the traditional service of thanksgiving at St. Paul's, "customary for our Kings after any extraordinary

[1] J.C., viii, 5.   [2] Carte. 30, f. 611.

mercies received from God?" The last—but it may be presumed not the least—of the bishops' anxieties was to tender through Barwick "a just and due account to his Majesty (who was well acquainted with all that affair of the Church . . .) why it had met with no better success".[1] Barwick was warmly received at Breda by the King and his ministers, and preached in the Royal presence the following Sunday. It is clear from the sequel that a policy of discretion was decided upon as regarded any public display of Anglican expectations; the dignitaries of the Church of England were not in evidence at the King's reception at Dover and London. Furthermore, it is no less certain that the "just and due account of the affair of the Church" was given small credence; Hyde had now lost all respect for the bishops, and was looking to other quarters for leadership in the Church.[2]

[1] *Barwick*, 270–2.

[2] There is ample evidence that the bishops were sensible of Hyde's displeasure after the Restoration, and felt that they had been passed over in matters of preferment. Skinner wrote to Sheldon on August 17, 1662, "A word sticks with me . . . which my brother of Bangor [William Roberts] told me . . . that the Lord High Chancellor was pleased to say that the ancient bishops were not removed because they did not (as they were bound in duty) relieve their Mother the Church when she stood in most need in point of ordination. . . ." (*Tann*. 48, f. 25.) The Bishop goes on to defend himself as if the charge concerned a failure to ordain priests during the Interregnum; but almost certainly Hyde was referring to the affair of the consecrations. He uses the term "ordination" in this connection. (For example, in a letter to Barwick of June 27, 1659: ". . . I pray God, that his not being at liberty, be not the cause that nothing is done in the business of ordination. . . ." *Barwick*, 422.) We have seen also how bitterly he resented the bishops' negligence. He had an especial animus against Skinner: "You must forgive me to tell you", he wrote Barwick in September, 1659, "that I am deceived if the Bishop of Oxford make good his word, or if he be not less disposed to it [i.e. the business of the Church] than most of the Function." (*Ibid.*, 210; cf. Hyde's remark quoted on page 100 of this book.) When a contemporary biographer of Skinner notes that in 1660 the Bishop "was not translated to a richer see, which he much expected, [and this was] occasioned by a great and potent enemy at court" (*Lan*. 986, f. 88), it is not hard to guess the identity of the enemy.

Warner of Rochester poured out his complaints on the same score to Sheldon in September, 1660. Listing all his sufferings for the Church and services to the Crown, he concluded: "Reverend Sir, if you ask me why I write all this . . . know I pray, that . . . though I am utterly forgotten in all, yet that I have not forgot in any kind to discharge the part of . . . dutiful son to my Holy Mother the Church." (*Tann*. 49, f. 23.) Wood notes of King, Bishop of Chichester, that "being discontented because he was not removed to a better see (as it was re-

Meanwhile, having received the King's authorization, Morley was reluctantly undertaking the conferences requested by the Presbyterians. On May 4 he notified Hyde that he had seen "divers of the chief of the Presbyterian ministers", and summed up his first impression as follows:

"[I] have reason (as I think) to hope they will be persuaded to admit of, and submit to Episcopal government, and to the practice of the Liturgy in public, so they may be permitted before and after their sermons, and upon occasional emergencies, to use such arbitrary forms as they themselves shall think fit."

As to Hyde's suggestion that an offer of preferment might induce a more submissive temper among them, the Doctor commented:

"I do not perceive that any of them desire to be a bishop, at least not at first, but some of their friends tell me that if three or four of their leading men might be gratified with such other preferments as they may hold with their charges here in the City (as the Mastership of the Savoy, the Provostship of Eton, or some of the chief prebends of Paul's or Westminster) they would be a great means to bring over their whole party; which though I hope it be not so powerful as absolutely to hinder, yet it is strong enough I fear to give the King much trouble."

He was convinced that the real difficulty would be that of Presbyterian ordination, "which we cannot acknowledge to be lawful, nor will they, I am afraid, be brought to acknowledge to be unlawful, and much less to be mere nullities". Two "expedients" had occurred to him; "the one, that no notice be taken whether there have been any such ordinations or no". The other he held "much the better *salvo* of the two, if they can be brought to it"—"hypothetical re-ordination by bishops . . . which . . . as it will be a provision against the nullity of such ordinations, so it will not conclude them to be nullified, but only irregular and uncertain". These alternatives he had communicated to Duppa and Sheldon, "as likewise of the taking off of the leading men amongst them by preferring of them, though one whom you will see shortly [probably Barwick] be much against it". All these proposals, however, must be seen in the light of Morley's definite assertion: "In the meantime I engage nor undertake for nothing, but only by a friendly and familiar manner of conversing with them, endeavour to gain upon them, and

ported), he became a favourer of the Presbyterians in his diocese". (*Athen. Oxon.*, ii, 432.) Of the nine bishops surviving, only three were advanced at the Restoration—Juxon, Duppa, and Frewen—and of these only Duppa played a rôle of any importance in the affairs of the Church.

to get an interest in them." He met the Presbyterians' uneasiness "that the King had taken no notice of them, nor of the service they had done him" by the assurance that the King was indeed sensible of this service, and that "they would have no cause to repent of it".[1]

This letter suggests that Morley was more sanguine on the subject of Presbyterian intentions than the facts justified. There is no other evidence that the moderate party as a whole ever indicated willingness to settle with Episcopacy on the basis of these very limited concessions. Lord Mordaunt was much nearer the truth when he informed Hyde on May 9: "[Dr. Morley] has prevailed with Reynolds and Calamy to comply as to Episcopacy and the Liturgy with little alteration, but as yet they cannot undertake for their brethren."[2] It is noteworthy that Baxter fully confirms the Doctor's assertion that he did "engage nor undertake for nothing"; he gives the following account of his interview:

"Because I heard that Dr. Morley was a moderate orthodox man, and had often meetings with Dr. Manton and others, whom he encouraged with pacificatory professions, and that he had greatest interest in the King and the Lord Chancellor, I had a great desire to have one hour's discourse with him, to know whether really concord was intended. And when he gave me a meeting . . . I found that he spake of moderation in the general, but came to no particular terms, but passed by what I mentioned of that nature. But speaking much for liturgies, against extemporary church prayers, he told me at last that the Jansenists were numerous among the Papists, and many among the French inclined to peace, and that on his knowledge, if it were not for the hindrances which Calvin had laid in the way, most on this side the Alps would come over to us. And this", Baxter concludes drily, "was all I could get from him."[3]

The Presbyterians, it is evident, were not content with the comfort administered in Morley's academic discussions and vague assurances. On the day the Doctor penned his report, James Sharp was writing to Scotland: "The Presbyterian ministers of the city, after several meetings, have resolved to send over next week some ministers from the city, Oxford, and Cambridge, to congratulate the King . . . [and] if it be possible, [to request] that he would write to both Houses by way of prevention, that they would secure religion in reference to some points."[4] These clergy were entrusted with an address to the King signed by some eighty of the London ministers met together in Sion

---

[1] *Clar.* 72, f. 199; portions of this letter are printed in *S.P.C.*, iii, 738, but an important paragraph is omitted.

[2] *S.P.C.*, iii, 744.   [3] *Rel. Baxt.*, 218.   [4] *Wodrow*, i, 22.

College on May 7, and four days later they set off for Holland in the company of the commissioners from Parliament and the City of London.[1] It was an imposing delegation of divines, including from London Edward Reynolds, Edmund Calamy, William Spurstowe, Thomas Case, and Thomas Manton, and from Yorkshire Edward Bowles, chaplain to Lord Fairfax. A Royalist agent wrote urgently to Ormond: "I humbly offer it as my opinion, that their reception with civility and affection may very much conduce to the King's real service; for they are men who have an exceeding great influence upon the most considerable persons in London, and indeed over all England. . . . I hear . . . that they are all for a moderated Episcopacy."[2]

This démarche was regarded by Morley with much suspicion. His earlier optimism was less evident in the letters of introduction he forwarded at this time. Sir John Holland he commended as "a friend of the Church, which hath yet need of more patrons than as yet it hath", and Sir Robert Howard as "a true son of the old Church of England, which for aught I can see yet will have need of many such to defend her from these heretics and schismatics that do and will oppose her".[3] One rumour concerning the Presbyterian mission had particularly alarmed him. As early as April 13 Sharp had reported to Douglas, "there is some talk that for the more reputable settling of the Church of England, a synod will be called from all the Reformed Churches".[4] This idea was still in the air a month later, and on May 10 Morley wrote: "Those [ministers] that are coming to his Majesty with purpose of bringing a letter to him, I presume have other instructions, as namely, to treat with and draw unto their party the Presbyters of those parts, as likewise to offer some propositions to his Majesty concerning a synod, and other particulars. . . ."[5] A letter from Lord Mordaunt to the King was more explicit: "Dr. Morley desires me humbly to beg of your Majesty, in case the Parliament press a Synod of the three nations, and the assistance of foreign divines, that your Majesty please not to consent to it . . . and as to the foreign divines, he beseeches your Majesty to engage them to

[1] *Ibid.*, 31, note; *Register* of Sion College, London, vol. A, f. 204.
[2] *Orm.* I, ii, 337–8.
[3] *Clar.* 72, ff. 316, 352.
[4] *Wodrow*, i, 19. Douglas, it is interesting to note, commented in reply: "Instead of a synod of foreign divines, the bottom of all [should] be the assembly at Westminster their procedure, and there is little need of the help of foreigners in that matter." *Ibid.*, 20.
[5] *Clar.* 72, f. 316.

persuade the Presbyterians here to submit to such a present government as your Majesty shall settle by bishops. . . ."[1] The latter advice Morley repeated to Hyde on May 12: "It will (as I told you before) in my opinion be of very great importance to draw something from the Dutch and French Presbyterians, though it be an acknowledgement of the lawfulness only of Episcopal government, which I think none of them will stick at, and that will be enough to oblige the Presbyterians in point of conscience to submit to it, being established by lawful authority, as it is. . . ."[2]

The Presbyterian delegation was cordially received by Charles, then at the Hague. There was first a formal audience, in which the divines presented the letter of the London ministers, recounted their services to the Royalist cause, and "professed they were no enemies to moderate Episcopacy, only desired that such things might not be pressed upon them in God's worship which, in their judgment who used them, were acknowledged to be matters indifferent, and by others were held unlawful". The King, according to Hyde, "spake very kindly to them", and referred them to his general promise of toleration in the Declaration of Breda.[3] But having seen all their previous plans for obtaining guarantees fail, and feeling that they had now "no reserve nor hope, but in his Majesty's good disposition and clemency",[4] they were determined, if possible, to gain from the King more definite pledges. Three days later, at their request, they were permitted to speak with him "two by two, in private".[5] Hyde describes them as taking a stiff line with the King, virtually insisting that he should renounce his customary Anglican habits in public worship on his return. The Prayer Book and surplice, they claimed, would give great offence and scandal to a populace now unaccustomed to the old ways. The King rejected these demands "with some warmth", declaring that "though he was bound for the present to tolerate much disorder and undecency in the exercise of God's worship, he would never in the least degree discountenance the good order of the Church in which he had been bred, by his own practice". For the first time the Presbyterians were confronted with the implications of the Anglican tradition in exile—"he had always used

---

[1] *S.P.C.*, iii, 743–4. A similar proposal discussed in the King's Council in May, 1649, had greatly agitated Dean Steward and other exiled Anglicans. Cf. E. Scott, *The King in Exile* (Lond. 1904), 100.

[2] *Clar.* 72, f. 352.   [3] *Hyde I*, vi, 3042 ff.   [4] *Wodrow*, i, 31, note.

[5] *Ibid.*, 31, note.

K

that form of service [the Prayer Book], which he thought the best in the world . . . in places where it was more disliked than he hoped it was by them . . . he was sure he would have no other used in his own chapel". The surplice also "had been still retained by him".[1] It is likely that in writing this account a decade later, the Chancellor allowed his animus against the Puritans to colour his narrative; for, according to general impression at the time, the delegation returned to England well content with its reception.

Sharp, who was also at the Hague, wrote that they were "much more satisfied" of the King's moderation and "great respectiveness towards them" in the private audiences, and Baxter recalls that the King's "encouraging promises of peace" were such "as raised some of them to high expectations".[2] "The ministers of London received much satisfaction from his Majesty, who discoursed with them two by two", reported *Mercurius Publicus* in similar vein, "since which his . . . chaplains and they have given several visits to one another, and do very friendly comply together."[3] The fact that the Anglicans were in possession of the field was suggested on Sunday, when that veteran of the Laudian party, Dr. Thomas Browne, "confessor and closet clerk" to the Princess of Orange, read Common Prayer, and an Anglican from London, Dr. Nathaniel Hardy, preached before his Majesty. The good doctor's text perhaps savoured more sweetly to those of his own party: "Awake and sing, ye that dwell in the dust" (Isaiah 26: 19).[4] Rumour in England credited the mission with great success. In Worcester, Henry Townshend wrote in his diary: "The Presbyterians that went to the King to move him for the settlement of Presbytery received, it seems, such satisfaction that they craved his Majesty's pardon, and left him to settle the Church and the State as he pleased."[5] Dr. Thomas Smith in London heard that Charles had promised the commissioners to "make it his care that both Episcopal divines and Presbyterians should mutually condescend".[6] At the Hague, only that dispassionate observer Mr. Pepys detected a less amicable spirit: "At Court, I find that all things grow high. The old clergy talk as being sure of their lands

[1] *Hyde I*, vi, 3042 ff.
[2] *Wodrow*, i, 31, note; *Rel. Baxt.*, 218.
[3] *Merc. Pub.*, No. 22, p. 341, Saturday, May 26, 1660.
[4] *Add.* 19,526, f. 33; W. Lower, *A Relation of the Voyage of Charles II in Holland* (Hague 1660), 73; *Merc. Pol.*, No. 39, p. 637.
[5] *Town.*, 43–4.
[6] J. R. Magrath (ed.) *The Flemings in Oxford* (Oxf. 1904), i, 133.

again, and laugh at the Presbytery . . . there being nothing now in any
man's power to hinder them and the King from doing what they have
a mind, but every body willing to submit to any thing."[1]

Though the visit of the Presbyterian delegates occasioned none of
the ill consequences Morley had feared, notice was nevertheless taken
of his advice to seek the support of foreign divines for the re-establishment of episcopacy in England, and thereby anticipate any appeal from
the Puritans. There was a convenient precedent for such a scheme. Early
in 1660 testimonials of the King's firm Protestantism had been sought
from leading Huguenot divines for dissemination in England. The Presbyterian Earl of Lauderdale had been active in the affair through his
agent, Sir Robert Moray. The latter had interested the three Jersey
ministers, Durel, Brévint, and Le Couteur—"intermédiaires naturels . . .
[avec] le pastorat reformé qui leur avait fraternellement ouvert ses
rangs".[2] Letters were obtained without difficulty by the French
Anglicans from such leading divines as Jean Daillé, Raymond Gâches,
Charles Drélincourt, and Jean Maximilien de l'Angle; on March 12
Moray wrote to Lauderdale: "With the next post there goes over four
or five very good letters from three of the ministers here, wherein they
say handsome things of the King's firmness to our religion."[3] The documents were immediately published under the title, *Certain Letters
Evidencing the King's Steadfastness in the Protestant Religion*, and according to Baxter, "the fears of many at that time were much quieted".[4]

It was natural, therefore, for Hyde to refer Morley's suggestions to
this same group of intermediaries. The cherished policy of Durel and
his fellows, as we have seen, was to alienate the Huguenots from the
Presbyterians in Britain, and they seized on the proposal with enthusiasm.[5] The help of Sir Robert Moray was once more enlisted by

[1] *Pepys*, i, 61.
[2] F. de Schickler, *Les Eglises de Refuge en Angleterre* (Paris 1892), ii, 205.
[3] *Burnet*, i, 159, note 1; cf. *C.S.P.C.*, iv, 660.
[4] *Rel. Baxt.*, 215.
[5] It is noteworthy that Morley in 1650 had proposed a similar scheme to
Hyde in the hope of moderating the demands of the Scottish Presbyterians on
the King—i.e. the King's submitting four questions to the Presbyterians of
Holland and France, respecting (1) the employment of excommunicated persons; (2) the employment of Catholic subjects; (3) Presbyterian government;
(4) the lawfulness of episcopacy. The measure of change accomplished since
then by the activity of the Jersey group is indicated by Hyde's response: "If they
could be drawn to return any answers or advice, it should be such as would give
you a deadly wound." (*S.P.C.*, ii, 519.)

Brévint's patroness, Mme de Turenne. "I was displeased with [the scheme] at first," wrote Moray to Lauderdale on June 7, "yet I was soon pacified when I saw a fair occasion presented to get the judgment of so considerable a part of this Church synodically, not doubting but the declaring of some, and so considerable persons, for episcopacy, the King will thereby be the more easily induced to do what is desired, as indeed he hath reason."[1] A number of the clergy, including Morus, Daillé, Drélincourt, and Gâches, had been approached, and had responded favourably; but to obtain an official synodical decision was Moray's real ambition. The National Synod of the Huguenot Church having been abolished by Louis XIV in 1659, a provincial gathering was to be held at Charenton in July. The difficulty was that Protestants were forbidden intercourse with foreign countries even in purely ecclesiastical affairs; the Synod might not address a corporate body outside the realm. However, the interest of the Marquis de Ruvigny, Deputy General of the Reformed Church, had been enlisted, and Moray hoped that if Charles wrote a letter requesting a declaration, his royal cousin might make an exception. This was his purpose in writing to Lauderdale: "I am sure you will consider it as one of the noblest opportunities God ever put into your hands for doing Him, His Church, your King, your country, and your conscience service. . . . It is Morus's judgment the synod will certainly declare, if the King write such a letter. And nothing can be more fair or more satisfactory".[2]

Since the contemporary records of the Church at Charenton have disappeared,[3] we are ignorant of what occurred at the meeting of the Synod. It is doubtful if Charles sent a letter, and if the Synod had acted favourably, some notice of its decision would have been taken in England. But in obtaining the support of individual divines, the Jersey Anglicans were completely successful. The most prominent Huguenot

[1] O. Airy (ed.), *The Lauderdale Papers* (Lond. 1884; Camden Soc.), i, 29.
[2] *Ibid.*, 29–30. Cf. A. Robertson, *Life of Sir Robert Moray* (Lond. 1922), 105 ff. The motives of Lauderdale and Moray in this affair are obscure, as both belonged to the Presbyterian party in Scotland at this time. Robertson (*ibid.*, 105 ff) suggests that they had realized that the choice for the Presbyterians lay between persecution and comprehension within the Anglican system, and that they hoped in this manner to induce the Puritans to accept Episcopacy. But Moray seems to suggest that the purpose of the mission is to persuade the King himself to establish Episcopacy, which would put this theory out of court.
[3] Bulletin, *Société de l'Histoire du Protestantisme Français*, vol. 37, p. 667.

clergy in France wrote to Brévint or Durel, strongly advocating the re-establishment of episcopacy, and deploring their own want of bishops. Jean Maximilien de l'Angle and Etienne le Moyne of Rouen; Moïse Amyraut and Raymond Gâches of Charenton; and Gayon of Bordeaux were among the number. Charles Drélincourt went so far as to publish his *Lettres sur l'Episcopat d'Angleterre* in Paris that year. The letter of Pierre du Bosc of Caen to Brévint is typical of the others:

"J'aprens qu'il [Charles II] veut rétablir l'Episcopat, mais en le rendant si modéré et si réformé, qu'on y verra tout l'air de l'ancienne discipline de l'Eglise. C'est là un dessein digne de luy: c'est là ce qui luy acquérra les bénédictions du Ciel et de la Terre, et qui luy gagnera l'aprobation et l'estime de tous les gens de bien. . . . Nous reconnoissons que cet Ordre a d'insignes avantages, qui ne se peuvent rencontrer dans la Discipline Presbitérienne. . . . Il ne faut donc pas tirer consequence de nos Eglises de France à celle d'Angleterre. Car, en celle-cy la Réformation ayant commencé par les Prélats et par les Evêques, il ne faut pas s'étonner si le gouvernement épiscopal y a toujours continué. Et s'il se trouve des gens assez amateurs de l'égalité Presbitérienne . . . pour vouloir choquer cet Ordre ancien, et le renverser de fond en comble, au dépens du repos de l'Etat et de l'Eglise, ils ne peuvent manquer d'en être blâmés."

Brévint replied enthusiastically:

"Le Roy et tout le clergé devroient vous rendre grâces publiques de votre excellente lettre. Il n'y a rien de mieux dit, ni plus à propos pour notre affaire. Et assurément, Monsieur, que nous n'en demandons pas davantage."[1]

[1] P. Legendre, *Vie de Pierre du Bosc* (Rotterdam 1694), 21 ff. Most of the letters were printed by Durel in *A View of the Government and Publick Worship of the Reformed Churches beyond the Seas* (Lond. 1662). The following are noteworthy (pp. 125, 127, 133–4, 143):

(Raymond Gâches) "Le nom de schisme peut faire plus de mal à l'Eglise en une seule année que tous les excès de l'authorité épiscopale en un âge. . . . Plût à Dieu que nous n'eussions d'autre différence avec les évêques de France que leur dignité! Combien volontiers je me soumettrais à eux! Comment se fait-il donc que ceux de vos Presbitériens s'opposent tant à l'Episcopat modéré?"

(Etienne le Moyne) "Véritablement je ne croy pas qu'il soit possible de garder la paix ou l'ordre en vostre Eglise sans preserver la dignité Episcopale. Et je confesse que je ne comprends point de quel esprit peuvent estre ceux qui s'opposent à ce gouvernement, et qui le décrient d'une si cruelle manière. Car je défie qui que se soit de m'en faire paroistre un plus convenable à la raison, plus convenable mesme à l'Escriture Sainte, et dont Dieu se soit servi plus utilement pour l'establissement de sa vérité et pour l'amplification de son Règne. . . . Et comment donc s'emporter contre ce gouvernement? Et quelle folie de croire qu'ils pourront utilement secouer un gouvernement qui, l'espace de tant de

There is probably a reflection of this affair in the King's Declaration on Ecclesiastical Affairs of the following October, but apart from depriving the Presbyterians of the moral support they expected from abroad, the letters had little influence on the course of events. The moderate Puritans, by this time, were already resigned to some form of episcopacy. But they were certainly aware of the scheme, and greatly irritated by its outcome. Sharp wrote on June 28: "I saw this day a letter from one in Paris, that some learned Protestants in France, and of the professors at Leyden, were writing for the lawfulness of Episcopacy; and, if the King would write to the assembly in Charenton, July next, there would be no doubt of their approving his purpose to settle Episcopacy in England."[1] Though the Huguenot clergy evidently envisaged "moderate Episcopacy", as opposed to "Prelacy", their tone was extremely critical of the English Presbyterians, and was correspondingly resented by them. Wood records that William Jenkyn dissuaded Louis du Moulin from translating into Latin a compilation of the letters, as being an injury to the Puritan cause.[2] In 1662 Henry Hickman issued a bitter rejoinder entitled *Apologia pro Ministris in Anglia (vulgo) Nonconformists*; a French translation, addressed to the Huguenot Church, was published at Geneva the following year. He upbraided those pastors

"qui au lieu de verser de l'huyle sur la playe n'ont que contribué à son inflamation, et au lieu de s'appliquer à adoucir l'amertume de nos douleurs, ils n'ont fait que l'augmenter . . . en écrivant en faveur du party Episcopal, et en fortifiant, en tant qu'en eux est, nos adversaires."[3]

In England, meanwhile, Morley and his associates continued quietly to prepare the way for Anglican re-establishment. A letter to Hyde in

siècles, a obtenu au milieu de leur Eglise? Faut-il pas estre bien brouillon pour se résoudre à ces extrémités?"

(Jean Maximilien de l'Angle) (Durel's translation from the Latin) "My heart did leap for joy when I was told that your Liturgy and ancient discipline should be restored again. I cannot tell what those haters of the peace of the Church mean that prattle up and down, and talk as if the French Churches were great adversaries to the Episcopal Order. . . . God forbid, Sir, that we should have such a perverse and rash opinion. I am sure that neither M. Daillé nor M. Amyraut, nor M. Bochart, nor any of my colleagues of Rouen ever approved of it."

[1] *Wodrow*, i, 46.   [2] *Athen. Oxon.*, ii, 733.
[3] [H. Hickman], *Apologie des Puritains d'Angleterre à messieurs les Pasteurs et Anciens des Eglises Réformées en France* (Génève 1663), 138.

the middle of May gives a further glimpse of the Doctor's methods. The winning of certain key Presbyterian leaders, he felt, would induce large sections of the party to submit to an Anglican régime. Following an interview with one Bodbuck, "a clergyman of the old stamp", he reported: "He tells me a great part of the Presbyterian party of the north lies in Lancashire, where he hath so much interest as he hopes (if it be thought fit to employ him there to that purpose) he may be instrumental for the reducing of many to the Church." Even more important was Edward Bowles in Yorkshire: "In the whole north of England . . . he is, as it were, the Patriarch, and in particular wholly governs the Lord Fairfax. I would I could say he was as well affected as the former, but certainly he is not so disaffected neither, but he may be gained, especially in this conjuncture, being not divided from us in point of conscience, but in point of interest only. And truly, my Lord, he is worth the gaining at any reasonable rate; for in gaining him, you gain all the Presbyterians both lay and clergy of the north, as Mr. Lowder, a very well affected and very knowing person assures me. . . ."[1] Thomas Wharton, writing to Ormond on May 10, echoed this estimate of Bowles, and added further: "His designs are to bring Episcopal men and Presbyterians to such a condescension in things which are not absolutely necessary, as that there might be no jarrings, but all agree for public good and peace. . . . He has been Episcopal in his judgment all these times, as I am credibly informed . . . and, I think, may be as instrumental in the King's service as any man in his profession that I know. . . ."[2] It is impossible to see in these activities of Hyde's agents no more than a disinterested effort to heal the breach between the two chief religious parties. Morley, as he did not hesitate to say, was seeking allies "to defend [the old Church of England] from these heretics and schismatics that do and will oppose her".[3]

The curtain was now to rise on the last act in a century-long drama— the final struggle of Anglican and Puritan for supremacy in the Established Church. On May 25 the King landed at Dover, and was greeted by a thunderous welcome from the thousands who lined the beach and looked down from the cliffs. General Monk and most of the high dignitaries of the realm were on hand to make obeisance, and Charles accepted their homage with gracious cordiality. He received from a Presbyterian minister the gift of a Bible, exclaiming to the infinite

---

[1] *Clar.* 72, f. 352.   [2] *Orm. I,* ii, 338–9.   [3] *Clar.* 72, f. 352.

delight of posterity: "It was the thing that he loved above all things in the world."[1] No Anglicans represented their Church in the official delegation of welcome. On the next evening, however, as the King tarried in Canterbury, a clerical visitor was shown into his chamber. It was a meeting for which Edward Hyde had long hoped and planned. There was a friend of whom he had written, "upon [your] advice and example I shall most absolutely guide myself", and to whom he had declared in October, 1659: "When you meet, as meet you will, I think you will be satisfied with [the King], and nobody is like to do so much good upon him as you are, for sure he reverences nobody more."[2] Of what passed between the King and Gilbert Sheldon we have no record other than a tale repeated two years later in Scotland: "When the King was at Breda, it was said he was not averse from establishing the Presbytery; nor was the contrary peremptorily resolved till the Saturday at night, in the cabin council at Canterbury."[3] It is not improbable that then, in the shadow of the mother Church of England, a discussion took place between Charles, the Lord Chancellor, and Sheldon that was to have lasting consequences in the religious history of the nation.

On the basis of the evidence set forth in this chapter, what conclusions can be drawn regarding Anglican policy before the Restoration? Hyde's basic position seems clear and consistent. Essentially he remained the constitutional Royalist of 1641, with a fixed conviction that there could be no settlement of the nation's troubles other than the acceptance by all parties of the ancient constitution. Only by acknowledging this as the source of law and justice, could each element within the commonwealth secure its inherent rights and safeguards, and the chaos of mutual distrust and opposing interests resolve into the harmonious common life of a healthy organism. "In this lay his strength," writes Professor Feiling, "that from 1641 to 1660 he pursued a single purpose, to restore the King and the Church on the old foundation of 'those admirable and incomparable laws of government' bequeathed by Queen Elizabeth."[4] The Church indeed, not less than King, Lords, and Commons, must be restored to what was lawfully hers. On this point strong religious feeling combined with political theory to make Hyde immovable. Writing to Lord Hatton in 1648, he inveighed bitterly

---

[1] E. Scott, *The Travels of the King* (Lond. 1907), 475.
[2] *Add.* 4162, f. 20; *Tann.* 51, f.159.   [3] *Baillie*, iii, 484.   [4] *Feil.*, 70.

against all schemes for 'moderate Episcopacy', and declared with un-usual passion:

"For my part, I do in my soul believe, that the true, conscientious affection for Episcopacy, as it was a part of the government of England . . . drew more good men from the other party than any one branch of policy, reason, or allegiance; and truly . . . I would not, to preserve myself, wife, and children from the lingering pain of want and famine (for a sudden death would require no courage) consent to the lessening any part, which I take to be in the function of a bishop, or the taking away the smallest prebendary in the Church, or be bound not to endeavour to alter any such alteration."[1]

Here was the original and irreconcilable difference with the Presby-terians. That party was wedded to the ideal of a Restoration based on the concessions made by Charles I at the Isle of Wight. Hyde had affirmed in 1649 that such terms were outside the pale of discussion, as violating the constitutional rights of King and Church,[2] and we have seen how boldly he maintained this essentially Anglican position during the years of exile. In April, 1660, he showed surprise that his old enemies could still harbour illusions on this point, and wrote to Lady Wil-loughby: "Sure if the Presbyterians please themselves with an imagina-tion of binding the King to hard conditions by sending high proposals to him, they are not so wise as their experience might in all this time have made them."[3] In reality, the Presbyterian leaders had no illusions about Hyde; but they were still willing to believe that the Chancellor's influence was not all-powerful with the King.

For this faulty calculation, the Puritan party was not entirely to blame. As it became increasingly clear that Presbyterian co-operation would be needed to effect a Restoration, Hyde stooped to veil his aim with a politic discretion, and to make friends with the mammon of unrighteousness. The Royalists certainly did not take their stand on an unequivocally Anglican platform in the spring of 1660. Instead, every effort was made to evade the religious issue by recourse to vague talk of toleration, and reference of the matter to a Parliamentary decision. But if Anglican aims were not proclaimed from the housetops, they are clearly revealed in the negotiations described in this chapter. Hyde's real policy was indistinguishable from that of the Laudian party, and the Laudian clergy were his instruments for putting it into effect. To such men as Morley, Barwick, Sheldon, Hammond, and Cosin, he

[1] *S.P.C.*, iii, 1 ff. [2] Cf. *ibid.*, 83. [3] *Clar.* 71, f. 214.

gave his unreserved confidence and communicated his innermost thoughts; they in turn looked upon him as the unfailing champion of the Church.

In 1659, when the Royalist cause still faced an uncertain future, Hyde tried desperately to secure the Church against its most immediate peril —the lapse of the Episcopal Order. The strength of his feeling is shown by the urgent letters despatched to Barwick, and by the pressure he evidently brought to bear upon the King to force the bishops to action. The Royalist position at this period was such that the Chancellor's religious policy could be only defensive in character. A new phase opened when Monk's intention was made known to the Court in March, and thereafter the Anglican agents were employed in what may be described as an offensive against the dominant Presbyterian party. Anglican tactics in these months have seemed ambiguous to some historians, and have been occasionally construed as a policy of *bona fide* conciliation towards the Presbyterians; but this interpretation is hard to reconcile with expressions used by the Chancellor and his agents. Hyde intended by "arts and artifices" to create a "schism" between the moderate and rigid Presbyterians, believing that the former, diplomatically handled, could be "converted . . . to a piety towards the Church". "To promote that temper", Morley and Barwick were authorized to hold out the inducement of good preferments to those "who being recovered, will have both reputation and desire to merit from the Church". Morley described this move as "the taking off of the leading men amongst them by preferring of them". In other words, the plan of offering bishoprics and deaneries to leading Presbyterians was, at least in origin, not an indication of Hyde's desire for a comprehensive settlement; it was a weapon of attack on Presbyterian solidarity, to be used entirely in Anglican interests.

Nor was Morley sent to England, as has been sometimes stated, to inaugurate conferences for the settlement of Anglican and Puritan differences. Both agents were exceedingly reluctant to engage in conferences when these were requested by the London ministers; and Hyde finally conveyed the King's sanction in terms consistent with his previous instructions—"that you may reduce them [i.e. those of the Presbyterian party] to such a temper, as is consistent with the good of the Church". Furthermore, it is clear that Morley made no promises that the old order and practice of the Church would be modified to meet Puritan demands—"I engage nor undertake for nothing. . . ." The only concessions which he even discussed were the use of extempore prayer in addition to the prescribed liturgy, and the method by which the deficiencies of Presbyterian ordination might be rectified. In short, in so far as the Anglicans held out a prospect of comprehension in the restored Church, it was nothing more nor less than the measure of comprehension which had previously existed. They doubtless felt that they had conceded much in promising to forget old scores, and welcome the Puritans back to their old place within the Establishment. The Chancellor severely condemned the anti-Puritan zeal of the Laudian extremists, but he did not disavow the views of "those good men", merely finding their passion "unskillful" and capable of doing "mischief" to the Church's cause. Every effort was made to avoid any word or action which might unnecessarily provoke the Presbyterian party; "by a friendly and familiar manner of conversing with them", wrote Morley, "[I] endeavour to gain upon them, and get an interest in them." The political situation as viewed by the Royalists remained too delicate and uncertain for discussion of an issue as explosive as that of the church settlement. Beyond cautious and skillful preparation of the ground, nothing must be attempted until the King had come safely into his own again. If Anglicans would only practise the virtue of discretion, as Hyde remarked to Cosin, "the Church will be preserved in a tolerable condition, and by degrees recover what cannot be had at once".

Something further must be said of Presbyterian policy. If this party followed a natural and perhaps inevitable line in the rapid shift of the balance of power, its tactics were nevertheless singularly unfortunate. The attempt in March, 1660, to force an arbitrary religious settlement on the nation was rash in the extreme, for it was obvious to all men that the Long Parliament no longer held a popular mandate. The determination to re-impose Presbyterianism by wholesale legislation belied the earlier professions of the moderate clergy that they would agree to a free Parliament and assembly of divines. Men like Calamy and Ashe seem to have been equally implicated in this action with their more fanatical brethren. It is small wonder that Anglicans felt their old enemies had not greatly changed, and had no compunction in working for an equally drastic settlement in their own favour. When later the Presbyterians tried to secure religious guarantees from Charles, the concessions sought were always closely related to plans for limiting the Royal authority. In short, the party continued blindly, if conscientiously, to pursue its own advantage, and to retain power in the hands of a Puritan oligarchy. This policy of bringing in the King "on terms" merely confirmed the old prejudice in Royalist minds that Presbyterianism was really incompatible with Monarchy, and attached to the party a vague stigma of "sedition" which was soon to be a serious handicap. Within less than a year such ballads as this were being sold on the streets of London:

> *A Presbyterian is such a monstrous thing*
> *That loves Democracy and hates a King.*
>
> *And in plain truth; as far as I can find,*
> *He bears the self-same treasonable mind*
> *As doth the Jesuit, for though they be*
> *Tongue-enemies in show, their hearts agree,*
> *And both professed foes, alike consent*
> *Both to betray the Anointed Innocent;*
> *For though their manners differ, yet they aim*
> *That either may the King or Kingdom maim:*
> *The difference is this way understood,*
> *One in sedition, th'other deals in blood.*
> *Their characters abridged if you will have,*
> *Each seems a saint, yet either proves a Knave.*[1]

Finally, there is clear evidence that the party was still persisting in the short-sighted policy of its members in exile. Such was the hostility to the Chancellor that in order to overthrow him, Presbyterians were willing to combine with the Roman Catholic zealots at the Louvre, and serve the interests of Queen Henrietta. On April 23 the French Ambassador reported: "Tout le party presbytérien n'est pas contraire [à la Reyne d'Angleterre]; quelques-uns des principaux appréhendent moins son auctorité que celle du chancelier Hyde et sont bien résolus de le déstacher d'auprès du Roi." He added on May 28: "J'en ai traicté … avec des plus considérables Presbytériens, qui se sont ouvertement déclarés du party de la Reyne et contre le Chancelier, dont le crédit leur donnoit de l'ombrage."[2] These assertions are confirmed by that staunch Calvinist in Scotland, Robert Baillie, who lists among the advantages enjoyed by his party "at the beginning"—"the Queen and her party was on our side".[3]

---

[1] *The True Presbyterian without Disguise* (Lond. 1661), pp. 1, 6.
[2] P.R.O., *Transcripts* 3/107, May 3 and June 7, 1660. (N.S.)
[3] *Baillie*, iii, 444.

With the strong anti-Presbyterian prejudice which persisted among Anglicans throughout the Interrgnum, the construction placed upon these manœuvres can be easily imagined. With some reason, it seemed to churchmen that the Puritans had been moved not so much by a revival of loyalty to the Crown as by the consideration of their own interests, and had turned to the idea of a Restoration merely as a *pis aller*. They poured scorn on the Presbyterians' claim to have been the primary agents of the King's return, and there grew up almost immediately an Anglican tradition disparaging the rôle of their ancient enemies.

"The Presbyterians", wrote a contemporary chronicler, "though their cause was pretended chiefly, and as the main occasion of managing the late wars against the King, yet since had been overtopped by an army of sectaries whom they had hired to be their servants, but now proved their masters: and therefore, these seeing themselves frustrated in their designs and ends, exclaimed much against this present state of affairs—of which themselves in a great measure were the occasion—and rather through their oppression under the cruel and tyrannical sectaries, than for any love they did have to Kingly Government, wished and contrived to bring it in some wise to its former estate again."[1]

Similarly, a pamphleteer of 1661:

"From henceforth [i.e. from the time of Monk's intervention] their business was, not so much to bring in his Majesty (which no endeavours of theirs could greatly expedite, or obstruct), as to contrive and limit the manner of his entrance, that it might serve their purposes. . . . To the Presbyterians, this single character, that they acted all along like prudent men, who knew a better use to be made of conscience than by suffering for it, and that having tried all expedients, they at length inclined to the bringing in of his Majesty, lest he should have come in without them."[2]

Thus, the brief period of political co-operation between Anglicans and Presbyterians did nothing to heal the breach and soften the old enmity between them. Instead, the ill-fated policy of the latter had given new grounds for Royalist and Anglican distrust. On the side of church relations, nothing had been accomplished towards agreement on a mutually satisfactory settlement. The Laudians were intent only on a restoration of the Church they had known and loved; the moderate Puritans, still not fully aware of their helplessness, played with hopes of

[1] *Add.* 19, 526, f. 36.
[2] *A Lively Portrait of our New Cavaliers: commonly called Presbyterians* (Lond. 1661), 12.

preserving the Presbyterian system in an Episcopal dress. A bitter struggle lay ahead whose course and outcome neither party could then foresee. Yet in one sense the Anglicans had already won their victory on the day when Charles II resumed the throne of his ancestors, unfettered by conditions, and his chief minister Sir Edward Hyde took up the reins of government.

CHAPTER IV

THE RECAPTURE OF THE ESTABLISHMENT
JUNE, 1660 TO MAY, 1661

TUESDAY, MAY 29, 1660, saw one of the greatest scenes of joy in London's history. Escorted by troops of splendidly uniformed horsemen and foot-soldiers, and announced by a fanfare of trumpets, Charles entered the capital through streets bright with flowers and hanging tapestries. The way was lined with the train-bands and livery companies holding back the crowds of cheering spectators—"such state and such acclamations as I want words to express!" reported one of them.[1] At an honoured place in the procession, preceded by kettle drums and trumpets, walked twelve Presbyterian ministers, their Geneva gowns and Puritan hats looking very "sad" in the brilliant spectacle.[2] As the King reached Ludgate Hill, he came upon the whole company of city ministers assembled on a platform before St. Paul's. Here he was solemnly presented with a Bible "worth covering and clasps an hundred and fifty pounds," and accepted it with the pious declaration that "the greatest part of that day's solemnity he must ascribe to God's Providence, and he would make that book the rule of his life and government".[3]

Farther along, he paused before another group of clergy, unobserved by most chroniclers of the day. These were the sequestered Anglican divines of the city, who offered him a second Bible, bound up with the Book of Common Prayer.[4] The monarch and his train proceeded to Whitehall, where the Lords and Commons paid their homage. In the evening, Anglican dignitaries hopefully awaited his arrival at West-minster Abbey for a service of thanksgiving—assembled were "the Bishops of Ely, Salisbury, Chichester, and Rochester, in their episcopal habits, assisted by divers others of the long oppressed clergy". But

[1] J. R. Magrath (ed.), *The Flemings in Oxford* (Oxf. 1904), i, 131.
[2] *Stoughton*, 71.
[3] *Sion College Register A*, f. 204; *Add.* 10, 116, f. 100; J. R. Magrath, *op. cit.*, i, 132.
[4] *Add.* 19, 526, f. 34.

Charles was not ready to show his hand so plainly, and "by the weariness he had contracted through the toil (however grateful) of that day's action, he was diverted from his intention of going thither". The bishops, without the gratification of the Royal presence, "there sang Te Deum in praise and thanksgiving to God Almighty for his unspeakable mercy in delivering his Majesty from many dangers, and after so long a time of exile and banishment, the so miraculously and happily restoring him to the possession of his crown and Royal Dignity".[1]

The twelve months following the restoration of the monarchy were the crucial stage in the evolution of the church settlement. It was during this period that the Anglicans, working quietly but purposefully under the powerful patronage of the Lord Chancellor, regained control of the Establishment. The nature of the settlement was not determined by negotiations with the Puritans nor by the deliberations of Parliament, but by the *fait accompli* which was the crowning achievement of Laudian policy, and which the nation had tacitly accepted before the Savoy Conference opened or the Cavalier Parliament convened. The completeness of the Laudian victory is undisputed; but to what extent this triumph was fortuitous, and to what extent the outcome of an astutely planned strategy, has been a matter of debate. Even more difficult to determine are the exact rôles played by the King and his chief minister, and the import of the efforts at conciliation which they publicly sponsored. After the return of the exiles, evidence on these matters becomes painfully scanty, and the flow of correspondence diminishes to vanishing point. The leaders of Church and State were now gathered in the capital in daily contact, and the volumes of Clarendon Papers no longer disclose Hyde's private thoughts. The circle of those in a position to know the real tenor of religious policy was restricted to a few important leaders, and if that policy designed other ends than those openly professed, there was small occasion to commit the fact to paper. Only by recourse to clues in scattered letters and tracts, by attention to the less prominent aspects of Laudian activity during the crucial months, and, above all, by giving due weight to that party's consistent stand during the Interregnum, can a judgment be reached with some measure of certainty.

The political situation at the beginning of the reign gave Anglican

[1] Sir E. Walker, *Account of the Preparation for the Coronation of Charles II* (Lond. 1820), 21; Sir R. Baker, *Chronicle of the Kings of England* (Lond. 1674), 734.

leaders every reason for caution. A sense of insecurity and a suspicion of widespread disaffection assailed the government constantly for the next few years, and was a psychological factor of untold weight in all its calculations. From a modern viewpoint, it appears obvious that the Restoration inaugurated an era of peace and stability which answered the wishes of the vast majority of the nation. But the extent of Royalist reaction was not then apparent. It seemed unlikely that the forces of radical sectarianism rampant under Cromwell had been permanently quelled, and doubtful if the Presbyterians felt more than a conditional loyalty to the Crown. In the background was the menacing danger of the Army, its anti-royalist traditions and sectarian enthusiasm well known. Monk's prestige and diplomacy had secured its acquiescence in the Restoration; but how long, in his new trappings of Duke of Albemarle and leading courtier, could he retain control? Only when the 35,000 troops received payment of arrears and were finally disbanded in February, 1661, did statesmen begin to breathe more easily. But sufficient evidence still appeared of plotting and unrest among fanatics to keep the government in a state of apprehension. Incidents like Venner's uprising in London in January, 1661; attempts to seize Berwick and Newcastle that spring; and a plot in the west country the following autumn seemed at the time convincing proof of great danger. Nor was this feeling minimized by the sensational reports of informers and *agents provocateurs*.[1] To politicians who saw "a conspirator in every Puritan and an incendiary in every disbanded soldier",[2] the church settlement appeared the issue most fraught with peril. The restoration of episcopacy meant the risk not only of exasperating anti-prelatic prejudice, but of alienating those who had a vested interest in the confiscated church lands. "Il y a . . . desjà des mécontents", remarked the French Ambassador in June, 1660, "et la Religion pourra bien augmenter un jour le nombre, si le Roi s'attache, comme l'on croit, à restablir les Evesques."[3] Small wonder that the problem was approached in the early months cautiously and with veiled intent, and every precaution taken to avoid a crisis with the powerful Presbyterian party.

[1] Abundant evidence of the government's chronic uneasiness, and of the way in which this was fostered by alarmist reports appears in *C.S.P.D.*, 1660-1, *passim*, the evidence is summarized and discussed in *Feil.*, 107 ff; *Stoughton*, 229 ff.; *Burnet*, i, 326.

[2] *Feil.*, 107.

[3] P.R.O., *Transcripts* 3/107, f. 265.

L

Another uncertain factor in the situation was the sentiment of the Convention Parliament. In an article in the *English Historical Review* for 1907 Miss L. F. Brown has examined the religious divisions of that body, and demonstrated that churchmen held a small majority over the Presbyterians from the beginning, but were outnumbered when the Presbyterians and Independents combined on any issue.[1] The enmity between these two groups operated to favour Anglican predominance, but the balance of power was always precarious, and the government could place no confidence in Parliamentary support of its ecclesiastical policy. According to Hyde, "the party of the Presbyterians was very numerous in the House of Commons . . . but the spirit of the time had of itself elected many members . . . of a very different allay; who together with such as were chosen after his Majesty's return, were numerous enough to obstruct and check any prevalence of that party, though not of power enough to compel them to consent to sober counsels."[2] Such a judgment, however, was possible only after the session had ended.

The Church party undoubtedly contained many an old Royalist who had damned the bishops in the early days of the Long Parliament. A taste of revolution is efficacious in changing reformers into reactionaries, and Anglicans remembered bitterly the rapidity with which the attack on prelacy had developed into an assault on the whole Church system. By 1660 criticism of episcopal government seemed an unsavoury pastime with horrid associations of religious and political anarchy, and bishops could now claim the indulgence with which the lesser of two evils is usually regarded.

But the chief source of Anglican strength in the House came from "the young men" who had been educated by the Laudian clergy; the French Ambassador observed: "la plus part des jeunes gens [sont] des plus affectionnés."[3] So perturbed were the Puritans by this phenomenon that they printed and circulated a collection of speeches made in the Parliament of 1641 against Episcopacy, alleging that "there are many hundred persons of considerable quality in the nation, either now entering, or already entered upon the stage for action . . . who are displeased with what the Parliament and nation did against Episcopacy, because

[1] *E.H.R.*, xxii, 51 ff.: L. F. Brown, "The Religious Factors in the Convention Parliament".

[2] *Hyde II*, i, 479.

[3] P.R.O., *Transcripts* 3/107, f. 278.

they only know what they did, but not why; and who are favourers of bishops and that party, as knowing only how much they suffered, not how much they had offended."[1]

Unfortunately for "that party's" peace of mind, the episcopalian zeal of the new generation was offset by growing slackness in attendance as the summer drew on. One of Ruvigny's reports to Mazarin provides a refreshing glimpse of young squires joyfully throwing off the cares of government, as they yielded one by one to the lure of the English countryside in midsummer, and set off for home.[2] This defection came near to wrecking Laudian plans.

Though the Presbyterian party had seen its immediate designs frustrated during the spring, it remained a political force to be reckoned with. In the country at large its popularity had doubtless waned since its moment of triumph in the forties. But in the seat of government its strength was still formidable, supported as it was by the powerful merchant class which governed the city. From the standpoint of the religious struggle, however, the Puritans were weakened by Hyde's policy of welcoming their political leaders into the new government. Old Parliamentarians like the Earls of Manchester, Leicester, and Northumberland, as well as younger men like William Morrice, Ashley Cooper, Sir John Robartes, and Arthur Annesley, took places in the Council beside the old Cavalier statesmen, and were given important ministerial offices. So great indeed were the favours showered on these new converts to Royalism that the needy Cavaliers who flocked to Court were soon aghast. Their joy at the miraculous turn of affairs speedily changed to sullen resentment, as they cursed the Chancellor's policy of reconciliation. "Those who gaped for preferment and offices in this great change fail of their account", wrote one observer, "for they were divided between the old servitors abroad and the new cavaliers at home long ago, and before either could hope for so happy a change; and at present all gratifications and favours are the Presbyters' portion—if any of the King's party get anything it is inconsiderable."[3] Before the end of June men were repeating with bitter relish the famous quip "whether it were not fit his Majesty should pass an Act of In-

---

[1] *A Landskip: or a Brief Prospective of English Episcopacy d awn by three skillful hands in Parliament,* 1641 (Lond. 1660), Pref. to the Reader, n.p.
[2] P.R.O., *Transcripts* 3/107, f. 278.
[3] *Suth.,* 194.

demnity for his enemies and of Oblivion for his friends", and a more learned wit celebrating his grievance in the distich,

> Te magis optavit rediturum, Carole, nemo,
> Et nemo sensit te rediisse minus.[1]

The effect of this wooing of the Presbyterian lay leaders was to give them a stake in the new régime, and to detach them from Puritanism as a political creed. Barwick had predicted to Hyde in April: "As for the grandees of that party, they [will] come in of themselves, when they see the tide begins to turn,"[2] and he proved a true prophet. From now on, the support given to the Puritan clergy by the "grandees" was luke-warm. They felt a growing embarrassment at connection with a party soon labelled "factious" and "seditious" by the Court, and endeavoured to keep their new-found loyalty above suspicion. The Presbyterians were thus losing an important element of political strength at the very time when the Laudian party was consolidating its lay support; but only gradually did they become aware of the drift of events. In the beginning, as a Nonconformist historian observes, "their . . . proposals . . . had the tone rather of concession than of demand, and embodied not what would induce them to remain in the Church, but what might, they thought, satisfy all moderate Episcopalians".[3] One Puritan divine, however, was more discerning.

"For ecclesiastical [affairs]", he noted on June 20, 1660, "the question is be-tween Episcopacy and Presbytery. You see that things are come to the old con-dition, all other parties yielding to these two as the most considerable. . . . I look upon the Presbyterian cause as to means, in a worse condition than at the beginning, because then the Parliament was for them: but now the greater part is content; their adversaries being cruel, and it being uncertain what the King's will is, though his practice makes him to be suspected of inclining to Episco-pacy; and further, the crisis of time is such, as that most of the nation are so weary of former wars that they will undergo anything . . . [rather] than to engage in new troubles."[4]

---

[1] Ibid., 205; W. W. Wilkins, Political Ballads (Lond. 1860), i, 162. Cf. two popular ballads published in London in 1660, The Cavalier's Complaint and Echo to the Cavalier's Complaint.

[2] Clar. 71, f. 110.

[3] D.A.U., Hist. Intr., p. 105.

[4] J. Gailhard, The Controversy between Episcopacy and Presbytery Stated and Discussed (Lond. 1660), 2–3. Ralph, i, 15–16, gives this summary: "[The Presbyterian Party] were in position, which they were very desirous to keep, had friends in the Court, the Army, and the Parliament; and had besides the

All these circumstances help to explain why the government, in close collaboration with the Laudian party, embarked on an ecclesiastical policy which expressed itself on two levels.[1] Two attitudes were possible as to the current state of affairs. On the one hand, it could be argued that since all legislation which had not received Royal assent was rendered void by the restoration of the Monarchy, the Church of England automatically resumed its old position with all rights and privileges. The sole exception to the revival of the *status quo ante* would be the right of bishops to sit in the House of Lords, for Charles I in 1642 had signed the Act abolishing this. But such a view, whatever its legal force, was much too drastic to be frankly acted upon. That it corresponded to the conviction of Hyde and the Laudian clergy, expressed in no uncertain terms during the Interregnum, we cannot doubt. In recent negotiations, however, the Royalists had avoided any suggestion that the return of the King meant automatically an Anglican triumph. For such a dénouement the nation was unprepared, and at first there was no open indication that the government contemplated it. The other theory, insisted on by non-Anglicans, was that the Declaration of Breda, with its promise of toleration and its reference of the religious question to Parliament, had in effect suspended the old ecclesiastical laws, and opened the way for their alteration. For some months the King and his Chancellor, as well as the High Church leaders, paid lip service to this general expectation. At the same time they proceeded quietly and cautiously to put into effect the measures necessary for the recapture of the Establishment by the church party. So gradual was the shifting of the balance between these two contradictory policies, that it is impossible to point to a particular moment when the government

merit of their late services to plead. . . . They found it difficult to make their friends act heartily for them. On the House of Commons they placed their principal dependence."

[1] Baxter's appraisal of Anglican policy at the Restoration is worthy of note: "When they [the Prelatic party] came in, it was necessary that they should proceed safely, and feel whether the ground was solid under them before they proceeded to their structure: the land had been but lately engaged against them; the Covenant had been taken even by the lords and gentlemen of their own party at their composition: there was the Army that brought them in (who were Presbyterians as to the most of the ruling part) to be disbanded: and how knew they what the Parliament would do? . . . How could they know these things beforehand? Therefore it was necessary that moderate things should be proposed and promised. . . ." *Rel. Baxt.*, 287.

disavowed the one and proclaimed adherence to the other. Yet by May, 1661, it was apparent to all that the Church of England was once more in possession of its rights, and that the strictly legal view had been fully implemented.

Throughout the month of June matters proceeded in a way calculated to reassure the Presbyterians. Immediately on his return, the King, at the request of Parliament, issued a proclamation temporarily maintaining all incumbents in their benefices. Drawn up in the Commons on May 28, and published by Charles, June 1, it declared:

"We, taking notice that several riots have been committed and forcible entries made upon the possessions of divers of our subjects, ecclesiastical as temporal, who have been settled in the said possessions by any lawful or pretended authority; and that without any order of Parliament or legal eviction. . . . We, therefore, by the advice of our Lords and Commons . . . do by this Proclamation command, publish, and declare that no person or persons, ecclesiastical or temporal, shall presume forcibly to enter upon or disturb the said possessions, or any of them, till our Parliament shall take order therein, or an eviction be had by due course of law."[1]

Shortly thereafter, the King received in public audience a delegation of the bishops, consisting probably of Wren, Duppa, Warner, and King. Coming "to salute and welcome his Majesty home, and to give him their paternal benediction", they sought assurance that he "would adhere constantly to the establishment of them, as his Royal Father had done before him". Charles was gracious but discreet. He replied that "as his heart and mind was always most chiefly addicted and inclined to Episcopal government, so he would labour to his utmost to see them restored and established; only, considering the present state of affairs, and the several interests and animosities of several parties . . . first it were fit he should be advised by his Parliament herein, to gain their consents, that so he might stop the mouths of those who were ready to accuse him of exercising tyrannical or arbitrary power, and withal by this consent of Parliament might lay a more sure foundation as by a law, to establish their government whenever it should be set up."[2] It was clear notice that the King did not regard the old laws as operative. John Gauden, moreover, was delighted to learn for himself of the King's longing for conciliation, and wrote to the Marquis of Ormond, who had arranged an audience for him: "I find his Majesty's wisdom and gentleness so disposed to moderate counsels in church

[1] J.L., xi, 46.   [2] Add. 19, 526, f. 40.

affairs, that I doubt not of happy and speedy settling in that grand concern."[1]

Some ten or twelve of the moderate Puritan clergy were appointed Royal chaplains, including Reynolds, Spurstowe, Woodbridge, Wallis, Manton, Bates, Calamy, Ashe, Case, and Baxter. Several were invited to preach at Court during the summer, and it was tactfully intimated that they were not required to use the Prayer Book—"when it is their course to officiate, they are not tied to the Liturgy, but others having performed that service, they shall only preach", explained Sharp.[2] For a brief moment the harmony was threatened by the strict Presbyterian leaders, who made a final desperate effort to secure the settlement made by the Long Parliament in March. "Some of the ministers petition the Common Council to put the King in mind of the Covenant," noted the Anglican Dr. Thomas Smith on June 11, "but it is obstructed at the Council, and it is thought the Houses would not pass it."[3] The matter was in fact broached in Parliament. As Edward Gower informed Sir Richard Leveson: "We had the last week a great talk of the City's petition to the House of Commons against bishops, but it was crushed in the shell, for (as I hear by some Parliament men) it was spoken of in the House and much resented, which was the cause (the citizens having timely notice of it) it never came to light."[4] Sharp set down a fuller account on June 10:

"There were, last week and this, some endeavours for getting a petition in the name of the city that religion might be settled according to the league and covenant; but the inconsiderate and not right timing of that motion has exceedingly prejudiced that business, if not totally crushed the design, so as it occasioned a cross petition by the most considerable of the city, that in all petitions hereafter there might be nothing mentioned which had a relation to the league and covenant, and that nothing should be moved to this nature to the Common Council, till their meeting be full."[5]

---

[1] Carte 30, f. 705. [2] Wodrow, i, 42. [3] Le Flem., 26. [4] Suth., 204.
[5] Wodrow, i, 39. The petition is quoted in Z. Crofton, Berith Anti-Baal (Lond. 1661), Preface, n.p. Crofton gives the following account of it: "At a general meeting of the Covenant Presbyterians in and about the City of London, the cause of the Covenant was debated, generally owned in its opposition to Episcopacy, and by joint consent it was agreed to petition his Majesty and the Houses of Parliament. . . . This petition, however, by some State stratagems and Court complement, and overprudent cowardice of some, who contrary to the due order of all assemblies would never let it be reported, was prevented from being presented to his Majesty."

It was widely rumoured that the petition had been "set on foot and influenced by the Scots". The moderate divines dissociated themselves from this rash move, and refused to sign the petition.[1]

These clergy, long resigned to the compromise of moderate Episcopacy, engaged on a more promising line of action. At the Earl of Manchester's lodging their leaders conferred with the King,[2] and, disavowing the factiousness and disloyalty of "some fanatics", declared "the large hope which they had of a happy union among all dissenters by his means". Baxter in a lengthy address laid down three prerequisites for their acceptance of episcopacy: "1. By making only things necessary to be the terms of union. 2. And by the true exercise of church discipline against sin. 3. And not casting out the faithful ministers that must exercise it, nor obtruding unworthy men upon the people." It was a programme which left much scope for interpretation. The King, Baxter records, "gave as gracious an answer as we could expect, professing his gladness to hear our inclinations to agreement, and his resolution to do his part to bring us together; and that it must not be by bringing one party over to the other, but by abating somewhat on both sides, and meeting in the midway; and that if it were not accomplished, it should be along of ourselves, and not of him: Nay, that he was resolved to see it brought to pass, and that he would draw us together himself."[3] The divines present were requested to draw up proposals for agreement about church government, and were given to understand that the Anglicans would do the same. This step, Charles emphasized, was not in preparation for an "assembly of divines", but for an un-

---

[1] Le Flem., 26; Wodrow, i, 42.

[2] There was probably more than one such conference; Baxter says: "Either at this time, or shortly after, the King required us, etc." (Rel. Baxt., 231.) Sharp wrote on June 26 that a meeting between the King and Presbyterian ministers had taken place on that day (Wodrow, i, 45); a letter of June 16 in the Suth., 168, refers to such a conference as "the news of the day".

[3] Rel. Baxt., 230–1. According to Sharp, the King was much more explicit in his statement: "The King told the four Presbyterian ministers . . . he would have the Church of England governed by bishops. And when it was replied that they were not enemies to regulated Episcopacy, he bid them put in writing their concessions. . . . He promised that none of them should be pressed to conformity until a synod determined that point, and that all who had entered into livings whose incumbents are dead, should be continued, and others, before they were outed, should be provided for." Wodrow, i, 49. Baxter elsewhere partly confirms this; cf. Rel. Baxt., 241.

official conference "to advise with a few of each side, for his own satisfaction".[1]

"Hereupon," relates Baxter, "we departed and appointed to meet
from day to day at Sion College, and to consult there openly with any
of our brethren that would please to join with us, that none might say
they were excluded; some city ministers came among us, and some
came not; and divers country ministers who were in the city came also
to us. . . . In these debates we found the great inconvenience of too
many actors . . . for that which seemed the most convenient expression
to one, seemed inconvenient to another, and we that all agreed in
matter, had much ado to agree in words."[2] The disagreement among
the two groups of Presbyterians, which Baxter tends to obscure, is
more clearly brought out by Sharp: "Some friends of the Presbyterian
way are very solicitous about this business, fearing that what they [the
moderate divines] do now may conclude all their party, and lest they
fall into an error *in limine*, which cannot be retracted; that is, if they
give in their paper of concessions, those will be laid hold on, and made
use of by the other party as granted; and yet [that] they remit nothing
of their way, and so break all with advantage." Again, on July 12:
"The ministers have had several meetings at Sion College since my last;
they have many debates, and are not all in one mind."[3]

Two days before, however, the Presbyterians had presented their
proposals to the King. In the matter of church government, Archbishop
Ussher's scheme was "designedly adhered to" and accepted "as a
ground-work towards an accommodation"; it was interpreted as establishing "the true ancient and primitive Presidency . . . balanced and
managed with a due commixtion of presbyters therewith", in distinction from "that ecclesiastical hierarchy or prelacy disclaimed in the
Covenant". A new form of Common Prayer was requested, "as much
as may be in Scripture words"; or at least a revision and reform of the
old book, with "an addition . . . of some other varying forms in Scripture phrase, to be used at the minister's choice". Dispensation was asked
from ceremonies against which the Puritans had protested for the past

---

[1] *Ibid.*, 232.
[2] *Ibid.*, 232.
[3] *Wodrow*, i, 46, 50; cf. Z. Crofton, *op. cit.*, preface, n.p.: "I well know that
those who had immediate conference with his Majesty, professed in private
debates with their brethren another judgment of the Covenant and Episcopacy
than what is now reported of them."

century, as well as abolition of the Laudian "innovations".[1] Orally, the King was begged to suspend for the present all proceedings under the old Act of Uniformity, dispense the oath of canonical obedience and subscription, secure the recognition of those already in Presbyterian orders, and, finally, to revoke the recent appointments to benefices where the sequestered incumbent was dead and a Puritan in possession. Charles showed his customary graciousness and tact. According to Baxter, he gave assurance that the proposed conference would be held, though no Anglican spokesmen had appeared at this audience, and promised "that the Bishops should come down and yield on their parts". Baxter's recollection, however, is not always to be trusted; at the time, Sharp merely reported: "[His Majesty] ordered them not to communicate it [their paper of proposals] till he made his pleasure known . . . commended it as savouring of learning and moderation, and hoped it might give a good beginning to a good settlement in the Church."[2] There, for the moment, the matter rested.

In these preliminary dealings with the Presbyterians, it will be noted that Hyde and the Laudian party took no direct part. The Laudians, however, had not withdrawn into the background. Signs of their activity were evident to all, and there was a growing tendency to contrast "the high and furious drivings of the Episcopalians" with "the gracious disposition and moderation of the King".[3] By the middle of June, Sharp was deeply impressed "with how much the prelatical men do here signify", and while Douglas's letters abounded in hopeful prayers that the Lord would "root out that stinking weed [of prelacy] in His own time, whatever pains men take to plant it and make it grow", his friend in London was assuring him that "the Episcopalians drive so furiously, that all lovers of religion are awakened to look about them, and to endeavour the stemming of that feared impetuousness of these men".[4] Baxter's old opponent, Dr. Thomas Pierce, sounded the opening note of the Laudian campaign in St. Paul's Cathedral on the Sunday after the King's arrival.

"Until our bishops receive their right", he declaimed, "though we are glad to have our King, we may rationally fear we shall not hold him. For ask, I beseech you, of the days that are past, and ask from one side of Heaven unto the other, if ever there were any such thing as this, that a King could be happy without a Bishop?" He exhorted "this assembly, as the head and heart of the

[1] *Rel. Baxt.*, 232 ff.   [2] *Ibid.*, 241; *Wodrow*, i, 51.
[3] *Wodrow*, i, 37.   [4] *Ibid.*, i, 37, 38, 40.

Royal City" to petition for the restoration of Episcopacy, a divine institution. "Even the Parliament itself hath such a respect unto the City, that if you plead for God's spouse, as you have done for his Anointed . . . if you shall supplicate for a discipline which is as old in this land as Christianity itself, and stands established by thirty-two Acts of Parliament, and without which you cannot live unless by living under the breach of your greatest Charter, they will not only be apt to grant, but to thank you also for your petition."[1]

If Dr. Pierce's views, at the time, seemed bold and over-sanguine, it was soon apparent that such sentiments were not really frowned on by the Court. The King might speak graciously to his Presbyterian subjects, but his favour was showered on the Laudians. Sheldon was now Dean of the Chapel Royal, and Brian Duppa Lord Almoner. The chapel at Whitehall assumed a new appearance—"amongst other things", wrote Edward Gower on June 9, "there are twelve singing boys provided, and a pair of organs setting up where Noll's seat was." Mr. Samuel Pepys, no ardent Puritan, attended service, and was unpleasantly surprised: "I heard a cold sermon of the Bishop of Salisbury's, [Duppa,] and the ceremonies did not please me, they do so overdo them. . . ."[2] Other Court preachers included Sheldon, Bishop King, and Bishop Wren—next to Laud himself, in the old days, the bitterest object of Puritan wrath.[3] From Scotland came a cry of horror:"Behold your unhappy diurnals and letters from London have wounded me to the heart," Robert Baillie wrote to Lauderdale. "Is the Service-Book read in the King's Chapel? Has the Bishop of Ely (I fear, Dr. Wren), the worst bishop of our age after Laud, preached there? . . . Oh! where are we so soon? . . . It's a scorn to tell us of moderate Episcopacy, a moderate Papacy!"[4] But even more afflicting to Scottish ears was news of Dr. Herbert Croft's sermon on June 21. In blunt terms the preacher told the King "that for the guilt he had contracted in Scotland, and the injuries he was brought to do against the Church of England, God had defeated him at Worcester, and pursued his controversy with a nine years' exile; and yet he would further pursue him, if he did close with his enemies." Even the amiable Charles was moved to term Dr. Croft "a passionate preacher", and it speaks much for the Royal good nature that in two years' time that uncourtly divine was enjoying the see of Hereford.[5]

---

[1] T. Pierce, *England's Season for Reformation of Life* (Lond. 1660), 14 ff.
[2] *Suth.*, 204; *Pepys*, i, 86.   [3] *Town.*, 53; *Pepys*, i, 80; *Wodrow*, i, 37.
[4] *Baillie*, iii, 405–6.   [5] *Wodrow*, i, 44.

The lead given by the Court was reinforced by evidence of popular support for the old Church. "Petitions come up from counties for Episcopacy and Liturgy," Sharp mentioned on June 26. "The Lord's anger is not turned away. The generality of the people are doting after prelacy and the Service-Book."[1] "The discourse of the town", wrote Edward Gower soon after, "is of the petition from Somersetshire and Dorset for establishing the Church in the same splendour and cere-monies that she was in King James's and Queen Elizabeth's times".[2] On June 20 the King was presented with an address signed by seventy-eight of the nobility and gentry of Northamptonshire, including the Earls of Northampton, Westmoreland, and Peterborough, Viscount Mordaunt, and the Lords Thomond, Hatton, Despencer, and Rockingham, which petitioned as follows:

"Because we cannot conceive anything can so well provide the continuing safety of your Majesty and People, as the restitution of Religion under the ancient and apostolical government by bishops, according to the undoubted laws of this kingdom, so highly asserted by your Royal Father of blessed memory . . . we humbly implore your Majesty . . . for the full attaining of these great ends in the settlement of Church and State."[3]

The Humble Petition of the Nobility and Gentry of the Six Counties of North Wales, presented on June 28, was, from the Laudian viewpoint, equally gratifying:

". . . Though we cannot make the least doubt (being convinced thereunto by your Majesty's most pious and exemplary practice in matters of religion) but that your Majesty's first and chief care is for the resettlement of the Church upon the ancient foundation of truth and peace, yet seeing we have suffered so deeply in the contrary practice by some that of late have had the power over us . . . we beseech your Majesty . . . that you would be pleased to cause all those good and wholesome laws for uniformity in religion, the government of the Church, and the maintenance of the clergy, to be put in execution, which have been made since the Reformation, whether by your Royal predecessor Queen Elizabeth, or your Grandfather and Father of ever happy memory."[4]

[1] *Ibid.*, i, 44.
[2] *Suth.*, 199. The petition from the nobility and gentry of Somerset was de-livered to the King by the Knights of the Shire on June 9, and is summarized in *Merc. Pub.*, No. 24, p. 374.
[3] British Museum Library, vol. 669. f. 25, f. 47; cf. *ibid.*, f. 74, for a similar address from thirty-five of the clergy of Kent, presented on July 24, and *Kenn.*, 226, for address of the Clergy of Surrey, August 10.
[4] *Mer. Pub.*, No. 27, p. 418.

These addresses, so prompt to appear, were early tokens of the staunch support from the county gentry that, in future, was to be the mainstay of the High Church party. There can be little doubt that they gave welcome encouragement to a government officially professing one religious policy, and, in fact, nervously engaged on another.[1]

On all sides, bits of evidence mounted to prove that the re-establishment of the old system was determined on, and would not tarry for a decision of Parliament or an agreement with the Presbyterians. There was no hesitation, for example, over ecclesiastical policy in Ireland, and action taken there anticipated the course of events in England. In a land where the tradition of autocratic rule prevailed and Parliament was suspended, there was no need to temporize with the Puritan party, and the government showed its hand plainly. On June 1 Dudley Loftus had written to Ormond from Dublin, invoking his aid for the immediate re-establishment of bishops. "It would much conduce to the settlement of the Church", he suggested, "if you would recommend as many ministers of gravity and learning of the right stamp as you can procure to be speedily settled in the ecclesiastical benefices here," and he enclosed a list of available preferments.[2] On June 18, commissioners from Ireland were in conference with the King, and requested "that religion might be settled there as it was in the days of [his] grandfather and father; that Establishment being the only fence against schism and confusion."[3] Five days later, Sharp could report: "All the bishops in Ireland are nominate," and "Dr. Bramble" made Archbishop of Armagh and primate.[4] Though Ormond remained for a time in England, the settlement was carried out with a strong hand by his representative, the Earl of Orrery, and by the new year, dissenters had been wholly repressed, and the old Church firmly settled. At no time was the character of the settlement in doubt.[5] Jeremy Taylor, newly raised

---

[1] The French Ambassador Bordeaux suggested that these addresses were instigated by the Court: "L'on suscite à cest effect [i.e., à restablir les Evesques] des Resquestes au nom de quelques Provinces." P.R.O., *Transcripts*, 3/107, f. 265.

[2] *Carte* 30, f. 685 and f. 689.

[3] *Wodrow*, i, 43-4.

[4] *Ibid.*, i, 44.

[5] Cf. in *Clar.* 74, f. 92, "Declaration by the Lords Justices and Council of Ireland forbidding all Assemblies by Papists, Presbyterians, Independents, Anabaptists, Quakers, and other fanatical persons, all of them in contempt of his Majesty's Royal Authority and the established laws of the land, January 22,

to the bishopric of Down and Connor, could not sufficiently praise the churchly zeal of the Lord Lieutenant: "The Church whose mouth and heart are full of gratitude and honour to the memory of that great Strafford, quickly sees herself improved in growth and form under the piety and care of the greater Ormond!"[1]

There were other straws in the wind. The French Ambassador mentioned to Mazarin on June 14 the common belief that the King would re-establish the bishops, and added: "Il se fait des diligences pour destruire la répugnance des Troupes contre cet Establissment."[2] The last Sunday in June had been set apart by Parliament for a national thanksgiving for the King's restoration; shortly before that date a pamphlet was published with the order of service to be used, and having on its title page the suggestive phrase: "Set forth by Authority".[3] The contents were extracted *verbatim* from the Prayer Book and consisted of Morning Prayer, with proper psalms, lessons, and collects, together with the Litany and Ante-Communion. A prefaced rubric left no room for misunderstanding, and referred to the services, "as in the Book of Common Prayer". There was an immediate and angry reaction in Parliament over this "great abuse". Andrew Newport wrote to a friend, "the Presbyterians in the House are scandalized at it, and have appointed a committee to examine the printer by what order he did it.

1661." Cf. also letters of Orrery to Hyde, Jan. 16 and 23, 1661 (*ibid.*, ff. 52, 98). In the first letter Orrery states that he has declared to the Presbyterians "that His Majesty had in a most particular manner commanded my utmost care of the Church of Ireland, that the Church government being settled in this kingdom by law . . . such as would not conform thereunto must expect no settlement or public maintenance, and would do well to retire by choice before they were compelled unto it by necessity". In the second letter he remarks: "If God be pleased to bless what we have begun, it will not only expeditiously and effectually settle this divided Church, but have a good influenceon England and Scotland."

For a discussion of Ormond's ecclesiastical policy, cf. T. Carte, *Life of James Duke of Ormonde* (Oxf. 1851), iv, 14–16. Carte says that the bishops were appointed in August, 1660, but he is certainly in error. Dr. Griffith Williams had been appointed to the see of Kilkenny and Ossory by July 4, and Bramhall to Armagh by July 7. Cf. *C.S.P.D.*, 1660–61, 16; W. J. S. Simpson, *Archbishop Bramhall* (Lond. 1927), 224.

[1] *Carte* 45, f. 78.
[2] P.R.O., *Transcripts* 3/107, f. 265.
[3] The full title of the pamphlet was: *A Form of Prayer with Thanksgiving to be used on 28 June 1660 for his Majesty's Happy Return.* (Lond. 1660.)

The Presbyterians are very high upon the King's bestowing favours upon some of them by the General's recommendation".[1]

Another significant item was reported by Sharp on July 7: "The English lawyers have given in papers to show that the Bishops have not been outed by law." He had noted previously: "The calling of a synod is put off."[2]

The final and conclusive evidence of the liaison between the government and the Laudian party was only guessed at by contemporary observers, but to-day lies plainly revealed in the Calendar of State Papers for 1660. From the time of Edward III, appointment to the vast majority of Crown benefices had been vested in the Lord Chancellor. Control of these presentations under the Great Seal was now placed by Hyde in the hands of the Laudian leaders; the first indication of this appears under the date of June 19. A petition on behalf of Abraham Allen for the rectory of Westmeane, Hants., bears the notation:

"His Majesty is pleased to refer this petition to Dr. Sheldon, Dr. Earle, and Dr. Morley, or any two of them, who are to inform themselves of the petitioner's merits, and certify his Majesty thereof, and then his Majesty will certify his further pleasure."[3]

A favourable judgment by these divines is recorded, with an order of June 22 granting the petition. In the weeks following, the identical procedure was followed in connection with some forty-two requests for preferment, and in many more instances with combinations of two of the three names. Obviously, these three intimates of the Chancellor formed a standing committee to ensure the appointment of clergy whose loyalty and orthodoxy could be guaranteed. To this end careful precautions were taken; petitioners were evidently notified that they must provide certificates signed by prominent divines of Laudian stamp. To most petitions are affixed testimonials like the following:

"These are to certify whom it may concern that . . . Daniel Vivian, clerk, Doctor of Laws, is known to be an honest and orthodox man, of sober life and conversation, rightly principled in matters touching church government, and one that hath done and suffered much in the cause of his late Majesty of blessed memory, and for his loyalty to his Majesty that now is.

John Cole, D.D.   John Gardner, B.D.
Thomas Bradley, D.D.   Oliver Lloyd

[1] *J.C.*, viii, 78; *Suth.*, 154.   [2] *Wodrow*, i, 50, 45.
[3] P.R.O., S.P. 29/4, f. 94.

Timothy Thurscross, B.D.   Daniel Lloyd
Bruno Ryves   William Bean
Peter Ingram, S.T.B.   Richard Osgood

"I presume the persons that have subscribed this certificate being all of them well affected, and divers of them to my knowledge men of great worth, learning, and integrity, have attested nothing but what they know to be true, and therefore I think it a sufficient information to qualify the petitioner for the King's favour in what he sues for.

"(Signed) George Morley."[1]

"These are humbly to certify whom it may concern that the bearer hereof, Kenelm Manwaring, clerk, is a person of holy life and conversation, orthodox in judgment, conformable to the ancient doctrine and discipline of the Church of England, and hath been in these late revolutions faithful and loyal to his Sacred Majesty . . . and a great sufferer.

Robert Mason   Robert Sanderson   Bruno Ryves
George Wilde   George Hall   Richard Ball
Nathaniel Hardy   Matthew Smallwood   Timothy Thurscross
                    John Barwick

"I am well assured by the testimony of these very credible persons that Mr. Kenelm Manwaring is very worthy of the favour he desires from his Majesty.

Gilbert Sheldon.
John Earle."[2]

Nothing could be more revealing than an examination of the list of sponsors; of the thirty-six clergy who provided more than one testimonial, all but one can be identified as members of the Laudian party.[3] Thus, under the aegis of the government, this party within a few weeks

[1] P.R.O., S.P. 29/11, f. 67 (1).
[2] P.R.O., S.P. 29/10, f. 19 (1).
[3] The following list of sponsors and the number of certificates provided has been compiled from the names cited in C.S.P.D., 1660-61, 59 ff. Only one name, that of Thomas Richardson, cannot be identified. Gilbert Sheldon (65), George Morley (39), John Earle (27), John Cosin (12), Robert Sanderson (12), Bishop Duppa (10), Edward Martin (10), John Barwick (8), John Pearson (7), Bishop King (6), Humphrey Henchman (5), Richard Ball (5), Bishop Warner (4), Jeremy Taylor (4), Henry Ferne (4), Nathaniel Hardy (4), Bruno Ryves (3), George Wilde (3), Henry Bridgeman (3), Thomas Richardson (3), Thomas Paske (3), Robert Mossom (3), Guy Carleton (2), Emmanuel Utye (or Ute) (2), Brian Walton (2), Matthew Nicholas (2), Bishop Roberts (2), Thomas Bradley (2), Edward Layfield (2), Bishop Wren (2), Edward Sparke (2), George Hall (2), Bishop Sydserf (2), Bishop Skinner (2), Timothy Thurscross (2), Edward Wolley (2). For brevity's sake I have omitted the names of those signing one certificate only; they are equally Laudian in character, with the exception of John Gauden and Edmund Calamy.

Such men as Skinner, Warner, and King were not, of course, considered

of the Restoration was enabled to use the Crown's patronage to establish its members in strategic posts. No regard was paid either to the King's Proclamation of June 1 or to the fact that the Puritan incumbent could frequently claim that his sequestered predecessor was dead.[1] By the middle of July, James Sharp was noting gloomily: "There are universal complaints of the ejection of many honest ministers throughout the land, and the re-admission of many not well qualified. . . . All offices in the Church and Universities are just filling with men of that [episcopal] way."[2] There was special need for haste in constituting the cathedral chapters, for any move toward filling the bishoprics must wait until the chapters could perform their canonical rôle. The government's concern is illustrated by the King's letter to the Dean and Chapter of Exeter:

"As we desire to contribute all we can to the recovering of the Church out of its languishing condition occasioned by the distempers of the late times, so it is our most princely care and design in order thereunto to promote such men who in the late sad times have been conspicuous both in their loyalty to us and conformity to the Church. . . ."

—on that ground he recommended Dr. Henry Byam for a canon's place, void by decease of Edward Cotton.[3] A contemporary chronicler records: "The King first filled up the chapters in every cathedral with prebendaries or canons of known worth and loyalty," and as early as July 13 Henry Townshend wrote in his diary: "The Church of Canterbury by dean and prebends settled for the election of a new Archbishop."[4] By the end of August the work was virtually complete.[5]

Laudians in pre-Civil War days, but at the Restoration they naturally aligned themselves with the party anxious to restore episcopal rights. Cf. the observation of the Puritan John Corbett: "There were also many more moderate Episcopal divines that were formerly reckoned half Puritans, and upon that account kept from preferment till about the beginning of the Long Parliament, some of them were made bishops for the support of episcopacy. These being exasperated by the late Wars, and the issue there of violent changes in government, and their own sufferings, which happened beyond our first expectations, were set at a greater distance from us." *The Interest of England in the Matter of Religion* (Lond. 1660), 108.

[1] Cf. *J.C.*, viii, 97, 138.   [2] *Wodrow*, i, 51–2.
[3] P.R.O., S.P. 29/11, f. 119.   [4] *Add.* 19, 526, f. 40; *Town.*, 54.
[5] Appointments to cathedral chapters, with dates, are given in *Kenn.*, *passim.*
In St. Paul's Cathedral, for example, the Dean, Matthew Nicholas, was in-

M

However little Hyde and his colleagues cared to advertise this activity, it could not escape notice. Sharp sounded a constant warning to his friends in Scotland: "All is wrong here as to church affairs; Episcopacy will be settled here to the height. . . . The Episcopal men have the wind of the Presbyterians and know now to make use of it. . . . The managing this business by papers will undo them [i.e. the Presbyterians]; those motions about their putting in writing what they would desire in point of accommodation are but to gain time, and prevent petitionings, and smooth over matters till the Episcopal men be more strengthened."[1] The Florentine Resident, Salvetti, despatched an analysis of the official policy to his government on June 23:

"La fazione Presbiteriana struggesi sempre per rendersi più potente et per havere in consequenza in mano loro tutto il potere et governo dello stato; et benchè pare che il Re discerna bene la lor ambizione et spiriti turbolenti, non proceda con tutto ciò per ancora contra di loro con rigore alcuno, ma cerca più tosto di moderarli con promettere ad ogniuno libertà di conscienza. Dall'altra parte, la fazione Episcopale se li opponga con ogni maggior zelo et diligenza, conoscendo molto bene li d'essi tenori esser tanto differenti et distanti dalla religion Protestante che sia impossibile che ambi sossistono in uno istesso stato senza la disturbanza di tutto il Regno, et si teme che l'antipatia et differenza tra di queste due religioni—o siano potenti fazioni—non sia per nuocere più al Re et suo quieto governo d'ogni altra cosa: moltadimeno habbiamo gran ragione di sperare che il Re sia con la solita sua prudenza per guadagnare et vincere poco a poco insensibilmente la fazion Presbiteriana, et così prevenire la ruina che minacceria latramente et al suo stato et persona."[2]

There were "discontents and grumblings" among the Presbyterians,

stalled July 10; Robert Pory, Canon Residentiary, on July 20; the Precentor and sixteen of the canons during the month of August. *Ibid.*, 202–3.
    The restoration of Anglican rites and the purging of Nonconformist fellows also proceeded rapidly in the Universities, and was largely achieved by the end of 1660. Cf. F. J. Varley (ed.), "The Restoration Visitation of the University of Oxford", *Camden Miscellany*, vol. xviii (Lond. 1948); *C.S.P.D.*, 1660–1, 199, 488; R. Gunther (ed.), *Further Correspondence of John Ray* (Lond. 1928), 17–18. *Matt.*, *C.R.*, 181, 352, 405, also introduction, xiii–xiv.
    [1] *Wodrow*, i, 44 ff., 53.
    [2] *Add.* 27, 962 P, f. 676. "The Presbyterian faction are ever consumed by a desire of becoming mightier and of holding thus in their grasp the whole power and government of the state; and notwithstanding that the king discerns well, as it seems, their ambition and turbulent spirit he proceeds not against them with any rigour but seeks rather to govern them by promising to each one liberty of conscience. At the same time the Episcopal faction opposes them with all the greater zeal and diligence, knowing full well their precepts to be so different and

but Anglican clergy throughout the land were correspondingly elated and encouraged. The Anglican "conformists" of the Commonwealth, without waiting for formal authorization, began to reintroduce the Prayer Book. "The state of the Church of England [in this summer] was this," wrote Henry Gregory. "Those who were Episcopalians read the Common Prayer (at his Majesty's first return or before) for most of them, and others beginning by degrees; but the Presbyterians refusing the Common Prayer, acted according to their Directory, or read some form of their own composing; and . . . there was no church government exercised."[1] The movement to restore the Liturgy was spontaneous and gradual. As early as May 12, a Durham parish register records: "On which day, I, Stephen Hogg, began to use again the Book of Common Prayer."[2] The Lords restored its use in their House on May 31, with the cautious proviso "that no penalty, prejudice, or reflection shall be upon any that are not present at prayers".[3] On July 8 Evelyn made the general observation: "From henceforth was the Liturgy publicly used in our churches," and Simon Patrick states: "Many ministers began of themselves to read the Common Prayer." He himself, after preparing his congregation and preaching on the subject, did so on July 22.[4] The Liturgy was first used at Peterborough Cathedral at the end of July, at York by August 26, and at Worcester on August 31.[5] Samuel Pepys, attending service at his parish church, St. Olave's, on November 4, noted characteristically: "Mr. Mills did begin to nibble at the Common Prayer . . . but the people had been so little used to it, that they could not tell what to answer."[6] It is possible,

---

far-removed from the Protestant religion that it is impossible the two exist in one and the same state without disturbance of the whole kingdom, and it is feared that the antipathy and differences between these two religions—or mighty factions—are like, more than aught else, to do hurt to the King and to his quiet government; much the less have we any great cause for hoping that the King with his wonted restraint is like to win over the Presbyterian faction or gradually to conquer them by imperceptible means and thus to prevent the ruin widely threatening his person and his realm."

[1] *Add.* 19, 526, f. 41.
[2] J. Tanner, *English Constitutional Conflicts of the 17th Century* (Camb. 1947), 225.
[3] *J.L.*, xi, 50.
[4] S. Patrick, *Autobiography* (Oxf. 1839), 37–8; *Evel.*, ii, 149.
[5] *Kenn.*, 229; *Suth.*, 199–200; *Town.*, 59.
[6] *Pepys*, i, 105.

however, to overestimate the spread of the practice in 1660; as late as March of the following year a Londoner, Thomas Stone, wrote to his father: "I think there are many more churches that have not the Common Prayer read in them than that have it."[1]

Similarly, the return of the sequestered clergy to their former parishes in large measure anticipated Parliamentary action. Many of the Puritan incumbents, foreseeing the inevitable, quietly relinquished possession; the chronicler already quoted asserts: "Many ministers that were put out of their places for their loyalty to his Majesty were this month [June] restored to them again."[2] But pressure could be brought to bear on the intruders, as we learn from the correspondence of John Cosin, ejected in years gone by from the rectory of Elwick in County Durham. Cosin was not the man to wait patiently for the slow process of law, and had urged the local justice, William Blakiston, to dislodge the Puritan incumbent. Blakiston reported on July 21:

"I was at Elwick, where we met with that impudent intruder Bowie. . . . When I told him what we were come about, and how I did understand that he had quit his claim . . . he did utterly deny any such thing. . . . So I told him my mind very freely, which did a little disorder him, and so went to the town where we met most of the parishioners, and wished them to keep their tithes in their own hands, till the title was tried, which they all consented to . . . [Bowie] urged the King's Proclamation against forcible entries. I replied, he did not well understand the meaning of it, for it was not intended to favour the intruders more than to convict them openly by law, as their own conscience had done privately, I hoped."[3]

Bowie was not legally deprived until October 11. Joseph Crowther, presented by the Crown in June to the rectory of Tredington, Worcestershire, "for two or three Lord's Days preached at one end of the church while Mr. Durham [the incumbent] preached at the other".[4] An even more dramatic scene enlivened worshippers when Robert Clarke returned to his former church at Andover, Hampshire, and according to contemporary account, "Sunday morning went to the church at full congregation . . . and going through the body of the church drew the eyes of all upon him, and comes up into the reader's pew, and puts the intruder aside, and told him: 'Sir, the King is come into his own, and will reign alone, and I am come to my own too and will officiate without an assistant!' and so taking a book out of his

---

[1] P.R.O., S.P. 29/32, f. 144.   [2] *Add.* 10, 116, f. 103.
[3] *Orns.*, ii, 5–6.   [4] *Matt., C.R.*, 174.

pocket, went on with the Liturgy, and an excellent sermon of forgiving injuries."[1] It is difficult to estimate the extent of this movement in the early months, unsanctioned as it was by Parliament; but Baxter remarks that "before this time [July 10], by the King's return many hundred worthy ministers were displaced, and cast out of their charges because they were in sequestrations."[2] The leading authority on the subject, Mr. A. G. Matthews, concludes that some 695 incumbents were ejected by the end of the year.[3]

The growing tension between Presbyterians and Anglicans is reflected in the sudden increase of controversial tracts on religious issues during the summer of 1660. In the month of June, these are still comparatively rare, but significantly in the first week of July *Mercurius Publicus* advertised three books: *English Episcopacy and Liturgy asserted by the great Reformers Abroad*, *The Idea of Government, Monarchical and Episcopal*, and *Collection of sundry Petitions presented to the late King in behalf of Episcopacy, Liturgy, and Suppression of Schismatics*.[4] Thereafter, as recorded in the catalogue of the Thomason Collection, the stream of such publications rapidly became a flood. The implications of the Covenant, episcopal government, presbyterian ordination, liturgy and ceremonies, and church lands, were discussed with growing bitterness and partisanship. On both sides, the large proportion of reprints of pre-Civil War pamphlets indicates how little the terms of controversy had changed since the 1640's, and makes clear that the conflict was merely the final phase of a century-old struggle. Edward Bowles, for example, when asked by Calamy to write down the Presbyterian exceptions to the Liturgy "backed with arguments", replied: "I have thought of it, but when I had done so, I found so much of that nature in the papers of the old Non-Conformists that I thought it superfluous."[5] As might be expected in a situation where the Church party increasingly held the advantage, the attack was largely from the Puritan side, with a full-scale revival of old grievances. But Anglican controversialists were quick to take the field in defence of the old ways,[6] and the authentic

[1] *Matt., W.R.*, 181.
[2] *Rel. Baxt.*, 241.
[3] *Matt., C.R.*, Intr., xii–xiii.
[4] *Merc. Pub.*, No. 28, 457.
[5] Dr. Williams' Library, *Baxter MSS.* IV, f. 172.
[6] As an example, we may trace one thread of the controversy. On August 3, Cornelius Burgess and other Puritan divines published a manifesto directed to Parliament, *Reasons showing the Necessity of Reformation in the Church of*

voice of the Laudians was again heard in the land. John Rowland, a Kentish rector recently back from exile, could scarcely have been more provocative in a tract of August 8:

"Moses and Aaron must be together", he declared, "the King and the Priest, the Crown and the Mitre, the Prince's Sceptre and the Bishop's Crosier, or else the Sceptre will be soon made to stoop to the Presbyterian Ferula.... Methinks it is high time bishops should be restored with more power than formerly, which will be but moderate Episcopacy, in regard of the great increase of schisms and heresies, and the dangerous times we are fallen into." As for those Presbyterians who wished a reformation in doctrine, worship, and discipline—"their best way will be, if they mean peaceably, to make their addresses to the reverend bishops, and by their advice, if there be any thing that will not agree with these men's queazy stomachs, something may be more fully explained to give them satisfaction, which I believe for my part is impossible for any men to do, they are so inconstant in their judgments and resolutions."[1]

The bishops, indeed, showed themselves to be somewhat of this mind. As we have seen, the Presbyterians had submitted their pro-gramme to the King on July 10; some days after, they received the considered reply of the surviving prelates. To Baxter, expecting "promised condescensions of the Episcopal divines", it seemed "but a paper of bitter oppositions, by way of confutation of our former pro-posals". Its studiously moderate language scarcely warrants the epithet "bitter", but it was in essence a traditional Anglican defence of the *status quo ante*. The general tone was indicated in an opening sentence: "In sundry particulars ... we do not perceive what farther security can be given, than is already provided for by the established laws of this realm." The Presbyterian proposals for a "moderate Episcopacy" were firmly resisted; but to lessen the fear of "prelacy", the Anglicans stated that "bishops, and all ecclesiastical governors, ought to exercise their government not arbitrarily, but according to law", and "if any bishops

England. This was answered on August 20 by John Pearson in *No Necessity of Reformation of the Public Doctrine of the Church of England*, and by Henry Savage, D.D., on September 5 in *Reasons showing that there is No Need of such a Reforma-tion, etc.* Puritan rebuttals were (Sept. 11) *Some Necessity of Reformation, etc.*, or a *Reply to Dr. Pearson*, by William Hamilton, and (Sept. 13) *No Sacrilege nor Sin ... with a Postscript to Dr. Pearson*, by Cornelius Burgess. On September 20 appeared *An Answer to Dr. Burgess ...*, by John Pearson, and on December 13, 1661, a final tract, *Defence of the Liturgy of the Church of England in answer to Reasons Showing the Necessity, etc.* (Anon.)

[1] J. Rowland, *A Reply to the Answer of Anonymous to Dr. Gauden ...* (Lond. 1660), 24, 50–1.

have [done], or shall do, otherwise than according to law, they were and are to be answerable for the same". The apologia for the Prayer Book was one with which most churchmen would sympathize; but extempore prayer before and after the sermon was held permissible, and the bishops expressed themselves as "not against revising of the Liturgy by such discreet persons as his Majesty shall think fit to employ therein". The general principle of ceremonial was upheld; in regard to particular points, it was desired that kneeling for Communion and observance of holy days be continued, and other disputed points referred to the King. The bishops disavowed the wish to impose any "innovations . . . or ceremonies which have no foundation in the laws of the land", and hoped that "all men would use that liberty that is allowed them in things indifferent, according to the rules of Christian prudence, charity, and moderation". They concluded with the opinion that to concede all Presbyterian demands would merely prove "the seminary of new differences" by provoking the dissatisfaction of "much the greater part of his Majesty's subjects", and by encouraging further demands from the more radical dissenters. In short, the document refused any essential modifications of the old system, but emphasized the comprehensiveness which could be enjoyed within it. Since the Presbyterians eventually decided to make no rejoinder, lest it "turn a treaty of concord into a sharp disputation", the negotiations lapsed for the time being.[1]

As the summer progressed, the focus of the religious struggle gradually shifted to Parliament. Early in May, before the King's actual return, the House of Commons had begun to concern itself with the Church question. On the ninth of that month a bill was reported "for establishing ministers settled in ecclesiastical livings", but it remained in committee, and the only action taken was that which occasioned the King's Proclamation of June 1.[2] On June 27 another bill, "for the maintenance of the true Reformed Protestant Religion, and for the suppression of popery, superstition, profaneness, and other disorders and innovations in worship and ceremonies", was read for the first time.[3] The weeks of delay and the frequent postponement of this bill's second reading give colour to Hyde's assertion:

"That party in the House that was in truth devoted to the King and to the old principles of Church and State, which every day increased, thought not fit

[1] Rel. Baxt., 242-7.   [2] J.C., viii, 19, 33, 47.   [3] Ibid., 76.

so to cross the Presbyterians as to make them desperate in their hopes of satisfaction; but, with the concurrence with those who were of contrary factions, diverted the argument by proposing other subjects of more immediate relation to the public peace . . . and the model for religion to be debated and prepared by that committee which had been nominated before his Majesty's return to that purpose; they not doubting to cross and puzzle any pernicious resolutions there. . . ."[1]

But it was apparent to one observer that the Puritans could not be put off indefinitely. Thomas Gower wrote on June 30: "The Presbyters begin to stir, and discover their opposition to ceremonies, and their desire to keep out the old ejected clergy, and 'tis believed as soon as the Act of Indemnity is finished that you will hear of greater opposition in that nature."[2] Salvetti had the same impression: "Di queste parti posso confirmarli che la fazione Presbiteriana cresca giornalmente et che divenga sempre più attiva nella propagatione delli lor interessi."[3]

Thus, it is not surprising that on July 6 the House finally decided to resolve into a Grand Committee to consider matters of religion on each following Monday.[4] On July 9 and 16 two lengthy debates occurred which throw considerable light on the course of the struggle between the two parties. The bill before the House, for "the maintenance of the Protestant Religion", was apparently a Puritan measure, and specified no other doctrinal requirements for membership in the Establishment than that faith set forth in the Old and New Testaments. "The original of the paragraph", acidly remarked Sir Heneage Finch, "was from Cromwell, and he did hope they would not cant after him." An Anglican, Sir Trevor Williams, opened the debate by moving for the inclusion of the 39 Articles; this proposal was interpreted by both sides as involving the re-establishment of episcopacy, probably on the basis of Article 36. As far as can be judged from the account preserved in a Parliamentary diary, the Anglican strategy was to prevent any Parliamentary decision in the matter, but if this failed, to insist on the inclusion of Williams's amendment. Lord Falkland thought "it not fit to debate the whole bill . . . but to leave the doctrinal part to a synod". Mr. Peckham was for "not altering our Religion without proper judges of it, as by a synod". Sir Heneage Finch, leader of the Church

---

[1] Hyde II, i, 331–2.   [2] Suth., 194.
[3] Add. 27, 962 P, f. 680. "Of these two parties I can confirm that the Presbyterian faction are increasing daily and becoming ever more active in the furthering of their interests."   [4] J.C., viii, 82.

party, eloquently expounded the orthodox Laudian view, declaring that "not one letter of the bill made good the title of it; that the Religion of our Church was not to seek, but we have enjoyed it long, and therefore should not now be inquiring for it." However, he moved that the question "should be referred to an assembly of divines, for which they ought to petition the King; for he knew no law for altering the government of the Church by bishops." As for liberty of tender consciences, "no man knew what it was!" Later, he intimated that if "the faith grounded upon Scripture and the discipline according to the laws were put into the paragraph", he would consent to the bill. Other Anglicans like Sir Thomas Widdrington, Thomas Grove, and Edward Stephens warned against "anticipating the King, who was then consulting about it [i.e. the church settlement]".

The Presbyterians, though prepared to accept a "circumscribed" Episcopacy, strove valiantly to divide the question of doctrine from discipline. Mr. Prynne spoke "passionately" for the original bill, holding that a Synod's decisions "must be confirmed by the King and Parliament"—"he could not be for bishops, unless they would derive their power from the King, and not vaunt themselves to be *jure divino*". Mr. Bunckley declared that if the amendment were carried, "all ministers made since 1648 would be abolished". The final stages of the debate were protracted and bitter—"at last it was moved to adjourn it to another time, which was opposed by others; and the Committee sat an hour in the dark before candles were suffered to be brought in, and then they were twice blown out, but the third time they were preserved, though with great disorder." Judging from the example of Sir Anthony Ashley Cooper, the more politic of the new Puritan courtiers finally threw their weight on the Anglican side. The future Whig leader opined that "our Religion was too much mixed with interests, neither was it ripe now to handle the subject", and moved that the debate be laid aside. "At last, about ten at night it was voted 'that the King should be desired to convene a select number of divines to treat concerning the affair, and the Committee not to sit again until October 23'."[1] On July 20 the House of Commons approved this resolution, "but not without opposition".[2]

[1] *P.H.E.*, iv, 79–80, 82–4; cf. *Wodrow*, i, 52. The final paragraph of the account in the former work, under date July 9, obviously refers to the conclusion of the whole debate on July 16, and I have made use of it in that context.

[2] *J.C.*, viii, 95; *Suth.*, 155.

There can be no question that on this occasion, after a bitter struggle, Anglican tactics succeeded. The church settlement, it now seemed, was removed from a sphere in which Anglican predominance was dangerously uncertain, and reserved to the King, of whose intentions the Church party felt assured. Such was the interpretation of Edward Gower, who wrote to a friend on August 4:

"The only tug is betwixt Episcopacy and Presbytery; the young men (though the old men who are generally Presbyterians are more cunning) are careful not to be outvoted in this point; and though the Presbyter would have the Church settled in Parliament, the other party are resolved to put it off with delay, and by that means compass their design, which is to have it settled by a Synod, where things may be fairly canvassed, after the dissolution of this Parliament."[1]

The question of Parliament's rôle, however, was not to be decided by a single victory; though the fact that the young Anglican squires now began to drift away from the capital suggests that they believed the matter safely disposed of. As disillusionment over the government's intentions increased among Puritans, their party in the Commons became the more determined to obtain legal safeguards. On July 21 a petition from "sundry poor ministers of the Gospel" was presented in the House, protesting against ejection; by a vote of 125 to 106 the Presbyterians carried a resolution to have it read. As an immediate consequence, the Bill for Settling Ministers, left in committee since May, was ordered to be reported within four days' time.[2] This action coincided significantly with a bitter attack on Laudian policy, which "divers ministers in sundry Counties in England" publicly addressed to Parliament in a tract entitled *Reasons Showing the Necessity of Reformation*. The petitioners declared that:

"It is far from our thoughts to oppose or disparage orthodox doctrine, a well-composed Liturgy, rites for decency and order, ordination of ministers, Apostolical Episcopacy, or due rules of discipline." But they maintained strongly that "neither the Articles of Religion; the Books of Common Prayer or Ordination; the jurisdiction of bishops, claimed before 17 Charles I, nor so much as their being as bishops, sithence; nor those Canons so much contended for, are indeed established by law", and that "none of these, as they now stand, ought to be confirmed and settled".

[1] *Suth.*, 204.
[2] *J.C.*, viii, 97.

They made plain their grounds of apprehension:

"It is already too obvious that too many (notwithstanding all pretences or moderation) do already fly higher than ever . . . some, in stickling for the Liturgy commonly used; some, still holding up sole ordination by, and sole jurisdiction of bishops, and all Canons, not only made in England, but in Rome itself (if not repugnant to our laws); labouring to possess the people that all these are settled by law, and therefore to be continued and imposed without alteration."

Parliament was begged to review "all these things, after the example of the Parliament in 3, 4 Edw. VI", with the assistance of "some of the most moderate and able persons of the different parties".[1] The widespread alarm and resentment among Puritans which this tract illustrates undoubtedly occasioned the renewed activity of their sympathizers in the House.

On July 27, the Bill for Settling Ministers was reported by William Prynne, and three days later was read the second time.[2] Though the bill was to be fought over at intervals for the next six weeks, the opening debate is unfortunately the only one recorded in the *Parliamentary History*. But it makes sufficiently plain that the issue of the Church settlement was now revived, for the terms on which ministers were secured in their livings could not but affect the doctrinal and disciplinary requirements of the Establishment. Prynne's bill was a clear challenge to the Laudians. Sequestered clergy who were not adjudged "scandalous" by official commissioners, and who were not pluralists, might be restored to their livings; in all other cases, existing incumbents would be confirmed, without additional tests or requirements.[3]

The Anglican reaction was immediate and loud. Mr. Serjeant Littleton moved against the bill, since it "was to continue all scandalous ministers out, and not to remove all scandalous ones that were in". Edward Thurland moved that all incumbents be required to subscribe to the 39 Articles. Sir Thomas Meres seconded, and reminded the

---

[1] Cornelius Burgess and others, *op. cit.*, preface, n.p. Cf. *Suth.*, 168, for further evidence of Puritan protest.

[2] *J.C.*, viii, 104, 106.

[3] The provisions of the Bill are deduced from the ensuing debate; the only other information regarding it is given in a letter of Andrew Newport, June 20: "A Parliament man now tells me that the Committee of Religion today voted that all ministers that were put out of their benefices merely for their affection to the King, and were not otherwise scandalous, should be restored to their respective cures." *Suth.*, 154.

House that the Triers had placed many Anabaptists in good livings. Once more Finch argued for the strictly legal position in uncompromising terms. He moved the ejection of "all such ministers as would not conform to the laws of the land; saying [that] they could not punish the Papists with any justice, if they did not punish their own ministers for refusing to be regulated according to the law." As for those, he said scathingly, who had been presented to livings without regard to patrons' rights, and "were allowed to have grace but no allegiance", he moved "not to confirm any such, nor abate one of the 39 Articles or the Oaths to those that should stay in; but to leave them to their several patrons to be prosecuted according to the law." These views were enthusiastically echoed by a number of others—Sir John Masham, Sir John Bowyer, John Charlton, William Thomas, and John Barton. A constant refrain runs through all Anglican speeches—"none to have the benefit of their livings that would not conform to the law". Prynne agreed that incumbents should be required to take an oath of allegiance; but otherwise he and his fellows defended the bill with resolute insistence. On a division, the Anglican motion to throw out the bill was defeated, and it was referred back to committee.[1]

This debate marked a turning point in the party struggle. From now on, though the Anglicans fought a fierce delaying action in the House, they were consistently defeated in every attempt to modify the basic provisions of the bill, or to make it a less flagrant violation of Laudian principles. It is clear that from the beginning of August to the adjournment in September, the Church party had lost control in Parliament; this fact is reflected in the general gloom now for the first time apparent among the Laudians. On August 7, for example, Edward Gower wrote:

"Yesterday the House of Commons was very severe against the bishops, and made an order they should have no power to let leases not till they had taken

[1] *P.H.E.*, iv, 94–6. Miss L. F. Brown observes (*E.H.R.*, xxii, 59, *op. cit.*): "It was not the Presbyterian policy, but the policy of delay, which triumphed, for the bill went back to committee, there to remain for another fortnight." This interpretation is quite erroneous; it is abundantly clear from the speeches recorded that the Presbyterians moved to commit the bill, and that the Anglicans on the other hand endeavoured to defeat it without further delay. Cf. in *P.H.E.*, iv, 94 ff., the speeches on the Presbyterian side of Wheeler, Swinfen, and Hungerford; on the Anglican, of Masham and Charlton. The writer of this article entirely misses the significance of what was happening in the religious struggle in Parliament during August and September.

some order in that affair; this day they made the same, concerning deans, chapters, and prebends. . . . Here is a complaint at Court that the young men absent themselves from the House, and by that means give the old men, who are most of them Presbyterians, the advantage; nor pleasure nor profit ought to be thought of where business of such concern as this of church government and purchasers' estates are in debate."[1]

This turn of affairs undoubtedly dismayed the government, always sensitive to evidence of Puritan strength. Bishop Duppa wrote to Isham, also on August 7, complaining of the uneasy hesitation which now beset the Court's religious policy:

"Out of [your letters] I could extract a quintessence of better counsels than the Court alembics as yet seem either to promise or afford. . . . Could I see you in some nearness of place to him [i.e. the King] . . . I should say my *Dimittis* . . . and confidently expect that our many little confusions at Court would at last settle in such an order, as might assure us of more happiness than the tottering condition, which for the present we are in, can suddenly promise us."[2]

In a letter written a few days later to Sheldon, Duppa was even more concerned over the government's delays:

"I was summoned from hence [i.e. Richmond]", he informed his friend, "by his Majesty's command by his Secretary, who signified to me his pleasure was that I shall change my abode that I might be more useful to him, and in obedience to that command I have repaired nearer, but have not found opportunity given me, wherein I might be serviceable. What may be done now the Bishop of London is arrived (whose absence was the only honest apology we should have that nothing was done in behalf of the Church) I know not, but if nothing be, we have lost an excuse. You are the only person about his Majesty that I have confidence in, and I persuade myself that as none hath his ear more, so none is likely to prevail in his heart more, and there was never more need of it; for all the professed enemies of our Church look upon this as the critical time to use their dernier resort to shake his Majesty's constancy. . . . In the meantime, I am the more at ease, because I know you stand ready upon the place to lay hold upon all opportunities, and are diligently upon your watch *ne ecclesia aliquid detrimenti capiat.*"[3]

---

[1] *Suth.*, 204.

[2] *Duppa*, August 7, 1660.

[3] *Tann.* 49, f. 17. A curious letter in *Clar.* 73, ff. 182–4, hints at another reason for the hesitation at Court. Dated August 23, 1660, London, it is addressed in code to Abbot Montague and unsigned; it was evidently obtained and deciphered by a government agent. It is sufficiently interesting to quote at length: "I have received yours of the 25th. . . . The King bids me tell you that as far as he durst he still opposed the establishment of bishops, and appearing too much in so important a business, his friends begin to be unsatisfied; of late he

At the same time Mr. Secretary Nicholas was confiding to Joseph Kent in Tuscany:

"Since [his Majesty's return] things proceed daily to put on a better face; only those that concern the Church, finding much opposition and some small lets from the dregs of that unhappy rumour which first discomposed them, fall not so easily into their old channel."[1]

To de Vic in Brussels he wrote in the same vein: "All things continue quiet, notwithstanding some troublesome Presbyterians who by their froward practices endeavour the contrary."[2]

Meanwhile, the struggle continued in the House. Between August 14 and 20, the Commons' *Journal* records that debate on the Bill for Settling Ministers was postponed four times. Prynne, however, mentions that both on August 15 and 17 motions were made by Anglican members that "all ministers ordained by presbyters during our late troubles should be put from their livings and ministry, unless they were re-ordained by bishops within one month", a step which he held to be

hath expressed more warmth, not upon that score though, I imagine; but at an offer that Scotland absolutely refused to admit of an Episcopacy and that England begins to speak the same language, for London is drawing up a [petition] to resettle the honour of Presbytery—wherefore he thought it absolutely necessary to countenance bishops that they might the better take heart to oppose that other faction that would presently overrun all, and prove a much greater obstacle to his designs than any settled hated Episcopacy. In the meantime Lord Hyde is reconciling all differences, and hath written a treaty which the King calls a strange potage. If you can propose any expedient that, embroiling Episcopacy, will not advance Presbytery, it will be most welcome. . . . Your letters come very safe, and without the least suspicion of being opened."

A second letter of August 27 (*Ibid.*, f. 196) reads in part:

"I have little to add to my last more than that the King of England is in great expectation of the Earl of St. Albans' return, and then we shall know the Cardinal's final resolution as to the match, and this subject I find the King would rather have you enlarge upon, than that of the bishops, for money and a wife are the things he most wants—as for Episcopacy, you know it is his religion to promote it; but you need not fear he will proceed so rashly as to venture his Crowns."

But for the reference in the second letter, one would suppose the writer's meaning to be that the King, as a Roman Catholic, was reluctant to favour the interest of either of the two parties; *hinc illae lachrymae*. But an unsupported letter of this kind is too slight a basis for theorizing, and in any case, raises more questions than it answers. The "petition" referred to is described in *Suth.*, 168.

[1] P.R.O., S.P. 98/4, f. 81.   [2] P.R.O., S.P. 77/33, f. 117.

in line with "the extravagancies of some of our reviving English bishops and Episcopal clergymen".[1] The proposal was twice defeated, and on August 21 the same fate befell another anti-Presbyterian amendment to the bill. An attempt was made to exclude from livings any minister who had "by preaching, printing, or writing, declared his judgment to be against the administering of the Sacrament of the Lord's Supper to such persons as were not scandalous or ignorant, or [who] constantly refused to administer the sacrament". The vote on this motion was 148 noes to 127 yeas.[2] On August 22 and 23, the Presbyterians carried two motions of their own, the first restricting clergy to one benefice, and the second exempting incumbents from further payment of "fifths" to sequestered ministers.[3] On the day following, one concession was made to Anglican feeling; the commissioners, already empowered to debar sequestered ministers from their old livings if they were adjudged "scandalous", were now authorized to deprive existing incumbents on the same grounds.[4] This was a matter of obvious justice, and involved no principle at issue.

The same day's session saw the beginning of a crisis. The bill in its present form plainly jeopardized many of the appointments made by the Chancellor and his Laudian advisers. To avoid this serious reverse, the Anglicans offered a proviso "that nothing in this Act shall extend to the prejudice of any person or persons who by letters patent under the Great Seal dated before August 26, 1660, is entitled to any ecclesiastical dignity, benefice, or promotion".[5] Debate on the matter was postponed until the following Monday, and when the House met on that day [August 27], the Puritans were ready. A petition was offered "of divers distressed ministers, whose livings, though in dead places, are granted away under the Broad Seal of England . . . with a catalogue of the names of ministers dispossessed". A motion followed "that it be referred to a committee to examine and state matter of fact touching

[1] W. Prynne, *The Unbishoping of Timothy and Titus*, Second Edition (Lond. 1660), pp. 27 ff.

[2] J.C., viii, 129; cf. letter of Robert Young, August 23, in *Trevelyan Papers* (Camden Soc., Lond. 1872), iii, 287–8. The refusal of Presbyterian ministers to admit to the Lord's Supper those who would not accept their discipline was almost universal during the Interregnum; cf. W. A. Shaw, *History of the English Church*, 1640–60 (London. 1900), ii, 142–51.

[3] J.C., viii, 130–1.

[4] *Ibid.*, 136.

[5] *Ibid.*, 136.

what presentations have been passed under the Great Seal where the former incumbents are dead". When the House divided, the Presbyterians carried their proposal by the large majority of 140 to 86. The next day it was announced that a sub-committee had waited on the Chancellor to learn the facts, and had obtained from him lists of the appointments.[1]

The Presbyterian counter-offensive in the Commons had now become a grave threat to the government's whole policy, and Hyde himself stood in serious danger of Parliamentary censure. Herbert Thorndike wrote to Sancroft at this time:

"Manifest it is, that the Presbyterian party is at present at a great height in the Commons House—though manifestly far the less—not only by their diligence and assiduity, and the negligence and absence of the opposites, but also by their importunity and audacity, which must be counted still zeal for God's cause."[2]

There is good evidence that, in the face of the deterioration of the political situation, the government now made three decisions designed to safeguard its plans for the Church settlement. Parliament should be speedily adjourned; the re-establishment of the bishops undertaken during the recess; and, both to disarm the aroused Puritan feeling and to recapture the initiative for the Crown, negotiations with the Presbyterians be resumed. We may conveniently consider these steps in order.

On August 31 both Houses received a message from the King ordering a recess from September 8 to November 6, on the ground that many members desired "leave to go into the country". The real reasons for the move are clear; as many observers noted, the Anglican party in the

---

[1] *Ibid.*, 140. Hyde's explanation to the Committee is not recorded; but on September 13, he referred to the matter in his speech before Parliament: "His Majesty hath never denied his confirmation to any man in possession who hath asked it; and they have all had the effect of it, except such who, upon examination and inquiry, appeared not worthy of it; and such who, though they are pardoned, cannot yet think themselves worthy to be preferred." *P.H.E.*, iv, 127–8.

[2] *Harl.* 3784, f. 2. Thorndike wrote in the same letter: "The worst thing they [i.e. the Presbyterians in the House] have prevailed for, is that Presbyterian Orders shall qualify for livings whose incumbents are dead," and added, "this [was] fomented from the Court", without stating grounds for the belief. In view of all the evidence to the contrary, I can only judge that he was mistaken. Thorndike was too much of an individualist to be of the inner circle of Laudians, or *persona grata* at Court (cf. T. A. Lacey, *Herbert Thorndike*, Lond. 1929, 110 ff), and was therefore not likely to have firsthand information of Court policy.

Commons had been increasingly weakened by the defection of "the young men" to less onerous duties, and the pressure of the Presbyterians as a majority party had reached an alarming pitch. The new French Ambassador, the Marquis de Ruvigny, himself a Huguenot, summed up the situation concisely in a report to Mazarin:

"Ce Parlement se sépare pour deux mois, et le Roy d'Angleterre l'a ordonné; parceque touts les jeunes gens, et la plus part des plus affectionnés, s'en estoient allés chez eux pour la moisson et pour leur plaisir. On a craint que ce qui restoit ne fût pas bien assuré."[1]

The Commons received the King's message somewhat warily, and after conference with the Lords, sent reply that "there is in the said message a word of ambiguity, namely 'recess', and they desire to know what his Majesty intends therein, whether he intends it by way of adjournment or prorogation. If by prorogation, then it will determine this session, and all bills must be to begin again. But if it be by way of adjournment, then all things remain as they are." They left no doubt that they desired the latter course.[2] On the following Monday, the Chancellor reported that the King consented to an adjournment, but made the significant admission that his Majesty "in his own thoughts [was] inclineable to a session [i.e. prorogation]".[3]

Work on the Bill for Ministers was now pressed to a conclusion, and it was finally passed in the Commons on September 4.[4] On the matter of the Crown's presentations to benefices, an agreement was reached with the King, whom the Presbyterians had no wish to alienate. Appointments already made were accepted, and the House then thanked his Majesty for his promise "to take care of and provide for such ministers as are worthy and every way qualified for the work of the ministry, and shall be removed from their livings by virtue of this Act", pointedly desiring that he should proceed to take such action forthwith.[5] But there was no lessening of resistance to the Church party. On the same day a proviso was offered exempting from any benefit under the Act any minister "that shall either by preaching or printing, or any other way, openly declare his opinion against the public Liturgy and the

[1] P.R.O., *Transcripts* 3/107, f. 278.
[2] J.C., viii, 145; J.L., xi, 151-2.
[3] J.C., viii, 147; cf. the King's speech on September 13, P.H.E., iv, 122-3.
[4] J.C., viii, 149.
[5] Ibid., viii, 147, 149.

N

Episcopal government of the Church of England till it be abolished by a legal authority"; this did not survive its first reading.[1] Another amendment was offered "to refuse any benefit of the Bill to any who by the power of the Major Generals and by force of arms, and not by authority of Parliament or the Committee of Plundered Ministers, have intruded themselves". The fact that this also was voted down suggests that the Presbyterian and Independent members were now co-operating. Finally, on the last day of debate it was resolved that no one should be disqualified from holding office in the universities, regardless of college statutes, "for want of Episcopal ordination".[2]

The determination of the Lower House to obtain enactment of the measure is evidenced by frequent requests to the Lords on succeeding days to expedite their consideration of it, culminating in a curt message that "the counties are much unquiet by reason of so many good ministers having been ejected; therefore they desire their Lordships would please to give despatch to the Bill."[3] Because of the press of business, adjournment was delayed with the King's consent until September 13. On the tenth the Lords passed the Bill with considerable alterations; these were considered in the Commons on the same day, and for the most part rejected. The great desire for the passage of the Act, however, as well as the pressure of time, had their effect, and in a conference between the two Houses, the Lords secured several modifications. Most important were the omission of the provisions about "scandalous" ministers; extension of the period during which Crown appointments were confirmed; and the safeguarding of the patronage rights of the peers.[4] The government felt in no position to refuse the Bill, and at the adjournment on the 13th, it was presented by the Speaker and signed by Charles. Hyde's comment in his speech to Parliament was tinged with acerbity:

"His Majesty well knows that by this Act he hath gratified and obliged many worthy and pious men, who have contributed much to his Restoration . . . but he is not sure that he may not likewise have gratified some, who did neither contribute to his coming in, nor are yet glad that he is in: how comes it else to pass that he receives such frequent information of seditious sermons in the city and in the country—they talk of introducing popery, of evil counsellors, and such other old calumnies."[5]

---

[1] *Ibid.*, viii, 147.   [2] *Ibid.*, viii, 149, 151.
[3] *J.L.*, xi, 162.   [4] *Ibid.*, xi, 165; *J.C.*, viii, 161.
[5] *P.H.E.*, iv, 128.

The Bill which thus became law was to some extent a compromise measure, made more so than it would otherwise have been by the insistence of the Anglican House of Lords. But it must be understood as a Presbyterian measure making certain concessions to Anglicans, rather than *vice versa*. Four categories of Anglicans were admitted to livings: (1) The sequestered clergy. (2) Those previously presented by lawful patrons, but refused admission by the Triers "without lawful cause". (3) Those presented under the Great Seal between May 1 and September 9, 1660. (4) Those lately presented by patrons who were peers. All incumbents not affected by these displacements were confirmed in their livings. There were only two political disqualifications—clergy who had petitioned for the trial of the late King, and those who had opposed the restoration of Charles II were excepted. The measure of Anglican defeat is exhibited by the fact that there was only one ground of religious disability—public denial of the rightfulness of infant baptism. Thus, only Anabaptists were legally excluded from functioning as ministers of the Establishment; ordination by "any ecclesiastical persons" was expressly declared a sufficient qualification for office. The new Act made a serious breach in the Laudian position that the old laws still prevailed, and, if maintained, would drastically modify the traditional requirements of the Church of England.[1]

At approximately the same date that the decision to adjourn Parlia-

---

[1] I have not touched upon the subject of church lands as treated in the Convention Parliament, since the discussions on the bills mentioned sufficiently illustrate the character of the religious struggle. The disposition of these lands, however, was one more occasion of conflict between the two parties; cf. debate on the Bill of Sales, July 11, *P.H.E.*, iv, 80–2. On the day before adjournment the matter was entrusted to a Commission for Church Lands (*J.C.*, viii, 167), and eventually the lands were returned to the Church, with proviso that purchasers be allowed liberal terms of lease. Cf. Duppa's lament: "The King by his letters having commanded that not only old tenancy should be regarded, but that new purchasers should be satisfied, hath so tied our hands, that though I infinitely long after it, I cannot find anything so free to me as to dispose of it where I please." (*Duppa*, Dec. 12, 1660.)

The religious tension was also felt in other matters in Parliament. Cf. Thorndike's observation on August 17: "Above all there is speech of disbanding part of the Army, when a Bill for pole money shall be completed and levied to pay them off—which is therefore studiously delayed by those that would continue troubles. For when it is done, things may come to something of the face which they are like to receive." (*Harl.* 3784, f. 2.) The context shows that he is speaking of religious "troubles".

ment was made, the government set in motion the legal procedure for the translation and election of bishops—with the purpose, it may safely be presumed, of re-establishing episcopacy before the House of Commons was again in session. Bishop Duppa's disconsolate letter of August 11 is evidence that at that moment there was no indication that the step was imminent. But on Monday, August 27, he wrote to his friend Isham: "His Majesty's favour hath this week made [Richmond] part of my diocese, by translating me to Winchester," and a passing comment directs our attention to the significance of the date: "We grow weary of Parliament, for we find that our best friends have left us, and gone after their pleasures, and the Tartar only is left in the bottom."[1] The step once decided on, matters proceeded apace, though for the time being in relative secrecy.[2] Duppa was formally nominated to Winchester on August 28, Juxon to Canterbury on September 2, Frewen to York on the same day.[3] On September 10, two days after the scheduled adjournment of Parliament, the chapter at Winchester held its election; Juxon's took place at Canterbury on the thirteenth, the actual day of adjournment. The appointment of new prelates began with the nomination of Morley to the see of Worcester on September 20, Sheldon to London on the twenty-first, and Griffith to St. Asaph on the twenty-second.[4] The approximation of dates is *prima facie* evidence of the correlation between the two government decisions, but a letter written by Secretary Nicholas on September 13 is equally suggestive.

"The Parliament not being able to finish the several businesses they had in hand," he informed Sir Henry Bennet in Spain, "were forced to defer their adjournment till this day. . . . The great confusion of business being now over, the further settlement of the Church is thought of, and in order to it, his Majesty

[1] *Duppa*, Aug. 27, 1660.

[2] The first notice of the step I can discover, outside the inner circle of party leaders, is Salvetti's despatch of September 7: "Sabato la Majestà del Re col consenso del suo consiglio privato nominò due archivescovi, [etc.]. . . . Tutti gli altri saranno anche tra poco nominati et in consequenza non ostante la oppositione de Presbiteriani, la Religion Protestante sarà stabilita in questo Regno col maggiore splendore et libertà che mai." (*Add.* 27, 962 P., f. 712.) ("On Saturday the King's Majesty with the consent of his Privy Council appointed two archbishops. . . . All the others will soon be appointed and consequently, notwithstanding the opposition of the Presbyterians, the Protestant Religion will be established in this Kingdom with greater splendour and liberty than ever.") The news was reported in *Merc. Pub.* of Sept. 20 (No. 39, p. 601).

[3] *C.S.P.D., Addenda*, 1660–1685, 8, 10.   [4] *Ibid.*, 13.

hath now given order for making the Bishop of London Archbishop of Canterbury, the Bishop of Lichfield and Coventry Archbishop of York, the Bishop of Sarum Bishop of Winton, and divers other bishops are shortly to be also made and consecrated, notwithstanding the factious endeavours of some editious persons."[1]

It is noteworthy that Hyde in his speech before Parliament on that day declared his purpose "to acquaint you with some things his Majesty intends to do during this recess", and though he proceeded to a lengthy discussion of church affairs and of the King's plans regarding them, not a word was said of the design now well under way.[2]

The necessary preliminaries were completed in time for the first consecrations to take place on October 28, well before Parliament reconvened. Mr. Pepys, who had witnessed the ceremony of Frewen's translation on October 4, was not a little disparaging in his remarks on the public reception then accorded the prelates: "But, Lord! at their going out, how people did most of them look upon them as strange creatures, and few with any kind of love or respect."[3] Notwithstanding, the service later in the month was held with considerable éclat. In King Henry VII's Chapel in the Abbey, the Episcopate was conferred on Sheldon, Henchman, Morley, Sanderson, and Griffith; Duppa acted as chief consecrator, representing the Archbishop, and was assisted by Frewen, Wren, Warner, and King. Canon John Sudbury preached a sermon on the nature of episcopacy that must have confirmed Mr. Prynne's worst fears.[4] As the first consecration in the Church of England since the service in besieged Oxford sixteen years before, the scene was one to fire the imagination of worshippers, who must have recalled the long years of the Church's humiliation, when the future seemed a matter for despair. Now in rites symbolizing the renewal of a spiritual Mother loved and venerated as never before, a new generation of leaders was commissioned by men already figures from a distant and heroic past. Something of the emotion evoked on such an occasion breathes in Bishop Duppa's noble prayer:

"O Lord God, who out of Thine infinite mercy and goodness didst bring back the captivity of Sion, and in good part restore this then afflicted Church;

[1] P.R.O., *State Papers*, 94/44, f. 96.
[2] *P.H.E.*, iv, 127 ff.
[3] *Pepys*, i, 98.
[4] J. Sudbury, *Sermon preached at the Consecration of Gilbert Lord Bishop of London, etc.*, October 28, 1660, (Lond. 1660).

perfect, we beseech Thee, this Thy great deliverance. Hedge it about with Thy continual protection, with the custody of angels, with the duty of kings and princes, with the hearts and hands of nobles, and with the affections of all good people. Re-unite all our remaining divisions and reconcile our differences, that with one heart and voice we may praise Thee in Thy Holy Church; through Jesus Christ our Lord."

The service ended, the congregation proceeded to celebrations in more secular surroundings. At the Haberdashers' Hall, "the rest of the day was spent in a great feast . . . where dined all the bishops, and many doctors and clergymen who were of the bishops' judgment, and friends —many earls and lords—that were by the bishops invited; who had every man a ticket for this sumptuous feast!"[1] One may be permitted to hope that Mr. Pepys was also present. Seven more bishops were consecrated on December 2, and four on January 13; all the sees were then filled with the exception of Lichfield and Sodor and Man.

The character of the appointments is of interest, as presumably reflecting the real direction of government policy. Juxon, now old and feeble, had been for many years hopelessly out of touch with church affairs; but in the popular mind no man living could symbolize more effectively the old order which the Laudians sought to revive. For that reason, he was made a figurehead at Canterbury. It is instructive to read the pious effusions of *Mercurius Publicus* on the occasion of his translation:

"This day was a day of rejoicing to all that love that (whereof God is the author) Order in the Church. . . . Besides a great confluence of the orthodox clergy, many persons of honour and gentry gave God thanks for the mercy of this day; there being scarce a man whose heart was not touched with the sight of that holy Prelate, who is a person of such . . . apostolic virtues that God hath now shown He hath yet mercy left for the distressed Church of England. Consider . . . where, and in what times he was preserved; was made bishop of that great city when it was most giddy; kept the King's purse when necessities were deepest and clamours loudest; in highest places and greatest business, and yet universally beloved. . . . Remember his valiant piety at the death of Strafford and of Strafford's Master; and then you'll grant (what a martyred Sovereign sealed at his last breath) that this is the GOOD MAN, whom God and the King have now placed in the helm of the Church of England."[2]

This was a vivid recalling of the past not likely to soothe Puritan feelings. Brian Duppa had been the most active of the old bishops, and,

---

[1] *Merc. Pub.*, No. 44, p. 693; *Add.* 10, 116, f. 131.
[2] *Merc. Pub.*, No. 39, p. 601.

unlike most of his fellows, was *persona grata* at Court; his translation to Winchester caused no surprise. Frewen's appointment to York was a less obvious choice, for he was a man of little distinction, and so far as we know, had no special claim to favour. The choice, it may be noted, was considered 'strange' at the time.[1]

Without exception, the vacant bishoprics of importance were bestowed on leaders of the Laudian party. Sheldon went to London, Morley to Worcester, Cosin to Durham, Henchman to Salisbury, and Sanderson to Lincoln. Other appointments were of much the same pattern. Benjamin Laney was given the see of Peterborough, Brian Walton that of Chester, Gilbert Ironside Bristol, and Richard Sterne Carlisle. Exeter was offered to John Earle, and Gloucester to John Hacket;[2] on their refusal, the former see went to John Gauden, and the latter to William Nicholson. Gauden, as we have seen, was a leader of the moderate Episcopalians, and may have been appointed for that reason; he had also become a prolific Royalist pamphleteer in recent months, was a tireless place-hunter, and privately claimed authorship of the famed *Eikon Basilike*. Nicholson, on the other hand, was a thorough-going High Churchman. Nicholas Monk, brother of the General, and a peaceful conformist during the Interregnum, was nominated to Hereford in obvious compliment to the hero of the Restoration. The offer of bishoprics to the Puritans will be noticed later.[3] Sheldon seems to have had the principal part in the selection of the new bishops; Izaak Walton, who, as an intimate friend of Morley, had a reliable source of information, states: "Dr. Sheldon . . . was by his Majesty made a chief trustee to commend to him fit men to supply the then vacant bishoprics." Bishop Nicholson was under the same impression when he wrote to Sheldon in 1661: "In all gratitude I do acknowledge that next to his Majesty . . . your endeavours from an obscure man have advanced me to a place of honour and dignity."[4]

[1] *C.S.P.D*, *Addenda*, 1660–1670, 649; letter of Dr. Thomas Smith, Sept. 17, 1660.

[2] *Tann.* 48, f. 46; T. Plume, *Life of John Hacket* (Lond. 1865), 75. Carlisle was first offered to John Barwick, and Lichfield and Coventry to Dr. Richard Bayly (after it had been refused by Edmund Calamy); *Barwick*, 301; *Kenn.*, 272.

[3] Cf. pp. 193–4. Further Episcopal appointments in 1661–2 were Henry Ferne, Herbert Croft, John Hacket, Samuel Rutter, George Hall—all Laudians—and Seth Ward, a somewhat belated convert to the party.

[4] I. Walton, *Life of Dr. Sanderson* (Lond. 1678), 158–9; W. Nicholson, *Exposition of the Catechism* (Ed. Oxf. 1842), ix–x. Nicholson also adds his testimony

From the first, the Bishop of London exercised an unofficial primacy in the affairs of the Church, and as dean of the province acted in public functions for the ailing Archbishop. Even before the King's return he had been mentioned as the obvious successor to Laud if none of the old bishops was translated.[1] The intimate friend of Hyde and high in favour with the King, he was soon reputed to be a power at Court; second only to him in influence was the new Bishop of Worcester.

We come finally to the third link in the government's strategy— the re-opening of negotiations with the moderate Puritan clergy. It is a reasonable conjecture that this decision, like the other two, originated from the Parliamentary crisis at the end of August. It will be remembered that the House of Commons on July 20 had requested the King "to advise concerning matters of religion" with a number of divines, but for some weeks no action was taken. According to Baxter, he and his friends were suddenly notified that "the King would put all that he thought meet to grant us into the form of a Declaration", and that a preliminary draught would be submitted to them for comments. He gives no date, but implies that little or no time elapsed before the promised document was received on September 4.[2] At Parliament's adjournment on the thirteenth, Hyde announced the King's intention in the following words:

"What pains [his Majesty] hath taken to compose [religious differences], after several discourses with learned and pious men of different persuasions, you will shortly see by a declaration he will publish upon that occasion; by which you will see his great indulgence to those who can have any pretension from conscience to differ from their brethren."[3]

In view of the aggressiveness of the Presbyterian party in the House, and the further resentment which the re-establishment of bishops would undoubtedly occasion, it doubtless seemed wise to encourage the view that the church settlement was still an open question. The government certainly desired to take the religious question out of the

to the Royal favour enjoyed by Sheldon: ". . . the most excellent of princes shines upon you in so full a lustre, as if he hoped by you and those he hath chosen to assist you, to dispell all the clouds that have darkened the face of our Church these twenty years." But according to Burnet, Sheldon emphatically disclaimed responsibility for John Gauden's appointment. Cf. *Burnet*, i, 324.

[1] *Suth.*, 184.
[2] *Rel. Baxt.*, 259.
[3] *P.H.E.*, iv, 130.

reach of Parliament—witness Mr. Secretary's letter to Bennet on November 1: "Tuesday next the Parliament meets again, of which we may hope the better success, since the King hath removed the main bone of division, by taking into his own hand, and [by] his Declaration determining, the great point of church government." Similarly, Ruvigny had reported two weeks earlier: "Le Roy d'Angleterre m'a dit qu'il accommoderoit l'affaire des Eveques, des Presbitériens, et des Anabaptists avant l'Assemblée du Parlement."[1]

The draught of the Royal Declaration was eagerly examined by the Presbyterian divines; but though it set forth considerable modifications of the old Anglican system, they concluded "that it would not serve to heal our differences". A lengthy criticism was drawn up by Baxter, with a list of further concessions desired; of these, the most important were: (1) a definite promise that suffragan bishops should be appointed in the larger dioceses; (2) that bishops should not ordain or exercise disciplinary jurisdiction without the consent of the presbyters; (3) that Confirmation be administered "by the information and with the consent of" the parish minister; (4) that a more drastic revision be made of the Prayer Book than that indicated in the original draught, and that alternative forms of service be provided; (5) that kneeling at the Lord's Supper be made optional, and a more specific exemption from the other ceremonies provided. In addition, the King was requested to alter or omit a number of expressions in the Declaration which were found objectionable.[2]

Soon after, at the request of the Presbyterians, a conference was arranged between Baxter, Reynolds, and Calamy on one side, and Morley, Henchman, and Cosin on the other. "After a few roving discourses", records Baxter, "we parted without bringing them to any particular concessions for abatement, only their general talk was from the beginning as if they would do anything for peace which was fit to be done."[3] To a detached observer like Ruvigny, the prospect for agreement seemed small; he remarked to Mazarin on October 7,

---

[1] P.R.O., S.P. 94/44, f. 125; *Transcripts* 3/107, f. 293.
[2] *Rel. Baxt.*, 265, 275 ff. The relation of these alterations to the original draught is made clear in *D.A.U.*, 63 ff. The original also contained this clause, later omitted: "That such as have been ordained by Presbyters, be not required to renounce their ordination, or to be reordained, or denied institution and induction for want of ordination by bishops." *Ibid.*, 77.
[3] *Rel. Baxt.* 274.

"L'affaire des Evesques et des Presbitériens s'aigrit tous les jours; les uns ne veulent rien diminuer de leur jurisdiction, et les autres y désirent un tempérament."[1] On October 22, however, another and more formal meeting was summoned at Worcester House, Hyde's residence, and to this came the King himself, attended by some of the leading peers. The Laudians were present in force—Sheldon, Morley, Henchman, Cosin, Barwick, Hacket, Pierce, and Gunning, as well as John Gauden. The Presbyterians were represented by Reynolds, Calamy, Ashe, Wallis, Manton, Spurstowe, and Baxter. "The business of the day", states the Puritan leader, "was not to dispute, but as the Chancellor read over the Declaration, each party was to speak to what they disliked, and the King to determine how it should be, as liked himself."[2]

Accounts differ considerably as to what actually occurred. Baxter describes long and acrimonious arguments between the two parties, and says that he left the meeting "dejected, as being fully satisfied that the form of government in that Declaration would not be satisfactory". When the document was published three days later, actually embodying the terms insisted on by the Puritans, and now "such as any sober honest ministers might submit to", he "wondered at it, how it came to pass".[3] William Bates gives the same impression of a discordant meeting, relating that the Puritan proposals were "so displeasing", that Cosin protested:"If your Majesty grant this [i.e. that bishops exercise authority only with the consent of presbyters], you unbishop your bishops."[4] Anglican sources, however, present a curiously different version. ' There remains one thing, and but one, which we are not as yet agreed on," Morley wrote on October 23; "namely, whether such as are ordained by presbyters only should be instituted by the bishops."[5]

[1] P.R.O., *Transcripts* 3/107, f. 290.
[2] *Rel. Baxt.*, 276.
[3] *Ibid.*, i, 278–9. This was not a later impression on Baxter's part; cf. his letter to Hyde of November 1, 1660, quoted, *ibid.*, 282–3. The concessions added in the interim Baxter specifies as follows: "the word 'consent' put in about Confirmation and Sacrament, though not as to jurisdiction, and seeing the 'pastoral persuasive power' of governing left to all the ministers with the Rural Dean, and some more amendments". *Rel. Baxt.*, 279. In his letter to Hyde, he enlarged the last phrase to: "Subscription abated in the Universities, &c. . . . such happy concessions in the great point of parochial power and discipline, and in the liturgy and ceremonies, &c." *Ibid.*, 282.
[4] W. Bates, *Works* (Lond. 1723), "Funeral Sermon on Richard Baxter", p. 725.
[5] Quoted in *Lister*, iii, 110.

This point was not touched on in the Declaration issued. A letter despatched on the same day by Andrew Newport states: ' They are agreed in all matters, and very suddenly."[1] Hyde's account of the meeting is much the same: "Though it cannot be denied that either party did desire that somewhat might be put in, and somewhat left out, in neither of which they were gratified; yet it is most true, they were both well content with it [the Declaration], or seemed so."[2] In any event, the conference was brought to an abrupt end by an unexpected distraction. The young Duchess of York was reported to be in labour, and the King and Chancellor, prospective uncle and grandfather, hastily quitted the scene for a matter of more urgent interest.[3] Morley, Henchman, Calamy, and Reynolds were appointed "to put this agreement in such words as may best express the King's meaning" in order that the Declaration might be issued forthwith.[4]

Baxter recounts one episode in the course of this gathering that has received much notice. The Chancellor, referring to a petition for toleration from the Independents, desired the advice of the company on a final addition to the Declaration—that "others also be permitted to meet for religious worship, so be it, they do it not to the disturbance of the peace". No comment was forthcoming, until Baxter, suspecting he says, that "the liberty of the Papists" was aimed at, declared that he and his brethren distinguished "the tolerable parties from the intolerable"; for such as Papists and Socinians, "we cannot make their toleration our request". When Charles remarked that "there were laws enough against the Papists", Baxter countered that the question was "whether those laws should be executed on them, or not".[5] On the

---

[1] *Suth.*, 157.   [2] *Hyde II*, i, 481.   [3] *Suth.*, 157.

[4] *Lister*, iii, 110-11; Denzil Holles and Arthur Annesley, two Puritan laymen, were to act as assessors. Baxter declares: "His Majesty had all along told what he would have stand in the Declaration, and he named four divines to determine of any words in the alteration, if there were any difference; . . . if they disagreed, that [Annesley] and [Holles] should decide it." (*Rel. Baxt.*, 277-8.) My own surmise as to the discrepancy in the reports is that Anglican policy at this juncture required the publication of a document which should satisfy the Puritans; the conference was interrupted before the point of agreement was reached, and that Morley and Henchman, with Hyde's approval, afterwards added the alterations necessary for their purpose.

[5] *Rel. Baxt.*, 277. For the petition of the Independent Ministers mentioned by Hyde, cf. *Clar.* 73, f. 314. Salvetti had already informed the Florentine government on July 13, 1660, that the Presbyterians on the Monday preceding had laid before the King a petition against the Roman Catholics. The King,

basis of this interchange, the theory has been elaborated that the real aim of Charles throughout this period was to establish universal toleration, and that this opposition of the Puritan spokesman aroused his angry resentment against the whole party. Actual evidence of the King's views at this date is so slight that the theory is no more than an hypothesis. In the early months there is no ground for supposing that the King was not in accord with his Chancellor's religious policy; if his views were other than Hyde's prior to the passing of the Act of Uniformity, the fact was certainly not apparent to contemporaries. In the absence of evidence to the contrary, we can only assume that the policy followed by the government during 1660–2 was in fact designed by the Chancellor, and assented to by the King.[1]

"His Majesty's Declaration to all his loving subjects concerning Ecclesiastical Affairs" appeared on October 25, and was carefully studied. In it the King asserted that "we . . . have so far complied with . . . the distemper of the time, as to be contented with the exercise of our religion in our own chapel, according to the constant practice and laws established, without enjoining that practice, and the observation of those laws in the churches of the kingdom". The "present jealousies" had caused him to defer his intention of calling a synod, but "the im-

---

he wrote, showed some anger, and replied to them: "La carità e il megliore segno di religione et la fedeltà di buoni sudditi; l'una et altra ho sperimentato nelli cattolici et perciò io non veggo ragione de molestarli se viveranno pacificamente et conforme alle mie leggi." ("Charity is the best token of religion and loyalty of good subjects; both have I tested in the Catholics and hence I see no reason to molest them provided they live peacefully and in conformity with my laws.") With this reply, declares Salvetti, the Presbyterians were much dissatisfied. *Add.* 27, 962 P, ff. 688, 689. Cf. also f. 690.

[1] Corroboration is given this view by the fact that representatives of the French government in London were finally and reluctantly driven to the conclusion that the King at this time was entirely guided by Hyde in all matters of policy. "Que [M. de Ruvigny] sache bien", wrote Bartet to Mazarin on October 29, 1660, "la part essentielle que M. le Chancelier a à toutes les résolutions d'Estat qui se prennent; elle est telle que M. d'Aubigny, qui est dans son amitié, quoyqu'il ne soit pas dans sa confiance pour le gouvernement des affaires publiques, m'a dit que de toutes celles qu'il a entreprises depuis la restablissement du Roy d'Angleterre, soit publiques ou particulières, il n'en a manqué pas une. Et cela est une vérité si bien établie, qu'elle est ici connue de tout le monde. . . ." P.R.O., *Transcripts* 3/108, ff. 309–12. The whole letter is of great interest; cf. an even more detailed analysis of the relations between the King and Hyde, *Transcripts* 3/109, f. 37.

patience . . . in many for some speedy determination in these matters" had moved him "to give some determination ourself to the matters in difference, until such a synod may be called as may . . . give us such further assistance . . . as is necessary". The significant concessions to the Presbyterians were as follows. Suffragan bishops were to be appointed in every diocese, "sufficient for the due performance of their work". No bishop should ordain or pronounce ecclesiastical censure "without the advice or assistance of the presbyters". To provide an advisory council, the cathedral chapters were associated with an equal number of presbyters elected from the diocese by their fellows to assist in any important exercise of episcopal jurisdiction. Confirmation was to be duly administered "by the information and with the consent of the minister of the place", and in admission of persons to the Lord's Supper large scope was allowed for the exercise of the cherished "discipline". Alterations in the Prayer Book would be considered by a commission of divines "of both persuasions" which the King promised to appoint; in the meantime, no one was to be penalized for failing to use the Book. The question of ceremonies was likewise referred to a national synod, to be "duly called after a little time". For the present, all the disputed practices were made optional. Nor were the oaths of subscription or canonical obedience to be required for ordination or institution into livings; assent was to be made only to the Articles of Religion dealing with doctrine.[1] Such concessions as these had never before been offered by the Church of England to dissident Puritans, and it is small wonder that they were received by moderate men of that party with "humble and grateful acknowledgement". But if one reads the document with the question in mind, are the decisions set forth as final or merely *ad interim*?—no answer is possible. The Declaration defines its own intent with masterful ambiguity—to give some determination to matters in difference until a synod be called to give such further assistance as is necessary.

Among dissenters as a whole, the King's pronouncement had a mixed reception. At a meeting of the Presbyterian ministers of the capital, it was apparent that the more strict of that party could make no terms at all with episcopacy, and despite Baxter's pleadings, "some remained unsatisfied to the end".[2] Even those who joined in an address of thanks to the monarch requested two further concessions—"that re-

[1] *D.A.U.*, 63 ff.
[2] *Rel. Baxt.*, 284. "To me" in this edition is a misprint for "some".

ordination and the surplice in colleges may not be imposed"—thereby indicating a belief that the Declaration was not a final settlement. Ruvigny believed that the moderate views of Baxter and Calamy were not shared by most Presbyterians. He had reported to Mazarin on October 22:

"Il y a eu aujoud'hui une assemblée d'évesques et de Presbitériens chez M. le Chancelier Hyde: on ne doute point de l'ajustement présent, mais il y a à craindre que le grand corps [des Presbitériens] n'estant entièrement satisfait et ayant une grande inclination de brouiller, n'accuse bientost leurs Commissaires de les avoir trahis, et d'avoir esté gagnés par des bénéfices."[1]

The Independents saw no grounds for content in the limited indulgence now proposed, and their feeling of angry resentment against the Puritan leaders was merely increased.

"The Independents and Anabaptists", declares the historian Ralph, relying on an unnamed contemporary source, "were aggrieved by the King's Declaration . . . which contained a comprehension for the Presbyterians, and an exclusion for them. . . . Both were filled, says our Authority, with resentment and fury . . . to see the Presbyterians, who (they thought) had been as deep in rebellion as themselves, confirmed in the possession of what they had got in the iniquity of the late times. They clamoured in all places against the difference which had been made between them."[2]

The substance of this report is admitted by Baxter.

"The chief of the Congregational party", he writes, "took it ill that we took not them with us in our treaty, and so did a few of the Presbyterian divines; all whom we so far passed by as not to invite them to our councils. . . [They] raised it as a common censure against us that if we had not been so forward to meet the bishops with the offer of so much at first . . . we had all had better terms, and standing off would have done more good." He learned sometime after that a damaging fact had been revealed—"the Lord Chancellor had told them that their liberty was motioned before, when the King's Declaration came out, and that we spake against it, even I by name."[3]

This indifference to Sectarian interests was to cost the Presbyterian party dearly in the approaching session of Parliament.

The Laudians, so far as can be observed, regarded the Declaration as a master-stroke of policy, well calculated to relieve the dangerous state of tension. Morley, whose earlier sentiments will be remembered,

[1] P.R.O., *Transcripts* 3/108, Nov. 1 (N.S.) (Folio unnumbered).
[2] *Ralph*, i, 52 ff.
[3] *Rel. Baxt.*, 379–80, 430.

wrote to the Presbyterian John Lauder in emphatic approval: "I hope [it] will give abundant satisfaction to the honest and peaceably-minded men of both parties, and make them cease to be parties any longer, but unanimously to join against the common enemy the Papists."[1] Sir Edward Nicholas, most unbending of churchmen, wrote enthusiastically to de Vic in Brussels: "This week the King hath published his Declaration concerning Ecclesiastical Affairs, wherein his condescensions are so gracious that he hath now wholly taken away all ground of faction from the Presbyterians; and so moderated Episcopacy that 'tis supposed the most squeamish amongst them will not scruple it."[2] To Sir W. Curtius he gave an equally favourable account: "par sa douceur accoutumée et prudentes condescensions, [le Roy] a si bien gaigné les coeurs de son peuple que nous nous promettons dorénavant une tranquillité dans l'Eglise égale à celle de l'Etat."[3] Jeremy Taylor in a letter to Ormond praised the King's "most gracious concessions in his late excellent and princely Declaration".[4] Dr. Thomas Smith found it "welcome" and "highly acceptable", since "it cannot choose but give great satisfaction to all such as have anything of moderation in them".[5] These hosannas of the Prelatists might well have inspired Puritans to paraphrase a Royal witticism, and "confess it was their own fault they had been absent so long from the old Church, now hearing no one that did not protest he had ever wished for their return".

The Laudian party obviously valued the Declaration as a means of pacifying the Presbyterians, and of "taking away all ground of faction" from them; did they in any sense accept it as establishing the compromise they had so long and so resolutely opposed? Much indirect evidence on this point will emerge in the sequel, but we may notice now the attitude of John Gauden, who alone of the bishops-elect had advocated a settlement of this kind. Already during the summer he had affirmed: "His Majesty hath not a new Church to build, but an ancient and well-modelled one to restore."[6] In a work published in November, he wrote further:

"It is not to be doubted . . . that his Majesty's design in that indulgent Declaration was not to show any disaffection or disesteem . . . toward the ancient and

---

[1] Lister, iii, 111. [2] P.R.O., S.P. 77/33, f. 129.
[3] P.R.O., S.P. 29/21, f. 32. [4] Carte 45, f. 38.
[5] P.R.O., S.P. 29/21, f. 20.
[6] J. Gauden, Analusis, the True Sense and Solution of the Covenant (Lond. 1660), 22.

excellent Liturgy of the Church of England . . . but this temporary condescension was only in order to compose at present the minds of all his good subjects to some calm and Christian temper, until such further expedients might be applied . . . as should . . . wholly remove the uncomfortable dissensions of his loyal subjects of the Church of England in so great a concern as that is of religion."[1]

Another moderate churchman, Richard Henchman, writing on November 7, expressed the same judgment:

"His most excellent Majesty . . . sweetly and prudently indulged some forward and peevish children by his late seasonable Declaration concerning Ecclesiastical Affairs, that so (if possible) he may compose the spirits, and allay the rigidness of some violent tempers, till a learned and pious Synod can be convened to determine matters."[2]

It is not likely that Sheldon, Morley, and Cosin took a more literal view of the document than these liberal churchmen.

Opinion on the matter in the more informed circles in the capital is reflected in the despatches of foreign representatives. The Count of Nassau informed the States General on November 2: "From the enclosed Declaration your High Mightinesses will see the interim agreement which has been accomplished between the Prelatists and the Presbyterians, until the time when a National Synod shall be convoked to decide differences."[3] The Venetian Ambassador, writing the same day, pointedly connected the affair with the re-establishment of bishops:

"His Majesty having appointed bishops to fill up the vacant sees . . . they are steadily resuming authority in their dioceses." The consecrations on October 28 are then referred to. "As there are great disputes about this between Presbyterians and Episcopalians, a proclamation has come out prepared by the Council before the Court left, granting liberty of conscience to all these sectaries until a synod is convoked, which they intend to summon soon, in which they will discuss and establish many points of religion which are now controversial."[4]

Salvetti's despatch to Florence is similar:

"Il Re ha publicato . . . la sua dichiarazione toccante la religione che deve professarsi in questi Regni, nella quale per il presente conceda libertà di conscienza a tutte le sette di religione, dichiarando che nessuno sarà molestato per conto de Religione, pur che viva conforme alle leggi del Regno et non dia

---

[1] J. Gauden, *Considerations touching the Liturgy* (Lond. 1660), preface, n.p.
[2] R. Henchman, *A Peace Offering in the Temple* (Lond. 1660), preface, n.p.
[3] *Add.* 17, 677 X, f. 580.
[4] *C.S.P.V.*, 1659–61, 214–15.

scandolo. . . . Dichiara anco che intende fra poco di convocare un sinodo nazion-
ale . . . per il quale sinodo deve essere stabilita la forma di religione che deve
hora generalmente professarsi in questa Nazione, sotto pene che saranno dichi-
arate per un atto de Parlamento, che deve esser passato per il detto effetto."[1]

The Frenchman Bartet, as we shall see, was even less inclined to take
the terms of settlement *au pied de la lettre*.[2]

What reliance did the Presbyterians themselves place on the King's
assurances? Shortly before the Worcester House meeting, a seeming
gage of good faith had been given them in the offer of bishoprics to
Baxter, Calamy, and Reynolds.[3] There is no evidence for establishing
the real motive of the government in making this gesture; its significance can only be judged in the light of one's interpretation of Anglican
policy as a whole. Baxter makes clear that Morley and other Laudian
leaders were well aware of what was planned, and evidenced no displeasure.[4] If Hyde merely designed the strategy discussed with Morley
in the spring—"the taking off of the leading men amongst them by preferring of them"—undoubtedly it might still be used to good effect.
Baxter describes the reaction of his party to rumours of the offer:

"They wished that none of us should be bishops, yet they said Dr. Reynolds
and Mr. Baxter, being known to be for moderate Episcopacy, their acceptance
would be less scandalous. But if Mr. Calamy should accept it, who had preached,

[1] *Add.* 27, 962 P, f. 736. "The King hath published . . . his proclamation
touching the religion to be professed in these Kingdoms, wherein for the present
he granteth liberty of conscience to all sects of religion, declaring that none shall
be molested by reason of his Religion, providing he live in conformity with
the laws of the Kingdom and give no cause for scandal. . . . He declareth too his
intention of speedily convoking a national synod . . . by means of which synod
is to be established the form of religion to be professed in this Nation, under
such penalties as will be set forth in an Act of Parliament to be passed to the said
effect."

[2] Letter quoted on p. 198, *infra*.

[3] According to Baxter, he and the others were first approached unofficially,
but after the appearance of the Declaration, an offer was made to him personally
by the Chancellor. Baxter was to have the see of Hereford, Calamy of Lichfield
and Coventry, and Reynolds of Norwich. Manton was offered the Deanery of
Rochester, Bates of Lichfield, and Bowles of York. *Rel. Baxt.*, 281 ff. There is
some evidence that the see of Carlisle was offered to Dr. Richard Gilpin, another well-known Puritan divine. Cf. the Prefatory Memoir by A. B. Grosart
in his edition of R. Gilpin, *Daemonologia Sacra* (1867), xxxii. All eventually
declined except Reynolds.

[4] *Rel. Baxt.*, 274.

O

and written, and done so much against it . . . never Presbyterian would be trusted for his sake; so that the clamour was very loud against his acceptance of it: and Mr. Matthew Newcomen, his brother-in-law, wrote to me earnestly to dissuade him, and many more."[1]

Preferment would unquestionably have diminished the influence of these leaders; as Baxter aptly remarked to Hyde: "Men will question all my argumentations and persuasives, when they see me in the dignity which I plead for."[2] The government may well have reasoned that the sacrifice of a few of the sees to Puritans would be a small price for the further disruption of that party. Some words of Hyde in his memoirs certainly support this interpretation of the offer. Speaking of "the unhappy policy of making concessions to the dissenters", he remarks:

"If some few, how signal soever (which often deceives us) are separated and divided from the herd upon reasonable overtures, and secret rewards which make the overtures look the more reasonable; they are but so many single men, and have no more credit and authority (whatever they have had) with their companions, than if they had never known them, rather less."[3]

In any case, the affair of the bishoprics clearly reveals the misgivings of the Presbyterians in regard to the permanence of the settlement put forward. Baxter cites one of his chief reasons for declining the see of Hereford: "I feared that this Declaration was but for a present use, and that shortly it would be revoked or nullified."[4] The uncertain legal status of a Royal proclamation gave ground for uneasiness; a Presbyterian tract admitted to the world: "We ingenuously confess, that his Majesty's Declaration as it cannot make an obliging law, so it cannot dissolve the obligation of it [i.e. of the existing law]."[5] This feeling of insecurity led to a move which the Church party had not foreseen. The Puritans determined to press their advantage in Parliament, and force the enactment of the Declaration into law. Baxter challenged the Lord

---

[1] Ibid., 281. It is significant that within a year of his consecration, Puritans were reviling Reynolds as an "apostate"; cf. Math., 193-4.

[2] Rel. Baxt., 282.

[3] Hyde II, ii, 121.

[4] Rel. Baxt., 281. Baxter's final judgment of the Declaration's purpose is worth recording. In the situation in which the Anglicans found themselves, he says, "it was necessary that moderate things should be proposed and promised; and no way was so fit as by a Declaration, which being no law is a temporary thing, giving place to laws." Ibid., 287.

[5] H[enry] D[awbeny], A Sober and Temperate Discourse concerning the Interest of Words in Prayer (Lond. 1661), 60.

Chancellor, as an evidence of good faith, to lend his support; soon "Mr. Calamy and some other ministers [were] endeavouring with those they had interest in . . . to try if the Parliament would pass the King's Declaration into a law; and sometimes they had some hope from the Lord Chancellor and others."[1]

Accordingly, when the House reconvened on November 6 the matter was immediately broached, and the administration faced the disagreeable fact that all its efforts to remove the church settlement from the sphere of Parliament had been in vain. Thomas Gower expressed the indignation of most Anglicans when he wrote to a friend on November 17:

"The Parliament endeavours to put whatever the King offers or is about into an Act that their power may the least go along with the King's, to which purpose the Declaration at Breda, and that concerning church government are turning into Acts to oblige his Majesty to whatever he hath offered when circumstances of time, occasions, ceremonies, emergencies, and indeed necessity gave him reason to offer more than there was reason to expect."[2]

On the opening day, the Presbyterians in the House acted with considerable adroitness, offering a motion to return thanks to the King for his Declaration, and at the same time to prepare a Bill "for the making the same effectual". The embarrassment of churchmen was only too plain. The first part of the motion was accepted *nemine contradicente*; and Anglicans were then in the awkward position of explaining why the settlement so gratefully acknowledged should not be enacted by an approving Parliament. We may sympathize with their dilemma—to oppose legalizing the King's decision was virtually to impugn the Royal good faith, while to acquiesce was to assent to such a settlement of the Church as they had never dreamed of in the years of adversity. The protests were fumbling. Mr. Barton was against "making a law as yet, because the Declaration referred to a synod". Mr. Allen's advice was "not to do it too suddenly". Sir Thomas Meres spoke heatedly "against making any act at all"; what of the synod? Sir John Masham could only insist that he was "against taking it now into consideration". The Presbyterians were unmoved by such quibbling; Prynne proposed that a committee bring in a Bill, and "it was voted accordingly".[3]

[1] *Rel. Baxt.*, 384.
[2] *Suth.*, 195; the date given is October 17, but this is an obvious slip of the pen.
[3] *J.C.*, viii, 176; *P.H.E.*, iv, 141–2.

In the weeks following, the committee's report was several times postponed, and on November 22 the House was informed of the King's intention to dissolve Parliament on December 20. This decision, in Professor Feiling's opinion, may have been influenced by the revival of the religious conflict.[1] It was certainly a blow to the Puritans, who now based their hopes on the strong position they had achieved in the present assembly. Thomas Gower had commented on November 8: "The Presbyterian makes his advantage of all, and for aught I can see intends to make the Parliament long-lived by tediousness in settling the King's revenue," adding ominously: "Every day gives new light as well as discourse." Two weeks later he reported:

"Since the King declared that he would dissolve the Parliament, some of the old Presbyterians assembled and were drawing up reasons why the King should only adjourn and not dissolve, there being so much business on foot that it cannot in so short time be despatched . . . but upon better consideration, I heard, not an hour since, they have let it alone. They of late build much upon the Chancellor's favour, I hope without ground, though not without appearance; that party carrying all places and profits."[2]

On November 28 occurred the first reading of the Bill "for making the King's Declaration touching Ecclesiastical Affairs effectual".[3] It is apparent that on this occasion the Anglican party was prepared for the struggle. The House was full, and the boldness of the speeches attacking the Bill suggests that complete confidence now prevailed as to the government's wishes. Sir Alan Brodrick moved at once that the Bill be laid aside, in view of the King's intention to call a new Parliament and a Synod. Sir Clement Throckmorton declared bluntly that the Bill permitted "too great a toleration", and made the bishops "no more than *vox et praeterea nihil*". Meres agreed that it was a boon to all Papists and other heretics, and "would wholly remove all conformity in the Church". A Presbyterian retorted indignantly that "the King had taken much time and deliberation to consider it well before he published his Declaration", and then a Secretary of State, William Morrice, rose to reply. Morrice's role of providing a liaison between the Court and House of Commons is evident from a cursory study of the

[1] *Feil.*, 129.
[2] *Suth.*, 196; cf. p. 200.
[3] *J.C.*, viii, 194. L. F. Brown points out (*op. cit.*, 60–1) that consideration of this bill was blocked until the question of the King's revenue was settled the previous day.

Journals, and few could doubt that day that he spoke unofficially for the government.[1] Bland and deprecating, he was well stocked with useful metaphors: "The same man who was sick might be cured with a medicine at one time which would not help at another . . . some things are seasonable now which were not so at another." Indeed, "sometimes a wound would heal of itself if you applied nothing to it . . .". He opined that "time would rather do that good they desired than . . . to have [it] enforced by a Bill". The Bill should be laid aside.

The speeches that followed have an element of unconscious humour. Sir Solomon Swale was *for* the Declaration but *against* the Bill. "Since the government of the Church was despised," he lamented, "how were they fallen into confusion!" Puritans may have wondered how this charge could touch one document and not the other, but Sir Solomon moved happily on to a well-tried position; he desired "that the laws established might suffice". Sir John Masham made the illuminating suggestion that they were confronted with "an excellent Declaration metamorphosed into a very ugly Bill", and instructed the Puritans that "the King's intention was for a settlement of religion amongst us— which surely this Bill did thwart!" The virtues of the Declaration served only to magnify the horrors of the Bill. Mr. Prynne was finally move to outraged protest: "What a wonder it would be, after they had given the King thanks, to throw out the Bill!" The Anglicans, however, were not to be diverted by so obvious a red herring, and Mr. Thurland went on composedly, "it was very disputable whether such an excellent Declaration would make an excellent law"; indeed, he thought not, giving as it did "so great a toleration and endeavouring to lessen the Liturgy". Sir Heneage Finch, a law officer of the Crown, firmly stated his belief that the King desired no such bill. One Presbyterian interjected with a certain simplicity that "the Bill would not grate the bishops at all, because they were with the King at the framing the Declaration". This digression was properly ignored. At last, an old friend of George Morley, Sir John Maynard, brought this extraordinary debate to a conclusion. He intimated that an adverse vote on the Bill itself would be both tactless and regrettable, "because the King's Declaration on which the Bill was based was so pleasing to everyone". But since the measure proposed "gave too great a liberty", it must go no further; he moved "to put the question whether it should be read the second time".[2]

[1] Cf. W. Bates, *op. cit.,* 725; *Ralph,* i, 25.   [2] *P.H.E.,* iv, 152–4.

This was undoubtedly the crucial moment in the history of the church settlement. The size of the vote, one of the largest of the entire session, indicates how vital the issue was felt to be by both parties, and we may be certain that the truant Anglican squires had been marshalled back to their duties. Out of 340 votes cast, a majority of 183 opposed a second reading of the Bill. The Anglican margin of victory—26 votes— was thus extremely small, and the narrowness of the decision is further emphasized by Gower's information that some of the Independent members unexpectedly voted with the majority. "[The Bill] induced the greatest dispute of any yet", he wrote the next day, "and with much vehemency; but was thrown out. . . . The Presbyter strove as for life, and which you will wonder at, some of the old Commonwealth Party joined with the Cavaliers."[1] The Puritans had paid a bitter price for their careless disdain of the Sectarians. "John [Presbyter] is very angry," remarked Andrew Newport.[2] It was in fact the death-blow to Presbyterian hopes. Their failure to retain control of their last stronghold, the House of Commons, left them, as Andrew Marvell observed, "henceforth [to] rely only upon his Majesty's goodness".[3] But they had at least compelled the Anglicans to declare their real sentiments, and to admit openly that the Declaration "so pleasing to everyone" had commended itself to the Church party only as a temporary expedient of policy. Evidence that the Anglican laymen in Parliament were not more Royalist than the King and his ministers is given by Sir Edward Nicholas. The Secretary's gratification over the King's "gracious condescensions" has been noted; now he wrote to Bennet: "The Bill that was with great zeal brought into the House of Commons for passing the King's late Declaration . . . into an Act was last week happily thrown out, and now lies quashed with the violent passions of its promoters." To Sir Henry de Vic he expressed himself in similar fashion.[4] But the most illuminating report is that of the Frenchman Bartet, written to Cardinal Mazarin on November 30: "La . . Chambre Basse vouloit réduire en loy la dernière Déclaration du Roy touchant le faict de la Religion. Sa Majesté l'a empesché par ses amis, parce qu'il n'auroit jamais pu changer la loy, et qu'il fait estat de changer la Déclaration quand il le jugera à propos pour le bien de ses affaires."[5]

[1] *Suth.*, 196.   [2] *Ibid.*, 158.
[3] A. Marvell, *Works* (1875), ii, 26.
[4] P.R.O., S.P. 94/44, f. 142; S.P. 77/33, f. 136.
[5] P.R.O., *Transcripts* 3/108, Dec. 10 (N.S.) (unnumbered folio).

THE RECAPTURE OF THE ESTABLISHMENT

In the light of all the evidence, it is difficult not to believe that the truth of the matter is here summed up.

The Anglican victory in Parliament undoubtedly gave joyful re-assurance to the government, hitherto beset by grave hesitation as to how far it dared press its religious programme. Addressing Parliament at its dissolution on December 24, Hyde threw discretion to the winds when he reached the subject of religion, and revealed his true sentiments with astonishing boldness. His tone was almost that of an exultant *Nunc Dimittis* as he rejoiced over the Church's revival, so long the object of his plans and labours:

"We may tell those who still contrive the ruin of the Church, the best, and the best Reformed Church in the Christian world—reformed by that authority and with those circumstances a Reformation ought to be made—that God would not so miraculously have snatched this Church as a brand out of the fire, would not have raised it from the grave, after He had suffered it to be buried so many years by the boisterous hands of profane and sacrilegious persons under its own rubbish—to expose it again to the same rapine, reproach, and impiety. That Church which delights itself in being called Catholic was never so near expira-tion, never had such a resurrection! That so small a pittance of meal and oil should be sufficient to preserve and nourish the poor widow and her family so long, is very little more miraculous than that such a number of pious, learned, and very aged bishops should so many years be preserved, in such wonderful straits and oppressions, until they should plentifully provide for their own succession. . . . That that Church should again appear above the waters, God be again served in that Church and served as He ought to be, and that there should be some revenue left to support and encourage those who serve Him . . . may make us all piously believe that God Almighty would not have been at the expense and charge of such a deliverance, but in the behalf of a Church very acceptable to Him, and which shall continue to the end of the world, and against which the gates of Hell shall not be able to prevail!"[1]

Many of the members, as they hastened homeward at the Christmas season, must have felt something of the same triumph, and shared the happy content which Sir Justinian Isham made known to his Lordship of Winchester: "Now [am I] all overweighed with the public blessing of seeing our King and Religion I may now say re-restored!"[2]

If now for a time church affairs receded from the foreground of the political scene, re-establishment of the old system proceeded steadily at the parish level, and to this subject we must turn. In September of 1660 a publication appeared entitled *Acts of Parliament now in force establishing the Religion of the Church of England*, containing the text of

[1] *P.H.E.*, iv, 176. [2] *Duppa*, Dec., 1660.

the Elizabethan Acts of Uniformity and of Reformation of Disorders, with two relevant proclamations of James I and Charles I. The preface was significantly worded:

"Forasmuch as the reformed Religion of the Church of England settled by several Acts of Parliament . . . hath for divers years last past, by the schisms of Scottish innovation and Fanatic separation been most shamefully neglected and contemned; so as the legality thereof doth seem to be forgotten, and forasmuch as it oft cometh to pass that many a religious and well-minded person is not conversant with the laws of this land . . . it hath been thought expedient to reprint certain Acts of Parliament to that purpose, remaining still in full force and power, to the intent that everyone may be informed both of the duties and penalties by the Law enjoined."

Here was a bold proclamation of the Laudian position, and it was soon apparent that such views were not held merely by legalistic clerics. The seventeenth-century Justices of the Peace were officials managing all the details of local government, recruited from the local gentry, and possessed of wide powers. Since their appointment was in the hands of the Crown, many Cavalier squires like Isham had been quickly placed in office during the early months of the Restoration by a government desperately anxious to secure firm control of the country at large. The staunch churchmanship of these new incumbents had been overlooked when a Presbyterian majority placed administration of the new Act for Settling Ministers in the hands of the Justices. As Trevelyan remarks: "The Presbyterians did not know that in re-establishing squire-archy they were setting up a persecuting Anglicanism; for the squires whom they remembered had been haters of parsons and bishops."[1] They were speedily made aware of the silent revolution accomplished by the Laudian clergy in the years of leanness. On all sides, complaints of arbitrary action and minor persecution were heard from sorely harassed Puritan ministers. The tale of grievance which John Chester, rector of Witherley in Leicestershire, wrote to Col. Edward Harley on October 10 is typical:

". . . During our last continuance at Bucknall five or six Justices met according to the Act in order to settling or displacing ministers, and there was a warrant sent to my house in my absence to summon me in before them. . . . On October 9 they got one or two poor labouring men and one inn-keeper to swear that I had been against infant baptism and the King. . . . I was not permitted to hear my accusers examined and sworn, but after they had done I was called in and the oaths read to me, but I was not suffered to speak in my own defence, nor

[1] G. M. Trevelyan, *England under the Stuarts* (Ed. 1947), 278.

any for me. . . . Nor would the Justices suffer any cross question to be put to my adversaries. . . . Nor could I obtain a copy of the depositions against me, nor time to reply to them, for St. Paul had fairer usage from heathen than I from Christian magistrates. But 'tis not my case alone but the condition of divers able men, and I am informed they will out everyone that were settled by the former powers."[1]

Royalist magistrates were not inclined to take their tone from the studied moderation of the Court, with its promises of toleration and concession. Isham wrote to Duppa: "Here (as I doubt in many other places) some peevish spirits there are who will ever have (I can hardly say so well as) a chapel wherever God hath a church, and yet who expect a large dispensation from his Majesty's goodness and lenity. . . . Truly to speak my sense, where there is roughness to be used, as sometimes it must be, I think it may be better expressed by those who act under his authority than by himself."[2]

This ruthless determination to enforce the old Church laws without further delay was to be seen on all sides. The grand jury at the Winchester Assizes on September 13 gave thanks to his Majesty somewhat prematurely "for his care in the settling religion according to the government of the Church established in the reign of Elizabeth, James I, and Charles I, which they unanimously declared was by Episcopacy". Furthermore, according to the same report, "at the *nisi prius* bar was not one sequestered minister that brought his action against the intruder, but had a verdict from him with costs".[3] Beginning in September, prosecutions were undertaken against ministers in many parts of the country who refused to read the Prayer Book. Mr. A. G. Matthews notes cases tried during the autumn months, both in the Assizes and Quarter Sessions, in counties as widely scattered as Shropshire, Sussex, Staffordshire, Nottinghamshire, Cheshire, Middlesex, Devon, and Northumberland.[4] Other signs of nonconformity might also bring wrath upon the offender. John Crodacot of St. Saviour's, Southwark, was summoned before the Council on December 28, for not observing Christmas Day; and again, five days later, for having drawn "seditious conclusions against the doctrine and discipline of the Church of England". Matthew Mead, for inveighing against "sinful compliance with ceremonies" in a sermon in Stepney

[1] *Matt., C.R.,* 113–14.
[2] *Duppa,* Sept., 1660.
[3] *Merc. Pub.,* No. 38, p. 607.
[4] *Matt., C.R.,* I, 42, 143, 193, 203, 221, 315, 420.

Parish Church on September 16, found himself charged with sedition.[1] Only the convinced Puritan was likely to face this kind of pressure with equanimity, and we may surmise that the return to Anglican customs now proceeded apace.[2]

The indulgence granted in these matters by the King's Declaration of October 25 seems hardly to have dampened the churchly zeal of the Justices. Mr. Peniston Whalley, J.P. for Nottinghamshire, has left to posterity his remarkable gloss on that proclamation in his speech to the grand jury at the Quarter Sessions of the county, April 22, 1661:

". . . But some may object against the Penal Laws, his Majesty's gracious Declaration—which indeed ought to be held sacred with all good subjects— wherein he promises to remit what penalty they shall run into, *as far as concerns his Majesty*; the performance of which were impiety to suspect.

"In answer to which it must be taken notice of, that that Declaration is grounded upon the letter from Breda, which relates to 'tender consciences'; only it rests now therefore to examine what may be meant by 'tender consciences'. . . . If . . . only the conscience of the Nonconformist [be meant], yet I hope none is so uncharitable as to think his Majesty . . . meant that all Justices of the Peace should be forsworn, a thing they must be necessitated to, if, according to the best of their understanding, they do not put the Penal Laws into execution; and I know no reason why a man that will not break the King's laws may not be suspected to have as good a conscience as they that will not keep them. . . .

"There cannot be a more acceptable piece of service done to his Majesty, notwithstanding his Declaration, than putting the statute about Common Prayer in execution, for the opposers being a generation of men that seldom or never believe well of any, especially of Kings if they be of a contrary judgment, it may be presumed that they doubt much of the Royal performance, which indeed they cannot be assured of till trial: and how can they have that, till they be prevented, and lie under the punishment of the law, the remitting of which will make them love the King, by which in time they may prove good subjects—but that is scarce to be hoped for, because next to a miracle."

Mr. Whalley, it may be seen, in his flair for legal sophistry and abusive irony anticipated the great Jeffreys. His instructions to the jury, however, were blunt and to the point:

[1] *Ibid.*, 143, 347.
[2] For example, cf. the case of William Annand, who had been a conformist rector during the Interregnum. In the Epistle Dedicatory of *Panem quotidianum* (Lond. 1661), addressed "to the Lords, Knights, and Gentlemen, and Justices of the Peace of the County of Bedford", he wrote: "Receiving a command from your honours met together in your quarter sessions House in Bedford, October 2 [1660], for the public reading of the Liturgy of the Church of England", he had hastened to dust off his Prayer Book, and obey their instruction.

"You are to present all ministers, as well beneficed as others, that do not constantly upon every Sunday or other opportunity of religious worship, read the Liturgy of the Church established by law, commonly called the Common Prayer.

"You are likewise to enquire of all persons that have wittingly heard or been present at any other form of Common Prayer, administration of the Sacraments, making of ministers, or other rites, than what are expressed in the same book, or which are contrary to the Statute of 2 and 3 Elizabeth 6.1."[1]

Whatever may be thought of Mr. Whalley's reasoning on the intent of the Declaration, there can be no doubt that such views were widely prevalent. A Puritan tract published in April, 1661, declared:

"Many of us in several places have no benefit by his Majesty's Declaration, while some eager lawyers and justices still give the statutes in charge against us, and cause us to be indicted and prosecuted, openly telling the people that the King's Declaration is no law."[2]

Baxter implies that the indulgence proclaimed afforded Puritans some measure of protection during the year following, but adds:

"Some men were so violent at a distance in the country that they indicted ministers at the Assizes and Sessions notwithstanding the Declaration, taking it for no suspension of the Law. . . . The brethren complained to us from all parts, and thought it our duty, who had procured the Declaration, to procure the execution of it."[3]

Appeal was made by these harassed pastors not only to the prominent divines in London, but to influential patrons at Court. William Blagrave, for example, wrote from Woburn in Bedfordshire to the Earl of Bedford's chaplain on January 20:

"Both Justice and constables proceed still in their persecution of me. This morning, being the Lord's Day, the constable Dyer came to my house with a warrant from the Justice, viz. Mr. Wingate, just before church time, to tell me that they are to indict me if I will not read the Common Prayer Book. Next Thursday is the petty session held at Tuddington, where they will present the indictment. . . . I pray be pleased to move my Lord further in this business, that he will be pleased to interpose and prevail by his interest here, or else I am like to suffer very much."[4]

[1] P. Whalley, *The Civil Rights and Conveniencies of Episcopacy delivered in a charge to the Grand Jury, at the General Quarter Sessions held at Nottingham, April 22, 1661* (Lond. 1661), 11–12, as filed in P.R.O., S.P. 29/34, f. 79. It is interesting that a copy of this tract with an identical title page in the Cambridge University Library does not contain the first passage quoted.

[2] H[enry] D[awbeny], *A Sober and Temperate Discourse* (Lond. 1661), 61.

[3] *Rel. Baxt.*, 286.   [4] *Rawl*, 109, f. 12.

The Duke of Albemarle and the Earl of Manchester assisted John Shaw of Hull to present his complaint at Court.[1] Baxter and his fellows were put to "many ungrateful addresses" to the King and Lord Chancellor in behalf of the sufferers, but "when we petitioned for them, they were commonly delivered".[2] Hyde indeed seems to have maintained courteous and kindly relations with the moderate Puritan leaders, and when particular cases of persecution were brought to his attention, always intervened.[3] But apart from the Chancellor's obliging attitude in personal relations, there is no evidence that the government endeavoured to restrain the militant activity of the magistrates. On the contrary, Kennett hints that the campaign was secretly encouraged. "In September and October [1660]," he notes, "the Justices of Peace by instructions sent to them had met in their several divisions to give out orders for restoring the use and public reading of the Liturgy of the Church of England according to the laws in being."[4] Some such action is certainly suggested by the outbreak of prosecutions throughout England in those two months.

There was one factor which undoubtedly disposed Royalist leaders to favour the vigilant searching out of nonconformity. The deep-seated fear of plotting and uprisings tended to operate in a vicious circle. The government instinctively assumed that danger to the monarchy lay chiefly in the fanaticism of the sectarians; as the unrest of these groups would obviously be increased as the Laudian policy was put into effect, the tendency became irresistible to interpret religious discontent as political conspiracy. And as time went on, the Presbyterians were more and more given place besides the "Fanatics and Sectaries" in the categories of the official mind. So acute was the government's uneasiness that when some evidence of plotting did come to light from time to time, the relief at having something concrete to deal with was noticeable.

"The Fanatic party . . . have been designing their revenge in the nation's disturbance", wrote Nicholas to Bennet on December 7, 1660, "and though

[1] *Yorkshire Diaries and Autobiographies*, "Life of Mr. John Shaw" (Surtees Soc., Lond. 1877), 155.
[2] *Rel. Baxt.*, 286.
[3] For example, Manton was successful in securing his intervention in the case of John James of Ilsley, Berks. (Palmer, *History of Nonconformists*, i, 206–7), and Baxter enlisted his help for Adam Martindale (A. Martindale, *Life*, Chetham Soc. 1845, 153).   [4] *Kenn.*, 308; cf. also *Ralph*, i, 25, 32.

we had very early notice of it, yet it was suffered on purpose to ripen so perfectly, till it burst out within these few days by several discoveries from persons engaged in it; by which means not only the plot and its consequences are broke, but the King, God willing, will have a full occasion of cutting off by present justice and a continued severity that obstinate unreconcileable sect of men."[1]

The inevitable consequence of this state of mind was mournfully observed by the Puritan Edwards, writing a few weeks later:

"Great stir there is here about the Plot . . . whether there was any such plot at all I cannot learn. However, there is abundance troubled upon that account, as well here as in other places; many ministers and others that lived in good fashion formerly are reduced to hardship already."[2]

Venner's Insurrection, which occurred in London on January 6, seemed to the nervous Royalists much more than the desperate enterprise of a handful of Fifth Monarchist fanatics. Nicholas sent an account to Lord Winchelsea:

"I doubt not but your Lordship hath heard . . . some part of what hath occurred here most remarkable since your departure. The Fanatics had laid their plot throughout the kingdom, and actually broke forth in this city into some weak attempts to embroil affairs; but by the unanimous vigilance and activity of the whole nation having been frustrated, they are discouraged, we hope, from any further designs, and we at present (thanks be to God) enjoy a perfect quiet, for the preservation whereof his Majesty hath set forth a proclamation forbidding all private meetings and assemblies of the Fanatics and Sectaries."[3]

The proclamation in question was issued on January 10, though some move of this sort had been under consideration four days before the uprising took place.[4] By it, all meetings of "Anabaptists, Quakers, and Fifth Monarchy men, or some such like appellation" held "under pretence of worshipping God", were forbidden outside parochial churches or chapels.[5] An almost hysterical wave of alarm swept over the nation,

---

[1] P.R.O., S.P. 94/44, f. 149.

[2] P.R.O., S.P. 29/24, f. 43. Even the mild Sanderson shows signs of the same fever. On December 31, 1660, he wrote: "With what boldness some of the said [Presbyterian] ministers do in their ordinary Prayers and Sermons openly asperse the King and his government? and with what cunning other some of them do covertly and glancingly inject suspicions into the minds and thoughts of their credulous auditors concerning the same?" Preface to J. Ussher, *The Power communicated by God to the Prince* (Lond. 1661).

[3] P.R.O., S.P. 97/17, f. 180.

[4] *C.S.P.D.*, 1660–61, 515; Stoughton, 131.

[5] *D.A.U.*, 104–6.

and though the refusal of Quakers to take the oath of allegiance made them the chief sufferers, suspicion was widespread that all nonconformists were somehow implicated. Thomas Lamplugh, a future Archbishop of York, wrote to a friend: "I hear of a proclamation, but have not yet seen it, to suppress all meetings. I hope Presbyterians are included, for they have meetings too; I need not tell you what temper they are of."[1] As before, those in authority felt considerable relief at the opportunity for active measures, and Nicholas notified de Vic with much satisfaction: "Our late disturbances are now very well over, and have been so far of use to his Majesty's service, as that they have left the kingdom in a better posture to secure its own peace and happiness than they found it." On February 15 he had further news to send: "Writs are now preparing for the calling of a future Parliament, to meet on the 8th of May next."[2]

Meanwhile, the newly appointed bishops were beginning the difficult task of restoring Anglican discipline in their dioceses. Gauden wrote to the Chancellor from Exeter on January 25:

"What inconveniences I contend with, the bearer [Dr. Chancellor of Exeter] can witness, not only as to my private affairs, but also as to the public, for want of ecclesiastical authority and an uniform way of Liturgy; to which all sober people and ministers are much devoted; and many Presbyterians have expressed their readiness to conform."[3]

It was on the occasion of this bishop's enthronement that *Mercurius Publicus* had remarked cheerfully: "Ere long things will be better, for where the Bishop and Sheriff go hand in hand, God's service, the King's honour, and the People's happiness will be certain consequents."[4] Certainly the bishops seem to have felt no more hampered than the magistrates by the spirit of the King's Declaration. The Anglican cause was visibly in the ascendant, the support of the local gentry was enthusiastically given, and clergy who were content to move with the times were now clear as to which way the movement would be. "The expectations of all conformable men are so raised," wrote Bishop Henchman from Salisbury in March, "that they think themselves despised if a curate's place be offered them."[5] In Worcester diocese, Richard Baxter was beginning to feel at firsthand the weight of episcopal authority, as Bishop Morley and Sir Ralph Clare took thought for the spiritual

[1] P.R.O., S.P. 29/28, f. 56.   [2] P.R.O., S.P. 77/33, ff. 145, 148.
[3] Clar. 74, f. 103.   [4] Merc. Pub., No. 54, p. 834.
                    [5] C.S.P.D., 1660–61, 546.

welfare of Kidderminster.[1] Everywhere the requirement of episcopal ordination was being pressed, and on March 8 Samuel Wilson wrote in distress to his friend Sancroft of Bishop Sanderson's refusal to institute him without this qualification:

"I conceive I cannot maintain the honour of my ministry, at least in these parts where I am known [i.e. Lincoln], and where I have been public preacher in the cathedral these ten years last past, and also laid hands on others in their ordination. . . . If no such indulgence can be granted, I must make a resignation of my presentation, and reduce myself to a private capacity."[2]

Another Puritan, George Sanderson, confessed: "When I was at London, by the advice of many reverend friends (especially Dr. Reynolds, the Bishop of Norwich, who. . . both directed and encouraged my address that way) I went to the Bishop of Galloway [Sydserf], and had Orders from him, without rigid (and indeed feared) impositions."[3] So indeed did many others. Sydserf's casual practice in this matter became a scandal to his episcopal brethren, though Bishop Skinner himself achieved something of a record for those times by performing 103 ordinations at once in Westminster Abbey.[4]

Especially in London was the bishop's activity bewailed; here Presbyterianism was at its strongest, and here it was confronted by a resolute and uncompromising will. Sheldon did not shrink from a trial of strength with the leaders of the opposition, many of them divines he had conferred with on equal terms at Worcester House. William Taylor was given notice of his imminent ejection from the living of St. Stephen's Coleman, when he could not bring himself to accept re-ordination.[5] Thomas Manton found it advisable to receive episcopal institution to St. Paul's, Covent Garden, and when his parishioners petitioned the bishop to "use his episcopal power that we may have divine service celebrated . . . with such rites as by the laws of the land hath been most laudably ordered", the harassed incumbent was induced to read the Prayer Book.[6] But when Dr. Bates, at St. Dunstan's

---

[1] Rel. Baxt., 300, 374 ff.
[2] Tann. 49, f. 143.
[3] Rawl. 52, f. 97.
[4] Burnet, i, 236; Lan., 986, f. 89. Matthews lists fourteen ordinations of Presbyterian ministers performed by Sydserf, beginning on December 13, 1660; cf. Matt., C.R., 453, et passim.
[5] P.R.O., S.P. 29/32, f. 97.
[6] Kenn., 358; Merc. Pub. (1661), No. 8, p. 127; P.R.O., S.P. 29/32, f. 109.

in the West, and Dr. Jacombe, at St. Martin's, Ludgate, received the
bishop's orders to use the Service Book, they were less compliant, and
pleaded the benefit of the King's Declaration. That excuse, however,
"would not satisfy" Sheldon, and he notified the two divines that he
would send deputies to read the service as required. Dr. Jacombe firmly
declared that he would maintain his right by law, and refuse to permit
such intrusion; but Dr. Bates endeavoured a compromise by arranging
to have certain parts of the Prayer Book used.[1] The parishioners of
St. Mildred Poultry petitioned to keep their minister Mr. Wills, who
was probably not in episcopal orders; whereupon Sheldon answered
roundly that he would be unworthy of his office, "if he knew not better
who were fit for them".[2] Here, as elsewhere, such pressure was not
without effect. A Londoner reported: "Some of our ministers have
conformed for fear of losing their places; but blessed be God, we have
many able men that do withstand them . . . although we hear that the
bishops are in hopes to dethrone them when the Parliament sits."[3]
Even Baxter thought it wise, before exercising his ministry in London, to
obtain a licence from the bishop, and take an oath not to preach against
the doctrine of the Church or the ceremonies established by law—
though some of his friends charged him with "an owning of prelatical
usurpation".[4]

This vigorous regimentation of the London churches was the immediate cause of an outburst which profoundly shocked and dismayed
the government. The writs for a new Parliament had been issued on
March 9, and ten days later one of the first elections was held in the
Guildhall of the capital. Here, as citizens gathered to choose four burgesses for the City, a tumultuous scene took place in passionate protest
against the revival of episcopacy. The cries of "No bishops! No bishops!" echoed to the rafters, vividly recalling the popular demonstra-
tions against the Church twenty years before. Royalist candidates were

[1] P.R.O., S.P. 29/32, f. 109.
[2] Ibid., f. 116.
[3] Ibid., f. 139.
[4] Rel. Baxt. 302. The Anglican tone was also high at Court; the list of Lent
preachers is like a roll-call of the Laudians (cf. Kenn. 368). The three sermons
which the King ordered to be printed furiously attack the Presbyterian party;
cf. B. Laney, Ld. Bishop of Peterborough, Sermon preached before his Majesty,
March 9, 1661, (Lond. 1662); P. Gunning, The Paschal or Lent Feast Apostolical
(Lond. 1662); J. Hacket, Sermon preached before the King on March 22, 1661 (Lond.
1661), especially pp. 13, 16, 21.

greeted with insults and hisses, and four "sober Presbyterians" were voted into office by a majority of five to one.[1] The sensation was enormous. One witness wrote to the Mayor of Coventry: "You cannot imagine what an astonishment it hath been: certainly great weal or woe."[2] Mr. Pepys recorded in his diary: "The great talk of the town is the strange election . . . men that, so far from being Episcopal, are thought to be Anabaptists . . . [were] chosen with a great deal of zeal, in spite of the other party that thought themselves so strong."[3] The meaning of the portent was only too plain to Royalists; Andrew Newport told Sir Richard Leveson, "The late [elections] of the City much surprise us, some being chosen there that could never before find credit amongst them, nor had now . . . but for their known and remarkable opposition to the bishops."[4] Most alarming of all was the news that all varieties of Nonconformists had united in common resentment against the government's religious policy to defeat the official candidates. The Presbyterians were as jubilant as the Anglicans were perturbed—"What influence the City's choice will have on the country's", wrote one of the former, "you may know better than myself. But I think that if so be it all the Fanatics . . . can agree together, as here they did, to choose any sober Presbyterians, it will do well." "The bishops' interest fell before the conjunctive interest of honest men," asserted another; "we all agreed unanimously, and carried all clearly and fully, so much that their party is exceedingly vexed, and swear the Devil united the Presbyterians, Independents, and Anabaptists."[5]

The government's reaction was immediate. Stephen Charlton reported on March 23:

"As many letters as possible of those that were written into the country to incite them to follow the example of London were sent to the Court so that the King might see what was written. . . . The King intends to draw up some more forces about the City to strengthen his own guard, as also to reserve the militia in all counties; this being very needful, seeing the Presbyterians, Independents, and Anabaptists are leagued together in the plottings—their pretence being, as they give out, to be only against the order of bishops."[6]

The numerous letters thus abstracted from the mails, still preserved among the State Papers, made plain to the King and Council that the

[1] P.R.O., S.P. 29/32, ff. 113, 125. [2] *Ibid.*, f. 125.
[3] *Pepys*, i, 141. [4] *Suth.*, 159.
[5] P.R.O., S.P. 29/32, ff. 125, 146. [6] *Suth.*, 170.

successful *coup* had been instigated and planned by the more violent nonconformist ministers of the City.

"Mr. Caryll and other eminent ministers held a fast, and prayed heartily, and God has heard them." . . . "Crofton, a subtle witty man, bitter against the bishops . . . prosecuted his argument last Lord's Day, and there were more people than could get into the church." . . . "All who oppose prelacy are mightily followed, as Dr. Seaman and others. Mr. Graffen had two thousand in the streets, who could not get into the Tantling Meeting House, to hear him bang the bishops, which theme he doth most exquisitely handle. . . ."[1]

—these were the revelations studied by Hyde and Nicholas. The consequence most dreaded was the possible effect on elections throughout the country. One citizen recorded a wish all too commonly expressed in other letters: "We hope the sense of this famous and populous city in all affairs of this nature will be precedential to the whole kingdom, that a happy composure of our difficulties and a well-grounded settlement may follow, in order . . . to the security of religion in its power and purity, and the establishment of our civil rights upon firm foundations."[2] Pepys had also observed: "It do make people to fear it may come to worse, by being an example to the country to do the same. And indeed the bishops are so high that very few do love them."[3] The government was fully alive to this possibility, and as usual saw the episode in the setting of a formidable conspiracy. An indication of the Chancellor's state of mind is given in a letter to the Earl of Middleton, Lord Commissioner of Scotland, on March 26:

". . . The mad people are not without hope of conjuring up some evil spirit in your country to countenance their seditious designs here, and I do assure you knowingly, that after they had made their election last week of four the worst men they could choose for the Parliament, they sent two expresses, the one for Scotland, the other for Ireland, to acquaint their friends with their success, and with their further designs."[4]

Within three days of the election Zachary Crofton was committed to the Tower "for his intemperate writings and rude reflexions on the

[1] The letters are summarized in *C.S.P.D.*, 1660–61, Nos. 83–147; these quotations are gathered in *Stoughton*, 170–3.
[2] P.R.O., S.P. 29/32, f. 126.
[3] *Pepys*, i, 141.
[4] *Clar.* 74, ff. 290 ff.

King and bishops",[1] but measures of repression on a wide scale were clearly inadvisable in the midst of a general election.

The demonstration in the Guildhall occurred on March 19. On March 25 the King issued his warrant summoning representatives of the Anglican and Presbyterian parties to meet "in the master's lodging in the Savoy" to undertake a revision of the Prayer Book, "for the giving satisfaction to tender consciences, and the restoring and continuance of peace and unity in the churches under our protection and government".[2] It is difficult not to believe that there was a causal connection between these two events. Five months had passed since the King had promised to convene a synod. "Being often with the Chancellor," says Baxter, "I humbly entreated him to hasten the finishing of that work [i.e. the calling of the synod]."[3] But by this time many despaired of the conference. A Londoner, Thomas Stone, wrote to his father on election day: "There was a report that there should be a conference betwixt some of the Episcopalians and some of the Presbyterian ministers about church government and Common Prayer, but it never came to any effect that I can yet hear of."[4] We may readily believe that the government saw in the revival of this plan a means of giving new hope to the Presbyterians and of easing the religious tension. In a situation calling for immediate action, in which high-handed measures might well aggravate the danger of Royalist defeat, the convoking of the synod was an obvious step. The nation was informed that the church settlement was still *sub judice*, and that the King was prepared to act on the promise made in his Declaration.

Within ten days, however, the crisis was past, and the moment of panic seen to have been without justification. The London election had been a political freak; from all parts of the country poured in news that Royalist and Anglican candidates had carried all before them. The Presbyterians were reduced to an impotent minority, variously estimated from forty to sixty members.[5] In reality, as Dr. Trevelyan observes: "The few divines and politicians who in 1660 represented the Presbyterian cause, were leaders without an army."[6] The young men who had saved the Anglican cause in the Convention Parliament had come back in force—"which being told the King, he replied that [their youth] was no great fault, for he would keep them till they got

[1] *Kenn.*, 397.   [2] *D.A.U.*, 107 ff.
[3] *Rel. Baxt.*, 303.   [4] P.R.O., S.P. 29/32, f. 144.
[5] *Feil.*, 106.   [6] G. M. Trevelyan, *op. cit.*, 279.

beards".[1] Anglican statesmen felt a thankful reassurance, and Hyde wrote to the Earl of Orrery on March 31:

"Notwithstanding the alarums which the ill and malicious election of the burgesses for the City gave us, and some horrible malicious and seditious attempts and designs of some of the Presbyterian clergy, who in the presbytery invited the congregations to ask all over again which they did in the year 1640, yet you will find that the elections are well made throughout the kingdom, and I am confident we shall have a very sober Parliament. . . . I pray use all your interest with your friends that they will appear most warm and solicitous to pull up those bitter roots from which rebellion might hereafter spring, that they will advance the King's lawful royal power, and increase his revenues, and that since all is forgotten that hath been ill done, they will not suffer the memory of it to be revived."[2]

The expressions used in the beginning of this letter are significant, for they mark a further stage in the evolution of the official attitude towards the Presbyterians. Those in authority had been severely frightened, and though the experience was transitory, the effects remained. At least in appearance, the Presbyterians had joined forces with the "factious sectaries" in opposition to the government; and in that company, in the eyes of officialdom, they were to remain. "All the subtle artifices of the factious presbyters and sectaries cannot make the people either to dislike anything the King doth or to approve any of their schismatic ways," wrote Nicholas to Winchelsea on May 2,[3] and such sentiments were henceforth a commonplace. This attitude had at least some parallel in the public reaction to the election—witness the tone of *The Lay Subject's Lamentations on London's Perverseness in the Malignant Choice of some Rotten Members on Tuesday, the 19th of March,* 1661:

> Oh horrid Monsters! What strange news is here,
> What factious Locusts thus in swarms appear
> At Guildhall Gate, where they do freely vote
> For such vile scabs, who soon would cut the throat
> Of Justice, and would have all idle sport
> In churches used; Nay, they a tennis court
> Would make it, if they could (by lot or fate)
> Obtain the pow'r to rule in Church or State.
>
> Then Anabaptists they aloud do cry
> With Jack Presbyter 'gainst Episcopy.

[1] Ibid., 279.   [2] Clar. 74, f. 297.
[3] Hist. MSS. Com., Finch MSS. (1913), i, 117.

All good subjects by the choice suppose
They did appoint that day for to undo
Themselves, their King, aye and their country too.
But stay, methinks, I hear blind Justice say,
The vote is carried a contrary way;
The Independent voices do appear;
The Anabaptist and the Presbyter,
Many, of whom we may malignants make
Because they never yielded yet to take
The oath of true allegiance to their King,
Which well their persons might the question bring
With their estates; how can the vote
Of such stand firm, who have no note
Of Loyalty? . . . [1]

What always remained the inner conviction of the Laudian clergy and laity was now again trumpeted in the market-place—Puritanism was as dangerous to the Crown as it was destructive of the Church.

The renewed confidence given to the government by the Royalist triumph at the polls had an immediate result in church affairs. At Whitehall on April 10, it was "ordered by his Majesty in Council that the Lord Chancellor do forthwith give warrants to the Clerk of the Crown to draw up writs of summons . . . for Convocations . . . of the respective provinces in usual form".[2] That a Parliament had been called "without a meeting of the clergy at the same time" was, as Dr. Peter Heylyn had reminded the Chancellor, an "innovation".[3] We have seen that writs for the new Parliament were in preparation as early as February 15; but almost two months passed before the decision was reached to summon Convocation. According to Heylyn, the reason for this delay was rumoured to be "the distrust which his Majesty hath in some of the [Presbyterian?] clergy, and the diffidence which the clergy have one of another . . . [being] divided into sides and factions . . . at this present time"; and, further, "that the commission now on foot for altering and explaining certain passages in the public Liturgy shall

---

[1] P.R.O., S.P. 29/32, f. 146; cf. also *A Dialogue between the two Giants in Guildhall, Colebrand and Brandamore, concerning the late Election* (Lond. 1661) and *The True Presbyterian without Disguise* (Lond. 1661), issued on April 6 and April 4 respectively.

[2] *Lan.* 957, f. 42.

[3] Quoted in J. Barnard, *Life of Dr. Peter Heylyn*, reprinted in P. Heylyn, *Ecclesia Restaurata* (ed. Camb. 1849), i, clxxviii ff.

either pass instead of a Convocation or else is thought to be neither compatible nor consistent with it".[1] What one would infer to have been the real reasons for delay may be stated somewhat differently. In February the condition of the dioceses was not yet sufficiently settled to guarantee a wholly Anglican assembly. Uncertainty as to the temper of the country about the church settlement was an additional ground for hesitation. Finally, the summoning of Convocation would have immediately raised the question of the bi-partisan Synod, and this, we suggest, the government was not over-anxious to do.[2]

Heylyn, who had devoted much time and effort to searching out the old register of Convocation, and providing information as to the customary procedure, was in a fever of impatience, and only two days after the writs were authorized, wrote to Sheldon:

"I had some speech with [the Lord Archbishop] yesterday ... and found him willing to defer it [i.e. Convocation] longer than may stand with the safety of the Church; for questionless, some busy members of the House of Commons will thrust themselves into concernments of religion, when they shall find no Convocation sitting to take care thereof; and when it was replied that the intimating of a Convocation might prevent that mischief, I answered that I thought it would rather hasten it, and make them the more earnest to make use of their time before the prey would be taken out of their mouths by the actual coming together of so many divines, from whom they could not honestly pretend to extort the cognizance of those matters which belong properly to their calling. . . . Though there hath been much time lost since Monday last since I despatched the writ to Mr. Wren, yet it may possibly be redeemed if such of the Lords the Bishops as are now in town would put themselves unto the charge of sending to the Deans and Archdeacons of their several churches messengers of diligence and trust, and that your Lordship would be pleased to do the like to such other bishops as are retired into the country."[3]

Sheldon was never chargeable with lack of diligence where the interests of the Church were at stake, nor was he likely to be overborne by

[1] *Ibid.*, clxxix ff., Heylyn's letter is frequently assumed to have been the immediate occasion of the summoning of Convocation. But it is surely naive to suppose that the question had not been carefully considered by churchmen of the known views of Hyde, Sheldon, and Morley; or that they required the encouragement of Dr. Heylyn to take action when the moment was ripe.

[2] Baxter's evidence supports the first of these surmises. Cf. *Rel. Baxt.*, 333: "Had it [the Convocation] been called when the King came in, the inferior clergy would have been against the Diocesan and Imposing way: but afterwards many hundreds were turned out that the old sequestered ministers might come in, etc."

[3] *Tann.* 49, f. 146.

Juxon on matters of policy.[1] Clerical elections were soon under way, and the Presbyterians looked on with helpless disapproval. They had stated their view of the matter in a tract published the previous November:

"The carriage and constitution of our Convocations or National Synods is such that it is impossible to proceed to a reformation . . . by that way. What are they for the main but meetings of the one Party, consisting of bishops, deans, archdeacons, and other dependents on Episcopacy, and pre-engaged persons? So that there is as little hope for us of reformation in points of government from them, as was for the Protestants' side of a fair decision of their controversies in the Council of Trent."[2]

Edward Bowles wrote from York to Richard Baxter in similar vein on May 11: "I hear you are chosen of the Convocation at London, a meeting so constituted as if it were appointed only for the use of cathedrals. I wish you may do good in it. We have also chosen here, or rather they, for few that are called Presbyterians concerned themselves in the election, and the choice was accordingly."[3] The election of Baxter and Calamy as proctors by the London clergy was indeed the only *contretemps* suffered by the Laudian party, and that by a majority of three votes. Sheldon, however, bethought himself of the bishop's ancient right to select two names from the four receiving most votes, and so, says Baxter, "we were excused". Thus, a solidly Anglican Convocation would meet side by side with the Cavalier Parliament.[4]

[1] Almost the only clue we have of the Archbishop's viewpoint during his brief and nominal primacy is provided by a Puritan, Robert Dodd, who reported that when Juxon ordained him in 1660, he remarked that "he was not for going high against the Presbyterians; but others were of another mind". Quoted in *Matt., C.R.*, 166.

[2] *Complaints concerning Corruptions and Grievances in Church Government, by certain peaceably affected Presbyters of the Church of England in the name of their brethren* (Lond. 1660), 10.

[3] Dr. Williams' Library, *Baxter MSS.* IV, f. 172.

[4] *Rel. Baxt.*, 333. Baxter says: "Those ministers . . . ordained without Diocesans were in many counties denied any voices in the election of clerks for the Convocation. By all which means, and by the scruples of abundance of ministers who thought it unlawful to have anything to do in the choosing of such a kind of assembly, the Diocesan party wholly carried it in the choice." *Ibid.*, 333.

It was at this time, May 7, that the Anglican clergy in London gave a more successful demonstration of strength by ousting the Puritans from their stronghold of Sion College, and installing Dr. Robert Pory as president Cf. *Register*

A further impressive witness to Anglican predominance was observed on April 23, when Charles II was crowned in the Abbey with
the traditional pageantry. Archbishop Juxon, clad "in a rich, ancient
cope", was able to preside despite his infirmity, though the Bishop of
London assumed his role during part of the service. George Morley
delivered the sermon, and the other prelates performed the particular
duties of their offices in the elaborate drama. The King solemnly pledged
his word to preserve to the Church all her canonical privileges, and to
be a protector and defender of the bishops. Then, given precedence
before the Lords temporal, the prelates advanced one by one to kiss the
cheek of anointed Majesty.[1] To the throngs who witnessed the scene, it
seemed to solemnize the re-establishment of the Church no less than
the restoration of the Monarchy. Robert Baillie wrote sorrowfully
from Edinburgh: "The ceremony was very solemn, as ever any coronation before; our only grief was, that the bishops in anointing, crowning
and all, had so deep a hand."[2]

Mr. Secretary Nicholas, however, was contemplating the future with
complete equanimity. "We have great hopes that this will prove a very
happy Parliament," he wrote cheerfully to Lord Winchelsea in Turkey,
"there being few Presbyterians of it!"[3]

By May, 1661, the re-establishment of the Church of England was,
in all essentials, virtually complete. Within a year of the Restoration,
the plan of Hyde and his clerical allies had been consummated; the
Church had recovered by degrees what could not be had at once. The
role of Parliament in this work had been merely negative—the refusal,
after a prolonged internal struggle, to take a hand in the church settlement. But this very act of renunciation was an achievement of the
Laudian party. Only one reverse had marked the gradual reconstruction of the old ecclesiastical order. The Act for Settling Ministers had
overridden traditional Anglican requirements, and given legal tenure
in the Establishment to clergy who would formerly have been de-

of Sion College, A, f. 206. Baxter remarks: "Some of the Presbyterians upon
a petty scruple absenting themselves, the Diocesan party carried it, and so
got the possession and rule of the college." Rel. Baxt., 334.

[1] E. Ashmole, Narrative of the Coronation, P.R.O., S.P. 29/34, f. 51; E. Walker, op. cit., 97, 106 ff.

[2] Baillie, iii, 470.

[3] Hist. MSS. Com., Finch MSS. (1913), i, p. 118.

barred. As one looks back, the course of events seems at first sight to have been governed by a confused interplay between an official policy of conciliation and an instinctive movement of religious reaction. But if the story has been correctly interpreted, it is possible to discern an intelligible plan of action. Three separate crises mark the stages of Anglican advance, and each was accompanied by a similar reaction on the part of the government.

In June, 1660, the Royalists assumed power, well aware that the Restoration was partly due to Presbyterian influence. The religious sentiment of the country was uncertain, and the stability of the new régime far from assured. Negotiations for a comprehensive church settlement were therefore undertaken with Presbyterian leaders. The proclamation against forcible ejections, the appointment of Presbyterian chaplains, and the King's non-committal attitude towards the bishops were meant to reassure the Puritan party. Under cover of this feigned conciliation, the government proceeded at once to the first stage of its programme—the filling of strategic posts in the Establishment with the Laudian clergy, and the restoring of cathedral chapters preparatory to the election of bishops.

In the late summer, a new crisis arose, due largely to the steady encroachment of Anglicans on the Establishment, and to the consequent alarm of the Puritans. When negligence on the part of churchmen enabled the Presbyterian party to gain control of the House of Commons, strenuous efforts were made to protect the Puritan incumbents, climaxing in a scarcely veiled attack on the Court's ecclesiastical appointments. The government resorted to the same strategy as before, first obtaining a breathing spell by adjourning Parliament. Friendly negotiations were resumed with the Puritans, and public announcement made of a satisfactory settlement; the Royal Declaration was designed both to soothe the Puritans, and forestall further action by Parliament in the matter of religion. Preferment was also offered to leaders of the opposition. But once again, these measures were a strategic diversion for a further Anglican advance. Before the end of the recess, the restoration of episcopacy along the old lines was well under way, and pressure was being exerted on the parish clergy to comply with the old laws. This time the Puritans were not so easily reassured, and in a crucial struggle in the House of Commons the Church party was barely able to frustrate their counter-measure—the attempt to give the Royal Declaration legal force.

By March, 1661, indignation at the steady restoration of Anglican discipline had again reached a boiling point in the capital. The Guildhall election was an alarming proof of religious discontent, and for the third time the government hastened to relieve the tension by a conciliatory gesture. Within a week the warrant for the Savoy Conference was being perused by Londoners. But as before, the tender of a compromise settlement was not allowed to delay the progress of re-establishment. No sooner had fear of danger subsided than the Convocations were summoned to assemble in traditional manner, and the administrative machinery of the Church of England was at last fully operative.

This, in bare outline, is the strategy by which the Laudian party and its sympathizers achieved success within so brief a period, and disposed of the formidable problem of Puritan opposition. Admittedly, certain episodes in the story, seen apart from the context of the long-term policy, may be made to bear a different interpretation. For example, conclusive evidence of Hyde's state of mind in October, 1660, is not available; since human policy is always subject to inconsistency and unpredictable deviations, some historians have believed that the Chancellor and even the Laudian clergy were at that moment genuinely desirous of a comprehensive church settlement. But a considerable body of indirect evidence suggests strongly that never at any time was the government prepared to give security for its generous proposals; the favour it showed the Puritans was mostly in words, whereas the Anglicans profited steadily by its deeds. On the one occasion when the Puritan party attempted to translate the paper settlement into reality, the hostile reaction of the government was all too apparent. Nor is there reasonable ground, during this period, for distinguishing between the policy of Hyde and that of the Laudian clergy. No evidence exists of divergence between the political and religious leaders of the Royalist party—to all appearances Hyde and Sheldon were in full accord.

Thus, before the Cavalier Parliament assembled, the main objective of the Laudian party had been secured. The Church of England had made good its claim to its old position in the restored Monarchy, and the Establishment had reverted to its original ownership. Anglicans were in possession of the house; it only remained to regulate the household.

CHAPTER V

THE EXODUS OF THE PRESBYTERIANS
MAY, 1661 TO AUGUST, 1662

WITH great ceremony the new Parliament was opened by the King on May 8. In contrast to the handful of Peers who had made up the House of Lords a year before, more than a hundred were now present in velvet and ermine when the monarch entered their chamber, and took his seat upon the throne. The loyal members of the House of Commons crowded in below the bar to hear his Majesty declare in graceful phrases: "You will not wonder that the memory of the great affection the whole kingdom showed to me this day twelve-month, made me desire to meet you again this day, when I dare swear, you are full of the same spirit, and that it will be lasting in you. I am sure, as I can be of anything that is to come, that you will all concur with me, and that I shall concur with you in all things which may advance the peace, plenty, and prosperity of the nation."[1] It was left to the Lord Chancellor, now Earl of Clarendon, to refer to ecclesiastical matters, and his scathing words made evident that the memory of the London election in March still rankled.

"There are a sort of patients that I must recommend to your utmost vigilance, utmost severity, and to no part of your lenity or indulgence. . . . These are the seditious preachers . . . who, by repeating the very expressions, and teaching the very doctrine they set on foot in the year 1640, sufficiently declare that they have no mind that twenty years should put an end to the miseries we have undergone. What good Christian can think without horror of these ministers, who by their function should be the messengers of peace, and are in their practice the only trumpets of war? . . . If you do not provide for the thorough quenching these firebrands; King, Lords, and Commons shall be their meanest subjects, and the whole kingdom kindled into one general flame."[2]

The harsh indictment fell on receptive ears, and was a harbinger of wrath to come.

Held on the same day, the opening service of Convocation also re-

---

[1] *P.H.E.*, iv, 178-9. [2] *Ibid.*, iv, 184-5.

219

vived an ancient spectacle. The bishops and members of the Lower House, preceded by the verger with his mace, passed in solemn procession through St. Paul's Churchyard into the south door of the Cathedral. There they were met by the Dean and Chapter "in their several habits", and conducted to the choir. "All along after they entered the church", recorded *Mercurius Publicus*, "did the choir sing the Te Deum in English," and an echo of joyful praise must have uplifted many hearts that day. The service for the day being read by the Sub-Dean, an anthem and sermon followed. Dr. Thomas Pierce, who in this pulpit the year previously had so eloquently vindicated episcopal order, had the gratification of preaching to the restored Assembly of his Church. His Latin discourse was based on the text: "For it seemed good to the Holy Ghost and to us to lay upon you no greater burden than these necessary things" (Acts 15: 28). Curious to relate, the fiery Doctor was held to have "delivered himself very cautiously", and we are left to wonder whether this fact was due to the awfulness of the occasion or to the pitfalls of the learned tongue. Another anthem: "O Lord, grant the King a long life", ended the service, and then the members met for legal formalities in the vestry—"the goodly old [Chapter] House being by the impiety of Oliver Cromwell's horse guard rendered unfit for use". In the absence of Archbishop Juxon, Sheldon presided, and "in excellent Latin" addressed the Lower House, "desiring them to go together and choose their Prolocutor, whom they should present the Thursday following in King Henry the VII's Chapel".[1] The ceremony concluded, "the bishops walked through the streets in their rochets, and had the prayers of the spectators".[2]

Trivial incidents sometimes cast a revealing light on the shifts of popular opinion, and one such merits recording. Sir Richard Browne, an old Parliamentary general and a veteran leader of the Presbyterian party, had been elected Lord Mayor of London the previous October. His Royalist sentiments were now impeccable, but church leaders found the Puritan mayor less than accommodating. "This Lord Mayor of London is troublesome to the clergy of the old stamp," wrote Edward Gower in November, 1660; "the Bishop sent to him that the Church [St. Paul's?] might be fitted decently, and he would provide ministers to preach there. His answer was that he would make no pro-

---

[1] Dr. Henry Ferne, Dean of Ely, was elected, and was succeeded in February, 1662, by Dr. John Barwick, Dean of St. Paul's.

[2] *Le Flem.*, p. 27; *Merc. Pub.* (1661), No. 20, p. 305.

vision for any of the singing men, and when he saw the names of those he intended for preachers, if he liked them, they should have admittance."[1] But the ecclesiastical climate of the City was altering rapidly, and perhaps Sir Richard was smarting at his recent defeat in the Guildhall election. At St. Paul's on the Sunday after Convocation's opening, worshippers were offered an edifying spectacle. As "Common Prayer was read exactly, according to the rubric", the Lord Mayor and Aldermen were observed present, "very devout and canonical, standing up at the Doxology, and bowing at the name of Jesus". Moreover, his Worship was solicitous for the behaviour of others; he "ordered two men to go about and command all persons in his name to be uncovered during the whole time of divine service". "So that his Lordship, Major-General Browne", gleefully reported Dr. Thomas Smith to a friend in the country, "has become a very dutiful son of the Church of England."[2] Two months later, an even more emphatic proof of conversion was to be had. "The Lord Mayor", wrote the same cleric, "entertained the bishops very nobly, with good cheer, good looks, and good words. He told them he had invited them on purpose to let the Presbyterians know that he disavowed them and their principles."[3] *Tempora mutantur, nos et mutamur in illis*; the halcyon days of Royalist Puritanism were gone forever.

Since during the summer of 1661 three separate bodies were concurrently occupied with church affairs, we may turn first to events in Parliament. Destined to be remembered as the most Royalist and Anglican legislature which ever sat in England, the Cavalier Parliament gave early token of its sentiments. On May 17 the Commons resolved by a vote of 228 to 103 that the Covenant should be publicly and ignominiously burned by the common hangman; the Upper House concurred the following day.[4] Puritan members did not accept the insult meekly, and prolonged the debate in the Commons for five hours. "The opposers of the motion attributed the restoration of the King to it [the Covenant], and some others that said they had taken it, undertook to say they had served the King as well with that as others that were openly professed of his party—this made the heat much greater"; so wrote Andrew Newport.[5] But the London populace was delighted with the show provided at Westminster, Cheapside, and the old Exchange, and joined in tearing copies of the Covenant from the city

---

[1] *Suth.*, p. 200.   [2] *Le Flem.*, 28.   [3] *Ibid.*, 28.
[4] *J.C.*, viii, 254, 256.   [5] *Suth.*, 160.

churches to burn them "with great shouts and acclamations". The old Cavaliers looked on with a grim satisfaction, and Nicholas expatiated to Joseph Kent on the marvellous workings of Providence:

"In my last I acquainted you . . . what great expectations we then had from the future Parliament, which how far they are already answered you may guess from the enclosed print, wherein you have an account of some of their proceedings, especially of that just fate to which they have at length brought that monster of rebellion the Covenant, which having been the original incendiary of these nations was some days ago itself sentenced to the flames, which was actually executed yesterday by a signal instance of divine justice, and to the great joy of all good men here. The House of Commons are upon several wholesome Bills towards the completing a good and lasting settlement in this nation."[1]

The Puritan débâcle continued. All members of the Commons were required to receive the Sacrament according to Anglican rites on Sunday, May 26, at St. Margaret's; refusal would disqualify members from sitting in the House.[2] Consequently, Sir Richard Leveson was not surprised to learn that compliance with the order was unanimous, "excepting three or four, whereof two were our citizen burgesses, viz., Love and Tenison, who absented themselves. And Prynne was there, but would take it sitting, and the minister that gave the bread [Dr. Gunning] saw that he would not kneel, and refused to give it to him, and he that came after thought that the other had given him the bread, and gave him the wine sitting, and took no notice, by a mistake. . . ." Not surprisingly, Mr. Pepys observed that the episode was "thought very preposterous".[3] Next day the Royalist sense of humour was given play in the House—" 'twas moved . . . that Dr. Gunning might have the thanks of the House for his pains, and be desired to print his sermon; Secretary Morrice and Mr. Prynne opposed it; the former said it was a scandalous sermon, but the House ordered thanks, and in waggery some desired that those two opposers should be the persons ordered to carry them, but not so ordered."[4]

More serious matters were soon under consideration. On May 30 a Bill was brought in to restore the bishops to their seats in the Upper House, and two weeks later the measure had been approved and sent to the House of Lords. Pepys reported gossip to the effect that "they had not done [it] so soon but to spite Mr. Prynne, who is everyday so

---

[1] P.R.O., S.P. 98/4, f. 123; *Math.*, p. 166.   [2] J.C., viii, 247.
[3] *Suth.*, 171; *Pepys*, i, 167.   [4] *Suth.*, 160.

bitter against [the bishops] in his discourse in the House". Edward
Gower commented further: " 'Tis thought the Lords will scarce pass it
with so little difficulty; some do not stick to say they will oppose it
there."[1] Clarendon in his memoirs describes the efforts of the Roman
Catholic Earl of Bristol to prejudice the King against the Bill, and
declares that this intrigue seriously obstructed and delayed passage of
the measure.[2] But in actual fact, the Bill was enacted by the Lords with
unusual rapidity. Brought up from the Commons and read on Friday,
June 14, it had its second reading the next day, and passed the following
Tuesday (June 18).[3]

The Commons was now savouring the taste of ecclesiastical legislation, and on June 25, it undertook a bolder venture. A committee was
appointed "to view the several laws for confirming the Liturgy of the
Church of England . . . and to bring in a compendious Bill to supply
any defect in the former laws, and to provide for an effectual conformity to the Liturgy of the Church for the time to come". This was
in flagrant disregard of the fact that the Savoy Conference was even
then engaged on the question of Prayer Book revision, and was doubtless intended as such. The same committee was likewise "to look into
the Act that takes away the High Commission Court, and to report
their opinion how far the coercive powers of the Ecclesiastical Courts
are taken away, and to prepare a Bill for settling the same".[4] Duly
presented, this latter Bill passed the House on July 13; the Lords gave
assent on the 27th. By it the ordinary jurisdiction of bishops and their
courts regained legal status; but the lately acquired High Churchmanship of the squires was not equal to a full revival of the Laudian régime.
The Court of High Commission was not restored, the use of the *ex*

---

[1] *J.C.*, viii, 261, 270; *Pepys*, i, 168; *Suth.*, 203.

[2] *Hyde II,* ii, 100–3.

[3] *J.L.*, xi, 279, 281, 283. So difficult is it to reconcile Clarendon's story with
the actual facts that Lister supposed the Chancellor had confused the occasion
with some other; cf. *Lister*, ii, 111 (note). This seems to me highly probable,
and I suggest that the real basis of the tale is Clarendon's dispute with Bristol
in March, 1662, (cf. pp. 251 ff., *infra*), of which he makes no mention in his
Life. His account of his role in the passing of the Act of Uniformity is so misleading as to make a manipulation of facts quite credible. Clarendon was certainly anxious to cover up his part in promoting the King's dispensing power,
which was the occasion of his quarrel with the "mercurial" Earl, and, con-
ceivably, he transferred the well-known episode to a context in which he could
represent himself in a more desirable light.

[4] *J.C.*, viii, 279.

officio oath was forbidden, and the authority of the Canons of 1640 disallowed.[1] The Royalist gentry might now entrust their spiritual welfare to their Laudian allies, but they were resolved that the temporal power of the Church should derive solely from the will of Parliament. Nonconformists should have the satisfaction hereafter of knowing that their persecution was inflicted by strictly legal means.

As the parent of the later and more famous Act, the Bill for Uniformity passed by the Commons on July 9[2] is of some interest. It enforced the Prayer Book of 1604, and, according to the reconstruction of Professor C. A. Swainson, was a less stringent measure than that of the following year.

"Every person in possession of any ecclesiastical benefice was to read the Morning and Evening Prayer appointed to be read by that Book on some Sunday before Michaelmas Day, 1661: and he was to declare his unfeigned assent and consent to the use of all things prescribed by the Book. Every person refusing to do so was to be deprived of his preferment, and every person hereafter presented or collated to a benefice was to read the Prayers, and declare his assent and consent to the use of the Book within two months from his taking possession. All lecturers were to do the same on pain of imprisonment. All laws and statutes of the Realm in regard to uniformity were to be enforced in regard to this Prayer Book of James."[3]

Thus the clergy were not required, as later, to give assent "to all and everything contained in the Prayer Book"; nor were they required specifically to renounce the Covenant, and declare it unlawful "upon any pretence whatsoever to take arms against the King". So far as is known, mention was not made of the necessity of episcopal ordination.[4]

This Bill was sent to the House of Lords on July 10, and there, despite prompting from the Commons, it received no reading.[5] In view of the alacrity the Upper House had hitherto shown in approving Anglican legislation, the failure even to consider the Uniformity Bill may almost certainly be attributed to the government's intervention. To a statesman of Clarendon's cautious temper, it would have seemed wholly inopportune to enact the measure at the very moment when a Royal

[1] *Ibid.*, viii, 300; *J.L.*, xi, 323.

[2] *J.C.*, viii, 296.

[3] *Swain.*, 12–13.

[4] The requirement of episcopal ordination contained in the Prayer Book enforced may have been held sufficient safeguard.

[5] *J.L.*, xi, 305, 308.

Commission was charged with revision of the Prayer Book. Such a breach of the King's engagement to the Puritans would have been difficult to justify. Possibly, church leaders themselves were reluctant to surrender the opportunity of improving the old Prayer Book; the sentiment against revision chiefly derived from the laity, and the bishops from the beginning had accepted it in principle.[1] Finally, the new French Ambassador, D'Estrades, informed his master that Charles considered the time not yet ripe for a *coup de grâce* against the Presbyterians.

"Les Presbitériens, qui sont ceux qui ont rétabli le Roi d'Angleterre, croyant etre maltraités par la résolution qu'il a prise de rétablir les Eveques, il use de cette grande addresse pour les faire venir à ce qu'il désire, et jusqu'à présent il y a réussi."[2]

In September he amplified this view:

"Qu'à l'égard des Presbitériens il avait esté en son pouvoir de les pousser, le Parlement dernier ayant pris pour cela toutes ses résolutions, mais qu'il se voit empesché, ne croyant pas qu'il en fût encore temps, et se réservant de le faire au premier Parlement qui sera assemblé, et se promettant que ce sera utilement pour luy et pour le repos de son Estat."[3]

Nevertheless, when Parliament adjourned on July 30, the Anglican party had reason to be well satisfied with the work accomplished. Presenting the ecclesiastical bills to the King, the Speaker, Sir Edward Turner, achieved a most striking use of scriptural metaphor to convey the sentiments of the House to the Church's Supreme Governor:

"Thanks be to God, the Flood is gone off the face of this island. Our Turtle Dove hath found good footing. Your Majesty is happily restored to the government; the temporal Lords and Commons are restored to sit in Parliament, and shall the Church alone now suffer? *Sit Ecclesia Anglicana libera et habeat libertates suas illaesas!* In order to this great work, the Commons have prepared a Bill to repeal that law . . . whereby the bishops were excluded this House; these noble Lords have all agreed, and now we beg your Majesty will give it life. Speak but the word, Great Sir, and your servants yet shall live!"[4]

The King indicated his complaisance, and Parliament dispersed, to meet again on November 20.

[1] Cf. p. 167 *supra*.
[2] *Lettres, Memoires, et Négotiations du Comte d'Estrades* (Lond. 1743), i, 145–6.
[3] P.R.O., *Transcripts* 3/109, f. 110.
[4] *P.H.E.*, iv, 219–20.

Q

Meanwhile, what of the Savoy Conference? The Anglican and Presbyterian commissioners had assembled for the first time on April 15, and for four months their deliberations pursued a stormy and futile course. Baxter has left to posterity a voluminous account of the proceedings, and on his memoirs historians have almost exclusively depended in judging the affair. Despite honesty of intention, so passionate an advocate of one side found it impossible to view the motives and conduct of the other with any measure of objectivity. His thesis is summed up in one burning sentence: "We spoke to the Deaf; they had other ends [than unity and peace], and were other men, and had the art to suit the means unto their ends."[1] This conviction unconsciously dominates his narrative at every turn. Since our chief concern is rather to determine the viewpoint of the Laudian participants, we must endeavour, so far as possible, to look at the Conference through Anglican eyes. Fortunately, a letter of Dr. Henry Ferne, written four days after the meetings ended, provides a useful and fairly detailed account. Ferne was not a commissioner, but as Prolocutor of Convocation he was closely in touch with the course of events, and above all, would accurately reflect the opinions of Anglican leaders.

As we know from Richard Baxter, the Conference was formally opened by Archbishop Frewen, who immediately resigned leadership to Sheldon as one who "knew more of the King's mind". Sheldon has been frequently censured for insisting that since the Puritans were the advocates of change in the established Liturgy, theirs must be the first move—exceptions to the Prayer Book should be drawn up in writing, with alterations desired. Far from resenting this as an unfair strategy, Baxter declared: "In this I confess, above all things else, I was wholly of his mind, and prevailed with my brethren to consent"—adding: "I conjecture, upon contrary reasons." Thereupon, the Conference recessed until May 4, during which time Baxter devoted himself to the task of drawing up an "entire Liturgy" as an alternative to the old, while the other Puritan commissioners laboured over "an enumeration of faults" in the Prayer Book.[2]

At this point Dr. Ferne begins his account:

"The . . . commission for the review of Liturgy and ceremonies . . . has been [pursued] two days in a week at the Savoy for this long time, and for this last fortnight every day till it expired, which was on Thursday last, divers bishops

[1] Rel. Baxt., 336.   [2] Ibid., 305–6.

and many of our House giving attendance to it; the chief actor of the Presbyterian party was Mr. Baxter, who through the bishops' condescensions so often to debate the business with him, has every time returned more considerable to the general of that party (the *hoi polloi*). . . . To us that heard him, he seemed to show more boldness and ignorance than reason for the most part.

"The particulars of the whole business from the beginning are these. They had first time to bring in their exceptions against the Liturgy and ceremonies: which they gave in May 5, comprehended in ten sheets of paper, promising they would offer some forms for public use, and desiring they might, and every minister, have liberty to use either those or the forms of our Liturgy, with liberty also for conceived prayers if occasions required. Upon the receiving of their papers of exception, it was our work to consider what was to be *yielded*, what to be *answered* to their exceptions, what to be *added* to our Liturgy, if anywhere seemed defective.

"After divers meetings of divers bishops and some of our House (which as I said above was twice a week at least) we run through the whole Liturgy and their exceptions to every part;[1] agreeing what might be yielded to—which besides the whole alteration of the Epistles and Gospels into the new version were not many—and drawing up an answer to their several exceptions; which being read unto them and given them, they required time to consider and bring in their answer. This was about the 12 June. . . . In the first week of July, they brought in their form of Liturgy,[2] which beginning with a confession of extraordinary length, and their litany they put into one continued prayer, and in a word, the whole was larger and longer than our Liturgy."[3]

There is important evidence that it was at this juncture—and not, as the Puritan leader conjectured, before the Conference even began— that Anglicans reached the conclusion that the negotiations were really futile. One of the commissioners, John Hacket, wrote from Surrey

---

[1] This information refutes one of Baxter's biased conjectures; for he demonstrates at length to his own satisfaction "that the generality of bishops and doctors present never knew what we offered them in the reformed Liturgy, nor in this reply, nor in any of our papers, save those few which we read openly to them. For they were put up and carried away, and I conjecture scarce any but the writers of their confutations would be at the labour of reading them over. . . . So that it seems before they knew what was in them, they resolved to reject our papers, right or wrong, and to deliver them up to their contradictors." *Rel. Baxt.*, 335.

[2] Baxter gives the impression that the reformed Liturgy was submitted at a much earlier date, and accuses the bishops of delaying the disputes until the conference had almost expired. It may be seen from Ferne's account that Baxter's composition was not received until three weeks before the end, and that the Puritan rebuttal to the bishops' paper came in even later.

[3] *Add.* 28,053 (*Danby MSS*), f. 1.

to the Master of Emmanuel College, William Dillingham, on July 8:

"Since we parted at London, a composure of a Liturgy (some say it was Mr. Baxter's pen) was brought to the bishops. It was sent to me immediately to look it over, and in three nights' warning for my answer. I was sorry to see that it was so unconsonant, so quite different in the frame from our Liturgy. Which produceth this result, that since the disagreeing party keep such a distance from the old Reformed way, the ancient Prayer Book shall be held up with some few alterations and additions. This I communicate to yourself privately, till you see it really done, as I sub-intimate unto you."[1]

The Conference, however, was drawn out to its dismal end. "Our wandering discourses", says Baxter, were succeeded by "our as unprofitable disputes".[2] Dr. Ferne continues:

"The week after, they brought in their answer or reply to ours, which contained twenty-nine sheets of paper; at the delivery of which Mr. Baxter had the honour to be talked with by seven or eight bishops. But everyone being convinced that no good would come upon these general discourses; it was agreed that they should either show or prove something unlawful in the Liturgy and therefore necessary to be altered, or be concluded wilful. The Conference upon this point was referred to three and three; and only two bishops to be present for moderating the dispute. Mr. Baxter's instance (when they came to it) was kneeling at the Communion, which he acknowledged not sinful in itself or unlawful; but the imposing of it under penalty of being denied the Sacrament was unlawful, and this argument held several days.

"Mr. Baxter made sometimes strange syllogisms and as strange answers to some of ours. The last meeting he said more than once, he was persuaded that if it were not imposed, there would be more compliants to it; so it was seen what was to be expected from them that will not endure anything as imposed, and so overthrow all authority and order."[3]

It seems plain from these letters that the Anglicans, contrary to the generally accepted version, did entertain some hope of satisfying the more moderate Puritans, and did not embark on the Conference with a pre-determined attitude of *non-possumus*. The Laudians had already gained their primary objective, and we may suppose them desirous of comprehending within the Establishment the moderate men of the defeated party—of whom Reynolds was already an encouraging example—and anticipating a settlement on the basis of minor concessions and adjustments. Such an approach may seem to us completely unrealistic in view of the outcome of the Conference; but it should not

---

[1] B.M., *Sloane MSS.* 1710, f. 202.   [2] *Rel. Baxt.*, 376.
[3] *Add.* 28,053, f. 1.

be forgotten that many such Puritans did in fact find it possible to conform when the hour of decision came.

So far as the Savoy Conference was concerned, these hopes were
fruitless, and in the eyes of churchmen the blame was squarely fixed on
the shoulders of Richard Baxter. The Puritan leader had undoubtedly
dominated his party to an astonishing degree—by his own account,
making most of the decisions, and draughting all but one of the papers
submitted. The Anglican commissioners received an impression that
but for his intervention an agreement might have been possible. "Unto
those that came with him (Dr. Bates and Dr. Jacombe)," wrote Ferne,
"he seemed sometimes to speak more and more strict than they would
have him."[1] Bishop Morley asserted publicly: "His brethren have
several times declared themselves not to be of his opinion. . . . They did
show themselves unwilling to enter upon this dispute [i.e. in the closing
sessions of the Conference], and seemed to like much better another
way tending to an amicable and fair compliance, which was wholly
frustrated by Mr. Baxter's furious eagerness to engage in a disputation."[2]
If Baxter, as he himself explained, monopolized speech-making on the
Puritan side because he "was loath to expose [my brethren] to the
hatred of the bishops, but was willinger to take it all upon myself",[3] he
fully achieved his end. Since his unflattering vignettes of the bishops
are well known, it is not perhaps unfair to cite further their impressions
of Mr. Baxter. In Walton's inimitable phrases, he appeared "so bold,
so troublesome, and so illogical as forced patient Dr. Sanderson to say
[to John Pearson] with an unusual earnestness, that he had never met
with a man of more pertinacious confidence and less abilities in all his
conversation". Bishop Cosin observed with pent-up feeling: "Truly it is
high time he should hold his peace, for I think he hath tired both himself and many others with his much speaking."[4] Even the hitherto
amiable Lord Chancellor, Baxter noted, was "most offended at me . . .
and possessed with displeasure towards me upon that account, that I
charged the Church and Liturgy with sin. . . . I told him I had spoken
nothing but what I thought. . . ."[5] Certainly, Baxter's combativeness

---

[1] *Ibid.*, f. 1. Cf. *Rel. Baxt.*, 343.

[2] G. Morley, *Bishop of Worcester's Letter to a Friend for Vindication of Himself. . . .* (Lond. 1662), 13.

[3] *Rel. Baxt.*, 364.

[4] I. Walton, *Life of Dr. Sanderson* (Lond. 1678), 166–7; *Orns.*, ii, 36.

[5] *Rel. Baxt.*, 364–5.

and voluble self-assertion were highly exasperating to the Anglicans, and militated against any friendly rapprochement between the two parties.[1]

Though Convocation had been summoned without undue regard for the status of the Savoy Conference, it discovered that it could not ignore the existence of that body. At every turn, its deliberations were hampered by the fact of "the concurrent commission"—"which indeed", regretted Dr. Ferne, "was an antecedent commission to ours, [and] has been a great *Remora*". For the first month, he continued, "we had no commission for to debate anything in order to the altering or making of Canons, the commission before granted for review of the Liturgy causing some demur in the drawing up of a commission for the Convocation, by reason of a clause in the usual form [i.e. in the traditional writ to the Archbishop]."[2] The first weeks, therefore, were whiled away in the composition of special services to commemorate the martyrdom of Charles I and the restoration of his successor. On May 31, however, the government acted to remove the legal obstacle to more urgent business—"it was ordered by his Majesty in Council that the Attorney General should forthwith prepare a commission to authorize the Convocation to consult of matters relating to the settlement of the Church, and not to insert therein the clause of proviso: 'Provided always that the said Canons, Orders, Ordinances, Constitutions, Matters and Things of any of them so to be considered . . . be not contrary or repugnant to the Liturgy as established or the Rubrics in it, or the nine and thirty Articles, or any Doctrine, Order, or Ceremonies of the Church of England already established'."[3] This Royal commission was read in Convocation on June 7, and on June 19 a more specific licence to revise the Canons was received from the King.[4]

---

[1] Bishop Burnet commented acutely on this point: "As [Baxter] was his whole life long a man of great zeal and much simplicity, so he was most unhappily subtle and metaphysical in everything. There was a great submission paid to him by the whole party. So he persuaded them, that from the words of the Commission they were bound to offer everything that they thought might conduce to the good or peace of the Church, without considering what was like to be obtained, or what effect their demanding so much might have, in irritating the minds of those who were then the superior body in strength and number." *Burnet*, i, 320.

[2] *Add.* 28,053, f. 1.   [3] *Lan.* 957, f. 42.

[4] Some confusion has existed on the subject of these two communications; but a comparison between the commission quoted and that of June 19, quoted in Cardwell, *Synodalia*, 687–91, shows that the first was purely general in scope and the second a specific licence to revise the canons. Cf. *Swain*, 14.

Thereupon, says Ferne, "several committees were appointed to consider the old Canons, and to see what might be added. The several
heads inquired on were these: The Manners of the Clergy, Their
Apparel and Residence, Of Schoolmasters, Of the Exercise of Ecclesiastical Jurisdiction, The Repairing of Churches and Parsonage Houses,
The Furniture of Churches, The Preaching, Praying and Printing of
Heterodox Opinions. Several things are suggested and prepared upon
these heads, but it was thought fit not to conclude or constitute anything by way of Canon this session."[1] The subject of the Canons received attention at several later sessions, but for reasons that have never
been explained, the task was eventually abandoned.[2] It may be seen that
the assembly was well aware of the problems which two decades of
ecclesiastical chaos had produced. An additional step for dealing with
this situation was the preparation of a Book of Articles to serve as a
guide for episcopal visitations.[3]

The adjournment of Parliament and Convocation and the termina-
tion of the Savoy Conference made it possible for the bishops to set out
for their several dioceses in midsummer, there to engage on the formidable task of bringing some order and regularity into parish life, and
of reviving the machinery of diocesan administration. Even with
allowance made for Anglican bias, the picture drawn of religion in
England at the close of the Interregnum was a depressing one. Everywhere church buildings showed the ravages both of vandalism and
neglect; the traditional appointments for Anglican worship had of
course long since vanished in most places. Rectories and vicarages were
more often than not in a sorry state of dilapidation. Walker gives a
relevant anecdote of Richard Reynolds of Woodley in Devon, who,
as soon as the order of sequestration was served on him in 1644, "forthwith set himself to put his house in very good repair (saying): 'They will
always fear being dispossessed, and so let my houses run to ruin.'" This,

[1] *Add.* 28,053, f. 1.
[2] The matter is referred to in *Barwick*, where the biographer merely says,
somewhat mysteriously: "These preparations came all to nothing; for the
endeavours of many, though very hearty, were wholly frustrated by one or two
on whom this matter chiefly depended." *Op. cit.*, p. 326.
[3] The book was still unfinished a year later, when Bishop Skinner wrote to
Sheldon, June 26, 1662: "I well hoped to have seen that uniform Book of
Articles (viz., for Visitation) before this day, resting assured that no pretences
could take off your Lordship's resolution from what so much concerns the
honour and peace of the Church." *Tann.* 48, f. 14.

comments Walker, "was what most of the clergy who lived to be restored found to sad experience to be a great truth."[1] Puritan prejudice had reacted with particular severity against the cathedrals. Lichfield was little better than a ruin, while Worcester and Hereford were battered shells. In Exeter Cathedral a wall had been constructed to divide the interior into separate places of worship for Presbyterians and Independents.[2] Far more serious was the disintegration of corporate church life in the parishes, where the successive changes of ecclesiastical régime and the activity of the more extravagant sectarians had had devastating effect.

Doubtless typical of many areas was the account of conditions drawn up by clergy of the Archdeaconry of Northumberland:

"There is a great need of a visitation of the churches in these northern parts, many of them being either altogether unprovided of ministers, or provided with such as are, in effect, no ministers; and are so far from conforming themselves, that they preach against those that are conformed, and intrude themselves upon their charge, by baptizing children and marrying the persons of such as are enemies to the orders (sic) of the Church of England. And likewise the fabrics of many churches and chapels are altogether ruinous and in great decay, and cannot be gotten repaired without visitations. Besides, in many churches there be neither Bibles, Books of Common Prayer, surplices, fonts, Communion Tables, nor anything that is necessary for the service of God. Nor will the church-wardens (not being yet sworn) contribute any assistance for the supply of those defects."[3]

The horrified Archdeacon, Dr. Basire, lately returned from his peregrinations in the Near East, could only pray fervently that "God may assist us, reform them, and amend all".[4] But being assured by his

---

[1] *Walker*, ii, 341.

[2] T. Plume, *Life of John Hacket* (Lond. 1865), 79–80; I. G. Smith, *Worcester* (Lond. 1883), 264 ff.; H. W. Phillott, *Hereford* (Lond. 1888), 228; R. J. E. Boggis, *History of the Diocese of Exeter* (Exeter 1922), 410, 421.

[3] *Works and Letters of Dennis Granville, D.D.* (Surtees Soc., 1861), p. 251. This general picture is confirmed by the records of Bishop Sanderson's visitation of the Archdeaconry of Buckingham in July, 1662. Thirty-seven churches were declared "out of repair"; in a score of others the chancels were in a state of dilapidation. Virtually all the churches (some eighty-seven) were without surplices; thirty-four had no copy of the Prayer Book; ten lacked a carpet for the Communion Table; and nine had no Communion cup. Nine vicarages were out of repair, and two had fallen or been pulled down. Cf. E. R. C. Brinkworth, *Episcopal Visitation Book for the Archdeaconry of Buckingham*, 1662 (1947).

[4] *Orns.*, ii, 88.

Bishop [Cosin] "that the coercive power was now restored", he made ready, at the invitation of "that little remnant of the loyal canonical party in that jurisdiction", to hold a lengthy visitation.[1] His friend William Lucy, now Bishop of St. David's, assured him that his problems were not unique:

"I was in hope that the unhappiness of the Church had principally fallen to my share, but reading your last letter I find that I have fellow mourners for the same sad calamities. Papists have taken a great advantage upon these sad destructive times, which were of late brought into the Church by 'the propagators of the Gospel', as they were called—a sort of people, four or five, who rode up and down preaching; and all the parsonages sequestered. I have been informed that sixteen churches together have had no divine duty officiated in them for twelve years together. . . . These fanatics . . . fear as little our excommunication as the Papists, and indeed I find no sect much dreading it; but although I doubt every diocese (I am too sure mine) hath all sects in Amsterdam, and more by the Papists; yet I fear a secret Atheism more than all them, for I hope in time by degrees they will wear away with the reviving of ecclesiastic discipline, but Atheism will not be overcome but by apostolical men. . . . Complaints will do no good; we must act what we can with counsel, with menace, with deeds."[2]

As Nehemiah and the exiles, the returning bishops and clergy thus bewailed the broken walls and waste places of Jerusalem, and set themselves valiantly to take away the reproach. But some of them must have wondered with Mr. Abraham Cowley:

> Will ever fair Religion appear
> In these deformed Ruins, will she clear
> Th'Augean Stables of her Churches here?[3]

The measures passed by the Cavalier Parliament, however, had greatly strengthened Episcopal authority, and the bishops found themselves in a better position to undertake reform than had been the case the previous spring. Moreover, they had cause to be enheartened by the loyal and enthusiastic reception accorded them by the local gentry. Bishop Cosin wrote to William Sancroft on August 22 with much gratification:

"[At] my solemn reception into the Church [of Durham], and singing the Te Deum there . . . there was nothing wanting but your assistance. The con-

---

[1] W. N. Darnell, *Life and Correspondence of Isaac Basire, D.D.* (Lond. 1831), 222.

[2] *Ibid.*, 217-18.

[3] A. Cowley, *Ode upon the Blessed Restoration of Charles II* (Lond. 1660), 3.

fluence and alacrity both of the gentry, clergy, and other people was very great; and at my first entrance through the river of Tees there was scarce any water to be seen for the multitude of horse and men that filled it, when the sword that killed the dragon was delivered to me with all the formality of trumpets and gunshots and acclamations that might be made. I am not much affected with such shows, but, however, the cheerfulness of the country in the reception of their Bishop is a good earnest given for better matters, which, by the grace and blessing of God, may in good time follow here among us all."[1]

His friend and fellow-exile Bishop Morley met with an equally warm welcome at Worcester, which Henry Townshend described in his diary on September 12:

"Dr. George Morley . . . was solemnly brought into Worcester by my Lord Windsor, Lord Lieutenant of the County, and most of the gentry and all the clergy, there being ten trumpets then attending, and some volunteer militia horse, the trained bands of the city, and clergy band of foot in arms, giving divers volleys of shot. As soon as he had rested, within half an hour the Bishop with all the prebends, and the choir meeting him at the college steps in their formalities, sang to the Choir, where he was enthroned, performing the ceremonies. Then choir service. So to his Palace, where was noble treatment prepared."[2]

These festivities were a prelude to apostolic labours. Bishop Lucy wrote to Archdeacon Basire: "I am very glad to hear my Lord of Durham is so active as you describe him"; and in September Cosin sent the following account of himself to Sancroft:

"I am so full of the Bishopric affairs, that I have not the least leisure for anything else. Upon Sunday last I had a solemn Confirmation, with a sermon to that end before it; and yesterday I had another; for the company was too great to go through with them all in one day, yet I admitted none but those who were duly examined, and brought testimonies besides, subscribed by their own ministers. Busy I am about the reparations of my ruined houses, the very covering whereof with lead and slate (not yet half done) hath cost me more than £500. In the meantime, having been here five weeks, I have not sealed more than two leases . . . the purchasers have made the tenants so poor that they are not able to renew their farms. . . . The next Sunday I am here to attend an ordination, and the two first Tuesdays after Michaelmas an ordinary Synod of the clergy, one at Durham, and another at Newcastle; where I shall preach among them, and put them in some order, if by any fair means I can. My temporal Chancellor is here with me at his sitting in the Chancery Court. . . ."[3]

[1] *Orns.*, ii, 21.
[2] *Town.*, 78.
[3] W. N. Darnell, *op. cit.*, 218; *Orns*, ii, 31.

A month later he described the visit to Newcastle:

"where I stayed from Saturday to Thursday, preached there and communicated with many persons upon Sunday: I think the number of people at the sermon was no less than three or four thousand. On Tuesday I kept the Synod of the clergy, and made them my assessors in it, treating them so that I hope (and they assured me all as much) they are well pleased with their Bishop—even Mr. Durant himself, whom only I entreated and ordered to forbear preaching till he made it appear that he was an ecclesiastical person, as he is not, having neither episcopal nor presbyterial ordination."[1]

Other bishops were similarly occupied. Morley promptly instituted articles of inquiry into the canonical qualifications of incumbents in the Diocese of Worcester, and with his encouragement the dean and chapter had expended £6,000 on cathedral repairs by the end of the year.[2] Even Bishop Warner at length proceeded to visit the diocese of Rochester, where he issued "letters of inquiry for the reformation of the ritual", and at a Synod in the cathedral candidly addressed his clergy as follows: "It is twenty-five years since I visited this place, and in twenty of these the Bishop's power hath been utterly taken away, and in the last two years much suspended—no marvel then that the Bishop hath work enough to set all in order that is left undone or done amiss."[3]

One Puritan institution, at least, had proved its value to Anglicans during the Interregnum, and we learn from Henry Townshend that during the autumn "the Bishop of London set up four lectures in London, viz., one at St. Paul's on Wednesday, two at Christ Church, Thursdays, and three and four at [blank] and St. Dunstan's in the East, Fridays. So hath the Bishops of Salisbury and Worcester in their several dioceses." "Thin congregations, and every one must stand bare!" was the disparaging comment of the godly in the capital.[4] An interesting light is thrown on Sheldon's personal relations with Puritans from an incident recounted by John Shaw, incumbent at Trinity Church, Hull. Shaw was inhibited from preaching by the King's command in June, 1661, and heard that a complaint from Sheldon had occasioned the order. Journeying to London, he first had an interview with Charles, who gave him "good words".

[1] *Orns.*, ii, 35–6.
[2] I. G. Smith, *op. cit.*, 268, 273.
[3] *Archaeological Journal*, No. 81 (1864), p. 47.
[4] *Town.*, 81; *Math.*, 195–6.

"I then went to the Bishop of London", he continues, "and boldly asked him (for I had many friends in the Court, especially Secretary Morrice, who desired me to do so), why he, who knew me not, nor knew either good or bad by me, would complain of me to the King? To which (after he knew my name) he answered, that he had heard much of me; that I was a leading man among the clergy in the north, and that I was accounted no great friend to Episcopacy and Common Prayer. To which I answered that in all these times (when there was liberty enough for it) I had never said a word against either of them; 'though', said I, 'I say not this to flatter you, for if they had never come in, I would never have fetched them.' At last he asked me if I would have a living? To which I answered no; but I would endeavour to live without one as well as I could—not that I was unwilling to have accepted of a living, but not thus to have one from him, on his terms."[1]

The account certainly does not suggest that intransigence was all on one side, or that Sheldon was determined at any cost to rid the Church of its Puritan clergy.

Perhaps the clearest picture of the way the work of reformation was approached during the summer and autumn of 1661 may be found in the letter which Bishop Henchman of Salisbury wrote to Secretary Nicholas in October:

"I have now been in all the chief places in my diocese . . . partly to frame ecclesiastical affairs. . . . In church government I find no such discouragement but that I hope (if a small number of persons be removed) I shall regulate the clergy of this diocese in the same manner as they were governed twenty-four years since. Almost all those which give me some resistance are placed in benefices of his Majesty's donation originally, thrust into them in the time of the late disorders, and continued by the Act of the last year. I find very little trouble at Devizes though the people not good, for the minister is a learned prudent orthodox man; he stays there upon a small maintenance, hath refused good benefices that he may do good there. Until I can add to him in an ecclesiastical way I cherish him by mine own purse.

"At Marlborough are two ministers, neither of them regular: I relieved myself somewhat by appointing some neighbour ministers to preach weekly a lecture there. I cannot yet hope for good alteration in that town. I took the same course at Reading, where are two that will not yet conform, one of them Mr. Fowler, a busy turbulent man; yet these are content to submit to my appointment that at the weekly lecture Common Prayer be read. Newbury I have reduced to a better condition; though Mr. Woodbridge, the present parson, doth not conform, he is so far pliant that his curate shall read Common Prayer. At Wallingford one Pinckney, at Malmesbury one Gawen are busy turbulent men; I cannot with any skill or power that I have form those places

---

[1] *Yorkshire Diaries and Autobiographies in the 17th and 18th Centuries* (Surtees Soc. 1877), "The Life of Mr. John Shaw", 155.

into good order. In some private villages irregular and schismatical men do mischief; I take particular account of them, and know who in my diocese conform not, which I shall report when I attend on your Honour."[1]

This pastoral activity of the bishops was temporarily suspended when Parliament and Convocation reconvened in London at the end of November, 1661. In line with a tradition soon to be firmly established, the prelates were instructed that their Parliamentary duties must have priority over all others. Sheldon wrote to Cosin in September: "I shall give your Lordship an account of my readiness to serve . . . when we meet, which must be at the beginning of the Parliament; for the King expects it from all of our order, and when his great business for his revenue and that of the Church is over, any may have liberty to return to his diocese. He supposeth that none among us is so inconsiderable but that he hath interest enough in one or other to promote his business more effectually than can be done by a proxy."[2] Accordingly, when Parliament reassembled, twenty-three of the twenty-seven bishops were on hand.[3]

Anti-Presbyterian sentiment had noticeably heightened in the capital in recent months. According to Richard Baxter:

"Now our calamities began to be much greater than before. . . . We were represented in the common talk of those who thought it in their interest to be our adversaries, as the most seditious people, unworthy . . . to enjoy our common liberty among them. We could not go abroad but we met with daily reproaches and false stories of us: Either we were feigned to be plotting, or to be disaffecting the people. . . . And the great increaser of all this was that . . . a multitude of students that studied for preferment . . . found out quickly what was most pleasing to those whose favour they must rise by, and so set themselves industriously to reviling, calumniating, and cruelty against all those whom they perceived to be odious."[4]

Undoubtedly, the public was reacting to the belligerent Anglicanism of the Court and Parliament, and once more the authorities were scenting danger wherever there was religious discontent. Rumours of plotting and treason were legion,[5] and in December the House of Com-

---

[1] P.R.O., S.P. 29/43, f. 68. [2] Orns., ii, 26.
[3] J.L., xi, 332. [4] Rel. Baxt., 373.
[5] An analysis of evidence in the State Papers dealing with this subject is given in Chapter viii, pp. 229–43, of Stoughton; the author concludes: "Intercepted letters and other communications pregnant with alarm occur for the first six months of 1661, but they become much more numerous in the next half year." Ibid., 230.

mons notified the King that it "had received credible information from several parts of the Kingdom of divers designs and attempts to disturb the public peace", begging him "to take care for . . . the securing the peace of the Kingdom".[1] The government was anything but sceptical of the rumours; Nicholas had discoursed wrathfully to Clarendon in a letter of September 13:

"I can assure you that [the Presbyterians] are as bold and as insolent here in this city as ever they were since the Independents mastered them; I have intelligence that they are so united with the Anabaptists and Fifth Monarchy men as at their meetings of late they preach one after another in the same churches and meeting houses, and all persuading the people . . . their deliverance is near; and yet there is no law to punish them (as some say) that did not scruple notwithstanding the law, to fight perpetually against their Sovereign."[2]

The violent outpourings of Royalist pamphleteers and the ridicule of the Court further contributed to the discrediting of the Puritans. Roger L'Estrange, whose caustic and ribald style recalled the Marprelate tracts of Elizabethan days, was using every unscrupulous device of journalism to whip up the persecuting zeal of the Cavaliers. "The city church meetings", he wrote in August, "look but like authorized conventicles, the pulpits are profaned by unqualified and seditious lecturers . . . both Presbyterian and Independent. These lectures are increased both in number and boldness to a most scandalous and prodigious degree, even since the last recess of Parliament, not only to the hazard of the public peace, but to the infamy and dishonour of the English Church."[3] From many quarters, the public was invited to marvel at Puritan hypocrisy and effrontery—"their swallowing down the camel-sins of disobedience and perjury and oppression and sacrilege, etc., and yet straining hard at the gnats, a surplice, a ring, a cross, or a may-pole".[4] The success of the play-houses was an up-to-date version of Ben Jonson's *Bartholomew Fair*, in which the two satirized Puritans were made to represent Baxter and Calamy. The Court was vastly diverted, and the King came in person to enjoy the joke, attended by

[1] *J.C.*, viii, 324.

[2] *Clar.* 75, f. 191.

[3] R. L'Estrange, *A Caveat to the Cavaliers* (Lond. 1661), preface; cf. also his tracts, *Interest Mistaken, or the Holy Cheat* (Lond. 1661), *The Relapsed Apostate* (Lond. 1661), *State Divinity* (Lond. 1661), *A Whipp, A Whipp for the Schismatical Animadverter* (Lond. 1662).

[4] *The Merit and Honour of the Old English Clergy asserted . . . and the Demerit of the New Clergy discovered* (Lond. 1662), 98.

the Earl of Manchester and the Bishop of London. The godly, scandalized at the burlesque of Puritan manners and piety, "were greatly
astonished, wondering the house did not fall upon their heads!" Pepys,
inevitably present, when he found the play "so satirical against Puritanism", wondered that "they should already dare to do it, and the
King to countenance it".[1] But the Court was now callous to Puritan
sensibilities. The Frenchman Battailler reported to D'Estrades on
November 18: "Hyer il fut fait un sermon à Whitehall devant le Roy
par un évesque, qui estoit proprement comme une satyre contre les
puritains ou Presbitériens, dont toute la cour est demeurée fort satis-
faite."[2]

In such an atmosphere Parliament reassembled on November 20,
and Pepys watched the King proceeding to Westminster in his stately
barge. His Majesty's unexpected appearance was a graceful compliment
to the bishops, who, clad in lawn, chimeres, and caps, now filled the
bench vacant for twenty years past. "My Lords and Gentlemen,"
Charles declared, "I know the visit I make you this day is not necessary
... yet if there were no more in it, it would not be strange that I come
to see the Lords spiritual and temporal and the Commons of England
met together." Nor did his further announcement cause any dismay
among his hearers: "If we help one another, we shall with God's blessing master all our difficulties. Those which concern matters of religion,
I confess to you are too hard for me; and therefore I do commend them
to your care and deliberation, which can best provide for them."[3]
Anglican opposition to a Parliamentary settlement of the Church question had vanished overnight when the temper of the new House became apparent; there was every assurance that the matter was now in
competent hands.

In dealing with this session of Parliament, historians have tended to
focus attention on the Act of Uniformity, and an earlier episode has
almost escaped notice. As we have seen, the Commons had already
approved a Bill for Uniformity in the early summer; now the Church
party made plain that the memory of a humiliating defeat in the Convention Parliament of 1660 still rankled.[4] Within a week of the session's

[1] *Newc.*, 7–8; *Pepys*, Sept. 7, 1661. The best description of the performance is
in *Math.*, 177–8.
[2] P.R.O., *Transcripts* 3/109, November 28, 1661 (N.S.), folio unnumbered.
[3] *Pepys*, i, 207; *P.H.E.*, iv, 222, 224.
[4] Cf. pp. 171 ff., *supra*.

opening, one of the Anglican protagonists in that struggle, Sir Thomas Meres, was by order of the House reporting a "Bill for confirming the Act of the last assembly concerning Ministers".[1] It was immediately obvious that confirmation of that Act was the last thing the Commons intended. From November 29 to December 16 the House exercised its ingenuity on amendments to transform the measure into a veritable scourge for its original promoters. The Bill as finally passed reaffirmed the previous Act for Settling Ministers, with some fifteen amendments completely reversing its intent. Of these the most important were the following: (1) For a six months' period beginning February 1, 1662, all persons and bodies corporate might exercise patronage rights which had been overridden during the Interregnum, "anything in the original Act to the contrary notwithstanding".[2] (4) All ministers formerly holding a sequestered living were made liable for a full fifth part of the profits for the entire period of incumbency, and this might be recovered by the sequestered minister or his heirs "by action of debt at the Common Law". (7) All ministers who had publicly expressed any sentiment in favour of the former King's execution, either before or after the event, should be deprived. (8) Any surrender of benefice made during the Commonwealth by reason of "fraud, extreme poverty, force, or fear of imprisonment or sequestration" was voided. (9) Any minister "who by any articles of complaint by himself or any other did cause the former incumbent to be sequestrated" should be deprived. (10) Sequestered ministers who had held a plurality of livings should be restored to all of them. (13) Neither this nor the previous Act should confirm any minister not in episcopal orders by March 25, 1662, or who had omitted to administer the Lord's Supper in his church "according to the form of the Liturgy of the Church of England for one whole year last past".[3]

So little debate would seem to have been occasioned by these drastic privisoes that on December 14 the House obviously welcomed the intrusion of an old and pleasing controversy. Some discussion then arising "upon the precedency of the University of Oxford before Cambridge", the members divided. The sequel was, we fear, to be expected in an Anglican and Royalist Parliament—"The Ayes went out, and the

[1] J.C., viii, 321, 322.
[2] Ibid., viii, 325. It will be remembered how violently Anglican members insisted on the right of patrons in the original debate. Cf. p. 172, supra.
[3] J.C., viii, 330-2.

Noes that stayed in, finding themselves much outnumbered, yielded."[1] It was an agreeable interlude, serving to prove that even a Parliamentary decision lacks finality.

On January 8 the Bill and its long list of provisoes finally passed, and with some suggestion of irony the House agreed that it should be transmitted to the Lords under the title, "An Act for confirming Three Acts therein mentioned, with additions and alterations in the last".[2] The measure languished in the Upper House for several weeks, but after a request for expedition from the Commons on January 28, the Bill had its second reading the next day. A resolution was offered to confirm the original Act without the new provisoes, but the vote was evenly divided and therefore counted in the negative.[3] However, on February 3, after a debate in a committee of the whole House, the Lords confirmed the Act of the Convention Parliament without alterations.[4] Only the bald fact is recorded in the *Journals*, but thereby hangs a tale.

From many sources, we learn that the Puritan party had been not unnaturally appalled by the action of the Commons. Supremely dreaded was the possibility that Puritan incumbents would be forced to pay the arrears of fifths. Though this dole to the families of sequestered clergy had been a legal obligation under the Commonwealth, the majority of Presbyterians, it now emerged, had not felt called upon to honour it. Henry Newcome piously exclaimed in his diary on January 5, 1662: "Some wise men have dreadful apprehensions of the evil that is coming toward us. Sure this Act which we see copies of, should be spread before the Lord [in prayer?].... And will the Lord suffer these that are turned out to be utterly undone by the arrears of fifths, &c., and all to be snared by such desperate abjurations."[5] One Mr. Hooke wrote to a friend in New England: "There was lately an Act ready to pass as it was feared, prepared by the Lower House, to bring destitution to ejected ministers, which would have utterly undone thousands of them, their wives and children, and filled the prisons with innumerable debtors."[6] But to the surprise and joy of Puritans, a delivering angel in the form of the rotund Lord Chancellor intervened, and the fearful prospect was avoided.

[1] *Ibid.*, viii, 333. [2] *Ibid.*, viii, 341.
[3] *J.L.*, xi, 364, 372–3. [4] *Ibid.*, xi, 376.
[5] *Newc.*, 41; the latter phrase must refer to some proviso in the Bill not described in *J.C.*.
[6] *Math.*, 194.

R

It is, of course, the role of Clarendon that gives the affair its chief importance, for the rejection of the revised Bill in the House of Lords represents his first open attempt to stem the tide of Anglican reaction. The evidence on the matter is somewhat confusing, but merits careful examination. On February 8, 1662, Dr. Peter Pett despatched this account to Archbishop Bramhall in Ireland:

"There have been great animosities lately and heats in the House of Lords about the Bill for the Confirmation of Ministers that passed in the last Parliament in England—save only as to those livings where Lords had the *jus patronatus*, which the Commons in this Parliament would have had—the Lords have joined with them in exploding.[1] At first all the bishops in the House of Lords were against it [i.e. were against 'exploding' the measure sent up by the Commons], and most of the Protestant Lords temporal. But my Lord Chancellor was resolved to oblige the Presbyterians by keeping the Act [i.e. of 1660] from being repealed, and at last got seven of the bishops to join with him, five of which I have not forgot the names of, and they were the Bishops of London [Sheldon], Norwich [Reynolds], Exeter [Gauden], Lincoln [Sanderson], Worcester [Morley]. The Duke of York was likewise brought over by his father-in-law, and the Earl of Bristol was vehement in the thing, and all the Popish Lords.[2]

"The Presbyterian ministers sent Calamy, Baxter, and Bates that day to the Chancellor to give him thanks. Some of the Commons going to the King the day before, to desire him to express himself positively against the confirmation of the ministers, he said he had promised them at Breda the continuance in their livings; whereupon they said that the Commons might possibly, many of them, be tempted not to pass the Bill intended for the enlarging of his revenue, if his Majesty would favour the confirmation of the Presbyterian ministers—to whom the King answered that if he had not wherewith to subsist two days, he would trust God Almighty's Providence rather than break his word."[3]

So elliptical is Dr. Pett's epistolary style that we may doubt whether Bramhall received any clear notion of what was at issue. But our

[1] The sentence is confusing, but becomes clear when it is understood that "joined" has the sense of "joined in conflict". The Upper House had insisted on vindicating the patronage rights of its members, which in many cases had been disregarded under the Commonwealth. In such cases, Puritan incumbents were not confirmed by the original Act. But the Commons, then controlled by the Presbyterian Party, had disallowed any retroactive exercise of patronage rights in other cases, and thus protected the clergy who had been "illegally" beneficed.

[2] In view of the previous reference to "the Protestant Lords", the writer evidently means that Bristol and his co-religionists were vehement in supporting Hyde.

[3] *Rawd.*, 137–8.

acquaintance with the Bill makes the letter's purport clear. Plainly, both the King and Chancellor regarded the tactics of the Lower House as impolitic, and Clarendon with some effort persuaded the Laudian leaders to follow his line in opposing the measure.[1] To overthrow the work of the previous Parliament without any formal refusal of conformity by Puritan incumbents would have seemed a purely arbitrary act of vindictiveness on the part of the Anglican majority. Reserving a full discussion of Clarendon's attitude until later, we may readily see in the progress of the Act of Uniformity an important factor in the situation. This Bill had received its second reading in the Lords on January 17, and only awaited reception of the revised Prayer Book from Convocation for its further consideration. To cooler heads in the Church party, this would offer a much less exceptionable way for dealing with the situation created by the Convention Parliament—undesirable incumbents would be forced to disqualify themselves by refusal to conform under the new law, and there need be no pointed reversal of a Parliamentary decision. Such, at least, is the implication of the chronicler Henry Gregory:

"The House of Commons took some things into their consideration concerning the presentation of ministers to advowsons and the further settlemens of ministers; but the House of Lords thinking it inconvenient that the Commons should have a liberty of presenting ministers equal with the Peers, or that such particular matters should be determined before the grand business of a Liturgy and Ecclesiastical Government, did for that and other considerations dissent."[2]

The House of Commons viewed with evident displeasure the Lords' action in confirming the Act without the amendments, and after a conference with representatives of the Upper House, firmly rejected the expurgated Bill sent down to them.[3] Another conference was demanded, but no further notice of the matter appears in the *Journals*. According to Gregory, "after several conferences betwixt the commissioners of both Houses, the matter at present broke off", and he adds, "hereupon the Presbyterians in London and other places kept

[1] According to Puritan gossip, "[the Act was] stopped by the Chancellor, for which it is said he hath the ill will of the bishops". (*Math.*, 194.) Since this suggestion would inevitably arise in Puritan circles, it is not dependable evidence. The leaders of the episcopal bench sided with Clarendon in the actual vote; six months later they did not hesitate to oppose him when their convictions ran counter to his on a matter of policy.

[2] *Add.* 19,526, f. 48.

[3] *J.C.*, 367.

many days of thanksgiving that God had put it into the hearts of the Lords in Parliament to stand their friends."[1]

Before following the progress of the Act of Uniformity, it is necessary to turn back to proceedings in Convocation, which had resumed sessions on November 21. At this time, the King's letter was read directing the Assembly to "review . . . the Book of Common Prayer . . . and after mature consideration . . . make such additions and alterations . . . as to you shall seem meet and convenient".[2] To avoid delay, the bishops of the northern province, already in London, were accorded proxies to act for their synod.[3] The revision of the Book was carried on with extreme rapidity by the two houses, for the work had already been carefully prepared by the bishops. Calamy recounts that when the Clerk of Convocation, Dr. Allen, urged Sheldon before the opening session that "they might so reform the Liturgy as that no sober man might make exception", the Bishop's reply was, "that what should be, was concluded or resolved"; and the story gives a correct impression.[4] According to Clarendon, "the bishops had spent the vacation in making such alterations in the Book of Common Prayer, as they thought would make it more grateful to the dissenting brethren . . . and such additions, as in their judgments the temper of the present time and the past miscarriages required".[5] Mutual consultation on the subject took place at Ely House, the London residence of Bishop Wren, for several weeks before Convocation reconvened, where the bishops considered a prepared list of changes. These had been embodied by hand in a 1619 edition of the Prayer Book, still in existence in the library of Durham Cathedral, and known as the "Durham Book".[6] This material, further altered and corrected, was submitted to the Lower House as soon as Convocation began its work in November.

[1] *Add.* 19,526, f. 48.

[2] The letter, directed to the two primates, is quoted in *Swainson*, 15–16.

[3] The temper of the Convocation of York is indicated by a number of propositions which were ordered to be transmitted to the bishops in London. The first begins: "Whether, in case any alterations in the Liturgy should be decided upon, a public declaration should not be made, stating that the grounds of such change are different from those pretended by schismatics?" Quoted in J.W. Joyce, *England's Sacred Synods* (Lond. 1855), 712–13.

[4] E. Calamy, *Abridgement of Baxter's Life and Times* (Lond. 1713), 159.

[5] *Hyde II*, ii, 118.

[6] Cf. J. T. Tomlinson, *The Prayer Book Articles and Homilies* (Lond. 1897), 208; F. E. Brightman, *The English Rite* (Lond. 1915), i, cxcvi–cxcviii.

The whole subject of the revision has been fully treated in numerous works on the English Prayer Book,[1] and except for two points, the details need not concern us here. The first relates to those parts of the Durham Book which were not finally adopted, and leads to a significant conclusion. The Convocation of 1661 had assembled when the Laudian party was at the height of its influence, and the membership of both houses was overwhelmingly of that school. The King's mandate had apparently given *carte blanche* for dealing with the Prayer Book, and Bishop Wren had written, not without guile: "Never could there have been an opportunity so offenceless on the Church's part for amending the Book of Common Prayer, as now, when it hath been so long disused that not one of five hundred is so perfect in it as to observe alterations; and they who are likeliest to pry into it, do know themselves to have been the causers of it [i.e. of the revision]."[2] Accordingly, we might well expect the completed work to exhibit in a pronounced way the doctrinal and liturgical ideas characteristic of the Laudian revival in the previous half-century.

This is, in fact, an accurate description of the Durham Book with its original manuscript emendations. It was a composite production, embodying (1) the principal amendments of the Scottish Prayer Book of 1637, a book well known for its Laudian colour, and in which Bishop Wren himself had had a hand; (2) suggestions which Wren is believed to have drawn up in 1660; (3) a paper of "Particulars" submitted by Bishop Cosin, which in substance probably dated back to the reign of Charles I.[3] Unquestionably, the revision at this stage reflected the real views of the party in power, and if adopted, would have given the English Church a form of Common Prayer not far removed from the original Book of 1549. But for some reason the Laudian leaders themselves decided otherwise.

We need only glance at the proposals which concerned the office of

[1] The fullest study is in J. Parker, *An Introduction to the Successive Revisions of the Book of Common Prayer* (Oxf. 1877); convenient summaries of the changes made can be found in J. W. Joyce, *op. cit.*, 716–17, and in Procter and Frere, *History of the Book of Common Prayer* (ed. Lond. 1902), 196 ff.

[2] W. Jacobson, *Fragmentary Illustrations of the History of the Book of Common Prayer* (Lond. 1874), 45.

[3] The relative importance of the several sources is a difficult and controversial subject, though there is general agreement on the facts as stated in the text. The most authoritative discussion of the matter is in F. E. Brightman, *op. cit.*, cxc ff.

Holy Communion to see what was involved. The distinctive features of the "Durham" liturgy were:

(1) The addition of a detailed rubric on the place and furnishings of the Communion Table, "meet for the high mysteries there to be celebrated".

(2) The insertion of a rubric enjoining an oblation of the elements at the Offertory.

(3) The Prayer for the Church was introduced by the words: "Let us offer up our prayers and praises for the good estate of Christ's Catholic Church", and included a commemoration of the faithful departed and of the saints. It also referred to the congregation as "here assembled . . . to celebrate the Commemoration of the most precious Death and Sacrifice of thy Son and our Saviour Jesus Christ".

(4) In the Prayer of Consecration, the words "and sacrifice" were inserted after the phrase "continue a perpetual memory of that his precious death"; a specific invocation of the Holy Spirit "to bless and sanctify these thy gifts, etc." was added before the Words of Institution; and the canon was concluded by the 1549 Prayer of Oblation and the Lord's Prayer.

(5) The Prayer of Humble Access was inserted immediately before the act of Communion, and the Agnus Dei ordered to be sung during Communion.

(6) Rubrics provided for the reverent veiling of the elements after Communion; for a form of reconsecration when needed; and for the permissive use of wafer bread.[1]

The theological tendency of these innovations is unmistakable, and is completely in line with the Laudian viewpoint. But how were the suggestions actually dealt with? On the page of the Durham Book containing the new Order of Consecration is a note in the handwriting of William Sancroft, secretary of the episcopal committee: "My Lords the Bishops at Ely House ordered all in the old method."[2] The same negative course was taken in regard to most of the other "High Church" proposals. In the whole of the Prayer Book as finally revised, the Laudian influence is barely apparent; the only changes which might be described as such are:

(1) The substitution of the word "priest" for "minister" in certain rubrics, and "bishops, priests, and deacons" for "bishops, pastors and ministers" in the Litany. "Congregation" was also altered to "church" in some places.

(2) At the reading of the gospel and recitation of the Nicene Creed, the people were ordered to stand.

(3) A thanksgiving for the faithful departed was added to the Prayer for the Church in the Communion Service.

(4) Provision for additional consecration was made.

[1] Cf. Orns., ii, 52 ff.; E. Cardwell, History of Conferences (Oxf 1840), 390–1.
[2] J. Parker, op. cit., ccxxii.

(5) A phrase was added in the Office of Baptism for the blessing of the water

(6) The formulas for consecrating bishops and ordaining priests in the Ordinal were altered to specify the order of ministry intended.[1]

The decision to refrain from a Laudian type of revision was probably not unrelated to the second point to be noticed. Not only did the bishops forbear gratifying their own preferences, but they made a definite effort, on the other hand, to show tenderness to Puritan exceptions, where these did not challenge "some established doctrine or laudable practice of the Church of England". In the judgment of a leading authority on the Prayer Book, Dr. F. E. Brightman, "the *Exceptions of the Ministers* of 1661 had considerable influence on the revision [of 1662]".[2] Of the seventeen concessions made by the bishops at the Savoy Conference, all but three were embodied in the new Book. In addition, "some thirteen other of the *Exceptions* were recognized in the revision, and changes were made which satisfy in whole or in part the Puritan objections [on these points]".[3] Three further changes were occasioned by the Puritan Memorandum of 1641. The concessions are too numerous and involved to indicate in any detail, but perhaps the most important were:

(1) The use of the 1611 version of the Bible for the Epistles and Gospels.

(2) The adoption of a rubric requiring communicants to give notice "at least some time the day before".

(3) The directions as to the manual acts to be performed at the Prayer of Consecration in the Eucharist.

(4) The restoration of the Declaration on Kneeling found in the Prayer Book of 1552 (though now significantly altered in one phrase).

(5) The addition of a note on the use of the Cross in Baptism.

(6) The requirement of the curate's formal consent to the Confirmation of any parishioner.

(7) The addition of the phrase "or be ready and desirous to be confirmed" to the rubric after Confirmation.[4]

---

[1] The rubric prescribing the manual acts at the consecration of the elements is sometimes attributed to Laudian influence; but the Puritan ministers had complained of the lack of such direction in their *Exceptions*: "We conceive that the manner of the consecrating of the elements is not . . . explicit and distinct enough, and the minister's breaking of the bread is not so much as mentioned." *D.A.U.*, 130. Baxter's Liturgy had also specified the manual acts.

[2] F. E. Brightman, *op. cit.*, ccviii.

[3] *Ibid.*, ccviii.

[4] For a full discussion of the Puritan influence on the revision, cf. *ibid.*, cxcv, ccviii ff.

What lay behind this two-fold moderation on the part of Laudian churchmen? Clarendon asserts that on the subject of the revision "the bishops were not all of one mind". One group deemed it wiser to restore the old Book "without any alterations and additions", as "the best vindication the Liturgy and Government of the Church could receive". Any change, they held, would merely "raise new scruples in the factious and schismatical party". Others believed that "the doubts and jealousies of many conscientious men" might be removed, were the Church "to gratify them in those small particulars, which did not make any important difference from what was before".[1] Hyde's memoirs at this point are such a medley of history and homiletics as to raise doubts of the author's accuracy in reporting the views of others. But the actual revision does seem to reflect a compromise between these two opinions. On the one hand, there was no striking departure from the old Book—to the eyes of laymen it must have seemed scarcely altered at all. On the other, a number of changes "in small particulars" gave substance to the claim that Puritan exceptions had not been ignored. The bishops themselves expressly laid claim to "moderation", and in the preface to the new Prayer Book explained their attitude as follows:

"Of the sundry alterations proposed unto us, we have rejected all such, as were either of dangerous consequence . . . or else of no consequence at all, but utterly frivolous and vain. But such alterations as were tendered to us (by what persons, under what pretences, or to what purpose soever so tendered) as seemed to us in any degree requisite or expedient, we have willingly . . . assented unto. . . . Our general aim therefore . . . was . . . to do that which to our best understandings . . . might most tend to the preservation of peace and unity in the Church . . . and the cutting off occasion from them that seek occasion of cavil or quarrel against the Liturgy of the Church."[2]

Two other factors may have played a part. The situation which had originally given rise to the revision called for a moderating rather than a heightening of the Catholic tone of the Prayer Book. Furthermore, the Commons in the early summer of 1661 had given notice of its con-

---

[1] *Hyde II*, ii, 119–20.

[2] Walton declared that this preface was drawn up by Bishop Sanderson, that "for the satisfying all the dissenting brethren and others, the Convocation's reasons for the alterations and additions to the liturgy" might be declared. I. Walton, *Life of Dr. Sanderson* (Lond. 1678), sig. 15.

servative sentiment in liturgical matters.[1] But whether the restraint of Convocation was due to the wishes of the Anglican laity, or was really designed as a *bona fide* olive branch to the Presbyterians, it was of no aid in reconciling the two parties. Baxter indeed complained that "the Convocation . . . made the Common Prayer Book more grievous than before";[2] but apart from an increased use of the Apocrypha in the lectionary, it is not easy to find basis for the charge.

On December 20, 1661, the revision was finally approved and subscribed by the whole synod; but not until February 24 could an official transcription of the Book be completed for presentation to the King. On that day, Bishops Sheldon, Cosin, Duppa, Morley, and Ferne appeared before the Council, and "the Book of Common Prayer with the amendments and additions, as it was presented by the Lord Bishops, was read and approved and ordered to be transmitted to the House of Peers".[3] As noted earlier, the Lords had on January 14, 1662, at last taken up the Bill for Uniformity received from the Lower House the preceding July; and, fulfilling D'Estrades's prophecy, the government now showed readiness to promote the measure. On February 25 Clarendon was able to submit the new Prayer Book to the Lords, with a letter from the King recommending its enforcement "by the intended Act of Uniformity".[4] The Book was approved on March 17, and the House then began work on "alterations and provisoes" to the Bill before them. An impression is given by many historians that the House of Lords showed much greater generosity to the Presbyterians than did the Commons; but, in fact, most of the amendments now added increased

---

[1] Cf. also, in the warrant for the Savoy Conference, the King's instruction, ". . . but avoiding, as much as may be, all unnecessary alterations of the forms and liturgy wherewith the people are already acquainted, and have so long received in the Church of England". *D.A.U.*, 109.

There is a curious note in W. Nicholls, *Comment on the Book of Common Prayer* (Lond. 1710), note c, on "The Preface" n.p.: "It is inconceivable what difficulties the bishops at that time had to contend with about making the alterations. They were not only to conquer . . . the quick remembrance of their sufferings, together with the unreasonable demands of the Presbyterian party, but they had the Court to deal with likewise, who pushed on to all acts of severity, but were willing to let the odium thereof lie upon the clergy. And by the management of some great persons then in power, the minds of the Episcopal clergy and zealous conformists were so wrought up, upon the talk of these alterations, that the bishops . . . found it a difficult matter to manage the temper of their own friends." [2] *Rel. Baxt.*, 384.

[3] J. Parker, *op. cit.*, ccccvii ff.; *Lan.* 957, f. 45. [4] *J.L.*, xi, 392–3.

the stringency of the original Bill.[1] The date of enforcement was gradually advanced from Michaelmas to Midsummer Day; the eventual substitution of St. Bartholomew's Day was made necessary by the delay in passing the Act. The declaration of general assent to the Prayer Book was altered to specify "all and everything contained and prescribed in it". Subscription was required to all the Thirty-Nine Articles, rather than, as in the Act of Elizabeth, to those only "which concern the confession of the true Christian Faith and the doctrine of the Sacraments".[2] The original measure had left some discretion to the magistrates in enforcing the law; the Lords made literal enforcement mandatory. All incumbents were now required to subscribe the declaration "that it is not lawful upon any pretence whatsoever to take arms against the King . . . that I will conform to the Liturgy of the Church of England, as it is now by law established . . . that I do hold there lies no obligation upon me from the Oath commonly called the Solemn League and Covenant, and that the same was in itself an unlawful Oath". Finally, all who were not in episcopal orders by St. Bartholomew's Day, 1662, were to "be utterly disabled, and *ipso facto* deprived. . . ."[3]

The Peers' only title to mildness rests on two additional provisoes. One of these permitted a deprived incumbent, if certified "of peaceful disposition" by the bishop, to lay claim to a fifth part of his former stipend, at the King's pleasure.[4] The other arouses greater interest because of the identity of its sponsors. On March 17, the day the Lords began serious consideration of the Act, "the Lord Chancellor acquainted the House with a proviso recommended from the King, to be inserted in this Bill of Uniformity". It reads as follows:

"Provided always, in regard to the gracious offers and promises made by his Majesty before his happy restoration, of liberty to tender consciences. . . . Be it enacted that it shall and may be lawful for the King's Majesty . . . to dispense with any such minister . . . of whose more peaceable and pious disposition his Majesty shall be sufficiently informed and satisfied, that no such minister shall be deprived . . . for not wearing the surplice or for not signing with the sign of the cross in baptism, so as he permits some other minister to perform that office towards such children whose parents shall desire the same. . . ."[5]

[1] *Swain.*, pp. 29 ff., prints the Bill of Uniformity in the form it left the House of Lords, including the material later rejected by the Commons.

[2] *Swain.*, 48.   [3] *Ibid.*, 29 ff.

[4] *Ibid.*, 46; this proviso was approved on April 9, *J.L.*, xi, 425.

[5] *J.L.*, xi, 409; *Swain.*, 22–3, 44–5. Certain minor changes were made in the wording before the Bill passed the Lords.

After several days' debate, this proviso was referred to a committee. It is not again specifically mentioned in the *Journals*, but was certainly included in the amended Bill which the Lords passed on April 9.[1] The official records give no indication of the drama which occurred on March 19, and which filled much space in contemporary letters. Francesco Giaverina, the Venetian Resident in London, wrote to the Doge and Senate on March 21:

"There have been serious disputes these last days in the House of Lords between the Lord Chancellor and the Earl of Bristol, going so far that they exchanged very sharp words. The Chancellor proposed a clause in the Bill which is all but completed, in the matter of religion, tending to the advantage of the Presbyterians, urging that the King desired it, and that it was suggested in his name. Bristol, who is a Roman Catholic, opposed. He is a most eloquent orator, and the Chancellor's equal in prudence, wisdom, and sagacity. He showed that the King did not at all wish such a pernicious and scandalous point to be discussed in Parliament. Upon this the two attacked each other, and the dispute lasted several days, and is not settled yet, as the House is still debating whether the clause shall be inserted or not. Even if it should be carried by virtue of the authority of the Chancellor, who though no Presbyterian supports that party because it is strong, to have it on his side in case of need, there is not the smallest sign that it would be passed by the Commons, on account of the animosity of the majority there against the Presbyterians, and of their rancour against the Chancellor, for which reason they would oppose any deliberation which they knew him to favour."[2]

Dr. Pett's account to Bramhall doubtless brings us nearer to the truth:

"The Chancellor, when he brought in the forementioned proviso, said, he had instructions from the King so to do, and . . . my Lord of Bristol opposed him on the score of private piques, and said it was unparliamentary for the King to anticipate the freedom of the votes of a House of Parliament by the prejudging anything undebated. The Duke of York was eager in the same business with the Chancellor."[3]

The stormy interchange between Clarendon and Bristol was the sensation of London. Pepys heard of "the great difference that hath been between my Lord Chancellor and my Lord of Bristol", and he too prophesied that even if the Lords accepted the King's proviso, "it will hardly pass in the Commons".[4] A Puritan wrote with zest: "The Act for Uniformity . . . lies in the House of Lords, where there hath been falling out about it. The Chancellor would have had several provisoes put in, whereupon the Lord Digby [Bristol] and he had such jarring that Digby had like to have been sent to the Tower."[1] De Wiquefort sent news of the affair to the States General on March 31: "... il y eût de grandes paroles entre le Chancelier et le Comte de Bristol, où le D. de Yorke se trouvait intéressé et M. le D. d'Ormond. Le Comte de Bristol eût du meilleur, quoy qu'il s'y agît de l'honneur du Roy d'Angleterre: dans un sentiment tout contraire à ce que disoit le Chancelier."[2]

None of the accounts except Dr. Pett's gives any explanation of Bristol's motives. His erratic and extravagant character was such that he doubtless seized immediately on the favourable opportunity to discredit his old enemy and rival, engaged in the unpopular task of promoting the King's dispensing power. Bristol's charge that the Chancellor was misrepresenting the King's wishes was not more fantastic than the attempt a year later to indict Clarendon for high treason.[3] Plainly, however, both the King and his minister wished to secure some elasticity in the enforcement of the Bill. The indulgence proposed concerned two relatively minor points, but in practice would have given Charles considerable latitude in individual cases. There is evidence that early in March a petition on behalf of the Puritan ministers was presented to the King by a Lancashire divine, John Harrison, for some relief from the intended Act,[4] and this may have given occasion for the move. Of the attitude of the bishops in this affair and on the whole matter of the Act of Uniformity, there is little evidence; but there are a few hints that they were not averse to some degree of moderation in

---

[1] *Math.*, 188.

[2] P.R.O., S.P. 84/165, f. 161. There is also a somewhat confused despatch by Salvetti to Florence, which says that Clarendon made a violent attack on Bristol on the subject of the penal laws, and that Bristol threatened to beat the Chancellor. *Add.* 27,962 Q, ff. 176, 179.

[3] *Hyde II*, ii, 256 ff. Cf. Dr. Pett's gossip to Archbishop Bramhall (May 20, 1662) of Bristol's effort to discredit the Chancellor in private conversation with the King—"whereupon the King was not observed to check the Earl of Bristol for the liberty of speech, or to vindicate the Chancellor". Pett shows what was popular opinion at the time, mentioning "the belief and observation of several knowing persons here concerning the Lord Chancellor's interest being in a declining condition. My Lord of Bristol is every day more and more adored by people as judging him to grow daily more the King's favourite. . . . Sir Harry Bennet, who is looked on as no good friend of the Chancellor, is likewise looked on to be grown of late as great a favourite as any is." *Rawd.*, 164–5.

[4] *Newc.*, 66, 68, 71.

dealing with the recalcitrant. Sir Edward Seymour mentions that the Royal proviso was "countenanced" by four of the bishops.[1] Morley, Gauden, and Croft were members of the committee which recommended the allowance of fifths to deprived ministers, and on April 7 Morley also made an unsuccessful attempt to mitigate the terms of the oath against the Covenant.[2] In the House as a whole, there was considerable misgiving about the King's proviso; "it was mainly opposed by divers", wrote Seymour, and during the debate the question was put: "Whether a salvo shall be entered into the Book to save the privilege of this House upon the occasion of this proviso from the King."[3]

The Act of Uniformity was returned to the Commons on April 10, and there, as several had predicted, the two deviations of the Peers into the paths of mercy received short shrift. On the 22nd the King's proviso was rejected, and four days later the allowance of fifths met the same fate.[4] That the feeling was hot is revealed by a letter of John Wandesford, M.P. for Richmond, written on April 21:

"The Bill for Uniformity hath displeased both parties . . . engaged in the debate. The opposers against the amendments which are understood to favour the Presbyterians could not carry one [additional?] vote in favour of that cause, and the other party did engage earnestly to give them the benefit of a promise made in the Act by his Majesty."[5]

A week later, Richard Neile wrote to Cosin's secretary, Stapylton:

"The great devil that scareth them [the Parliament] is the Act of Uniformity which is now in the House of Commons, who have thrown out both the provisoes, which in one of yours you so rightly guessed. The Pu[ritan] Lords are much troubled at it, but the Commons are resolute, and will pass no bills of concernment (as for money or the like) till the Bill of Uniformity passed. . . . Dr. Sand[croft] saith, the Presbyterian ministers in Suffolk begin now to say that the Lords' House is the House of the Lord, and so they pray for it."[6]

By the end of the month the Bill had been tightened to a satisfactory pitch of severity; Pepys observed that it would "make mad work among the Presbyterian ministers".[7] A conference took place between

[1] *Hist. MSS. Com., 15th Report, Part vii, Somerset MSS.,* (1898), 94.
[2] *J.L.,* xi, 423, 424.
[3] *Hist. MSS. Com., 15th Report, Part vii* (1898), 94; *J.L.,* xi, 410.
[4] *J.C.,* viii, 402, 413, 414.
[5] P.R.O., S.P. 29/448, f. 18.
[6] Quoted in *Orns.,* ii, p. xviii.
[7] *Pepys,* i, 252.

the two Houses on April 30, and so persuasive was the eloquence of Mr. Serjeant Charlton in commending the rigorous views of the Commons that, upon report of his speech, the Lords concurred without more ado, and passed the Bill unprotestingly on May 8.[1] The final episode in its long history was the ceremonious occasion on May 19, when the Speaker of the House presented the measure for the King's assent, declaring: "Your Majesty having already restored the governors and government of the Church, the patrimony and privileges of our churchmen, we held it now our duty for the reformation of all abuses in the public worship of God, humbly to present unto your Majesty a Bill for the Uniformity of Public Prayers and Administration of Sacraments. We hope the God of Order and Unity will conform the hearts of all the people in this nation to serve him in this Order and Uniformity."[2] If the prayer witnesses sincerely to that longing for peace and order in the national religion which possessed churchmen at the Restoration, it indicates no less forcefully the gulf dividing their world of thought from ours.

The interval between the passage of the Act of Uniformity and its enforcement on St. Bartholomew's Day (August 24) is one of the few stages of the church settlement in which contemporary evidence is actually an *embarras de richesse*. Associated as it is with one of the noblest and most pathetic chapters in Puritan annals, it has not lacked historians to describe the plight of those ministers compelled by conscience to quit their livings, and enter upon a life of poverty and persecution. But for our purpose it is necessary to follow events on the Anglican side, and to seek an understanding of the conflict in policy which developed between Lord Clarendon and his Laudian allies.

Though the Church party in Parliament had now carried its cam-

---

[1] *J.L.*, xi, 442, 446–50. Charlton disposed of the King's proviso by charging (1) It is without precedent; (2) It would establish schism; (3) It would not gratify those for whom it is intended. Against the allowance of fifths he argued that it would be almost a reward for noncomformity, would imply fear of Presbyterian resentment, would do for the Puritans what they had neglected to do for sequestered ministers under the Commonwealth, and (somewhat inconsistently) most livings were too poor to permit this sacrifice of income.

[2] *P.H.E.*, iv, 245. It should be noted that the Commons accepted the revised Prayer Book without debate by a vote of 96 to 90, but only after the Book had been subjected to a careful scrutiny in committee, and with the affirmation that the alterations "might by the order of this House have been debated". *J.C.*, viii, 406–8.

paign against the Puritans to a victorious conclusion, Royalists were not all of one mind as to the strict enforcement of the law. As always, members of the government kept an anxious eye on signs of popular discontent, and since London remained the focus of Presbyterian strength, these were not far to seek. Neutral observers like Samuel Pepys were deeply troubled. He noted in June: "I confess, I do think the bishops will never be able to carry it so high as they do. . . . All people discontented; some . . . that the King do take away their liberty of conscience; and the height of the bishops, who I fear will ruin all again."[1] Lady Anne Halkett somewhat naively reflects the uneasy feeling of a different circle—she was highly dubious of the wisdom of Parliament "to determine of those ministers who will not be conformed to the government . . . intended to be established, when in most parts of the kingdom it meets with opposition. Questionless the generality of the kingdom is inclined to Episcopacy as being the ancient government of this Church, and what many of the laws are built upon; yet that will not persuade others to be of their judgment because they are possessed with a prejudice against it."[2]

Fear of Puritan resistance led to different reactions among Royalist leaders. Although we have noted some reason for believing that the bishops in Parliament had not been advocates of extreme severity towards nonconformists, there can be little doubt that once the Act of Uniformity was on the statute book, they were for enforcing it to the hilt. Sanderson, for example, whose liberal views towards Presbyterians had of old caused such distress to his friend Dr. Hammond, was now engaged on a visitation of his diocese, and wrote to Sheldon from Leicester on August 5:

"I find the clergy of different constitutions; the obstinate Presbyterians appear not. But of those that for their worldly interest will subscribe anything, there are, I fear, very many. I have discovered such palpable hypocrisy in the men of that faction, as I thought should not possibly have been found in men that pretend to godliness or tenderness of conscience. If those that are about the King, and plead for some indulgence towards these men did but so well understand their temper as we find them (and as by many instances I could discover to you) how full of malice and hypocrisy—I presume they would soon forsake their clients and leave them to the Law. Truly, my Lord, unless the laws be executed (and that with some severity) upon them; neither Church nor kingdom will ever be at peace."

[1] Pepys, i, 259, 262. [2] J. G. Nichols (ed.), Autobiography of Anne, Lady Halkett (Camden Soc. 1875), 112–13.

After describing the difficulties experienced by the clergy in combating enclosures and recovering tithes, he continued:

"My Lord, I am not able to relate unto you the grievances of the clergy in several kinds. Upon the whole matter, without restoring the Court of High Commission, I think all the pains particular bishops can take will contribute but little to the settlement of the Church in peace and prosperity."[1]

It is a little difficult to recognize Walton's "patient Dr. Sanderson" in these lines! Nor was Bishop Hacket in the mood for compromise when he wrote to Clarendon from Lichfield on August 23: "The two seditious preachers of Coventry, [John] Bryan and [Obadiah] Grew, will immediately give up their ministerial charge, but will still live in that town to bewitch the silly people. . . . I will be vigilant (as God shall give me understanding) to see that city well taught, and Shrewsbury also."[2] George Morley, lately translated to the see of Winchester, informed the Chancellor that he wanted no suspension of the Act in his diocese:

". . . I know not, without giving very great scandal to the well-affected both of the clergy and laity, how to suffer such men [i.e. 'obstinate nonconformists'] to stay and enjoy the profits of their livings, who will do nothing but preach as long as they do stay, and that so, as that the sooner they were silenced, the less mischief they would do. Neither can it be said for these country obscure non-conformists, as may perhaps be said for dispensing with those grandees at London, as namely that they have been instrumental to the restoring of the King, as that the silencing of them would very much disaffect any considerable persons either for their number or for their quality, and therefore . . . I do not see any reason to dispense with them here."[3]

The temper of some of the Anglican laity was, if anything, even more bitter and intransigent. The Earl of Northampton found occasion to read the King a blunt lecture on his tenderness towards the Presbyterians. Forwarding a scurrilous letter he had received, he observed that

"[it] hath in it the whole spirit of Pagan Presbytery, without the least tincture of Anabaptists' or Quakers' schism. By it your Majesty may see that those are the only implacable enemies; it is the Covenant they adore. As for the other,

---

[1] *Clar.* 77, f. 157. Sanderson was not the only Anglican who regretted the failure to revive the Court of High Commission. On April 11, 1663, John Sudbury, Dean of Durham, wrote to Archdeacon Basire: "Things go very well on in the Houses of Parliament. I believe you will shortly hear of a repeal of all acts made in the Long Parliament; and then the Star Chamber and High Commission will return of course." W. H. Darnell, *op. cit.*, 224; cf. *Rawd.*, 174.

[2] *Clar.* 77, f. 274.

[3] *Ibid.*, f. 307.

were they extinguished by your Majesty's displeasure, I should not fear but that those who for their own fanatic humours resist the laws of the land, and glory in their strength as if they had or meant to frighten your Majesty to condescensions—I think that your Majesty is not so low in the people's opinion nor so destitute of loyal subjects, but your command would if but pronounced, strike them to the dust. . . . Your Majesty, by this and other actions of that party, may plainly perceive they fled to your Majesty for succour, but as the serpent to the husbandman, who so soon as warmed, poisoned his house; for they, frozen by their perceived cheats on the people in their affections, and mastered by others . . . connived at your Majesty's restoration as a degree to their rise, and yours and Monarchy's eternal destruction and the Church's fall.

"The ecclesiastical part of reformation I shall leave to the Bishop [Hacket], though never more needed than here, both the possessors of the churches being transcendent in two most excellent qualities, ignorance and obstinacy—I may safely add the third, disaffection to the present government both in Church and State."[1]

Even more striking evidence of the bitterness against the Presbyterians among old Cavaliers is the fact that a man as sober and generous as Ormond could write to Sheldon in these terms: ". . . I hope a general conformity will follow, and wish so great and good a work may be yours. The Bishop of Derry [George Wilde], I presume, gives your Lordship an account of that place; he shall not want such assistance as I am able to furnish him with to convince his flock, and those (sic) are troops and companies."[2]

The policy of "no compromise" was, for different reasons, supported also by opportunist politicians like Bennet, St. Albans, Bristol, and Ashley Cooper. Henry Bennet, now rapidly advancing in the King's favour, and leader of the Royalist faction hostile to Clarendon, submitted his views to Charles in a memorandum drawn up early in the summer.

". . . It imports your Majesty, in this conjuncture, to strengthen your authority by all the means and ways the law allows you, since the dissatisfaction towards the present government . . . is become so universal that any small accident may put us into new troubles, though they should not as yet be thoroughly designed by those that wish for them. . . . Above all things, there must be avoided, by any compliance or easiness, upon what specious grounds soever, the giving the discontented parties a belief that they have created in your Majesty any fear of them; for they will effectively gain courage by it and those that are most faithful to you will lose it, and with whom [is] the present Parliament. . . ." Only after the Act of Uniformity had gone into effect, should the King "be pleased to declare, you will effectively employ yourself, at the next meeting of the Parliament, to obtain a mitigation of those things that are now complained of as

---

[1] *Ibid.*, f. 236. [2] *Carte.* 49, f. 137.

grievous; and then, I say, it will be reasonable . . . to use that easiness and compliance which, in the beginning, will be looked upon only as a mark of extraordinary fear, and hasten the discontented parties to attempt something upon your Majesty and your government. . . ."[1]

But the Lord Chancellor's mind was moving towards a different conclusion. In his address at the adjournment of Parliament, he had expressed the hope that "the moderation and wisdom" of the bishops would in a short time induce "the poor misled people" to return "into the bosom of their dear Mother the Church", and in a more general frame of reference had added: "the execution of these sharp laws depends upon the wisdom of the most discerning, generous, and merciful Prince, who . . . can best distinguish between the tenderness of conscience and the pride of conscience . . . and will never suffer the weak to undergo the punishment ordained for the wicked." But since the speech distinguished sharply between the nonconformist laity and their teachers, castigating "the frowardness and pride . . . the fraud and imposture of [those] seducers", there was no clear hint that Clarendon still advocated the exercise of a Royal dispensation for Puritan clergy.[2] On June 2, however, Mr. Secretary Nicholas must have read a report from one of his informers with some irritation:

"The Presbyterians, or some of them for the rest, presented my Lord Chancellor with a petition to get them favour with the King for a connivance or grace of toleration which they say his Majesty may do by his Prerogative, having in him the same power in his kingdoms of connivance, as the Pope in former times. I am informed Mr. [William] Cooper was their spokesman, and delivered the petition. My Lord promised them kindness from him in help to the King."[3]

---

[1] Clar. 76, f. 150; printed in Lister, iii, 198–201. For date, cf. V. Barbour, The Earl of Arlington (Washington 1914), 60.

[2] P.H.E., iv, 251–2.

[3] P.R.O., S.P. 29/56, f. 6. It was at this time, however, that Clarendon finally quarrelled with Baxter. Thomas Pares wrote to Lord Massereen on June 16: "Mr. Baxter went to the Lord Chancellor, who is said to have done this [i.e. promoted the Act of Uniformity] and many things else for all his pretensions; his Lordship told Mr. Baxter he might preach if he would, but he gave off because he was proud and factious and to occasion confusion now in the King's absence—that he preached humility, but did not practise it. Mr. Baxter told him he hoped others had not that opinion of him, and he knew not himself if he were." Carte 31, f. 532. The incident probably explains why Baxter took no part in the petition for indulgence in August; it also suggests that the Chancellor's usual suavity had given place to a nervous irritability.

We can easily believe that to the King's chief minister, the storm signals seemed ever more ominous as the fateful day of August 24 drew near. Pepys was writing fearfully: "I pray God the issue may be good, for the discontent is great." Signor Giaverina was warning the Venetian Senate: "It is impossible to foretell any good thing, as the bitter feeling has gone too far, and things are moving exactly as they were when the war began in the time of the late King."[1] From every part of the country came alarming reports of plotting soldiers, treasonable speeches, seditious meetings, and plans of a general rising at the end of August.[2] A Royal proclamation gave evidence of the government's nervousness; as Battailler explained to the King of France: "Sur ce qu'on a remarqué que quelques factieux qui avoient trempé dans les troubles passés, meslés parmi les sectaires, se servoient de l'Acte d'Uniformité pour fomenter dans Londres les désordres que l'établissement de la liturgie sembloit y devoir apporter, le Roy a donné un ordre depuis trois jours qui ordonne à tous ceux qui ont esté contre son service de sortir de Londres dans vingt-quatre heures et de n'en approcher que de vingt milles."[3] Giaverina, however, was not reassured; "it is greatly to be feared," he wrote, "that [such precautions] will not suffice, as there is certainly great appearance of fresh troubles."[4] The government soon reached the same conclusion, and Battailler's despatch on St. Bartholomew's Eve gave an alarming picture of military preparation:

". . . Depuis deux jours il y a ordre à la cavalerie de tenir ses places d'armes, et toute la nuict elle est détachée par brigades dans les rues pour dissiper les soulèvements desquels on est adverty. . . . L'on a fait mesme advancer des troupes aux environs de cette ville, et le régiment de cavalerie du Comte d'Oxford y est entré. Avec cela l'on croit estre en estat de rendre inutiles toutes les factions de ce party [Presbytérien]."[5]

Is it astonishing that in the face of this crisis the King and Chancellor reacted in a not unfamiliar way, and resorted to a well-tried device for relieving the tension? A last minute concession to the Presbyterians was

[1] Pepys, i, 275; C.S.P.V., 1661–1664, 185.
[2] C.S.P.D., 1661–1662, 396 ff.
[3] P.R.O., Transcripts 3/110, July 10, 1662 (N.S.), folio unnumbered. For the proclamation mentioned, cf. R. Steele, Tudor and Stuart Proclamations (Oxf. 1910), p. 405, No. 3362.
[4] C.S.P.V., 1661–1664, 161.
[5] P.R.O., Transcripts 3/110, Sept. 4 and Sept. 11, 1662 (N.S.). A similar impression of great danger and description of the military precautions may be noted in Salvetti's despatches, Add. 27,962 Q, ff. 225, 226, 227.

decided on—but this time without the consent of the bishops. A letter to the Earl of Bedford's chaplain, John Thornton, gives a Puritan version of what followed:

> "The diurnal gives you a true (though malicious) account of the late petition, but conceals the occasion, because it reflects much on the honour of the Lord Chancellor and another greater person. He and the Chancellor sent to Dr. Manton, etc., and asked them why they did not petition, telling them that the King thought they were sullen, and had some design in hand, assuring them also that the King would give an indulgence to Dr. Manton, Dr. Bates, Mr. Calamy, and some few more; wherefore they petitioned in that form that you read. . ."[1]

Clarendon's move was made only a few days before the law took effect; Henry Newcome wrote in his diary on August 23: "I received a letter from Mr. Ashurst which gave us an account that past all expectation there was some indulgence to be hoped for in some cases."[2] The London ministers acted immediately to inform their brethren in the country of the good news, and circulated the following notice: "His Majesty will write to all the bishops that it is his pleasure that those ministers that cannot subscribe shall notwithstanding be allowed to preach, if the Common Prayer be read in their churches. This favour was obtained by non-subscribers, particularly by Dr. Jacombe, Dr. Bates, Mr. Calamy, Dr. Manton."[3] This message had no other basis than the Chancellor's verbal assurance, for the petition he recommended was not presented until three days after St. Bartholomew's— Wednesday, August 27.[4] It read as follows:

---

[1] *Rawl.* 109, f. 87. The bottom of this letter, with name and date, is torn off; but it was obviously written early in September, 1662. The information fits in perfectly with the other facts known, and is to some extent corroborated by Baxter: "Mr. Calamy and the other ministers of London, who had acquaintance at the Court, were put in hope [i.e. during the spring of 1662] that the King would grant that by way of indulgence which was before denied them; and that before the Act was passed, it might be provided that the King should have power to dispense with such as deserved well of him in his Restoration, or whom he pleased; but that was frustrate. And after that, they were told that the King had power himself to dispense in such cases, as he did with the Dutch and French Churches: and some kind of petition . . . they drew up to offer the King." He adds a note: "If I should at length recite the story of this business, and what peremptory promises they had, and how all was turned to their rebuke and scorn, it would more increase the reader's astonishment." *Rel. Baxt.*, 429.

[2] *Newc.*, 113.   [3] *Mer. Pub.* (1662), No. 35, p. 579.

[4] *Newc.*, 115-6. Newcome wrote on August 28: "I was sent for to the ministers at Mr. Greene's. We perused Mr. Heyricke's letter, whereby we

"May it please your most excellent Majesty. Upon former experience of your Majesty's tenderness and indulgence to your obedient and loyal subjects we, some of the ministers of London, who are likely by the Act of Uniformity to be thrown out of our public services in the ministry because we cannot conform to all things in the same Act required, have taken the boldness humbly to cast ourselves and our concernments at your Majesty's feet, desiring out of your princely wisdom and compassion you would take such effectual course, whereby we may be continued in our station to teach the people obedience to God and your Majesty, and we doubt not but by our dutiful and peaceable carriage therein, we shall not render ourselves altogether unworthy of so great a favour."[1]

The fullest and most reliable account of what followed is given us, curiously enough, in *Mercurius Publicus*:

"This petition was preferred to his Majesty on Wednesday last . . . whereupon his Majesty . . . caused the Lords and others of his . . . Privy Council to meet the next day (which was Thursday last, August 28) at Whitehall, to consider and answer this petition. For which purpose 'twas ordered that Gilbert, Lord Bishop of London, and as many of his brethren the bishops as were yet in town should be summoned thither; but the bishops (except the Lord Bishop of Exeter [Seth Ward] who was left behind sick) were all gone to their respective dioceses; so as the Lord Bishop of London was to answer all, and stand alone in the gap—which that incomparable prelate did to that height of prudence and Christian resolution (of both which at present there was absolute necessity) that by the very petitioners' own confession 'twas in vain to move farther, and they wish their petition had never been born. For . . . his Lordship having shown what a strait he was thrust into, either to observe the law established, and therefore become a mark for all that Party, in whose jaws he was to live, and who now were all let loose upon him; or else to break the statute, in affront to that Parliament who so lately, solemnly, and deliberately made it, and were yet in being to punish the violaters, and this Act so much the darling of that Parliament, and indeed of all the good people of England—his Lordship made it evident how the suspension of this law, at this conjuncture, would not only render the Parliament cheap, and have influence upon all other laws, but in truth let in a visible confusion upon Church and State. Which his most Sacred Majesty . . . the Duke of York, and . . . the Privy Council in their great wisdom considered, and left the law established to its due execution, there being no room for the pretended dispensations. So as the country Presbyterians (who by instructions from London were drawn to depart their livings) do now scarce pray for their brethren Petitioners."[2]

understand that . . . the ministers in the dark waited with the petition on Monday, and could not get it delivered, and came away more dissatisfied than they went." Cf. *Merc. Pub.* (1662), No. 35, p. 579.

[1] *Merc. Pub.* (1662), No. 35, p. 579.

[2] *Ibid.*, pp. 579–80. This version has unusual value for two reasons. We have contemporary Puritan evidence that it is "a true (though malicious) account of

This account of course suppresses the role of Clarendon in the affair, though its very omissions are suggestive. Some of the missing details, however, are supplied by letters of Daniel O'Neill to Ormond. The Duke's agent wrote first on August 28: "Here has been a design to have dispensed with some part of the Act of Conformity, but the bishops and my Lord Chancellor cannot agree upon it, which has bred a difference very prejudicial to both, and to our settlement. . . ." By September 2, he had learned more:

"Here has been great disputes at Council whether the Presbyterian ministers should be continued in their livings as the King promised from Breda, or that the Act of Parliament should be left in its force. The Bishop of London, who it was thought fit to be advised with, did not only advise that the Presbyterians should not have the satisfaction to have their ministers continued, but declared in the behalf of all the bishops that they would not comply with any resolution that should be taken contrary to the sense of the Act. This, with the zeal of the Duke of York, persuaded his Majesty to do nothing in prejudice of the Act, nor I believe will not, for much of his apprehension is over."[1]

But perhaps the most revealing bit of evidence to survive is Sheldon's wrathful letter to Clarendon two days after the event:

". . . And now, my Lord, not being able to wait upon you today as I intended, and having this occasion to send, give me leave to complain of your great unkindness upon Thursday in offering to expose me to certain ruin by the Parliament, or the extreme hatred of that malicious party in whose jaws I must live, and never giving me the least notice of it. You cannot blame me if it be sadly resented. . . ."[2]

the late petition"; cf. letter quoted on p. 260, *supra*. In addition, Sheldon's letter to the Chancellor of August 30 (cf. above) summarizes the same arguments, and indeed makes use of an identical phrase, "that . . . party in whose jaws I must live". Since it was rare for a debate in Council to be reported in a public journal, we can only infer that the account was inspired by Sheldon himself, or by a source close to him. Bishop Parker's frequently quoted narrative of the affair (*History of His Own Time*, Lond. 1727, 29 ff.), is merely a paraphrase of the report in *Merc. Pub.*

[1] *Carte* 31, f. 602; MS. 32, f. 3. It emerges from O'Neill's second letter that the Chancellor found himself in a strange *galère*: "You will hardly believe it, but it's very true, that the powerful Lady [Castlemaine] is, next one of your friends [Clarendon], the fiercest solicitor these ministers have; she has fallen out with the King for denying that to her, that at Council was resolved should not be done."

[2] *Clar.* 77, f. 319.

Finally, a letter from Sir Henry Bennet to Ormond on September 9 completes the picture by disclosing the attitude of the politicians in the Council:

"The not concluding any mitigation fit upon the Act of Uniformity will, we believe, fasten our own party and the Parliament better to us; whereas the indulgence that was proposed would certainly have disobliged them, and not gained the other [Presbyterian?] party, which would have been an unhappy middle to have affected."[1]

From these sources a perfectly consistent story can be reconstructed. Once the King and Chancellor had resolved upon an indulgence, care was taken to provide a favourable occasion by encouraging the most prominent and respected Puritan divines in the nation to petition for it.[2] The circumstances of Clarendon's interview with these clergy leave little doubt of his confidence that the King would impose his will in Council. Since Bishop Morley was plainly aware of what was brewing,[3] it is significant that Sheldon was summoned to the meeting "without the least notice" of the intended move. Doubtless the two schemers planned to confront him with a virtual *fait accompli*, and counted on his submitting, however reluctantly, to the inevitable. If so, they badly miscalculated; for Sheldon was the last cleric in England to play the docile and obliging prelate when he conceived the interests of the Church at stake. In Feiling's phrase, he was capable of "a front of iron",[4] and now, skilfully and without hesitation,

[1] *Carte.* 221, f. 9.
[2] We have seen (p. 258, *supra*) that a petition for indulgence had already been presented by William Cooper in June; but it was doubtless felt that there would be more weighty reason for action if one were presented by the more prominent London divines. A slightly different version is given by John Angier, Puritan minister of Denton, Lancashire: "August 20. Was a day of general seeking God in reference to the state of the church, that very day several ministers were before some of the Council and received encouragement to go on in the ministry. A letter read to them from the King to the Bishops that no man should be troubled for Nonconformity at least till his cause were heard before the Council. The news came to Manchester by Saturday post and was that night dispersed by messengers sent to several places. By means hereof many ministers that intended not to preach fell to their work, which caused great joy in many congregations." (Oliver Heywood, *Life of John Angier of Dentan,* Chetham Society, 1937).
[3] Cf. his letter quoted on p. 256, *supra*, written from Winchester on the day of the Council's meeting, August 28.
[4] *Feil.,* 127.

he played the one card which could infallibly defeat the King's intention. Speaking for himself and the entire episcopal bench, he threatened
to ignore a Royal Declaration of Indulgence, to take a stand on the
"law established", and, by implication, to appeal to Parliament. If he
deftly clothed his threat in oblique references, the meaning was clear
enough—"the strait he was thrust into to break the statute, in affront
to that Parliament who so lately, solemnly, and deliberately made it . . .
the Act so much the darling of that Parliament . . . the suspension
would render the Parliament cheap. . . . No, they could not comply
with any resolution contrary to the sense of the Act!" We may well
believe that such an attack, even without the zealous intervention of
the Duke of York, would "persuade his Majesty to do nothing"; a resourceful prelate was dealing with a realistic King, who could recognize
and accept defeat. There would be another day when James, still zealous
but less wise, would fight the issue with a weaker churchman, and discover none the less that it was not the Bishop but the King who courted
"certain ruin".

Naturally, to the Royalist Party Sheldon was the hero of the hour.
While *Mercurius Publicus* loudly acclaimed "that height of prudence and
Christian resolution" with which "that incomparable prelate" did
"answer all, and stand alone in the gap", O'Neill was dilating to the
Duke of Ormond on "the wisdom and courage of the Bishop of London, who behaves himself like St. Ambrose".[1] Nicholas thought that
the victory won by Sheldon's "great prudence . . . hath much satisfied
all the Royal party and the generality of the people, and will . . . render
the face of the Presbyter less insolent". He praised "the laudable care"
with which the Bishop had arranged for immediate replacements in the
parishes vacated by nonconformists; and even the sceptical Pepys was
constrained to admit: "The Bishop of London hath taken good care
that places are supplied with very good and able men, which is the only
thing that will keep all quiet."[2]

Gilbert Sheldon was indeed one of the few post-Reformation
primates to stand somewhat in the tradition of Langton and Becket.
His love of princely state and his munificent benefactions were not un-

---

[1] *Carte* 32, f. 25.
[2] *Ibid.*, MS. 47, f. 359; *Pepys*, i, 283. Bishops Hall in Chester and Henchman
in Salisbury also had substitutes ready for the vacant churches, and other bishops
probably took the same precaution. Cf. *Merc. Pub.* (1662), No. 36, p. 598;
Clar. 77, f. 298.

paralleled among Stuart and Hanoverian bishops; but in a combination of other qualities—courtliness and political finesse, driving energy and single-minded devotion to the Church, above all, readiness to defy the Royal will—he is reminiscent of the great medieval churchman.

Unfortunately, there was also in him the other and darker side of the same ecclesiastical tradition. If men would not accept the Church of their own free will and love, then force should compel them to come in, for the good of their souls and the welfare of the State. Two quotations from his letters are supremely revealing, and betray the state of mind which soon led him to commit his Church and Party to a hateful and futile policy. To Cosin he protested that autumn: ". . . The Presbyterians . . . cry out, 'Persecution, persecution', unless they may do and say what they list." In 1663 he wrote to Ormond: " 'Tis only a resolute execution of the law that might cure this disease—all other remedies have and will increase it—and 'tis necessary that they who will not be governed as men by reason and persuasion, should be governed as beasts by power of force; all other courses will be ineffectual, ever have been so, ever will be!"[1] Already, in Restoration England, this ruthless creed was awaking an uneasy doubt in Christian consciences; Sheldon was the product of a world which, if not dead, was fast dying.

For the moment, the satisfaction of churchmen was scarcely troubled by scruples or misgivings. The exodus of the Puritans seemed the glorious end of a weary struggle that had afflicted the nation for a century. Clarendon's attempt at a last minute indulgence had served only to embitter the sufferers under the law, and many on both sides believed that the Presbyterians had been victims of a clever stratagem. O'Neill informed his patron:

"The hopes the Presbyterian ministers had from Court of their continuance after Bartholomew . . . made the greatest and the most considerable of their number to decide that they would quit their livings rather than conform. The bishops took their advantage, and provided others for their livings. Now the poor fellows exclaim against the Court, and say that the hopes given them was to cheat them; that some of your friends that I know were very zealous for their continuance contrived it; whether it was by art or chance I know not, but sure I am, the surprise is very great, for most of all that quitted would now conform, but are answered as the foolish virgins were."[2]

[1] Orns., ii, 97; Carte 45, f. 151.
[2] Carte 32, f. 3.

But the new Bishop of Exeter, Dr. Ward, discerned a deeper and more wonderful meaning as he reflected on the whole affair:

"I trust", he wrote to his brother of London on September 20, "that God will be pleased to put into the hearts of our Governors a steady resolution to improve the present advantage to a perfect settlement. Next to the miraculous restitution, it was a wonder that the spirit of giddiness should so seize upon the enemies of the Church, and cause them to do that work themselves, which could hardly have been done any other way—that some few of them at London should deceive the whole party, so as to make a universal riddance of them at once—surely, my Lord, this was the Lord's doing!"[1]

Despite Royalist fears, St. Bartholomew's Day passed without alarming incident, and even in London, the enforcement of the Act was accomplished quietly and with little evidence of popular discontent.[2] According to Mr. A. G. Matthews, approximately 936 ministers were deprived at this date throughout the country for refusing conformity; with the addition of those already displaced since the Restoration, the total number of ejections estimated is 1,760.[3] Panic in the capital quickly died away, and Nicholas, ever a barometer of the government's mood, could write to Ormond on August 30 with belated detachment:

"There is much discourse of designs to rise, but when we come to examine the grounds of those rumours, we see little cause to apprehend it, and for my part I believe it a report raised only by the subtle Presbyterians, who (I have reason to believe) instigate the Quakers, Anabaptists, and Independents to rise or to make an appearance of some intention to make an insurrection, that they may lead the King and Council to yield to a dispensation of the Act of Uniformity."[4]

---

[1] *Tann.* 48, f. 43.

[2] A Puritan wrote of the state of the capital: "The tumults in London are nothing so bad as common fame represents them, though some disturbances the new preachers had by the boys, and by none else, in three or four churches." *Rawl.*, 109, f. 87. With the exception of a sensational letter in *Math.*, 201, all accounts agree that the change of ministers was effected with surprising ease. Cf. *C.S.P.D.*, 1661–1662, 488; *Pepys*, i, 290–1; *Mer. Pub.* (1662), No. 34, p. 570; No. 35, p. 577, 590; No. 36, p. 598. It is amusing, however, to contrast two versions of the popular reaction: "There was scarcely a good sermon in all London. The people dislike the Book of Common Prayer, and disdain it. They came into the meeting places, and hallowed and laughed at them who read it." (*Math.*, 201.) "The city is satisfied with their new pastors, and their churches are as full as ever, and the people behave themselves as decently as the orders of the Church prescribe." (O'Neill to Ormond, *Carte* 32, f. 25.)

[3] *Matt.*, *C.R.*, Introduction, xii–xiii.

[4] *Carte* 47, f. 359.

A few weeks later, the Duke received further reassurance from O'Neill:

"Every day we lose more and more our apprehensions of the Presbyterians. Those ministers that most threatened fire and sword, finding the zeal of their congregations vanish in sighs and words, now cry out against their credulity and their own folly, and begin to be received into the bosom of their Mother the Church. Where there are discreet bishops, the most penitent are provided for. For the present, the people of London are as well pleased as can be desired, and I have Sir Richard Browne's word, that he knows nothing that does not oblige him to believe the people will give all obedience to the Act of Conformity. This example will govern the Presbyterians not only all over this kingdom, but on that side, if you take the same course the bishops took here, which I doubt not is the only [course] to deal with that obstinate party, that hitherto no benefit nor indulgence has gained from their principles."[1]

By the end of September even Pepys was admitting his error: "Things are all quiet. . . . For aught I see the [Presbyterian] clergy are gone out very peaceably, and the people not so much concerned therein as was expected."[2]

Only the Lord Chancellor remained gloomy and depressed. A letter to Ormond on September 1 discloses the state of mind that had led him to attempt a compromise. "Your work I hope will be easier than you expected; I cannot say ours will be so," he lamented. "The very severe execution of the Act of Uniformity which is resolved on, may I fear add more fuel to the matter that was before combustible enough. But we are in, and must now proceed with steadiness, and so must you, and I wish I were as confident that we shall do so, as that you will."[3] Even more valuable for determining Clarendon's motives in the August crisis is Bishop Morley's letter of September 3. It is in reply to one which the Chancellor must have despatched shortly after the Council meeting of August 28, and deserves to be quoted at length.

"I have your Lordship's you were pleased to send me by my Lord Culpeper, and am heartily sorry to find by it that your Lordship should have such sad apprehensions, who are not naturally apt to be surprised or affected with them, and therefore I am afraid there be too great cause for them. But I wonder that Major General Browne should be of opinion that any toleration or indulgence to the Presbyterian ministers should be necessary, considering I have been often told when it was in debate at Hampton Court whether there should be such an indulgence granted or no, he was so much for the negative that he said the granting of it would undo him and the rest of the King's party in the City. . . . I am sure those that have the militia in this County seemed to me to be much

[1] *Ibid.*, MS. 32, f. 35.   [2] *Pepys*, i, 290–1.   [3] *Carte* 47, f. 3.

troubled, when they heard that such an indulgence was granted. I know the Presbyterians are a powerful and rich party, and I believe if they should join with the rest of the sectaries and other discontented persons, they might give a great shock to the present settlement; but I do not think that they are such zealots that for anything done, especially done by law, to their ministers, they will hazard their great wealth and their lives to boot by forfeiting the Act of Indemnity, as they must do, if they mingle with or abet any that shall openly oppose or secretly undermine the present government.

"Neither have they now the advantages they had formerly, when they had a Parliament, the Navy, all the magazines of arms, and the strongest garrisons in the kingdom, together with the unanimous assistance of all Scotland, and the militia of London wholly for them—so that they cannot begin a war with a great assurance that they shall prevail in it; but are sure (if they do not prevail) to be undone by it; and I think they have not showed themselves to be men of that courage as to hazard all upon such uncertainties.

"To conclude, I hope God that hath restored the King and his Church so miraculously (how unworthy soever we are of so great a mercy, or how ungrateful soever we have been for it) will not so soon suffer His as well as our enemies to prevail against either of them. And therefore, pray, my Lord, resume your old courage and your old cheerfulness; for certainly if we be not wanting ourselves, God will not forsake us in so good a cause as this. And perhaps He will not permit the wisest counsels to prevail, that He may have the glory of the whole work unto Himself."[1]

The Chancellor's original letter could hardly tell us more than this. Plainly, the question of a dispensation had been fully debated in Council and resolved against, when Clarendon at the last moment suddenly raised the issue anew. For once, his political acumen seems to have deserted him. Harassed by the growing threat to his ascendency at Court, and by an awareness that he had alienated the old Cavaliers through his liberal attitude to the "new Royalists", he may have hesitated to incur the bitter enmity of yet another faction. But unquestionably the Chancellor's obsession with the danger of civil strife was the principal reason for his conduct; he failed to analyse the temper of the Presbyterians as dispassionately as Morley, nor could he match the cynical calculations of a politician like Bennet. There is no evidence either now or at any time, however, that he felt sympathy for the Puritans or had any theoretical preference for a policy of ecclesiastical comprehension or toleration. "I am not much in love with your Presbyterians," he remarked to Mordaunt in 1659;[2] and it was an admission he might equally have made at any point in his career. Indeed, it was

[1] *Clar.* 77, f. 340.
[2] *Letter Book of John Viscount Mordaunt* (Lond. 1945), 111.

his consistent mistrust of "the factious and seditious ministers" which led him to magnify the immediate danger, and hesitate to drive the enemy to desperation. If we may judge from all his previous handling of the church question, Clarendon shrank from a ruthless application of extreme measures; his was the policy of "little by little", of gaining by degrees what could not safely be had at once.

In one respect, it must be admitted, the minister's proposal now went beyond any of his earlier moves to pacify the Puritans. In the other crises, the concessions offered had been more apparent than real; they had depended on a future implementation, and had in no way hindered the progress of Anglican plans. But whatever may be said of the limited dispensing clause sponsored in Parliament that spring, the Indulgence of August, 1662, would have rendered impossible the bishops' task of enforcing uniformity, as Sheldon clearly saw. According to the note sent out by the committee of London ministers, the Indulgence allowed "non-subscribers" to retain their livings and continue preaching if they secured readers to officiate at Common Prayer. Accounts differ as to whether the permission applied to a select number of Puritan clergy, or to the whole body.[1] In either case, the bishops, already deprived of the support of a High Commission Court, would have found their efforts to administer the law checked at every turn. In the final event, the Anglican victory would have proved illusory, and from a churchman's standpoint, Sheldon was not exaggerating when he declared that the Chancellor's proposal would "in truth let in a visible confusion upon Church and State".

The question therefore arises—did Clarendon intend the Indulgence to be permanent, or was it in his eyes merely an expedient to ease a menacing situation? There is no evidence to warrant a conclusive answer; but if we have interpreted his religious viewpoint and policy correctly, it is difficult to believe that he was now ready to sacrifice Anglican interests to Presbyterian scruples, and take the unprecedented step of giving a permanent licence to nonconformity within the Estab-

[1] Hyde states in his memoirs (*Hyde II*, ii, 147 ff.) that the scheme was to suspend the execution of the Act of Uniformity for three months, and historians often follow his account. Cf. *Feil.*, 105; J. R. Tanner, *English Constitutional Conflicts in the 17th Century* (Camb. 1947), 229. Nowhere is his biography less trustworthy than when it deals with the Act of Uniformity, and on this point he is contradicted by all the contemporary evidence, as indicated in the text. It is not impossible, however, that a three months' operation of the indulgence was what he privately envisaged at the time.

lishment. It seems much more probable that his action at Bartholomew-tide was a hasty, frightened move to tide the government over one more crisis, and made without thought of long-term consequences.

It is significant that, four months later, when fears of an uprising had quieted, and the King actually issued a Declaration of Indulgence, Clarendon's stand was what we should expect. On January 31, 1663, a week before Parliament met and voiced its violent disapproval of the Declaration, he gave an account of his attitude to Ormond. During his recent "indisposition", he wrote, Sir Henry Bennet had acquainted him with the King's resolution to issue an Indulgence.

"I made many objections against several parts of it, and some doubt of the seasonableness. . . . Some time after, he came again to me, told me he had made such alterations as he thought would answer all my objections, and that the King resolved that it was time to publish it, and then read it again to me. I told him, by that time he had writ as many declarations as I had done, he would find they are a very ticklish commodity; and the first care is to be that it shall do no hurt. This is all I know of it."[1]

As is well known, the Chancellor took a leading part in the Parliamentary attack on the Indulgence in February. If Professor Feiling is right in describing his position as one of "opposition to attempts undermining the very principle of Uniformity",[2] we can hardly suppose that the minister's sponsorship of the previous Declaration represented his considered policy.

An account of Anglican policy in the summer of 1662 would be incomplete without discussion of one further point. Did the bishops actually hope and scheme for the ejection of Puritan sympathizers from

---

[1] *Lister*, iii, 233. This letter was occasioned by one which Bennet had written to Ormond on January 13, giving an account of the matter which Clarendon now repudiated. Bennet had declared: "Nobody can affirm with more truth than I, that my Lord Chancellor had it [the Declaration] distinctly read twice to him, period by period, and not only approved it, but applauded the contents of it, and assured me it was entirely according to his mind. Your Grace may judge by this, how falsely it is suggested that his Lordship was not privy to it." *Ibid.*, iii, 231–2. Lister (ii, 204 ff.) makes an interesting comparison of these contradictory accounts, and gives good reasons for preferring Clarendon's version.

It is of course possible that Clarendon's attitude was affected by his rivalry with Bennet; but it is hard to believe that he would openly have opposed the King and further damaged his own position, if the Royal policy were one with which he honestly sympathized.

[2] *Feil.*, 130.

the Establishment, or did they accept the loss reluctantly as the price of securing a measure of uniformity and order? On the basis of words attributed to Gilbert Sheldon, a tradition became common in Nonconformist history that from the beginning the Laudians laid their plans with the former end in view. The tale first appears in William Bates's funeral sermon on Baxter, preached in 1691: "When the Lord Chamberlain Manchester told the King, while the Act of Uniformity was under debate, that he was afraid the terms of it were so rigid that many of the ministers would not comply with it, [Sheldon] replied: 'I am afraid they will'."[1] A story told at second hand thirty years after the event is not convincing evidence, and in this case its implication is certainly misleading.

To suggest that Sheldon and his fellow bishops looked on the new Act as a welcome instrument to purge the Church of its Puritan clergy is to misunderstand the Laudian attitude to uniformity. The High Church party had never exhibited intolerance of theological differences in the Establishment, or shown an inclination to regiment the clergy into acceptance of a particular doctrinal system. The ideal of a comprehensive national church, requiring assent only to Creeds and Scripture, and leaving wide room for divergence of opinion on secondary matters, had been accepted without question by Laud,[2] and was never seriously challenged by his followers. But equally in line with Elizabethan tradition was the insistence that the indispensable safeguard of the Church's unity was a prescribed common worship and a minimum standard of ceremonial. "Unity cannot long continue in the Church when uniformity [of worship] is shut out at the church-door," declared Laud, and: "No external action in the world can be uniform without some ceremonies. . . . Ceremonies are the hedge that fence the substance of religion from all the indignities which profaneness and sacrilege too commonly put upon it."[3] The attitude of the bishops in 1662, therefore, represented no new departure in Anglican policy—the Puritan clergy must yield an outward conformity to the requirements of the Prayer Book, or quit the Church whose lawful authority they defied.

There is ample evidence that here was no move on the part of the Laudians toward theological exclusiveness. The charge that the bishops

---

[1] W. Bates, *Works* (Lond. 1723), 725.

[2] Cf. E. C. E. Bourne, *The Anglicanism of William Laud* (Lond. 1947), 99 ff., 154 ff.; J. W. Allen, *English Political Thought, 1603–1660* (Lond. 1938), 192 ff.

[3] W. Laud, *Works* (Oxf. 1847–60), iv, 60; ii, xvi.

"feared" the Puritans might conform is belied by the efforts made during the summer to induce the clergy of that party to meet the legal requirements and remain within the Church. Sheldon advertised a special ordination in St. Paul's Cathedral on August 21, "that none might plead impossibility or want of notice", and we are told that on the day appointed, "he ordained many priests and deacons, divers whereof had before been under the hands of the Presbytery only". Cosin arranged an ordination in Durham on the 17th for the same purpose.[1] Morley described to Clarendon his efforts to win over "one Platt, minister of the parish where Sir Richard Anslow dwells", who could not conscientiously renounce the Covenant. "I said what I could in the presence of Sir R. Anslow to persuade him . . . with as much reason and kindness as I think became me. I am sure he seemed to be very thankful to me for it, though he was not persuaded by it." Though the minister at Farnham was not in episcopal orders, and had "exceedingly corrupted that place . . . and scrupled at . . . the whole ecclesiastical regimen and form of worship, I endeavoured to satisfy his scruples also". To conferences of this sort he invited all the Puritan clergy in the diocese "publicly and privately, and promised a fair reception and friendly manner of conferring with them".[2]

Bishop Sanderson offered Matthew Sylvester "considerable preferment" if he would conform.[3] Despite his angry words to the Chancellor, Hacket was "urgent" with the two firebrands in Coventry, Dr. Bryan and Dr. Grew, to conform and offered the latter a prebend in

[1] *Merc. Pub.* (1662), No. 33, p. 554; No. 34, p. 563; No. 35, p. 585.

[2] *Clar.* 77, f. 307. Cf. also an interesting account of Morley's visitation of the diocese of Winchester that autumn, and his attempts to persuade nonconformists to subscribe. *Ibid.*, MS. 73, f. 217.

Morley's later attitude to dissenters has been variously interpreted, for on several occasions he interested himself in projects for comprehension. Cf. *Rel. Baxt.*, Pt. iii, 84, 156. But a letter of his to the Earl of Anglesey, July 4, 1672, throws light on the matter: "You know what I was for in the late sessions of Parliament (I mean not a comprehension but a coalition or incorporation of the Presbyterian Party into the Church as it is by law established), and I am still of the opinion that it is the only effectual expedient, to hinder the growth of Popery, and to secure both parties; and I am very confident that there are no Presbyterians in the world (the Scotch only excepted) that would not conform to all that is required by our Church, especially in such a juncture of time as this is." *Carte* 69, f. 447. In other words, Morley's position was essentially the same then as in 1662.

[3] *Sand.*, vi, 337.

his cathedral. He persuaded twenty-three Presbyterian incumbents to submit to reordination, and his biographer adds that he "sent for Anthony Burgess, as he did for several other worthy but dissatisfied ministers in his diocese, hoping to gain upon them", though without success.[1] Bishop King was "importunate" with Matthew Woodman to remain in the Church, and "promised him his utmost interest for the deanery of that diocese".[2] Bishop Cosin was "more earnest to get [John Lomax] to comply with the ecclesiastical settlement than any preacher in the country". Piers of Bath and Wells persuaded John Humphrey to accept reordination.[3] The list could be amplified to great length; Kennett, for example, covers five folio pages with similar evidence, which he has mostly gleaned from Calamy's work on the ejected ministers.[4] It seems quite clear that the bishops as a whole regarded with honest regret the exodus of so many conscientious and worthy divines, and so long as the required minimum of outward conformity was secured, were anxious to comprehend the Puritan party within the Establishment. In this they were entirely faithful to the attitude of Laud himself.

The second stage of the church settlement, as we have reviewed it in this chapter, presents several points of contrast with the first. During the early months of the Restoration, Anglican energies were absorbed in disputing control of the Establishment with the Presbyterian party, initially in possession of the field. So long as the issue was in doubt, we have seen that the Church party had no mind for compromise; the "rights" of the Church were at stake, and in Laudian eyes, these were not subject to discussion. But by May, 1661, the victory was complete, and with the collapse of Puritanism as a political force, the Presbyterians had ceased even to be dangerous rivals. The nature of the religious problem was thus radically altered. The question was no longer, what compromise would the Presbyterians accept? but what terms would the Anglicans grant? The certainty of Parliamentary support gave the Laudian leaders a sense of freedom in formulating these terms, and it is worth noting that the requirement of episcopal ordination was not a major issue between them and the moderate Puritan

[1] *Vict. Co. Hist., Warwick*, ii, 44; *V.C.H., Derby*, ii, 30; T. Plume, *op. cit.*, 121.
[2] Matt., *C.R.*, 544.
[3] *Ibid.*, 327, 284.
[4] *Kenn.*, 813–18, 917–18.

T

group. The subject was not dealt with in the King's Declaration on Ecclesiastical Affairs, which Baxter deemed a sufficient basis for agreement, nor was it a bone of contention in the later discussions. Possibly because many of the Puritan divines were already in episcopal orders, their difficulties were of another sort.

We have shown evidence for believing that the bishops did not enter upon the Savoy Conference in a wholly intransigent frame of mind, and hoped that minor concessions in matters of liturgy and ceremonial might satisfy the opposite party. Under the influence of Baxter, the Presbyterians resolved to present their demands without abatement, and any chance of reconciliation between the two groups disappeared in an outburst of mutual recrimination. Nevertheless, the bishops did not write off all hope of appeasement. From the Laudian standpoint, the revision of the Prayer Book the following autumn was on extremely conservative lines, and showed unmistakable marks of deference to Puritan prejudice. The more temperate attitude of the bishops in this second period is further illustrated by the fact that after May, 1661, the real impetus in the drive against nonconformity passed from the episcopal bench to the House of Commons.

For it was now that the force of Royalist and Anglican reaction in the country at large became the controlling factor in the religious situation. Whereas, in the initial stage, the course of events had been patently directed from above in a calculated and careful strategy, the government found it increasingly difficult to control the rank and file of its supporters. The belligerent Anglicanism of the House of Commons not only showed itself in the degradation of the Covenant and the imposition of a sacramental test on its members. More serious was the fact that it hastily draughted a Bill of Uniformity before the ministry was ready for it, and further embarrassed the government by demanding an arbitrary reversal of the Bill for Settling Ministers passed in the Convention Parliament. These onslaughts against the Puritans were checked, perhaps rather on the ground that they were premature than that they were excessive. But the pressure from below could no longer be contained, and the gradual progress of the Act of Uniformity through Parliament in the spring of 1662 is marked by the increasing severity of its clauses.

Though there are some signs that the bishops favoured a less rigorous policy, the very slightness of the evidence suggests that they gave no strong lead in either direction. But once the Act was approved by King and Parliament, Church leaders took their stand as formerly on the law of the land, and firmly opposed all tampering with its provisions by arbitrary Royal dispensations. It is no less certain that diocesans laboured to retain the vanquished Puritans within the Church. If the terms of peace were high, it is still true that the Laudians preferred a peace that would include the Puritans in their midst to a victory that would drive them from the Church.

Clarendon had been no less intent than the clergy on the full restoration of the Church, and we have concluded that during the earlier period there was complete solidarity between his policy and theirs. But once the great end was achieved, the Chancellor, as a responsible statesman, naturally showed himself more sensitive to political considerations than did ecclesiastics. The Venetian minister remarked with discernment, "the Chancellor, though no Presbyterian, supports that party because it is strong, to have it on his side in case of need"—though "deal tactfully" would be a more accurate term than "support". The acute sense of political instability which Clarendon shared with other government leaders led him on successive occasions in 1662 to oppose drastic action against the Puritans. But so far as the evidence goes, not until this intervention would have contravened the established law, and introduced confusion into the work of enforcing order and conformity, did it conflict with episcopal policy. Thus, Professor Clark's comment that during these months "Clarendon's attitude was less consistently Anglican . . . than he and his apologists afterwards claimed"[1] needs some elucidation. His tactics were "less Anglican" than those of the House of Commons only in the sense that he believed Puritan disaffection to be a graver political hazard than did they, and that he persisted in the more gradual and cautious policy of dealing with it which they had abandoned. The evidence suggests that the difference was of means and not of ends, and the whole tone of Bishop Morley's letter, written after the crucial disagreement in August, assumes that the Chancellor's fundamental aims are still at one with those of the bishops: "Certainly if we be not wanting ourselves, God will not forsake us in so good a cause as this."[2]

[1] G. N. Clark, The Later Stuarts, 1660-1714 (Oxf. 1947), 19, note 2. The remark is made with reference to articles by K. Feiling in E.H.R., xlii, 407; xliv, 290.

[2] Though Clarendon's statement in his Life (ii, 150) has little evidential value in view of his general misrepresentation of the August crisis, it is perhaps worth

Historically, of course, it is impossible to separate the Act of Uniformity from the vindictive legislation enacted soon after against the Puritans by the same Parliament, and supported by many of the bishops. The church settlement of 1662 will always share the stigma which attaches to the so-called "Clarendon Code". But since the issues of comprehension and toleration are in essence quite distinct, and since action on the one has endured permanently, while legislation on the other lasted in its full severity less than thirty years, we are justified in considering the Act of Uniformity on its own merits. Historians as a whole have passed a harsh judgment on the Laudian unwillingness to widen the limits of comprehensiveness along the lines of the Royal Declaration, or to accept Puritan demands at the Savoy Conference. Many within the Church of England to-day would agree that an opportunity was tragically lost of retaining the more moderate dissenters in the national Church, and that the sacrifice was made for an ideal of little value. The final refusal in 1662 to come to terms with the Continental Reformation was in this view a major blunder, and productive of many future ills.

Another judgment is possible, however, and is perhaps most forcibly stated by writers who would regard the Laudian position with some detachment. A modern Congregationalist scholar, for example, has remarked:

"That the Puritan outlook was a limited one; that its comprehension within the Church, on the terms its representatives proposed, was only possible by a sacrifice of the wider comprehension of Protestant and Catholic attempted in the Anglican compromise; that the bishops had an arguable case in refusing to countenance what they regarded as a radical change in the character of the Church—considerations of this wider and more impartial character did not come within [Calamy's] purview; it was hardly to be expected that they should."[1]

Similar reservations are expressed by a recent secular historian:

"Had the prelates been willing to make a few concessions, it is said, the grim ejections of 1662 need never have taken place. It is a debatable point. The changes

quoting. Mentioning the resentment of "some of the bishops" at his attitude on that occasion, he declares emphatically: "Yet he [i.e. the Chancellor] never declined in the least degree his zeal for the government of the Church, or the interest of those persons [the bishops]; nor thought they could be blamed for their severity against [the dissenters]. . . ."

[1] *Matt.*, *C.R.*, Introduction, xix.

which the Puritans wished to make in the Liturgy would have opened the door to the introduction of a most uncompromising Calvinism, in which the variety of opinion and interpretation allowed under the old Prayer Book would have disappeared. . . . By rejecting such demands, the [Savoy] Conference at least preserved the catholic character of the Church."[1]

Such reflections suggest at least that the matter is not so simply stated as Professor Clark would have us believe: "Against the hardening bigotry of the Anglicans he [Baxter] could do nothing."[2] The Laudians firmly rejected the scheme of comprehension offered by a section of the Puritans; they did not decry the ideal of comprehensiveness. On the contrary, they believed and constantly asserted that within traditional Anglican limits a wider range of belief and practice was possible than in any other religious settlement, and later history has not disproved their claim. Because of their stand, the Church of England, alone among post-Reformation bodies, remained constant in its refusal to commit itself to a rigid system of doctrine and practice, and preserved that tension of authority and freedom, of variety and order, which is its unique heritage in the Christian world.

[1] E. W. Kirby in "The Reconcilers and the Restoration, 1660–1662", *Essays in Modern English History* (Harvard 1941), 74. For a similar view, cf. D. Ogg, *England in the Reign of Charles II* (Oxf. 1934), i, 199.

[2] G. N. Clark, *op. cit.*, 19.

EPILOGUE

THE importance of the church settlement of 1662 has always been recognized, but, as we suggested earlier, the form which it took remains something of a problem to historians. In one aspect it marked a surprising reversal of religious sentiment among the Cavaliers since the days when prelacy was first attacked in the Long Parliament. In another, it represented a puzzling deviation from the policy of conciliation which Clarendon followed in the restoration and stabilizing of the monarchy. The explanation, we have maintained, is to be found in the activity of the Laudian party during the crucial years 1649–62, and we are now in a position to summarize the conclusions reached.

The foundations of the Laudian triumph were firmly laid during the years of the Interregnum. In 1649, when the strong hand of Oliver Cromwell gave order to the nation, Anglicans faced the problem of adjustment to a new régime, the outcome of successful revolution in Church and State. The Protector's leniency during the first years of his rule made possible the rallying of a movement which had been thoroughly shattered by the measures of a Puritan Parliament. The most urgent question was that of its relationship to Cromwell's loosely organized and inclusive State Church—should Anglicanism persist as a distinct though outlawed tradition, or should it acquiesce provisionally in the abolition of the episcopate and Prayer Book, and become a conservative element in the new Establishment? The wide differences of outlook in the old Church made it difficult to agree on a common policy, and the matter was further complicated by the fact that only a third of the clergy had been actually expelled from their posts.

The Laudian party represented that section of Anglicanism which could not be assimilated in any general union of Protestants. The essentially Catholic interpretation of the Anglican settlement had deeply influenced the younger church leaders, and these men opposed Cromwell's programme on theological as well as political grounds. Circumstances combined to give the Laudians a clear field as spokesmen of the Anglican tradition. They alone could claim full loyalty to the Church of England as it had formerly existed, and, unlike their conforming brethren, they had no motive to temper zeal with discretion in their propaganda for the old faith. The refusal of the surviving bishops to accept responsibility and assume spiritual jurisdiction ended the hope that the various types of Anglicans might preserve a corporate unity, and leadership therefore passed to the men whose aims were consistent and aggressive, and who would risk danger and persecution to achieve them. So completely did the High Church group become identified with Anglican resistance that it lost consciousness of being an ecclesiastical party, and saw itself as "the faithful remnant of the old Church of England".

Laudian policy was not so much calculated as instinctive—to commend Anglicanism as the religious aspect of the Royalist creed, and to stake the future of the Church of England on a restoration of the monarchy. Sir Robert Shirley stated the axiom that "whoso in these times of persecution professes himself a son of the Church will also by the same principles be a loyal subject", and against the Cromwellian state, churchmen of this school kept up a relentless hostility. Loyalty to the King was taught as a religious duty, and the clergy who remained in England were always ready to act as political agents. In various ways this uncompromising Royalism served to re-establish the fortunes of the old High Church party. Intimate relations were formed with the exiled Court, and a strong claim laid on the future favour and gratitude of the King. A new and stronger sense of churchmanship among the Cavalier gentry was their natural reaction to the Puritan attack on the Church, and this temper was assiduously fostered by the tracts and theological works of the Laudian clergy. As chaplains and tutors in Royalist households, these divines implanted in the younger generation a fervent devotion to the Church, gaining for High Church principles a source of political strength hitherto lacking.

If the Laudians in England made capital of their loyalty to the Crown, it remained for another group to ensure the Crown's continued support of the Church. The clergy who sought refuge in exile were almost exclusively of the High Anglican school, and kept in close touch with their friends at home. During the years when a pro-Anglican policy seemed more of a hindrance than an advantage to the Royalist cause, these men worked to defeat the counsels which urged on the young King either a Presbyterian or a Roman Catholic alliance. Charles's treaty with the Scots in 1650 was a heavy blow, but after the defeat at Worcester the following year, the Anglican party rapidly regained its influence. Henceforth, Hyde, Nicholas, and Ormond were the counsellors to whom the

King chiefly deferred, and they were on terms of intimacy with the exiled clergy. Their insistence that the Royalist programme called for a return to the old Constitution carried with it the corollary that the Church should recover her ancient rights, and on this point logic was reinforced by strong devotion to the Anglican tradition. Divines like Cosin, Morley, and Bramhall were active in promoting this spirit among the refugees, and by a confident vindication of the Anglican position they largely frustrated Romanist attempts to absorb the forlorn remnant of the English Church. At the close of the Interregnum, they had good reason for satisfaction—Royalist policy was controlled by men who regarded the interests of Crown and Church as inseparable.

The government's espousal of the Anglican cause was apparent as early as May, 1659. Hyde in the King's name then undertook prolonged negotiations for ensuring the episcopal succession by further consecrations in England. Though the design was finally balked by the timidity and inertia of the bishops there, the Chancellor's letters made plain his deep concern for the future of the Church, and his will to restore it to "a great lustre". It was also evident that to the Royalist leaders, Anglicanism had become identified with the Laudian party; Hyde's clerical agents were exclusively of this group, and the choice of new bishops in 1659 showed the same bias.

With Monk's rise to power, and the emergence of the Presbyterian party as a vital factor in plans for a Restoration, the religious question became acute. An avowal of an Anglican policy by the exiled government was seen to be impracticable, and Charles took refuge in vague promises of toleration and a future settlement by Parliament. Any accommodation with the Presbyterians had been bitterly rejected by the Laudian party in the past, and there was no will to compromise now. George Morley was despatched to England ostensibly to reassure the Puritans and curb the "unskilful" threats of Anglican extremists in the capital; but Hyde and his agents were actually engaged in an effort "to break the design" of the rival party by fomenting division between the moderate Presbyterian divines and their stricter brethren. The evasive tactics of the Anglicans, aided by Monk's pressure for an unconditional Restoration, enabled the Royalist government to assume power in May, 1660, unhampered by any concrete engagement to the Presbyterians.

The influence which the Laudian party had acquired both in the inner circle of Royalist statesmen and among the landed gentry soon revealed itself in a formidable combination. In the Convention Parliament, where religious sentiment was too evenly divided to risk a decision on the church question, the Anglican laity fought a dogged delaying action, and were largely successful in neutralizing the role of that assembly. The government used the time gained to full advantage, and despite uncertainty as to the temper of the country, and persistent fear of sectarian uprising, displayed a remarkable tenacity in pressing the restoration of the old Church. Until the monarchy was firmly established, it dared not alienate the Presbyterian party; yet it was impelled to action by its entente with the Laudians, and by the conviction that the Church was legally entitled to her old position. Hyde obviated the difficulty in two ways. Political favour was showered on the Puritan nobles, and their opposition circumvented by the prize of high position and Royal favour. Secondly, with the connivance of the Laudian clergy, the Chancellor played skillfully on the willingness of one section of the Presbyterians to accept a compromise church settlement.

We have examined in detail the use of this strategy in the various crises which marked the advance of Anglican re-establishment. On each occasion the dangerous pressure of Puritan resentment was disposed of by the renewal of negotiations and the assurance of an agreed settlement. While the hopes of the Puritans were fixed on this mirage, the real plan was gradually put into effect. Cathedral chapters and important benefices were filled with carefully chosen clergy; the surviving bishops were quietly restored to office, and the Laudian leaders appointed to vacant sees; steady pressure was exerted by magistrates throughout the country to secure the conformity of the parish clergy; and the Convocations were finally revived on a purely Anglican basis in May, 1661. Within a year of the Restoration, the Puritan party had been hopelessly outmanoeuvred, and could rate only the offer of bishoprics to Presbyterian leaders and the summoning of the Savoy Conference as positive (though dubious) achievements.

The second stage of the church settlement was thus inaugurated by the triumph of the Laudian clergy in the Establishment, and of the Anglican laity in the Cavalier Parliament. Both in the ecclesiastical and political spheres, the Presbyterians were now helpless. Parliament lost no time in giving legislative sanction to the Laudian *fait accompli*, but did so with a discriminating and self-regarding zeal. Strict Anglican conformity should be imposed on the nation; but its enforcement was henceforth to be the affair of the legislature, and not an independent prerogative of the Crown and the episcopate. The political strength of the High Church party was bought with a price—the Church surrendered to Parliament its last shred of independence.

Once assured of a full restoration of Anglicanism, the leaders of the Church adopted a more conciliatory attitude towards the Puritans. The issue was no longer whether the latter should re-shape the Establishment, but whether they could be persuaded to remain within it. The attitude of the Laudians to the Savoy Conference and to the revision of the Prayer Book revealed the hope that minor adjustments might satisfy moderate dissentients, and up to the final breach on St. Bartholomew's Day, 1662, the bishops exerted themselves by individual persuasion to keep a conforming Puritan party in the Church.

On the treatment of obstinate nonconformists, it was soon apparent that Clarendon and the House of Commons held conflicting views. Still fearful that the religious unrest might provoke a renewal of civil war, the Chancellor clung to the cautious policy which had proved so successful in the past, and during 1662 opposed or tried to modify the drastic measures supported by Parliament. There is no evidence that the Laudian clergy intervened actively in the matter until the final crisis in August, when the Act of Uniformity had become law, and its operation was threatened by a proposed Declaration of Indulgence. Then Sheldon and his colleagues exerted a decisive influence. The dilatory tactics and disabling compromises of their patron were firmly rejected, and the prelates took their stand with Parliament in requiring that the problem of nonconformity in the Church be settled once for all.

The ecclesiastical settlement which thus took effect has been rightly regarded as a major landmark in English church history, and remains as a permanent achievement of the Laudian party. The Church of England would continue to be the meeting-place of diverse traditions, but, broadly speaking, its essential position and the limits of its comprehensiveness were finally established by the decision made in 1662. If a century before Anglicans had solemnly affirmed that "the Church of Rome hath erred", the Laudian triumph resulted in a judgment of equal moment—that the *Ecclesia Anglicana* was of another spirit than Geneva. In the Elizabethan settlement the Reformation had been given a peculiarly English expression, and we may interpret the settlement of 1662 as an equally characteristic version of the counter-Reformation.

Professor Powicke has affirmed that "the one definite thing which can be said about the Reformation in England is that it was an act of state",[1] and this comment is as applicable to the final phase of the religious upheaval as to its beginning. Indeed, there is a curious historic parallel betwːen the work of Cranmer and Laud. Each suffered martyrdom for the cause he typified, overwhelmed by a tide of religious reaction. Their respective movements underwent total eclipse, but a faithful remnant employed the years of persecution and exile in preparation for the future. Then, the advent of a new régime enabled the zealous minority, by the use of Fabian tactics and government patronage, to impose its will on the nation. Like all Church history the story of the formative years of the Church of England is seldom entirely edifying. In the stormy course of a century of struggle, noble ideals were too often corrupted by political intrigue, and heroism marred by intolerance and dissimulation. In this respect the final episode is of a piece with the rest, and if we would claim that the preservation of the Anglican heritage in its fullness was due to the work of the Laudian party, it must be with the conviction that the Lord who rules the destinies of the Church can turn even the wrath of man to his praise.

[1] F. M. Powicke, *The Reformation in England* (Lond. 1941), p. 1.

APPENDIX

LIST OF CLERGY IN EXILE, 1645–1660

Note

EXCEPT in a few cases, the names of those clergy who took refuge in the Anglican colonies in America have not been included. There was a considerable number of such men; cf. the reference of Sir William Berkeley, Governor of Virginia, to the Cavalier clergy: "The persecution in Cromwell's tyranny drove divers worthy men hither." (G. M. Brydon, *Virginia's Mother Church*, Richmond, 1947, 142, note 12.) The names of many of them may be found in Goodwin's volume (see below).

On the other hand, I have included the several Puritan ministers who were exiled for Royalist activity during the Commonwealth, and identified them as such. In some cases, it is impossible to determine whether the fellows of colleges were in Holy Orders; Barrow and Beaw, for example, were not ordained until the end of the period. Where the matter was in doubt, I have listed the names.

I am indebted to the Rev. A. G. Matthews of Oxted, Surrey, for corrections and additions to this list.

AITKEN, JAMES: Chaplain to the Marquis of Hamilton, and rector of Birsay in Orkney. Fled to Holland 1650, returning to Scotland 1653. Bishop of Moray 1677. (J. Dowden, *Bishops of Scotland*, Glasgow, 1912, 418; *C.S.P.D.*, 1660–61, 226.)

ALLESTREE, RICHARD: Student of Christ Church. Became Royalist agent, travelling between England and the Continent. Captured early in 1660. After Restoration, canon of Christ Church, and Regius Professor of Divinity at Oxford. (*D.N.B.*)

ALSOP, JOHN: Rector of Fordham, Essex; sequestered 1643. Chaplain to Laud, after whose death fled to France, where he died. (*Matt.*, *W.R.*, 145.)

ANGUISH, RICHARD: Rector of Starston, Norfolk; ejected 1644. Lived at Montserrat for five years, and served under Prince Maurice. Restored, 1660. (*Matt.*, *W.R.*, 263.)

ARNWAY, JOHN: Archdeacon of Coventry; imprisoned for Royalist activity, and exiled to the Hague 1649. Migrated to Virginia, where he died 1653. (*D.N.B.*)

ASTLEY, HERBERT: of Magdalene College, Cambridge. At Univ. of Padua 1651; living in Tunis 1652. In 1653 was serving the English merchants at Leghorn, and in 1654 appointed chaplain *pro tem* to the Levant Company in Aleppo. Dean of Norwich, 1670. (*Tann.* 52, f. 128; MS. 285, ff. 145, 147; *Brown*, 158; *Pearson*, 56; *Alum. Cant.*, i, 45.)

BANKES, CHRISTOPHER: Fellow of Peterhouse, Cambridge; ejected 1645. Became a Roman Catholic, and entered the English College at Rome 1642. Ordained 1647, and returned to England 1649. (*Alum. Cant.*, i, 79.)

BARGRAVE, JOHN: Fellow of Peterhouse; ejected 1643. Travelled in Italy 1646–60; admitted to Univ. of Padua 1647. After Restoration, Canon of Canterbury. (*D.N.B.*; *Brown*, 155.)

BARROW, ISAAC: Fellow of Trinity College, Cambridge, until 1655, when forced to leave England because of Royalist sentiments. Travelled in France, Italy and Near East until 1659. On return, ordained by Bp. Brownrigg. Later, Master of Trinity. (*D.N.B.*; P. H. Osmond, *Isaac Barrow*, Lond. 1946.)

BARWICK, JOHN: Preb. of Durham. Acted as Royalist agent from beginning of war. Imprisoned in Tower 1650–2; active in negotiating episcopal consecrations in 1659. Dean of St. Paul's, 1661. (*D.N.B.*)

BASIRE, ISAAC: Archdeacon of Northumberland; travelled in France, Italy and Near East. Lived in Transylvania until Restoration. (*D.N.B.*)

BAYLY, THOMAS: Sub-dean of Wells, emigrated in 1650. Travelled in Flanders and France, became a Roman Catholic, and settled at Douai. (*D.N.B.*)

BEALE, WILLIAM: Dean of Ely; went into exile 1646. Was Hyde's chaplain on mission to Spain, and died in Madrid 1651. (*D.N.B.*)

BEAUMONT, GEORGE: Minister to the Merchant Adventurers at Rotterdam in 1650; of the English Church at the Hague, 1651–60. Also, chaplain to the Queen of Bohemia. At Restoration preb. of Westminster and Dean of Derry. (*Steven*, 311; *Morley*, p. ix; *Alum. Cant.*, i, 118; *Merc. Pol.*, No. 29, p. 482; *Thurl.*, vii, 228, 246 *et passim*.)

BEAW, WILLIAM: Fellow of New College, Oxford; deprived 1648. Served as Royalist agent in Denmark, and took part in invasion of Poland as officer in Swedish Army. Ordained after Restoration; Bishop of Llandaff, 1679. (*Athen. Oxon.*, ii, 1179; N. Sykes, *Church and State in the 18th Century*, Camb. 1934, p. 16.)

BELL, WILLIAM: Fellow of St. John's College, Oxford; ejected 1649, when he emigrated to France. Returned to England 1655. After Restoration Archdeacon of St. Albans. (*D.N.B.*)

BIDGOOD, JOHN: Fellow of Exeter College, Oxford; ejected 1648. Went to Padua, where studied medicine. Returned 1660. (*Alum. Cant.*, i, 149.)

BISPHAM, WILLIAM: Preb. of Chester; "driven beyond the seas". (*Walker*, ii, 11.)

BOCKENHAM, ANTHONY: Fellow of Pembroke College, Cambridge. In Leghorn 1652; later in Constantinople, and temporary consul at Smyrna 1659–60. Rector of Helmingham 1663. (*Matt.*, *W.R.*, 328.)

BOLDERO, EDMUND: Fellow of Pembroke College, Cambridge; sequestered from rectorship of Westerfield, Suffolk, 1647. Chaplain to Montrose, imprisoned, and banished abroad. At Restoration, rector of Hadleigh, Suffolk. (*Matt.*, *W.R.*, 328; *C.S.P.D.*, 1660–61, 117.)

BRAMHALL, JOHN: Bishop of Derry; travelled in western Europe, 1646–60. Archbishop of Armagh, 1660. (*D.N.B.*)

BREVINT, DANIEL: Refugee from Jersey, ordained in Paris by Bishop Sydserf, 1651. Became chaplain to Turenne. Later, Dean of Lincoln. (*D.N.B.*)

BROUGH, WILLIAM, D.D.: Dean of Gloucester, "chaplain to the Queen's family in Holland, and returned with her to Oxford". Reinstated 1660. (*D.N.B.*; *C.S.P.D.*, 1660–61, 14.)

BROWNE, THOMAS, D.D.: Canon of Windsor; ejected before 1645. Emigrated to Holland, where became chaplain to the Princess of Orange. Reinstated 1660. (*D.N.B.*; *Merc. Pol.*, No. 39, 637.)

BULLEN, DANIEL: Minor canon of Canterbury. In Middleburgh 1652; also travelled in France and Italy. Rector of Elwick, Co. Durham, 1660. (*Matt.*, *W.R.*, 212; *C.S.P.D.*, 1660–61, 438.)

BURNET, ALEXANDER: Kentish rector; deprived 1650, when fled to the Continent. Acted as agent to Charles II; apprehended in London, but escaped. Bishop of Aberdeen, 1663. (*D.N.B.*)

BYAM, HENRY: Preb. of Exeter. In Jersey at its surrender to Parliament 1651, when fled to France with two sons. In England 1655. Preb. of Wells, 1660. (*D.N.B.*; *Matt.,W.R.*, 310.)

CADE, THOMAS, D.D.: Chaplain to the King in exile. At Univ. of Padua 1656; at the Hague 1659. Mentioned by Pepys as "a merry mad parson". (*Harl.* 3783, f. 248; *Brown*, 161; *Pepys*, May 17, 1660.)

CARLETON, GUY: Vicar of Bucklebury, Berkshire. Escaped from imprisonment in Lambeth House to Holland, where he lived during latter part of exile. Acted as Royalist agent. Bishop of Bristol, 1671; of Chichester, 1678–85. (*D.N.B.*)

CAWTON, THOMAS: Puritan rector of St. Bartholomew's, London; deprived for Royalist activity 1651, and left England. Pastor of the English Church at Rotterdam until his death in 1659. (*D.N.B.*; *Nich.*, iv, 70–2.)

CHALFONT, RICHARD: Fellow of Lincoln College; chaplain to the Merchant Adventurers at Rotterdam from 1646 until his death in 1648. (*Matt.*, *W.R.*, 27.)

CLARE, ANDREW, D.D.: Rector of Walton, Lancashire; sequestered 1645. Lived in Paris, and sometimes officiated at the Embassy Chapel. Rector of Cranford, Middlesex, 1658; died before the Restoration. (*Matt.*, *W.R.*, 229.)

CLERK, JOHN: Vicar of North Mimms, Hertfordshire; migrated to the West Indies. Restored 1660. (*Walker*, ii, 219.)

COOPER, WILLIAM: Vicar of Ringmer, Sussex. Chaplain to the Queen of Bohemia at the Hague, 1644–8. Puritan, and ejected from St. Olave's, Southwark, 1662. (*Matt.*, *C.R.*, 134.)

CORKER, FRANCIS: Vicar of Bradford, Yorkshire. Escaped from imprisonment in Lincoln Castle, spent two years in Holland, and a year in Scilly. Returned to England before 1657; restored 1662. (*Matt.*, *W.R.*, 391.)

COSIN, JOHN: Dean of Peterborough; became chaplain to Anglicans at Queen Henrietta's court in Paris, 1645–60. Bishop of Durham, 1660. (*D.N.B.*)

CRASHAW, RICHARD: Fellow of Peterhouse; expelled 1643. Went to Paris, where became Roman Catholic. Died in Rome 1649. (*D.N.B.*; for Anglican ordination, cf. *Church Quarterly Review*, cvi, No. 211, p. 143.)

CREIGHTON, ROBERT, D.D.: Canon of Wells; sequestered 1645, and emigrated 1646. Lived in Utrecht, and was tutor to Sir Ralph Verney's son. Bishop of Bath and Wells, 1670. (*D.N.B.*; F. P. Verney, *Memoirs of the Verney Family*, Lond. 1848–53, iii, *passim*.)

CRESSEY, HUGH: Canon of Windsor; left England 1644, and became a Roman Catholic in Rome 1646. (*D.N.B.*)

CROFTS, JOHN: Rector of West Stow, Suffolk; ejected 1644. Served in Royalist Army, and may have been the Crofts in Danzig, 1651. In England 1655. Dean of Norwich, 1660. (*Matt., W.R.*, 332.)

CROWTHER, JOSEPH: Preb. of St. Paul's. Chaplain to the Duke of York in exile. At Restoration, chancellor of St. Paul's. (*Walker*, ii, 50; F. C. Turner, *James II*, Lond. 1948, *passim*.)

CROYDON, THOMAS: Fellow of Trinity College, Cambridge. Lived in Padua, practising medicine, 1647–50. (*Matt., W.R.*, 41.)

DALTON, THOMAS: Rector of Dalham, Suffolk, Chaplain to the Levant Company in Constantinople 1654. Prebendary of Durham 1660. (*Pearson*, 15; *Alum. Cant.*, ii, 6.)

DAVENPORT, GEORGE: Student of Emmanuel College, Cambridge. In Holland and Paris after 1655. At Restoration became Cosin's chaplain, and rector of Houghton-le-Spring, Durham. (*Harl.* 3783, f. 178; *Tann.* 52, f. 103; G. D'Oyly, *Life of William Sancroft*, Lond. 1821, i, 52, 90 ff.)

DAVIDSON, CHARLES: Died at Antwerp, 1658. (*C.S.P.C.*, iv, 69; possibly referred to in *C.S.P.D.*, 1660–61, 546.)

DUNCON, ELEAZOR: Preb. of Durham and York; sequestered 1644. Chaplain to Levant Company at Leghorn, 1650; also at Smyrna 1652. Living in Saumur 1655, and visited England as Royalist agent. Resumed chaplainship Leghorn, and died there 1660. (*D.N.B.*; *Matt., W.R.*, 141; *Pearson*, 30.)

DURANT, NATHANIEL: of Jesus College, Cambridge. Chaplain to the Levant Company at Constantinople 1638–42; at Smyrna 1642–51. (*Pearson*, 14, 29–30).

DUREL, JOHN: Ordained by Bishop Sydserf in Paris 1651; became chaplain to the Duc de la Force. After Restoration, Dean of Windsor. (*D.N.B.*)

DURIE, JOHN: Ordained by Laud in 1634. Chaplain to the Princess of Orange at the Hague, 1641–3; minister to the Merchant Adventurers, Rotterdam, 1643–5. Travelled in western Europe 1654–7 to promote schemes of church reunion. (*D.N.B.*; J. M. Batten, *John Durie*, Chicago 1944; *Add.* 34,015, f. 52.)

EARLE, JOHN, D.D.: Chancellor of Salisbury; left England in 1646. Lived first at Antwerp. Succeeded Steward in 1651 as principal chaplain to the King, whom he accompanied on his travels. Bishop of Worcester, 1662; of Salisbury, 1663. (*D.N.B.*)

EATON, NATHANIEL: Former minister in Massachusetts and Virginia. Returned to England 1646, and in 1647 was studying at the University of Padua.

Though Puritan, conformed at the Restoration, and became rector of Bideford, Devonshire. (*D.N.B.*)

ELBOROUGH, JEREMIAH: Rector of Throcking, Herts., 1623–6; minister at the English Church in Utrecht 1634; and chaplain to the Merchant Adventurers at Hamburg through period of exile. (*Steven*, 339; *Thurl.*, iv, 322; *Alum. Cant.*, ii, 92.)

FEATLEY (or FAIRCLOUGH), JOHN: Rector of Langar, Notts. Migrated with his family to St. Christopher's in the West Indies 1643. Returned 1655, and at Restoration made precentor of Lincoln, and chaplain to the King. (*Walker*, ii, 47; *Kenn.*, 230; *Alum. Oxon.*, ii, 488.)

FLEETWOOD, JAMES: Preb. of Lichfield. After 1655 in France as chaplain to the Duke of Richmond and Lennox. Bishop of Worcester, 1675. (*D.N.B.*)

FOLLIOTT, EDWARD: Rector of Alderton, Northamptonshire; became minister of Hampton Parish in York Co., Virginia. (*Alum. Oxon.*, ii, 513; *Good.*, 269.)

FORBES, JOHN: Deprived 1641 as professor of theology, Univ. of Aberdeen, for support of episcopacy. Emigrated to Holland 1644, where served English congregations 1644–6. Died in Scotland 1647. (*Grub.* iii, 107.)

FRAMPTON, ROBERT: Ordained by Bishop Skinner during the Commonwealth. In 1655 became chaplain to the Levant Company at Aleppo, where he remained until 1670. Bishop of Gloucester, 1681. (*D.N.B.*)

FREWEN, ACCEPTED: Bishop of Lichfield; escaped to France after 1652, when Cromwell placed £1,000 on his head. Returned to England before Restoration. Archbishop of York, 1660. (*D.N.B.*)

FULHAM, EDWARD: Preb. of Chichester. Imprisoned 1641, later fled to Italy. Rector of West Ilsley, Berks., 1662. (*Matt.*, *W.R.*, 297.)

GATFORD, LIONEL: Rector of Dennington, Suffolk. Imprisoned, banished to Jersey, where he became chaplain to Hyde. Returned to England from Continent about 1655. Vicar of Plymouth, 1660. (*D.N.B.*)

GAWEN, THOMAS: Preb. of Winchester. Travelled in Italy for part of Interregnum as tutor. After Restoration became a Roman Catholic. (*D.N.B.*; *C.S.P.D.*, 1661–62, 311.)

GOFFE, STEPHEN: Chaplain to Charles I, and preb. of Canterbury. Became a Royalist agent; in 1651 in Paris was converted to Roman Catholicism, and joined the Oratorians there. (*D.N.B.*)

GOTOBED, WILLIAM: of Trinity College, Cambridge; chaplain to the Levant Company at Smyrna 1640–42, and at Constantinople 1642–9. Rector of South Pickenham, Norfolk, 1657; ejected 1658. Restored 1660. (*Pearson*, 14, 29; *Alum. Cant.*, ii, 225.)

GURGANY, JOHN: Chaplain at Merton College, Oxford, and naval chaplain until 1646; "forced to go abroad till the Restoration". Canon of Salisbury, 1660. (*C.S.P.D.*, 1660–61, 261, 346; *Alum. Cant.*, ii, 257.)

GWYN, JOHN: Vicar of Cople, Bedfordshire; became minister of Ware Parish, Gloucester Co., Virginia. (*Good.*, 276; *Alum. Oxon.*, ii, 624.)

HALL, RICHARD: Rector of St. Mary Steps, Exeter. Went abroad and became Roman Catholic, but recanted on his return to Exeter in 1660. Rector of St. Edmund, Exeter, 1665. (*Matt.*, *W.R.*, 114.)

HAMILTON, ARCHIBALD: Archbishop of Cashel; *c.* 1642 emigrated to Sweden. Died in Upsala 1659. (*D.N.B.*)

HAMILTON, WILLIAM: Fellow of All Souls' College, Oxford. Probably the Hamilton mentioned by Evelyn as serving the Embassy Chapel in Paris, 1651, as he is associated with John Lloyd, another fellow of All Souls'. (*Matt.*, *W.R.*, 23; *Evel.*, ii, 44.)

HAWLES, ANTHONY: Chaplain to the Earl of Pembroke; became chaplain to the King in exile. Lived at Leghorn six years, later at Smyrna and Constantinople. Returned to England 1657, when he was nominated by Duppa, Archdeacon of Salisbury. At Restoration, Canon of Windsor. (*Athen. Oxon.*, ii, Fasti. Oxon. 135; *C.S.P.C.*, iv, 463; *Add.* 34,015, f. 54.)

HEAVERS, JOHN: Fellow of Clare College. Acted as Sir Robert Shirley's agent in carrying information to the King in exile. (*Matt.*, *W.R.*, 36.)

HILL, NATHANIEL: Vicar of Renhold, Bedfordshire. At Univ. of Padua 1648; chaplain to the Levant Company at Aleppo 1650–4. Admitted to the rectorship of Fordwich, Kent, by Triers in 1657. (*Matt.*, *W.R.*, 65; *Brown*, 156; *Pearson*, 21, 56.)

HONYWOOD, MICHAEL: Rector of Kegworth, Leicestershire; crossed to Holland in 1643. Lived first at Leyden, and during most of exile at Utrecht. Dean of Lincoln, 1660. (*D.N.B.*)

ISAACSON, WILLIAM: Vicar of Swaffham Bulbeck, Cambridgeshire; ejected 1644. Chaplain to the East India Company in Madras, 1645–61. (*Matt.*, *W.R.*, 82.)

JAY, GEORGE: Preb. of Lichfield; sequestered 1644. In Brussels 1655, and returned to England 1656. Dean of Peterborough, 1660. (*Matt.*, *W.R.*, 280.)

JOHNSON, SAMPSON, D.D.: Rector of Fobbing, Essex; was abroad when sequestered 1645. With Hyde in Jersey 1646; a prisoner in St. James's Palace in London, 1655. Restored 1660. (*Matt.*, *W.R.*, 156.)

JOHNSON, WILLIAM: Rector of Warboys, Huntingdonshire. Went to Danzig as chaplain to Merchant Adventurers, 1648; returned 1649. Shipwrecked on second voyage to Danzig. Also travelled in Holland and France. (*Matt.*, *W.R.*, 207; cf. preface to his book, *Narrative of a great Deliverance at Sea*, Lond. 1648.)

JOHNSON, WILLIAM: Fellow of Queens' College, Cambridge; chaplain to the Queen of Bohemia at the Hague 1644. Later, Archdeacon of Huntingdon. (*Nich.*, i, 305.)

JONES, THOMAS: Rector of Offwell, Devonshire; served in Royalist army as chaplain to Sir Ralph Hopton. Fled to Rotterdam, where he died before 1651. (*Matt.*, *W.R.*, 116.)

U

KILLIGREW, HENRY, D.D.: Chaplain in the Royalist Army; lived on Continent during exile as chaplain to the Duke of York. Preb. of Westminster, 1660. (*D.N.B.*)

KING, JOHN: Dean of Tuam. At the Hague in 1650; accompanied the King's party to Scotland that year as secretary to the Duke of Buckingham. Later acted as agent between King and Marquis of Ormond. (S.R. Gardiner, *Charles II and Scotland in* 1650, Edin. 1894, 122, 140 ff.)

KNELL, PAUL, D.D.: of Clare Hall, Cambridge; chaplain to regiment of cuirassiers in King's army. Preached before Charles II at the Hague in 1649. Vicar of Newchurch, Romsey Marsh, 1660. (*D.N.B.*, *Kenn.*, 299.)

LANE, WILLIAM, Rector of Aveton-Gifford, Devonshire; sequestered 1645. Fled to France, where he worked at Torbay as stone quarrier; returned to England, and died before the Restoration. (*Matt.*, *W.R.*, 117.)

LANEY, BENJAMIN: Master of Pembroke College, Cambridge; emigrated to France after 1645, where he was in attendance on Charles II. Bishop of Peterborough, 1660; of Lincoln, 1663; of Ely, 1667. (*D.N.B.*)

LE COUTEUR, PHILIP: Receveur royal in Jersey; emigrated to France about 1651, and during exile acted as pastor to Huguenot Church in Caen. Dean of Jersey, 1660. (J. Durel, *A View of the Government . . .*, Lond. 1662, 93-5.)

LEECH, WILLIAM: Fellow of Magdalene College, Cambridge. Travelled in Italy and France during Interregnum. (*Matt.*, *W.R.*, 38.)

LE GROSSE, ROBERT: Sequestered London rector. Went abroad 1647-8; sent into Italy from Toulon by Prince Rupert "about some affairs concerning his Majesty's service". Lived at Leghorn for many years, also at Cairo. In Leghorn 1660. (*Nich.*, iv, 93-5; *C.S.P.D.*, 1659-60, 346; preface to his book, *Sion's Exultation*, Lond. 1660.)

LESLIE, HENRY: Bishop of Down and Connor. Preached before Charles II at Breda in 1649. Returned to Ireland before the Restoration, when he was translated to Meath. (*D.N.B.*)

LESLIE, ROBERT: Son of preceding; lived in Virginia during the Commonwealth. Bishop of Dromore, 1660. (*Good.*, 287.)

LEWIS, WILLIAM, D.D.: Preb. of Winchester; sequestered 1644. Emigrated 1646, when he was registered at the Univ. of Padua. Living in France 1653. Master of St. Cross Hospital 1660. (*D.N.B.*, *Matt.*, *W.R.*, 186.)

LINDSEY, JOHN: Vicar of Blandford Forum, Dorset; sequestered 1646. Twice imprisoned, and spent three years in France, returning to England before the Restoration. Reinstated 1660. (*Matt.*, *W.R.*, 134.)

LLOYD (or FLOYD), JOHN: Fellow of All Souls' College; ejected after long absence 1650. Was chaplain to Lord Culpeper on mission to Moscow 1650; in Paris, 1651. Later acted as chaplain to Charles II, and engaged in Royalist activity. (*Walker*, ii, 99; *Kenn.*, 218; *Thurl.*, iv, 167; *Ibid.*, vii, 337; *Nich.*, i, 185. Dobson confuses him with Dr. William Lloyd, Bishop of Llandaff; cf. *Evel.*, ii, 44 note.)

LONDON, RICHARD: Fellow of Caius College. Studied medicine at the University of Padua, joined the Roman Church, and died at Genoa 1647. (*Matt.*, *W.R.*, 37.)

LOVELL, RICHARD: Rector of St. Peter's, Sandwich, Kent. Became chaplain and tutor to the Duke of Gloucester, and accompanied him abroad in 1653, where he remained until the Restoration. (*C.S.P.C.*, ii, 215; *Alum. Oxon.*, iii, 941.)

LOWEN, JOHN: Student of Christ Church. House of Lords granted him pass in 1646 to study in Leyden for three years. (*Matt.*, *W.R.*, 25.)

MADEN, RICHARD: Rector of St. Mildred Poultry, London; sequestered before May, 1645. Minister successively at Dordrecht, Utrecht, Amsterdam, and Rotterdam (1660–80). (*Matt.*, *W.R.*, 53.)

MALLORY, PHILIP: Vicar of Norton, Durham; sequestered 1644. Sailed to West Indies in Prince Rupert's fleet, and afterwards became minister of Lynnhaven Parish, Norfolk Co., Virginia. Restored 1660. (*Matt.*, *W.R.*, 142; *Good.*, 291.)

MAPLET, JOHN: Principal of Gloucester Hall; travelled in France and Holland during the exile as chaplain to Lord Falkland. Reinstated at Restoration. (*Athen. Oxon.*, ii, 466.)

MARSHALL, THOMAS, D.D.: Student of Lincoln College, Oxford. Went abroad 1647, became minister to Merchant Adventurers at Rotterdam 1650. Followed his congregation to Dordrecht, 1656, where he remained until 1672. Later, Dean of Gloucester. (*D.N.B.*)

MARTIN, EDWARD: President of Queens' College, Cambridge; emigrated about 1652. Lived at Paris with Lord Hatton, and was in Utrecht 1656. In Caen 1659. Dean of Ely, 1660. (*D.N.B.*)

MEWES, PETER: Archdeacon of Huntingdon. Emigrated to Holland in 1648, and acted as Royalist agent. Bishop of Bath and Wells, 1672; of Winchester, 1684. (*D.N.B.*)

MICHAELSON, JOHN: Rector of Chelmsford, Essex; sequestered in 1642. Fled to Holland, but forced by poverty to return to England before the Restoration. Reinstated 1660. (*Matt.*, *W.R.*, 158.)

MILESON, RICHARD: Archdeacon of Suffolk. Fled to Continent, where he became a Roman Catholic. (*Walker*, ii, 57.)

MITCHELL, DAVID: Rector of St. Giles', Edinburgh; deprived 1638, and went to England. Eventually took refuge in Holland, where he supported himself in Rotterdam as a watchmaker. Bishop of Aberdeen, 1662. (J. Dowden, *Bishops of Scotland*, Glasgow 1912, 400.)

MORAY (or MURRAY), ALEXANDER: Scottish clergyman, with Charles II in his invasion of England in 1652. Said to have been in exile with the King; became first rector of Ware Parish, Gloucester Co., Virginia. In 1672, nominated by the King first Bishop of Virginia; but the plan to establish an overseas diocese proved abortive. (G. M. Brydon, *Virginia's Mother Church*, Richmond, 1947, pp. 183–4.)

MORLEY, GEORGE, D.D.: Canon of Christ Church; ejected 1648, and went to Paris the following year. Lived in France and Holland during exile, was chaplain both to Hyde and the Queen of Bohemia. Bishop of Worcester, 1660; of Winchester, 1662. (*D.N.B.*)

NALTON, JAMES: Puritan rector of Rugby, Warwickshire. Withdrew to Holland for six months in 1651 because of complicity in Love's plot. Joint pastor with Cawton of the English Church in Rotterdam. Ejected from St. Leonard's, Foster Lane, London, 1662. (*Matt., C.R.,* 361.)

OTWAY, THOMAS: Chaplain to Lord Hopton during War. Taken prisoner, banished to West Indies, returned 1660. Bishop of Killala, 1670; of Ossory, 1680. (*D.N.B.*)

PALMER, THOMAS: Vicar of Bedminster, Somerset; became minister of Hungar's Parish, Virginia, about 1647. (*Good.,* 297; *Alum. Cant.,* iii, 301.)

PIERCE, THOMAS: Fellow of Magdalen College, Oxford; ejected 1648. Travelled in France and Italy as tutor to the Earl of Sunderland, returning to England, 1656. After Restoration, Dean of Salisbury. (*D.N.B.*)

POLWHEEL, DEGORY: Fellow of Exeter College, Oxford. With Charles II in Holland and France until 1650, when he returned to England. (*Walker.* ii, 115.)

POWELL, THOMAS: Rector of Cantreffe, Brecknock; sequestered during the Civil War. "He shipped himself beyond the seas for a time." At Restoration, Canon of St. David's. (*Athen. Oxon.,* ii, 254.)

PRICE, WILLIAM: Fellow of Jesus College, Oxford. Became minister with Maden of the English Church in Amsterdam from 1648 until his death in 1666. (*Walker,* ii, 120; *Thurl.,* ii, 319, 374.)

PROWSE, EDWARD: Vicar of Long Benton, Northumberland; sequestered before July 1646. Imprisoned and in exile. Restored 1660. (*Matt., W.R.,* 290.)

PULLEN, JOHN: Fellow of Magdalene College, Cambridge; ejected 1644. "Obliged to seek sustenance abroad, and persecuted there by Sec. Thurloe for corresponding with his Majesty's Court." In Italy with Eleazor Duncon during later part of exile. At Restoration, preb. of Lincoln. (*Kenn.,* 47; *C.S.P.D.,* 1660–61, 220; *Alum. Cant.,* iii, 406.)

ROGERS, SAMUEL: Fellow of Queens' College, Cambridge. Appointed chaplain to the Levant Company in Constantinople, 1653. Preb. of Salisbury, 1661. (*Pearson,* 15; *Alum. Cant.,* iii, 480.)

ROWLAND, JOHN: Rector of Footscray, Kent; ejected 1642. Chaplain to Sir Jacob Astley's regiment in the Royalist Army; afterwards crossed to the Netherlands. Wife also overseas in 1646. Reinstated by 1661. (*Matt., W.R.,* 224.)

ROWLAND, WILLIAM: Curate of St. Margaret's, Westminster. At the time of the rebellion went to Paris, where he became a Roman Catholic. (*Athen. Oxon.,* ii, 241.)

RYVES, BRUNO, D.D.: Dean of Chichester. Made at least one trip to the Continent after 1649 to carry funds to Charles II. Restored 1660. (*D.N.B..*)

SANCROFT, WILLIAM: Fellow of Emmanuel College, Cambridge. In 1657 went to Amsterdam and Utrecht; at the University of Padua 1660. Archbishop of Canterbury, 1678. (*D.N.B.*)

SEFTON, JOHN: Rector of Burton, Sussex, c. 1652. Fled to the East Indies, and returned before 1660. Afterwards Canon of Chichester. (*Matt.*, *W.R.*, 360.)

SHERINGHAM, ROBERT: Fellow of Caius College; ejected 1651. Taught Arabic and Hebrew at Rotterdam, and was chaplain to the Princess of Orange. (*D.N.B.*; *Nich.*, ii, 13.)

STAMP, WILLIAM, D.D.: Vicar of Stepney, London; sequestered before 1645. Accompanied Prince of Wales on his flight to Continent. Lived at Paris, later became chaplain to the Queen of Bohemia, and died at the Hague 1653. (*D.N.B.*; *Merc. Pol.*, No. 37, Feb. 16, 1651.)

STARLING, HENRY: Rector of Homersfield, Suffolk. "Died in his passage to Virginia." (*Walker*, ii, 367.)

STEPHENSON, JAMES: Rector of Tormarton, Glos., where he sheltered his former patron, the Bishop of Ardagh. Ejected for refusing the Engagement 1650, removed to Holland, where he studied medicine at the University of Leyden. Returned to England before 1656. Puritan, ejected in 1662 from incumbency of Martock, Somerset. (*Matt.*, *C.R.*, 463.)

STEWARD, RICHARD, D.D.: Dean of St. Paul's. In attendance on Prince Charles from 1646. In Jersey 1650; died in Paris 1651. (*D.N.B.*)

STILES, JONAS: Vicar of Stokenham, Devon; ejected 1647. Fled overseas; at the Univ. of Padua 1648, where he became M.D. Restored 1660. (*Matt.*, *W.R.*, 124.)

STONE, WILLIAM: Minister of Wimborne Minster, Dorset; ejected 1646. Admitted at Univ. of Padua 1652. Restored 1661. (*Matt.*, *W.R.*, 137.)

SYDSERF, THOMAS: Bishop of Galloway; came to Paris about 1644, and lived there during the Interregnum. In Edinburgh, March 1657. Translated to Orkney, 1661. (*D.N.B.*; *Rawl.* D 317, f. 238.)

SYMMONS, EDWARD: Rector of Rayne, Essex; sequestered 1643. Fled to France 1645, and returned to England 1647. Later in same year House of Lords granted him pass to France. Died in London 1649. (*Matt.*, *W.R.*, 164.)

TEAKLE, THOMAS: Scholar of Corpus Christi College, Oxford. Fled to Virginia in 1649, where he became minister of Nassawadox Parish, Northampton Co. (*Matt.*, *W.R.*, 27; *Good.*, 310.)

THORNDIKE, HERBERT: Fellow of Trinity College, Cambridge. In England during most of period, but in Utrecht with Honywood 1659. Preb. of Westminster, 1660. (*D.N.B.*; *Harl.* 3783, ff. 244, 246.)

TIRWHITTE, THOMAS: Fellow of St. John's College, Cambridge. Lived in exile. Reinstated 1660. (*Walker*, ii, 148.)

TOZER, HENRY: Fellow of Exeter College, Oxford; ejected 1648. Became chaplain to the Merchant Adventurers at Rotterdam until his death in 1650. (*D.N.B.*)

TURNER, JOHN: Vicar of Treneglos, Cornwall; sequestered before 1647. Fled overseas, but returned for want of money. (*Matt.*, *W.R.*, 101.)

URQUART, ROBERT: Rector of St. John's, Newcastle; "went beyond seas, turned papist, and died in a convent". (*Walker*, ii, 389.)

VANE, THOMAS, D.D.: Rector of Crayford, Kent, and chaplain to the King. Became a Roman Catholic in Paris in 1645. (*D.N.B.*; *Verney Memoirs*, ii, 215.)

WALKER, OBADIAH: Fellow of University College, Oxford; ejected 1648. Lived in Rome during the Commonwealth; after the Restoration became master of his college, and a Roman Catholic under James II. (*D.N.B.*)

WARING, ROBERT: Camden Professor of History at Oxford; Student of Christ Church. Deprived 1648, and travelled in France with Sir William Whitmore. Returned to England, and died in 1658. (*D.N.B.*)

WASE, CHRISTOPHER: Fellow of King's College; deprived. Emigrated, and served in the Spanish Army against the French. Returned to England before 1654. Headmaster of Tonbridge School, 1662. (*D.N.B.*)

WATSON, RICHARD: Fellow of Caius College; ejected 1642. Chaplain to Lord Hopton in Paris until 1652; subsequently lived at Caen. After Restoration, preb. of Salisbury. (*D.N.B.*)

WELDON, ROBERT: Rector of Stoney Stanton, Leicestershire; "forced to leave the country". (*Walker*, ii, 400; *Alum. Oxon.*, iv, 1594.)

WELLER, RICHARD: Fellow of Emmanuel College, Cambridge; was in Leghorn as a refugee in 1645. (*Matt.*, *W.R.*, 36.)

WINCHESTER, ROBERT: of Trinity College, Cambridge. Chaplain to the East India Company at Surat and Fort St. George 1648–51; chaplain to the Levant Company at Smyrna 1654–9. (*Alum. Cant.* iv, 435; *Pearson*, 30.)

WISHART, GEORGE: Lecturer at St. Nicholas, Newcastle; ejected 1642. Chaplain to Montrose, and fled with him to Norway 1646. Travelled with his patron through Europe; later became chaplain to the Queen of Bohemia, and minister to the Scots congregation at Schiedam 1650. Bishop of Edinburgh, 1662. (*D.N.B.*)

WISHART, ROBERT: Rector of Wyke Regis, Dorsetshire; "was many years in banishment." (*Walker*, ii, 395.)

WOLLEY, EDWARD, D.D.: Rector of Adderley, Shropshire, and chaplain to Charles I; emigrated about 1646. Attended Charles II in exile, returned to England 1655. Bishop of Clonfert, 1665. (*D.N.B.*)

WOOD, THOMAS, D.D.: Rector of Whickham, Durham; ejected 1651. Travelled in Italy during the Protectorate. Bishop of Lichfield, 1671. (*Athen. Oxon.*, ii, 1176.)

WOODHEAD, ABRAHAM: Fellow of University College; left England about 1645 to travel with pupils in France and Italy, and became a Roman Catholic. (*D.N.B.*)

YERBURY, HENRY: Fellow of Magdalen College, Oxford; ejected 1648. Studied at Univ. of Padua, and became an M.D. Returned to England from France May 1657. Reinstated at Restoration. (*Walker*, ii, 123; B.M., *Add.* 34,015, f. 81.)

NOTE ON SOURCES

FOR the Commonwealth period, the chief sources for a study of Laudian activity are three collections of letters. The most important series is deposited in the British Museum (*Harleian MSS.* 6942), and consists of letters written to Gilbert Sheldon by Henry Hammond, George Morley, and others. Liberal extracts are quoted in a series of articles by Nicholas Pocock in *Theologian and Ecclesiastic*, 1848–53, though the editor went no further than the year 1654, and by no means exhausted the material. Hammond's letters are undated, and in most cases I have followed the years assigned by Pocock. Supplementing this collection are a number of letters by Sancroft, Duppa, and other churchmen in the *Tanner MSS.* of the Bodleian Library. Finally, there is the correspondence between Bishop Duppa and Sir Justinian Isham, 1650–60, deposited with the Northamptonshire Record Society at Lamport Hall. I am greatly indebted to Sir Gyles Isham, Bart., for the use of typed transcripts of these letters; the originals are mostly undated, and I have followed his chronology throughout.

The *Clarendon MSS.* in the Bodleian are a primary source for the history or the Church in exile; the collection is calendared as far as April, 1660, in four published volumes. Otherwise, I have chiefly depended for material on standard works: *The Nicholas Papers* (4 vols.), *The Ormond Papers* (2 vols.), *The Thurloe State Papers* (7 vols.), the *Works of John Cosin* (5 vols.), and the *Works of John Bramhall* (5 vols.). Clarendon's *History of the Rebellion and Civil Wars*, Evelyn's *Diary*, and Cosin's *Correspondence* were also useful. For the negotiations described in Chapter III, the *Clarendon MSS.* are again the chief source. Many of the important letters have been printed in the *Clarendon State Papers* (3 vols.) and in an appendix to the *Life of John Barwick.*

Material for a study of the Laudian party after the Restoration was more difficult to obtain. Until the final stage of the church settlement, letters by the leading churchmen are almost non-existent, and the disappearance of Bishop Sheldon's correspondence during this period is a particularly grave handicap. The two best-known sources, *Reliquiae Baxterianae*, and Hyde's *Continuation of His Life*, could be used only with great caution. Both Baxter and Hyde wrote from the standpoint of a later period than the events described; the former inevitably judged Laudian policy as an outsider and an opponent, while the latter was so intent on vindicating his defence of Anglican interests that he frequently misrepresented the facts.

Fortunately, there are various collections of letters by men who were acutely interested in church affairs at this time. Large extracts and summaries from the letters of John Sharp, commissioner in London of the Church of Scotland, are printed in the first volume of Wodrow's *History of the Church of Scotland*, and these cover the period January to July 1660. *The Mather Papers*, printed by the Massachusetts Historical Society, and *The Letters of Robert Baillie* also furnish material on the Puritan side for supplementing Baxter. The *Sutherland MSS.*

calendared in the Historical MSS. Commission volume for 1876 are invaluable for studying Royalist views during the first year of the Restoration. Equally important are the regular reports of foreign ministers living in the capital; these show considerable insight into the government's religious policy. Transcripts from the French archives are deposited in the Public Record Office; reports of the Venetian Resident are published in English translation in the *State Papers Venetian*, 1659–61, 1661–64; transcripts of the Florentine Resident's letters are in the British Museum *Add. MSS.* 27,962; and of the Dutch Minister in *Add. MSS.* 17,677. Certain interesting details are contributed by two contemporary manuscript chronicles, also in the British Museum—an anonymous one in *Add. MSS.* 10,116, and a "Narrative of Remarkable Affairs", by Henry Gregory, Rector of Middleton-Stoney, in *Add. MSS.* 19,526. A number of important letters have been copied from the *Clarendon MSS.*, the *Carte MSS.*, and *MSS. Rawlinson Letters* in the Bodleian Library; from the *Sloane MSS.* and *Additional MSS.* of the British Museum; and the *State Papers, Domestic Series*, in the Public Record Office. Particularly valuable as revealing the viewpoint of one who was a member of the government and an intimate friend of Hyde are the news letters written by Sir Edward Nicholas to English representatives abroad; these notes are scattered in the different collections of Foreign State Papers in the Public Record Office. Use has been made of the printed diaries of Pepys, Henry Townshend, and Henry Newcome, and of the files of *Mercurius Politicus* and *Mercurius Publicus* in the Bodleian Library. The *Journals* of the Lords and Commons and Cobbett's *Parliamentary History* have supplied most of the material for the discussion of the church policy pursued by Parliament.

A more general field of evidence exists in the numerous broadsides, tracts, and theological works issued by Anglicans and Puritans. These sometimes throw a useful light on party policy, and the introductory prefaces in many cases furnish important details on the current situation, both political and ecclesiastical. I have made as wide a survey as possible of this material, using the resources of the Cambridge University Library, and the Libraries of Trinity College and St. John's College, with frequent reference to the Thomason Collection of seventeenth-century tracts in the British Museum.

My obligation to modern works is indicated in the footnotes, but two books should be singled out. Mr. A. G. Matthews's scholarly *Walker Revised* has made available a wealth of detailed information on the fate of the Anglican clergy during the Civil War and Commonwealth, and I have found it indispensable as a work of reference. I have also made constant use of Prof. Keith Feiling's *History of the Tory Party*, 1640–1714, as a guide to Royalist political policy.

BIBLIOGRAPHICAL ABBREVIATIONS

Add.	Additional MSS., British Museum.
Alum. Cant.	J. and J. A. Venn, *Alumni Cantabrigienses* (Camb. 1922–7).
Alum. Oxon.	J. Foster, *Alumni Oxonienses, Early Series,* (Oxf. 1891–2).
Athen. Oxon.	A. Wood, *Athenae Oxoniensis* (Ed. 1721).
Baillie	*The Letters and Journals of Robert Baillie,* edited by D. Laing (Edin. 1842), 3 vols.
Barwick	*The Life of John Barwick,* by P. Barwick (Lond. 1724).
Bramhall	J. Bramhall, *Works* (Oxf. 1843–55).
Brown	H. F. Brown, *Inglesi e Scozzesi all' Università di Padova* (Venezia 1921).
Burnet	*History of His Own Time,* by Gilbert Burnet, edited by O. Airy (Oxf. 1897), 2 vols.
C.S.P.C.	*Calendar of the Clarendon State Papers,* edited by O. Ogle, W. H. Bliss, W. D. Macray, F. J. Routledge (Oxf. 1869–1928), 4 vols.
C.S.P.D.	*Calendar of State Papers: Domestic Series.*
C.S.P.V.	*Calendar of State Papers: Venetian.*
Clar.	Clarendon MSS., Bodleian Library.
Carte	Carte MSS., Bodleian Library.
Cosin	*The Works of John Cosin,* edited by J. Sanson (Oxf. 1843–55), 5 vols.
D.N.B.	*Dictionary of National Biography.*
D.A.U.	*Documents relating to the Act of Uniformity* (Lond. 1862).
Duppa	Duppa Correspondence: Northamptonshire Record Society, Lamport Hall.
E.H.R.	*English Historical Review.*
Evel.	*Diary of John Evelyn,* edited by A. Dobson (Lond. 1906), 3 vols.
Feil.	*The History of the Tory Party,* 1640–1714, by K. Feiling (Oxf. 1924).
Good.	*The Colonial Church in Virginia,* by E. L. Goodwin (Milwaukee 1927).
Grub	*Ecclesiastical History of Scotland,* by G. Grub (Edin. 1861), 7 vols.
Harl.	Harleian MSS., British Museum.

Hyde I   *History of the Rebellion and Civil Wars in England*, by E. Hyde, Earl of Clarendon (ed. Oxf. 1827), 6 vols.

Hyde II   *Continuation of His Life*, by E. Hyde (Oxf. 1827), 3 vols.

J.C.   *Journals of the House of Commons.*
J.L.   *Journals of the House of Lords.*

Kenn.   *Register and Chronicle Ecclesiastical and Civil*, by W. Kennett (Lond. 1728).

Lan.   Lansdowne MSS., British Museum.
Le Flem.   Historical MSS. Commission, Report XII, Part vii: *Le Fleming MSS.* (Lond. 1890).
Lister   *Life of Edward, Earl of Clarendon*, by T. H. Lister (Lond. 1837), 3 vols.

Math.   Massachusetts Historical Society, 4th series, vol. viii: *Mather Papers.*
Matt., C.R.   *Calamy Revised*, by A. G. Matthews (Oxf. 1934).
Matt., W.R.   *Walker Revised*, by A. G. Matthews (Oxf. 1948).
Merc. Pol.   *Mercurius Politicus*, weekly issues, 1650-60.
Merc. Pub.   *Mercurius Publicus*, weekly issues, 1660-2.
Morley   *Several Treatises*, by G. Morley (Lond. 1683).

Newc.   *Diary of the Rev'd Henry Newcome* (Chetham Soc. 1849).
Nich.   *The Nicholas Papers*, edited by G. F. Warner (Camden Soc. 1886-1920), 4 vols.

Orm. I   *Collection of Original Letters and Papers of the Duke of Ormond*, edited by T. Carte (Lond. 1739), 2 vols.
Orm. II   Historical MSS. Commission: *Ormonde MSS.* New Series. (1902).
Orns.   *Correspondence of John Cosin*, edited by G. Ornsby (Surtees Soc. 1869-72), 2 vols.

Pearson   *A Biographical Sketch of the Chaplains of the Levant Company, 1611-1706*, by J. B. Pearson (Camb. 1883).
Pepys   *Diary of Samuel Pepys* (ed. Lond. 1924), 2 vols.
P.H.E.   *Parliamentary History of England*, edited by W. Cobbett (Lond. 1808).

Ralph   *History of England*, by J. Ralph (Lond. 1744).
Rawd.   *The Rawdon Papers*, edited by E. Berwick (Lond. 1819).
Rawl.   MSS. Rawlinson Letters, Bodleian Library.
Rel. Baxt.   *Reliquiae Baxterianae; or Richard Baxter's Narrative of His Life and Times*, edited by M. Sylvester (Lond. 1696).

Sand.	*Works of Robert Sanderson* (Oxf. 1854), 6 vols.
S.P.C.	*State Papers collected by Edward, Earl of Clarendon*, edited by R. Scrope and T. Monkhouse (Oxf. 1767–86), 3 vols.
S.P.D.	Public Record Office: State Papers, Domestic.
Steven	*History of the Scottish Church, Rotterdam*, by W. Steven (Edin. 1832).
Stoughton	*Church and State Two Hundred Years Ago*, by J. Stoughton (Lond. 1862).
Suth.	Historical MSS. Commission, Report V: *Sutherland MSS.* (Lond. 1876).
Swain.	*The Parliamentary History of the Act of Uniformity*, by C. A. Swainson (Lond. 1875).
Tann.	Tanner MSS., Bodleian Library.
Thurl.	*The State Papers of John Thurloe*, edited by T. Birch (Lond. 1742), 7 vols.
Town.	*Diary of Henry Townshend*, edited by J. W. Willis Bund (Lond. 1920).
Walker	*Sufferings of the Clergy of the Church of England*, by J. Walker (Lond. 1714).
Wodrow	*History of the Sufferings of the Church of Scotland*, by R. Wodrow (Glasgow 1828), 7 vols.

INDEX

Albemarle, Duke of: *see* Monk, General George

Alexander VII, Pope, 77

Allen, Abraham, 159

Allen, Isaac, 28

Allestree, Richard, 30, 88, 89, 94, 98-9, 105

Amyraut, Moise, 133, 134

Anabaptists, 157, 179, 185, 190, 205, 209, 212-3, 238, 256, 266

Anglican clergy: sequestration, 4-5, 13, 241; attitude to Cromwellian Establishment, 5-6, 14, 23-4, 27-30, 32-6, 40 ff., 278-9; moderate group, 27-8, 120-2, 148; use of lectureships, 12, 43, 235; apologetical writing during Interregnum, 32-8, 63-66; changed view of Royal Supremacy, 72-3; attitude to Royal Declaration of Oct. 1660, 190-2; restoration to benefices, 161, 164-5, 201, 240. *See also* Laudian Party

Annand, William, 202

Anne of Austria: *see* Queen Regent of France

Annesley, Arthur, 147, 187

Anslow, Sir Richard, 272

Army, Cromwellian, 6, 104, 115, 116, 145, 148, 149, 158, 179

Ashe, Simeon, 118, 139, 151, 186

Association Movement, 46-7

Aubigny, Lord, 78, 188

Baillie, Robert, xiii, 120, 122, 140, 155, 216

Balcarres, Earl of, 55, 107

Barksdale, Clement, 28, 39

Bartet, M., 188, 193, 198

Bartholomew's Day, St. (1662), 250, 254, 259, 260, 265, 266, 282

Basire, Isaac, 65-6, 85, 232-3, 234, 256

Bates, William, 111, 151, 186, 193, 207-8, 229, 242, 260, 271

Battailer, M., 239, 259

Barwick, John, 18-21, 30, 32, 88, 89, 91, 93, 94, 95, 96, 97, 103, 104, 105, 109, 113, 117, 123-5, 126, 138, 148, 160, 183, 186, 220

Baxter, Richard, 15, 16, 27, 29, 38, 40, 46, 83, 119, 120, 121, 130, 149, 165, 166, 184, 190, 204, 206, 208, 211, 214, 215-16, 237, 238, 242, 247, 249, 271, 274, 277; character, 119; interview with Morley, 127; conferences with Charles II, June 1660, 152-4; discussions of Royal Declaration, autumn 1660, 185-7; attitude to Declaration, 186, 189-90, 194-5; offered see of Hereford, 193-4; role at Savoy Conference, 226-30; relations with Hyde, 204, 229, 258; account of proposed Indulgence, summer 1662, 260

Bayly, Richard, 183

Bayly, Thomas, 36, 79

Benefices: sequestration of, 4-6, 241; Royal appointments to, summer 1660, 159-61, 175-6, 177, 179, 217, 281; ejection of Presbyterians from, 150, 161, 164-5, 170, 175, 214, 240, 266

Bennet, Sir Henry, 180, 185, 198, 204, 252, 257-8, 263, 268, 270

Bernard, Nicholas, 45-6, 121, 122

Bishops, Anglican, 255; failure to provide leadership during Interregnum, 25-7, 30, 279; negotiate with Hyde regarding new consecrations, 89 ff.; reluctance to perform consecrations, 90, 96 ff.; appointment of new bishops, 1659, 94-5; message to Charles II at Res-